Video-Based Rendering

T0174019

Video-Based Rendering

Marcus A. Magnor
Max-Planck-Institut für Informatik
Saarbrücken, Germany

CRC Press
Taylor & Francis Group
Boca Raton London New York

CRC Press is an imprint of the
Taylor & Francis Group, an **informa** business

AN A K PETERS BOOK

CRC Press
Taylor & Francis Group
6000 Broken Sound Parkway NW, Suite 300
Boca Raton, FL 33487-2742

First issued in paperback 2020

ISBN-13: 978-1-56881-244-1 (hbk)
ISBN-13: 978-0-367-65943-1 (pbk)

Library of Congress Cataloging-in-Publication Data

Magnor, Marcus A. (Marcus Andreas), 1972-
 Video-based rendering / Marcus A. Magnor.
   p. cm.
 Includes bibliographical references and index.
 ISBN 1-56881-244-2
 1. Digital video. 2. Computer animation. I. Title.

TK6680.5.M345 2005
006.6'96--dc22

2005050055

For Marian

Contents

Contents

Foreword

If you have seen any of the Star Wars movies, you will certainly remember the futuristic video technology in a galaxy far, far away. Video is projected into free space, visible from any point of view. Objects and people appear to be present in almost ghostlike fashion as three-dimensional entities. Princess Leia's call for help is recorded by R2-D2 for playback at the opportune time, whereas the brave Jedi knights virtually attend meetings, zapping their three-dimensional video personalities in real time across the galaxy. We are in awe of such technological marvel, willing to forgive that the grainy, low-resolution video looks slightly worse than 1950s television.

It's fun to ask what it would take to make this vision of the future a reality. First, one needs to capture and record three-dimensional objects and scenes. Then there is the issue of transmitting the data, presumably in real time, over the inter-galactic equivalent of WiFi (let's call it WiGa for now). And finally we need a display that projects three-dimensional images into free space, such that a viewer receives stereoscopic images anywhere in the viewing area without special glasses. (As far as we know, even Darth Vader doesn't have stereo glasses built into his helmet.)

This book will hopefully convince you that much of this technology (apart maybe from WiGa) is not as far fetched as it seems. You will read about recording people and stadium-sized scenes using large numbers of distributed cameras. A viewer can pick arbitrary views and even virtually fly around the scene. Other systems capture the light coming through a "window" in the scene using many (maybe more than one hundred) closely arranged cameras. The captured light can then be displayed on modern (even commercially available) screens that project stereoscopic images to multiple viewers (without funny glasses). These scenarios are known as interactive television, free-viewpoint video, and 3D television. They hold great promise for the future of television, virtual reality, entertainment, and visualization.

Why has this book been written now, and not ten years ago? To paraphrase Intel's Andy Grove, we are at an inflection point in the history of visual media. Progress in computers, digital storage, transmission, and display technology continues to advance at unprecedented rates. All of this allows video to finally break free from the confines of the two-dimensional moving picture. Advances in computer vision, computer graphics, and displays allow us to add scene shape, novel view synthesis, and real-time interactivity to video. This book will show you how to do it.

If sales of computer games and the popularity of stereoscopic movies are any indication, we are all fascinated with new forms of visual media that allows us to get a better sense of presence. This book is a snapshot of what is possible today. I am sure it will stimulate your imagination until, someday, we may watch a three-dimensional rendition of Star Wars projected into our living rooms.

Arlington, MA   Hanspeter Pfister
May 2005

Preface

This book is about a new interdisciplinary research field that links computer graphics, computer vision, and telecommunications. Video-based rendering (VBR) has recently emerged from independent research in image-based rendering, motion capture, geometry reconstruction, and video processing. The goal in VBR is to render authentic views of real-world–acquired dynamic scenes the way they would appear from arbitrary vantage points. With this ambition, VBR constitutes a key technology for new forms of visual communications such as *interactive television*, *3D TV*, and *free-viewpoint video* in which the viewer will have the freedom to vary at will his or her perspective on movie scenes or sports events. To computer game developers, VBR offers a way out of the continuously increasing modeling costs that, driven by rapidly advancing hardware capabilities, have become necessary in order to achieve ever more realistic rendering results. Last but not least, virtual reality applications, such as training simulators, benefit from VBR in that real-world events can be imported into virtual environments.

Video-based rendering research pushes forward two scientific frontiers in unison: novel multi-video analysis algorithms are devised to robustly reconstruct dynamic scene shape, and adequate rendering methods are developed that synthesize realistic views of the scene at real-time frame rates. Both challenges, multi-video analysis and novel view synthesis, must be attacked in concert if our highly sophisticated visual sense is to be persuaded of the result's realism.

About This Book

Video-Based Rendering is an introduction to and a compendium of the current state-of-the-art in video-based rendering. Unfortunately, this immediately raises two fundamental problems. For one thing, it would be futile to attempt to do justice to all VBR contributions and related work that has been published in recent years. For another, the swift advancement in VBR research potentially assigns an expiration date to any printed material on the topic. To accommodate both concerns, the algorithms discussed in the following have been selected for their diversity and generality. Overall, the addressed techniques are believed to run the gamut of currently known approaches to video-based rendering.

There are several ways to read this book. To find a specific approach suitable for a given application, Appendix B compares different VBR techniques. Chapter 2 includes information on prerequisite techniques and various VBR-related issues. For a comprehensive introduction to video-based rendering, the book can be read from front to back, by which the different VBR concepts are encountered roughly in order of increasing complexity. Many references to scientific publications are included for additional information. So far, video-based rendering research has been mainly publicly funded, and most results are freely available on the Internet. To help find VBR electronic resources, a web site accompanies this book: http://www.video-based-rendering.org. It provides links to various VBR resources and is actively maintained to keep up to date with the latest developments in VBR research.

Synopsis

After introducing the topic, Chapter 2 discusses a number of prerequisite techniques that are related to or necessary for video-based rendering research. Chapters 3 to 6 are devoted to specific VBR algorithms. Chapter 3 addresses VBR approaches that rely on dense depth information. Time-critical VBR methods for widely spaced video cameras are presented in Chapter 4. Chapter 5 describes two approaches that make use of the continuous nature of any macroscopic motion. Chapter 6 discusses a VBR method that exploits a priori knowledge about scene content. The book closes with an outlook on future research and applications of video-based rendering.

With the exception of Spatiotemporal View Interpolation, Section 5.1, all algorithms are capable of rendering novel views at real-time frame rates on conventional PC hardware. Other than that, the discussed methods differ with respect to a number of criteria, e.g., online versus offline processing, small-baseline versus wide-baseline acquisition, implicit versus explicit geometry representation, or silhouette- versus photo-consistent reconstruction. To quickly evaluate the usefulness of an individual VBR technique for a specific application, each algorithm is briefly described and classified in Appendix B.

Acknowledgments

The VBR approaches described in this book have been proposed by various researchers. I thank Chris Buehler, Paul Debevec, Neel Joshi, Wojciech Matusik, Hartmut Schirmacher, Sundar Vedula, and Larry Zitnick for providing me with additional information on their work, going over the respective sections, and for allowing me to include their figures to better illustrate "their" VBR techniques.

Several algorithms discussed in this book have originated in the "Graphics–Optics–Vision" research group at the Max-Planck-Institut für Informatik. They are the work of Lukas Ahrenberg, Bastian Goldlücke, Ivo Ihrke, Ming Li, and Christian Theobalt, excellent PhD students who can convert ideas to working pieces of software, finding solutions to any theoretical or practical obstacle encountered along the way. Many figures in this book are reprints from our joint publications. I am lucky to have such a great research crew.

As I found out, finalizing a book in time is real team work. I am indebted to Gernot Ziegler and Michael Gösele who put a lot of effort into helping me identify and re-phrase unclear passages in the original manuscript. I also thank Alice Peters, Kevin Jackson-Mead and Sannie Sieper at A K Peters for their great assistance and fast work. Finally, I wish to express my sincere gratefulness to Hans-Peter Seidel, my mentor without whom I would not have discovered this fascinating and rewarding research field. It is to his persistent encouragement that the existence of this book is owed.

Chapter 1

Introduction

The visual sense is the most sophisticated, most advanced sensory channel connecting the real world to human consciousness. Its online analysis capabilities are enormous, and its reliability is proverbial. "Seeing is believing:" we are accustomed to unconditionally accept as objective reality what our visual system judges to be real.

It is the art of computer graphics rendering to "trick" the human visual system into accepting virtual, computer-synthesized images as being genuine. From its onset in the 1950s, impressive progress has been made in realistic image synthesis. Continued algorithmic advances, in conjunction with ever-increasing computational resources, have made possible ever more realistic rendering results. Whether on modern graphics hardware or on ray-tracing clusters, time-critical rendering applications today achieve a degree of realism that was unattainable only a few years ago. From animated feature films and special movie effects to computer games and training simulators, numerous new business fields have emerged from realistic rendering research.

With increasing hardware and software capabilities, however, rendering realism has become more and more dependent on the quality of the descriptions of the scenes to be rendered. More and more time has to be invested into modeling geometry, reflectance characteristics, scene illumination, and motion with sufficient detail and precision.[1] Increasingly, progress in realistic rendering is threatened to become thwarted by the time-consuming modeling process.

In response to this dilemma, an alternative rendering concept has established itself over the last decade: *image-based modeling and rendering*.[2] In image-

---

[1]The term *model* is used throughout the book to denote a description of a real-world scene at a level of abstraction that is suitable for generating novel views from different (arbitrary) viewpoints.

[2]See Shum et al. *Image-Based Rendering*. New York: Springer, 2005.

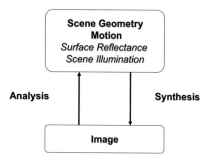

Figure 1.1. Image- and video-based rendering: From the description of a (time-varying) scene in terms of 3D geometry, motion, surface reflectance, and illumination, computer graphics rendering techniques are able to synthesize realistic images of the scene from arbitrary perspectives. Computer vision addresses the much harder, and in the general case even ill-posed, inverse problem of recovering the abstract scene description from real-world image data. In image- and video-based rendering, both sides, analysis and synthesis, are regarded collectively for best rendering results. To render a scene from arbitrary viewpoints, but under identical lighting conditions, only geometry and object motion must be reconstructed explicitly.

based rendering (IBR), natural scene appearance is not so much computed as it is looked up from a number of conventional photographs of a real scene [85]. In theory, IBR methods can display static scenes from arbitrary viewpoints with photorealistic quality at constant computational cost, regardless of scene complexity. The modeling process is replaced by image acquisition, which ideally takes only a fraction of the manual labor necessary for building a conventional model of the scene. While in conventional rendering images are synthesized from suitable descriptions of scene geometry, reflectance, and illumination, IBR is a "holistic" rendering approach in that the scene does not have to be dissected into its constituents for rendering. This strength of image-based rendering is, unfortunately, also its fundamental limitation: content cannot easily be edited anymore. Only if geometry, reflectance properties, and illumination are explicitly known can any of these components be altered separately and scene appearance recalculated (see Figure 1.1). *Computer vision* research explores ways to determine these more abstract scene descriptors from image data. Traditionally, however, research in computer vision is not predominantly concerned with generating novel, photorealistic views from the obtained model data. Rendering artifacts are the result. In contrast, IBR-driven *image-based modeling* and *inverse rendering* research has the goal, and the ultimate benchmark, of recreating visual realism.

Until recently, research into image-based modeling and rendering has concentrated on *static* scene content. This limitation in scope was owed primarily to the complexity and cost involved in acquiring input data for *dynamic* scenes.

Static scenes can be recorded with a single still-image camera by sequentially moving the camera from one viewpoint to the next. To capture the appearance of a time-varying scene from multiple viewpoints, in contrast, many video cameras must be deployed. In addition, the video cameras must be synchronized, and the enormous amount of image data must be either processed online or stored on appropriate mass storage media during recording for later processing.

While being able to render static objects realistically is already a valuable technological asset, the natural world around us is in constant motion, and the more interesting visual phenomena are changing over time. A comparison between still photographs and a video recording of some event makes evident the enhanced sense of visual realism that the temporal dimension brings about. This is why *animation* has become an important research area in computer graphics. Realistically modeling the motion of animated objects by hand, however, has proven to be exceedingly difficult. Human visual perception is very sensitive to unnatural movements of otherwise familiar real-world objects. Human gait, for example, depends on the build and weight of the person and changes with carried objects, ground consistency, even mood, among many other factors. If a character is to appear realistically animated, all these aspects must be correctly taken into account. Instead of attempting to artificially synthesize complex motion, animation specialists frequently pursue an approach equivalent to that of image-based rendering: they turn to the real world to *capture motion* from living subjects.

Video-based rendering unifies the concept of image-based rendering with the notion behind motion capture. It represents a new concept for modeling and displaying dynamic scene content. The ultimate objective in VBR is to photorealistically render arbitrary views of dynamic, real-world events at interactive frame rates. A number of intriguing new applications are expected to emerge from VBR research. In the telecommunications industry, conventional television is envisioned to be superseded by *interactive television* and *3D TV*. Instead of sitting passively in front of the television, the viewer will have the opportunity to decide for him- or herself from which vantage point to watch a movie or sports event. 3D TV technology may even enable watching the scene in three dimensions. For applications that do not require live broadcasting, *free-viewpoint video* will offer the freedom to watch movies recorded on DVD or next-generation storage media from arbitrary viewpoints. Video-based rendering is *the* enabling technology for the future development of visual media. Other fields of application for VBR techniques include interactive entertainment, virtual reality, training simulators, and other areas where visual realism in conjunction with real-time visualization are in demand.

Besides its application potential, research into video-based rendering also yields new insight into theoretical aspects of image analysis and synthesis. One

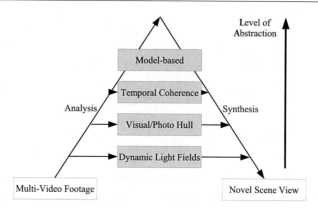

Figure 1.2. Video-based rendering: As input, multiple synchronized video sequences capture the appearance of a dynamic scene from different directions. Depending on camera arrangement, online processing requirements, and a priori scene information, different concepts are applicable to analyze the multi-video footage and to model dynamic scene content. Matching rendering techniques are then able to synthesize arbitrary new views of the scene in real-time.

fundamental challenge in VBR is finding ways to constrain and suitably regularize the shape reconstruction process. Temporal coherence and a priori scene knowledge can offer assistance towards this goal. For real-time visualization, suitable representations of natural, time-varying entities must be devised. To be able to mask reconstruction uncertainties, perceptual issues of the human visual system must be addressed, taking into account the psychophysics of video perception. Based on such theoretical considerations, viable solutions to the practical challenges of VBR are presented in the following.

Figure 1.2 illustrates the VBR processing pipeline, as well as the succession of chapters in this book. Video-based rendering actually begins with acquiring synchronized multi-video data as input. Chapter 2 highlights, among other related techniques, a number of issues that are critical for successfully recording high-quality footage. Two acquisition scenarios must be distinguished, differing in the number of simultaneously recorded video streams and/or the arrangement of cameras around the scene. If the distance between adjacent cameras is sufficiently small, images from neighboring video cameras exhibit high similarity, and the *dynamic light field* of the scene is densely sampled. Chapter 3 presents three approaches to render new views from such dynamic light field data. If, on the other hand, the cameras are arranged in a wide-baseline setup so that only a handful of cameras cover a large viewing angle, camera views differ substantially. Chapters 4 to 6 describe different VBR techniques that are able to render arbitrary scene views from wide-baseline data.

Chapter 2

Prerequisite Techniques

Video-based rendering is at the locus of different research disciplines. It can draw on a wealth of previous work in computer vision, graphics, and video processing. While all these areas are concerned with visual information, each one of them has been regarded so far as a separate research field in its own domain. In contrast, image data acquisition, analysis, and synthesis must all work in concert to achieve convincing visual realism in VBR. This chapter covers a number of related topics and gives details of secondary techniques that constitute necessary prerequisites for successful video-based rendering.

2.1   Acquisition

Video-based rendering begins with recording multiple video streams of real-world scenes. Input data acquisition is a crucial part of VBR, as it determines attainable rendering quality and, therefore, potentially also overall usefulness. To achieve optimal results, the acquisition set-up must be adapted to scene content and application scenario.

In image-based rendering, light fields of static scenes are customarily recorded by using a single still-image camera. Multiple images are recorded in sequence simply by moving the camera around the scene [169]. In contrast, acquiring the time-varying light field of a dynamic scene requires recording the scene *simultaneously* from different vantage points. Instead of a single still-image camera, multiple video cameras are necessary. In addition, all video cameras must be synchronized in order to be able to relate image content across cameras later. Such a multi-video acquisition system imposes challenging hardware demands that are constrained further by financial and logistical issues.

Synchronized multi-video acquisition systems have been built prior to VBR, primarily for commercial optical motion capture systems [214]. Such systems typically rely on high-speed cameras to track body markers of a person moving in a controlled stage environment. Multi-video acquisition for VBR, in contrast, must provide natural-looking, full-color images of the recorded scene. The recording might also have to take place outdoors. Accordingly, a suitable acquisition set-up consists not only of video cameras, but also of different mounting solutions, computational infrastructure, and illumination.

2.1.1 Imaging Hardware

A suitable video camera model for VBR acquisition has to meet specific requirements: the camera must be externally triggerable to make sure that the images of all video cameras are recorded at the same time instant, and the camera must be able to record in progressive scan mode (as opposed to interlaced half-images as customary for TV cameras) for full-frame processing. Additional desirable camera properties to achieve high-quality VBR results include: sufficiently high frame rate, good color recording properties, sufficient sensitivity to allow for short exposure times and/or high f-stop numbers, high dynamic range, as well as access to raw image data, i.e., access to pixel values that have not been preprocessed by the camera hardware internally. Meeting all of these conditions at the same time while avoiding the cost of building custom camera hardware requires some compromises.

Solid-State Imagers. For digital image acquisition, solid-state CCD [135] and CMOS imaging chips are used almost exclusively today. In comparison, traditional cathode-ray tube (CRT) cameras have a number of inherent drawbacks, such as non-linear response curve, inferior light sensitivity, higher electronic noise level, larger size, and higher cost. Solid-state imagers are characterized by their resolution, pixel area, light sensitivity, imaging noise, and quantum well capacity. The size of one pixel, or more accurately the grid constant of the regular 2D pixel array, Δx, is referred to as *pixel pitch*; see Figure 2.1. Light sensitivity varies with wavelength. For a given wavelength, chip sensitivity is specified by the conversion efficiency. The conversion efficiency factor denotes the percentage of photons that are able to excite electrons in the valence band across the silicon's band gap to the conduction band. Imaging noise is fundamentally present due to the temperature of the sensor. Additionally, the on-chip analog-to-digital converter introduces noise to the signal. The quantum well capacity specifies the maximum number of photons that can be accumulated per pixel. Together with the imaging noise level, the quantum well capacity determines the useful dynamic range of an imaging chip. In general, smaller pixels have a lower quantum well capacity leading to a limited dynamic range of typically no more than eight bits. Due to their different design, CMOS chips vary by fill factor, denoting the percentage of light-sensitive area of each pixel in comparison to total chip area covered by one pixel, while CCD chips differ in charge transfer efficiency, i.e, loss of signal during image readout. While CMOS chips are cheaper to manufacture and easier to control, so far, CCD chips are still superior with respect to imaging noise, light sensitivity, and the fraction of "hot" (faulty) pixels. With the advent of mass-produced CMOS-based webcams, however, CMOS imaging technology has been constantly gaining ground on CCDs in recent years.

Commercial Cameras.   Most VBR pioneering labs relied on the Sony DFW-V500 camera [259, 208, 209]. At that time, it was about the only commercially available digital color video camera that featured progressive scan mode and that could be externally synchronized. In external synchronization mode, the Sony camera achieves approximately 13 frames per second. It is fitted with a standard C lens mount. The color images are recorded by a single-chip, 1/3-inch, 640×480-pixel CCD chip using the Bayer mosaic technique [14]. All video cameras used so far in VBR research record color using this approach. A Bayer mosaic consists of a regular matrix of tiny red, green, and blue color filters right on top of the CCD chip. Plate I depicts the filter arrangement. Two green, one red, and one blue filter are arranged in a block of 2×2 pixels, following our visual system's emphasis on luminance information (approximately the green channel). As a rule of thumb, the effective resolution of a Bayer mosaic camera corresponds approximately to a full-color (e.g., 3-chip) camera with half as many pixels. On-board the Sony DFW-V500, color information is automatically interpolated to mimic full CCD-chip resolution. The camera outputs a YUV 4:2:2 digital video signal, i.e., the luminance channel has (interpolated) 640×480-pixel resolution, while the chrominance channels contain 320×240 pixels. Note that the output signal requires 50 percent more bandwidth than was actually recorded by the chip. The camera is connected to a host computer via the IEEE1394 (FireWire^{TM}) bus. The bus bandwidth of 400 MBits/s allows the controlling of two cameras from one host PC. The camera model features some additional on-board preprocessing, such as gain control and white-balance adjustment. Different sets of parameter values can be stored in camera memory for fast switching.

In recent years, other manufacturers have built externally triggerable video cameras, some of which have already been employed in VBR research. The *3D TV* system [207] is based on the Basler A101fc camera model. It records 12 frames per second at 1300×1030-pixel resolution on a 2/3-inch CCD chip. The camera can output raw pixel data, so transmission bandwidth of the FireWire^{TM}

	resolution [pixel]	synchronized frame rate	color format	chip	Ref.
Sony DFW-V500	640 × 480	13fps	YUV 4:2:2	CCD	[259, 208, 209]
Basler A101fc	1300 × 1030	12 fps	raw / YUV 4:2:2	CCD	[207]
PtGrey	1024 × 768	15 fps	raw	CCD	[345]
Omnivision 8610	640 × 480	30 fps	MPEG2	CMOS	[312]

Table 2.1. Specifications of camera models used in VBR research.

bus is used efficiently, and the conversion from Bayer mosaic data to, e.g., RGB color space can be controlled. The Basler models also feature the standard C lens mount.

The acquisition set-up of Microsoft's *Video View Interpolation* project [345] consists of PointGrey cameras that deliver 1024×768-pixel color images at 15 frames per second [130]. The video images are downstreamed via fiber optics cables to a custom-built storage system.

The use of CMOS imagers instead of CCD chips was pioneered in the "Stanford Multi-Camera Array" [312]. The system consists of custom-built camera heads using the Omnivision OV8610 CMOS imaging chip. The camera heads record 640×480-pixel color images in YUV 4:2:2 format at 30 frames per second. One control board per camera preprocesses the images and encodes the video data as MPEG-2 bitstreams. Up to 26 compressed video streams are downlinked via the IEEE1394 bus to one PC, where the bitstreams are stored on SCSI hard drives. As the Stanford Multi-Camera Array provides MPEG-compressed image data only, quantization noise and blocking artifacts deteriorate image quality, posing a challenge to further processing algorithms.

Table 2.1 summarizes the technical specifications of different camera models used so far in VBR research. Of course, new camera models with improved capabilities will continue to become available. The amount of data that can be processed using conventional PC technology, however, puts a limit on manageable acquisition resolution, frame rate, and color depth. With consumer-market PC memory, hard drive capacity, and CPU clock rate apparently levelling out in recent years, it may be surmised that VBR recording resolution and frame rate will not increase by orders of magnitude in the coming years from the level of the latest camera models in Table 2.1.

The Lens. Besides camera electronics, it is the lens that determines recorded image quality. No amount of processing on an image taken through an inferior lens can achieve the image quality of an appropriate, first-grade lens objective.

The standard lens mounts for video cameras are the so-called C- and CS-mounts for which a large palette of lenses are commercially available. To achieve the best possible recording results, the appropriate lens must be selected for the

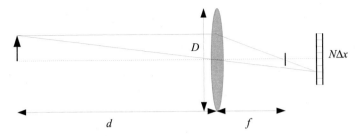

Figure 2.1. A camera lens is characterized by its focal length f and its maximal free aperture D, or minimum f-stop number $F = D/f$. To achieve the best recording results, lens parameters must be matched to pixel pitch (pixel dimension) Δx and overall imaging chip extent $N\Delta x$.

camera chip's specifications. Figure 2.1 illustrates the most important parameters of the lens-chip imaging system.

To avoid vignetting, the lens must be matched to the size of the camera's CCD sensor to evenly illuminate the entire CCD chip area $N\Delta x$. Typical video sensor sizes are 1/3-inch, 1/2-inch, and 2/3-inch, measured along the chip diagonal. Video camera lenses are specifically designed for these different chip sizes, with prices increasing from the small to the large illumination field. Lenses for larger sensors can be used in conjunction with smaller CCD chips, but not vice versa.

To make full use of camera resolution, the lens must produce images that are "as sharp" as can be imaged by the camera. In optical terms, the lens's *point spread function* (PSF) should approximately match the size of one pixel. For a good lens, its *Airy disk* diameter A depends on wavelength λ and f-stop number F:

$$A = 2.44\,\lambda\,F. \qquad (2.1)$$

The f-stop number, or f-stop, denotes the ratio of free aperture diameter D and focal length f of the lens, $F = D/f$. For green light ($\lambda = 500$ nm) and $F = 2.0$, a first-grade lens concentrates most intensity into a disc of $A = 2.44$ μm in diameter. Following the Rayleigh criterion, the smallest resolvable distance corresponds to the case when two point light sources are imaged $A/2$ apart. To record at maximum resolution, the sampling theorem dictates that at least two pixels must fall within this length. In summary, the largest permissible pixel dimension without sacrificing any theoretically attainable resolution is $\Delta x = A/4$. The f-stop of a lens objective can typically be varied to adjust for different light levels, so the Airy disk diameter increases with increasing f-stop number. If a lens is stopped down too much, its resolution can become worse than the pixel resolution of the camera, which would be a waste of available imaging resources. CCD pixel size Δx therefore limits the range of reasonable f-stops: the larger the CCD pixels, the smaller the f-stop number may be. On the other hand, if the Airy disk A is smaller than about four times the pixel size Δx, the recorded image is not adequately prefiltered, and aliasing artifacts occur. While the above argument is based on a single wavelength, the lens must also be corrected for chromatic aberrations to record sharp color images, which is the main reason excellent camera lenses are expensive.

The *knife-edge technique* constitutes a practical and convenient way to measure the effective resolution of a lens-sensor system [248]. It consists of recording the image of a straight edge that is oriented at a slightly slanted angle with respect to the CCD chip orientation. The slope of the imaged edge is determined, and all image scan lines are registered into a single, super-resolution edge profile. This edge profile is also referred to as the line spread function. The Fourier transform of the line spread function is the optical system's *modulation transfer function* (MTF). It captures the imaging system's response to (linear) spatial frequency. The resolution limit of an optical system is conventionally said to be the frequency at which the MTF has fallen to about 10 percent of its DC (maximum) value [314].

Besides controlling the amount of light that falls onto the image sensor and its effect on imaging resolution, the aperture stop (f-stop) has another important influence on imaging quality. It determines the depth of field, i.e., the depth range within which the scene is captured at full camera resolution. The depth range towards, $\Delta_{\min}$, and away from the camera, $\Delta_{\max}$, that is still imaged sharply depends on pixel size Δx, focal length f, f-stop F, and distance d:

$$\Delta_{\min} = \frac{\Delta x \, F \, d^2}{f^2 + \Delta x \, F \, d} \,,$$

$$\Delta_{\max} = \frac{\Delta x \, F \, d^2}{f^2 - \Delta x \, F \, d} \,.$$

For example, a camera with pixel size $\Delta x = 5 \mu m$ that is equipped with a lens featuring $f = 15$ mm focal length, focused at $d = 3$ m distance, and stopped down to $F = 4.0$ captures the depth range from $d - \Delta_{min} = 3m - 0.63m = 2.37m$ to $d + \Delta_{max} = 3m + 1.09m = 4.09m$ at full resolution. For $\Delta x = 5\mu m$, $F = 4.0$ is the largest f-stop number before sacrificing camera resolution at $\lambda = 500$ nm.

Some video objective lenses do not allow varying the focus. Instead, the focus is set by the manufacturer at the hyperfocal distance d_{hf} corresponding to some f-stop F and pixel size Δx:

$$d_{hf} = \frac{f^2}{\Delta x \, F} \,. \tag{2.2}$$

Such fixed-focus lenses give sharp images of objects at distances from about $d_{hf}/2$ to infinity. However, because the correct hyperfocal distance depends on CCD pixel size Δx, the lens must be specifically manufactured for that camera model. Lenses with adjustable focal distance offer a wider range of applications, e.g., they can also be used for close-up recordings. On the other hand, such lenses must be individually focused, which is a non-trivial task and can turn out to be a tedious chore for recording scenarios with many cameras. Also, if the focus changes between recordings, e.g., due to different room temperature or accidental touching, the cameras must be refocused, and potentially even re-calibrated (Section 2.1.5), before each recording session.

The focal length f of the camera lens and overall CCD chip size $N\Delta x$ determine the imaged viewing angle,

$$\alpha = 2\arctan\frac{N\Delta x}{2f}.$$

Typically, maximum distance from the scene, and therefore necessary viewing angle, is determined by the size of the recording studio. Wide-angle lenses offering angles larger than $40°$ to $50°$ potentially exhibit substantial radial distortion, which must be corrected for prior to VBR processing. Normal and telephoto lenses show less distortion, which makes camera calibration considerably easier. Zoom lenses with variable focal length are not recommended for VBR applications, simply because the cameras must be recalibrated whenever the focal length is changed.

One issue to keep in mind is whether the imaging chip is already equipped with an infrared-blocking (IR cut) filter. The silicon chip is highly sensitive to infrared radiation that is invisible to the human eye. If infrared light is not blocked, the images depict wrong object colors, and color calibration is not possible. If the camera is sensitive to IR, an infrared-blocking filter must be mounted onto the camera lens.

2.1.2 Recording Set-Up

When setting up the recording environment, camera mounts should be highly adjustable in order to optimally position and aim each camera at the scene. At the same time, the cameras must be installed in a rugged, stable fashion so they do not accidentally change position or orientation. This is because during acquisition, the location and orientation of all video cameras must remain fixed in order to capture calibrated image material. Frustrations and double work can be minimized by selecting appropriate camera mounting equipment.

Two different VBR acquisition scenarios must be distinguished. To record light field data for the *small-baseline* VBR techniques discussed in Chapter 3, the video cameras must be grouped close together. In contrast, the VBR approaches presented in Chapters 4 to 6 require input images that are acquired in a *wide-baseline* camera set-up.

Small-Baseline Camera Set-Up. To capture dense light field data of a dynamic scene, the synchronized video cameras are commonly arranged in a dense, regular grid. Equal distances between cameras simplify light field querying and interpolation later during rendering. Irregular camera spacings cannot later be adjusted for since translational changes in camera position cause parallax effects in the recorded images that cannot be corrected without scene depth information. A simple and cost-efficient way to mount multiple cameras in close arrangement was devised by Hartmut Schirmacher and his collaborators [259]. Their *Lumi-Shelf* system consists of a simple bookshelf to which six Sony DFW-V500 cameras are attached using clamps and conventional camera mounting heads. For larger rigs and more flexibility, Wojciech Matusik's *3D TV* system [207] and the Stanford Multi-Camera Array [312] built by Bennett Wilburn rely on a modular aluminum framing system [128]; see Figure 2.2. For individual camera head alignment, the latter system employs precision mirror mounts that are typically used in experimental optics [129].

To directly record the dynamic light field in the convenient two-plane light field parameterization (Section 2.3.2), the optical axes of all cameras must be aligned in parallel. However, exactly aligning the optical axes of many cameras is a very time-consuming occupation. Also, to make optimal use of camera resolution, it is often desirable to record the scene in a converging camera set-up. Light

Figure 2.2. The Stanford Multi-Camera Array consists of one hundred CMOS camera heads. The cameras can be arranged in a planar matrix with aligned optical axes to record dynamic scenes in the two-plane light field parameterization. *(Reprinted from [103].)*

field images that are not recorded with parallel optical camera axes can be rectified after acquisition by applying a projective transform to each camera image. Steve Seitz describes how to determine the projection transformation from point correspondences, as well as how to warp and resample the light field images [263, 262]. Suitably implemented, e.g., on graphics hardware, image rectification can be carried out on-the-fly at acquisition frame rates [332].

Wide-Baseline Camera Set-Up.   While small-baseline VBR techniques constrain acquisition camera positions to be close together, optimal camera placement is an important issue for wide-baseline VBR approaches. Because now, the scene is recorded from only a few viewpoints spaced far apart, the acquired video streams should contain as much VBR-relevant information as possible. If the dynamic scene does not exhibit any invariant symmetry characteristics, or viewpoints known a priori to be of little interest, available video cameras should be distributed such that the hemisphere around the scene is evenly covered. One example is the *3D Dome* at Carnegie Mellon University's Robotics Lab [247]. It consists of a geodesic dome structure, measuring five meters in diameter, made of metal struts and connectors. Fifty-one video cameras are mounted along the structure that are looking inward to record the stage area at the dome's center. A later version of the 3D Dome is the *3D Room*, composed of 49 cameras mounted along the four walls and the ceiling of a studio that measures 7 m × 7 m × 3 m [143]. Similar systems, albeit with fewer cameras, have also been built by other research groups [24, 208, 309, 178, 183, 206, 325, 38].

If possible, the camera heads should be placed far from the scene for several reasons:

- The use of wide-angle lenses is avoided.

- The cameras' depth of field can cover the entire scene volume.

- Projected pixel size varies less over the scene volume.

In the confines of a studio room, maximum distance from the scene is limited. Recording the scene from above can prove impossible if the ceiling height is that of a normal office room. On the other hand, limited ceiling height allows the use of telescope poles [200]. The poles can be jammed between the floor and ceiling at arbitrary positions in the room to serve as mounting rigs for the cameras; see Figure 2.3. This way, utmost camera positioning flexibility is achieved while providing sufficient stability and alignment robustness, e.g., against accidental bumps. To clamp the cameras to the telescope poles and to orient the cameras in arbitrary directions, mounting brackets with three-degrees-of-freedom camera heads can be used [200].

Figure 2.3. Camera mounting: the photo industry offers telescope poles that can be jammed between floor and ceiling, offering great flexibility in camera positioning. To affix the cameras to the poles, freely orientable mounting brackets are used. *((left) Reprinted from [291]. (middle, right) Reprinted from [176], courtesy of Ming Li.)*

Mobile Set-Up. A studio room restricts the type of dynamic events that can be acquired to indoor activities only. To record multi-video footage of events in their natural environment, a multi-video recording system is needed that can be folded up, transported to arbitrary locations, and set up almost anywhere without too much effort. This requires a compact and adaptable system for synchronized multi-video acquisition.

A prototype of a mobile multi-video acquisition system has been built by Lukas Ahrenberg [3]. The system is composed of several autonomous, portable laptop-camera modules that capture and store video data independent of any fur-

Figure 2.4. For a mobile multi-video acquisition system, each camera module must run autonomously. Built from consumer-market components, each unit consists of a laptop, camera, tripod, and battery pack. The complete module weighs less than 10 kg and fits into a backpack for convenient transportation. *(Reprinted from [3], © 2004 IEE.)*

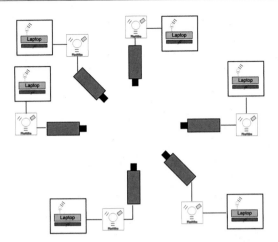

Figure 2.5. Modular acquisition system design: the laptop-camera units are controlled and synchronized via wireless LAN. *(Reprinted from [3], © 2004 IEE.)*

ther infrastructure; see Figure 2.4. The modules are built from off-the-shelf components only. Each module consists of a laptop PC with wireless LAN capabilities, a Sony DFW-V500 video camera, a 12V rechargeable battery, a FireWire™ card adapter, and a tripod.

A number of issues arise when adapting the equipment for use in a stand-alone system. One such challenge is the power supply for the camera. The Sony camera model draws its current from the FireWire™ cable. Laptop FireWire™ cards, however, do not exhibit the 12V output line that PC FireWire™ cards feature. In addition, the camera's energy consumption of about 4 watts would quickly drain the laptop battery and severely limit operation time. So instead, a Card-Bus adapter is inserted in the laptop's FireWire™ port that enables feeding an external power source to the FireWire™ cable. While the rechargeable 12V battery adds extra pounds to the module, the total weight of the complete unit is still less than 10 kg.

To synchronize multi-video acquisition, the camera modules are not physically connected by cable. Instead, a radio-based wireless network is used; see Figure 2.5. The 802.11 wireless local area network (WLAN) is run in ad-hoc mode, so that additional camera modules can be added or removed without the need to reconfigure the existing network. A client-server architecture is established among the laptops. The master laptop broadcasts instructions to all client modules via WLAN to remotely control the entire system. Due to limited availability of the drivers for the laptop's hardware components, the system is implemented using the non-real-time operating system Windows 2000.

The most important feature of VBR acquisition is synchronized recording. For the mobile system, camera triggering is accomplished via the wireless network employing software synchronization. To keep video frame capture in step, two different strategies can be pursued: either a triggering command is sent over the network for every frame, or only the start of the recording sequence is synchronized, after which each module must keep the pace by itself. The latter approach minimizes dependency on the communication channel and reduces the risk of unpredictable delays due to the non-real-time operating system. It turns out that the laptop-camera units are able to keep to the frame rate very precisely. Starting the acquisition for all units at the same moment, however, is critical. Synchronization time offsets are predominantly due to differences in receive and application time delay, i.e., the time it takes from the moment when a message arrives at the network interface until the operating system passes it on to the application, as well as the time it takes for the application to react to the message. These delays are, in essence, not controllable if the acquisition system runs on a non-real-time operating system. Repeated synchronization signal broadcast and feedback must be used to minimize synchronization discrepancies. Alternatively, exact clock synchronization can be achieved if each client laptop is equipped with a GPS receiver that provides an exact and absolute reference time signal. After having synchronized all laptop clocks, a start time for image recording is sent from the master to all client units. The client laptops wait until the specified time and only then begin recording. This way, synchronization errors introduced by the network are avoided altogether. Remaining synchronization differences are due to the application time delay, which, fortunately, turns out to be tolerable if recording at 15 fps.

The system is not designed to allow for online processing and VBR display in the field. Instead, each unit's video stream is saved for later processing. Because guaranteed continuous bandwidth to the laptop's hard drive is not sufficient to directly store the data, the video images are buffered in local memory. The laptops feature 1 GB of RAM, which is sufficient to capture about 80 seconds of video at 640×480-pixel resolution and 15 frames per second.. After capture, the images are losslessly compressed and written to the laptop's hard drive. Back home, the video streams are downloaded from the laptops to a central repository for further VBR processing.

To evaluate overall usability, the mobile recording system must be tested in the field. Plate II depicts the deployment of eight mobile camera units set up to record a craftsman in his shop. The equipment can be easily transported in a normal car and set up within two hours, including recording calibration sequences. Over a period of two hours, multiple sequences of multi-video footage are acquired using three different camera configurations. Set-up time to record in a new camera configuration takes about 20 minutes including calibration. When finished recording, packing up the equipment takes another hour. In summary, 30 minutes of multi-video footage employing three different camera configurations can be recorded in five hours. VBR rendering results obtained from the recorded sequence are shown in Plate III. Plate III(a) depicts original images of the multi-video data set. Using volume-based visual-hull rendering (Section 4.1), the craftsman can be interactively viewed performing his trade from arbitrary viewpoints; see Plate III(b).

2.1.3 Illumination

It is well known in photography that scene illumination has a strong impact on object appearance. In television studios, theaters, or at movie sets, scene lighting is the task of specialists. Remarkably, illumination has not yet been given serious consideration in VBR acquisition, even though VBR imposes strict requirements on scene lighting to ensure optimal acquisition:

- Intensity: scene foreground must be brightly lit to allow for short exposure times, which may be necessary to avoid motion blur. A brightly lit scene is also desirable to realize small internal video camera gain settings in order to keep electronic noise to a minimum while exploiting the cameras' full dynamic range. Also, high illumination levels allow for higher f-numbers, which increases the depth of field.

- Diffuse illumination: the lights should illuminate the foreground evenly from all directions. This way, large shadowed object regions are avoided, and shadows cast on the floor and walls are diminished.

- Placement: the light sources must be placed such that they do not cause lens glare in any camera.

- Natural spectrum: the lights must lend the scene its natural color appearance. Strong infrared emitters, such as incandescent light sources, or standard fluorescent tube light can falsify captured object colors.

Obviously, a large studio room with high ceilings is preferable because then light sources and acquisition cameras can be positioned at the periphery. Light sources are characterized by their output light intensity (luminous flux) and their *color rendering index* (CRI). The color rendering index ranges from 0 to 100 and indicates how well colors are reproduced by different illumination conditions in comparison to a standard light source (e.g., daylight). A CRI value of 100 represents identical visual appearance, while cool white fluorescent lamps may have a CRI value of as little as 60.

Different types of light sources are available for stage lighting. Arc lamps as well as tungsten-filament and halide light bulbs are based on thermal emission, creating a continuous, broad spectrum. Unfortunately, such incandescent light sources radiate excessive quantities of infrared light while emitting less energy in the green and blue part of the spectrum. To avoid yellow-tinted object appearance in the images, white balancing can be achieved by mounting appropriate filters in front of the lights. Conventional fluorescent lamps emit "cold" light, such that the red end of the spectrum is not suitably represented. Full-spectrum fluorescent lamps are available; however, fluorescent tube lamps typically flicker with the frequency of the power grid. Solid-state lights (LEDs, etc.) are just emerging as light sources for stage illumination applications. Halide metal vapor lamps (HMI) combine high illumination intensities with high CRI values. In an HMI light bulb, a DC electric arc burns in an atmosphere of mercury intermixed with halides of rare earth elements. HMI lamps exhibit a spectral energy distribution that resembles natural sunlight, including a substantial ultraviolet component that should be blocked via filtering. HMI lamps can deliver more than 10^5 lumens. Because the light-emitting area within the HMI bulb is confined to a small spot, a diffuser screen must be mounted in front of the light bulb to avoid sharp shadow lines.

2.1.4 Network Infrastructure

Depending on the application, the acquired multi-video footage is either processed on-the-fly for immediate display, or the images are stored on the hard drive for later retrieval and offline processing. In either case, because all camera models mentioned in Section 2.1.1 require a PC for control, multiple host computers must be integrated into one common network to provide sufficient bandwidth for the continuous stream of image data. Figure 2.6 depicts the layout of a typical set-up. Inter-PC communication can be conveniently realized via Ethernet^{TM}. For hardware-synchronized (gen-locked) recording, a separate line feeds the frame trigger signal directly into the cameras. A master PC sends out the synchronization signal and controls the host PCs. This client-server architecture allows for adding arbitrarily many cameras and PCs to the network.

The seemingly less demanding VBR scenario is to store the images for later processing. The huge amount of continuously arriving image data, however, imposes specific demands on continuous bus bandwidth to the storage device. The first VBR acquisition system at CMU recorded the video streams as analog signals on conventional video tapes [221]. Sustained write throughput of standard PCI-bus, IDE-controller hard drives is not sufficient to store uncompressed VGA-resolution images at video frame rates. The Stanford Multi-Camera Array relies

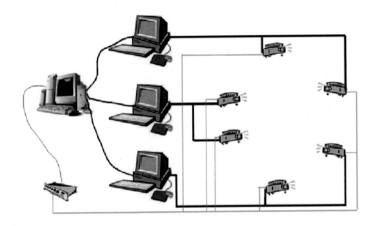

Figure 2.6. Client-server studio set-up: the cameras are connected to host PCs and synchronized via triggering cables. The PCs communicate with the server via Ethernet^{TM}. *(Reprinted from [291], © 2003 Eurographics.)*

on SCSI hard drives to store the video streams in compressed format [312]. A custom multi-drive system using fiber optical connectors was built by PointGrey Research Inc. for the *Video View Interpolation* system [345]. Storing uncompressed, high-resolution video streams using conventional PC hardware remains a challenge for VBR acquisition.

For online processing, data must be exchanged between client PCs and the display host. To keep the system scalable, as much computational load as possible must be delegated from the display host to the client PCs. A distributed client-server network facilitates on-line processing of the recorded multi-video imagery. On the lowest level, each client PC controls, e.g., two synchronized video cameras. Image resolution permitting, each client PC is able to perform low-level processing on both incoming video streams at acquisition frame rate. In a hierarchical network, the processed data from every two clients are sent on to one PC that processes the combined data further. The result is passed on to yet another computer in the next-higher hierarchical layer of processing nodes, until at the root of the hierarchical network the complete, processed information is available. For n video cameras, such a binary tree network requires $n - 1$ computers. The root node PC is the display server and renders the time-critical output image. At the same time, it is able to control the network. To limit network traffic for video texture transfer, the display server requests only those images from the respective camera clients that contribute to the target view. This way, network traffic and computational load are kept constant to accommodate arbitrarily many acquisition cameras. For VBR algorithms that can be parallelized to benefit from distributed processing, interactive performance is achieved using commodity PC hardware in conjunction with a standard 100 Mb Ethernet™ LAN [208, 259, 172, 207].

All time-critical VBR algorithms discussed in Chapter 4 are experimentally evaluated using a distributed set-up as shown in Figure 2.6. The network consists of four 1.1 GHz Athlon client PCs and one P4 1.7 GHz display server. Four client nodes each control two Sony DFW-500 cameras via the IEEE1394 FireWire™ bus. Camera resolution is 320×240 pixels RGB, acquired at 13 fps. The client nodes are directly connected to the display server via 100 Mb Ethernet™. While different VBR algorithms may require different graphics boards on the display server, the network infrastructure remains the same for all experiments.

2.1.5   Geometric Calibration

Multi-video footage by itself does not allow for much video-based rendering. To recover scene geometry information from the acquired data, images from different viewpoints must be related. This requires knowing camera locations and orientations (*extrinsic* parameters), as well as internal camera imaging characteristics (*intrinsic* parameters). The procedure to determine these parameters is known as *geometric camera calibration*. Figuring out calibration parameters directly by measuring the camera set-up, however, is not feasible. Instead, camera calibration is done by relating image projection coordinates of known 3D points. One standard technique of estimating extrinsic and intrinsic camera calibration parameters was first proposed by Tsai [297]. An implementation in C is available from Reg Willson's web site [316]. Another elegant calibration approach is Zhengyou Zhang's method [339] (he also provides a Windows executable file on his web site [340]). Because of the wide variety of possible camera configurations, the camera calibration routine must typically be manually adapted to the specific arrangement. Jean-Yves Bouguet has compiled a complete MATLAB toolbox that includes Tsai's and Zhang's algorithms as well as several more calibration algorithms suitable for various scenarios. It features a convenient user interface and can be downloaded free of charge from his web site [26]. The only constraint is that the toolbox requires a valid MATLAB license on Windows, Unix, or Linux. Alternatively, an implementation of the toolbox routines in C is included in the OpenCV library, which is also available free of charge [270]. The OpenCV library also features numerous additional routines, such as algorithms for automated corner detection.

Small-Baseline Calibration.   To calibrate a multi-camera set-up, one or more calibration sequences are recorded prior to (or after) actual VBR scene acquisition. Because in small-baseline configurations the cameras' respective fields of view almost coincide, intrinsic and extrinsic camera parameters can be determined from recordings of a single calibration pattern. The calibration object exhibits multiple feature points that are easy to detect and to identify, and whose 3D positions are known exactly. To obtain accurate intrinsic parameter values, especially concerning radial lens distortion, the calibration object must cover the entire field of view of all cameras. Because the 3D calibration points are not supposed to be coplanar, if a planar calibration pattern is used [339], its orientation must be varied during calibration sequence acquisition.

Wide-Baseline Calibration. For wide-baseline camera calibration, in contrast, it is impractical to construct a calibration object that is visible in all cameras and at the same time fills the cameras' field of view. Instead, intrinsic and extrinsic camera parameters are determined separately. Intrinsic calibration is done for each camera separately. As in small-baseline calibration, a sequence is recorded of a calibration object filling the field of view of the camera, from which the camera's focal length, optical center coordinates, and radial lens distortion are determined using only the intrinsic calibration part of any of the algorithms mentioned above. For extrinsic parameter estimation, a second calibration object is placed in the scene and is recorded from all cameras. With the already determined intrinsic camera parameters, position and orientation of all cameras can be determined from the calibration object's known 3D feature point positions.

Mobile Set-Up Calibration. For accurate results, the extrinsic calibration object should cover the entire visible scene. In a studio, the size of the stage is preset, and a suitable calibration object can be custom-built. For a portable system, however, camera arrangement and recorded scene size is different during every deployment. A robust, quick, and easy-to-use camera calibration procedure that performs well for arbitrary camera configurations and in a wide range of recording environments is desirable. For such applications, the use of a *virtual calibration object* has proven useful. A virtual calibration object is constructed by swerving an easy-to-localize object, e.g., a flashlight or a brightly colored ball, all around the scene volume [11]. A spherical marker object has the advantage that it also works in daylight, it has the same appearance from all directions, and its midpoint can be robustly determined from its image silhouette. If recorded in sync, video images of the same time frame depict the calibration object at a distinct 3D position in space. This 3D position serves as one calibration point. Chen et al. extend the virtual calibration object idea to the case of multiple unsynchronized cameras [44]. In contrast to a rigid calibration object, however, absolute 3D

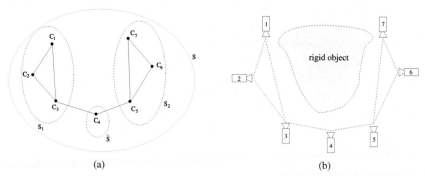

(a)   (b)

Figure 2.7. Graph-based extrinsic camera calibration: (a) example for a graph with non-empty sets S, S_k, $\bar{S}$, and (b) the corresponding camera configuration. *(Reprinted from [125].)*

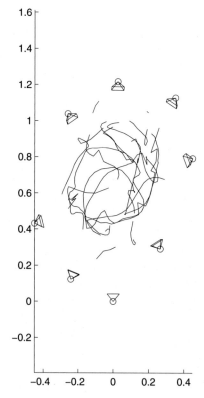

Figure 2.8. Top view of a reconstructed virtual calibration object (line segments) and the recovered camera calibration (frustum pyramids).

calibration point positions are not known, which leads to an indeterminate global scale factor for the camera set-up.

The virtual calibration concept does not require all cameras to see the calibration marker object simultaneously. The only requirement regarding the marker path is that the marker should be visible in at least two cameras at any time, and that every camera should record the marker sometime during the calibration sequence.

Relative position and orientation between camera pairs can be determined directly from pairwise image correspondences. To register all cameras into a common reference frame, a graph-based visualization is useful [125].

The graph $G = (V, E)$ reflects the relationship between cameras; see Figure 2.7(a). Graph nodes represent the cameras $C_i \in V$, while relative position and orientation between pairs of cameras $(C_i, C_j) \in E$ are represented by a connecting edge in the graph; see Figure 2.7(b). The graph is undirected since the relative position and orientation $(\mathbf{R}, \mathbf{t})$ for camera pair (C_i, C_j) automatically yields the relative position and orientation of (C_j, C_i) via $(\mathbf{R}^\mathbf{T}, -\mathbf{R}^\mathbf{T}\mathbf{t})$. Once the graph is constructed, it is searched for cyclic subsets $S_k \subseteq S$. The set $\bar{S} := S \setminus (\cup_k S_k)$ consists of all cameras that do not belong to any cycle.

First, the unknown scale factors for pairwise translation are determined independently for each S_k. Any cycle in the graph represents a closed curve in three-dimensional space. By exploiting the constraint that the scaled translations along any closed loop of the graph must sum to zero, a linear system of equations is set up for each cycle. The resulting linear system of equations is typically over-determined and can be solved in a least-squares sense. Since the obtained estimate is not directly related to the image-space measurements anymore, the reprojection error of the solution is not necessarily optimal. The overall shape of the set-up is, nevertheless, correctly recovered, and the result can be used as the initial estimate for subsequent bundle adjustment also to optimize camera orientation parameters [296, 109]. Using these partial registrations, parts of the virtual calibration object (e.g., the path of the tracked marker object) are reconstructed. The remaining step is to register all subsets S_k and all $C_i \in \bar{S}$ with each other to form one globally consistent calibration. Figure 2.8 depicts the reconstructed object marker path and estimated camera positions and orientations from a real-world calibration sequence.

2.1.6 Color Calibration

Two images of the same scene recorded from the identical viewpoint but with two cameras are almost always at least slightly different; see Plate IV. If optimal VBR results are to be obtained, this mismatch must be minimized prior to further processing and rendering. Conceptually, multi-camera color calibration consists of first linearizing each camera's individual response curve to obtain linear tristimulus values for each pixel. In a second step, individual camera color spaces are matched either to some common color space derived for the given scene illumination or to a standard reference color space.

A viable method to optimize internal camera settings and to calibrate color across cameras is described in Neel Joshi's report on radiometric calibration of the Stanford Multi-Camera Array [140]. The approach is fully automated and takes a couple of minutes prior to dynamic scene acquisition. It consists of two steps. First, the internal settings for gain and offset of each camera are adjusted. Then, sensor non-linearity, vignetting, and global color error minimization is performed in software. The method aims at obtaining a uniform color response from all cameras, not absolute color accuracy with respect to some color standard. Scene illumination is assumed to be static. The calibration technique is designed for a small-baseline multi-camera array such that a planar color calibration target can be recorded simultaneously from all cameras.

Before actual VBR recording, a 24-color GretagMacbeth ColorChecker™ chart is placed in the middle of the scene and recorded from all cameras [126]. The color patches are automatically identified by affixing the Macbeth chart atop a geometric calibration target. To reduce electronic noise, the pixels within each identified color patch are averaged over respective patch area as well as over several time frames. Internal gamma correction is turned off for calibration as well as subsequent VBR acquisition.

To adjust internal camera gain and offset settings, the Macbeth chart is recorded with different exposure times such that the white patch of the chart gets digitized to intensity values covering the linear midrange of the imaging sensors. For each camera, a straight line is fit to the recorded pixel values, separately for each color channel. Iteratively, the camera's internal gain and offset settings are varied such that the (extrapolated) zero-exposure pixel value is mapped to a preset minimum value (e.g., 12 pixel intensity units in all color channels). The white value at optimal exposure is mapped to a preset maximum value (e.g., 220 pixel intensity units). This way, the optimal exposure time corresponds to the case where full use is made of the cameras' dynamic range without clipping pixel color values.

Having determined the internal camera settings to be used during actual VBR acquisition, additional color calibration must be performed in software. To do so, in a second step, individual camera response is first linearized at the low and high end of the pixel value range. Again, the color chart's white patch is recorded for a range of exposure settings, and the recorded RGB pixel values are evaluated. Assuming that the exposure times are exact, the pixel values measured for short and long exposures are mapped to the extrapolated linear response curve determined from the mid-exposure times. Three look-up tables are established that map any recorded red-, green-, and blue-channel value to the full, linear imaging range, e.g., from 0 to 255 pixel intensity units.

To make use of all color patches, the radiometric falloff over the Macbeth color chart due to lens vignetting and non-uniform illumination must be accounted for. A large photographic gray card is placed in front of the Macbeth chart, covering the entire color chart. For each pixel, a scaling factor is computed from the gray-card image to correct the color-chart recording.

To minimize difference in color reproduction between cameras, a 3×4 color calibration matrix $\mathbf{M}_i^{\text{colcal}}$ is determined for each camera i. The matrices are computed by taking into account all 24 color patches j. The color chart is recorded at the exposure time used later during VBR acquisition. For each color patch, the recorded and falloff-corrected pixel values (r_{ij}, g_{ij}, b_{ij}) are averaged over all cameras i to yield average color-patch values $(\bar{r}_j, \bar{g}_j, \bar{b}_j)$. The color calibration matrices are used to best match recorded color-patch pixel values to the average color-patch value:

$$
\begin{pmatrix} \bar{r}_j \\ \bar{g}_j \\ \bar{b}_j \end{pmatrix} = \mathbf{M}_i^{\text{colcal}} \begin{pmatrix} r_{ij} \\ g_{ij} \\ b_{ij} \\ 1 \end{pmatrix}. \tag{2.3}
$$

The color calibration matrices $\mathbf{M}_i^{\text{colcal}}$ are determined from this overdetermined set of linear equations so as to minimize error in the least-squares sense, e.g., via singular value decomposition (SVD). By representing recorded color values using homogeneous coordinates, offset differences can be adjusted as well.

The VBR sequences are recorded using the optimal exposure time, applying the internal camera gain and offset settings determined during the first calibration step. Each recorded pixel value is looked up in the response linearization table and replaced with the tabulated value. Finally, global color correction is performed via Equation (2.3).

This approach is intended for small-baseline camera set-ups. If the color chart cannot be recorded simultaneously by all cameras, such that the chart must be recorded for each camera separately, chart illumination varies between cameras. The illumination differences complicate global color calibration considerably, suggesting matching patch colors to a ground-truth color standard. Calibration to a color standard, in turn, requires calibrating first the illuminating light's temperature, or even determining the detailed spectral energy distribution of the illuminating light sources; see Section 2.1.3. To obtain images from widely spaced cameras that are, to first order, similar in color, Neel Joshi and his co-workers advise to do only the first calibration step, placing the white target close to the cameras and recording out-of-focus [140]. If this is not feasible, they suggest to set internal camera gain and offset to the same values for all cameras instead of relying on the cameras' automatic gain and white balance feature.

2.1.7 Segmentation

Image pixel affiliation with either scene background or object foreground is a valuable clue for geometry reconstruction. Silhouette-based methods rely entirely on accurate image segmentation. To distinguish between fore- and background pixels from image data only, segmentation must be based on pixel color.

In professional applications, segmentation is traditionally realized via chroma-keying. The foreground is thereby recorded in front of a uniformly colored backdrop whose color does not resemble any color occurring on the foreground object. Typical backdrop colors are blue or green [309]. By labeling as background all pixels that are similar in color to the backdrop, the foreground can be quickly and robustly segmented. This simple method can be realized even with analog technology and is used for live broadcasts. (For example, the nightly TV weather forecast is commonly produced by recording the meteorologist in front of a uniform backdrop and compositing his/her color-segmented silhouette in real-time with the computer-generated weather chart.)

Particularly in small recording rooms, however, indirect illumination causes the background color of the walls and floor to reflect off the foreground object, resulting in an unnatural color tint of the object as well as segmentation inaccuracies. This effect is commonly referred to as *color bleeding*. Shadows cast by the foreground onto the background are another potential source of segmentation error. To avoid both problems, instead of using blue or green as the backdrop color, the studio walls and floor can be covered with black molleton and carpet; see Figure 2.9. This way, shadows become invisible, and no background color can reflect off the foreground. On the other hand, illumination conditions must be adjusted for the missing indirect illumination component from the walls and floor, and the segmentation algorithm has to account for dark or black regions that can also occur on the foreground object.

Retro-reflective fabric material is becoming popular to cover background walls and floor. Blue or green ring lights mounted on all camera lenses strongly reflect back from the material into the cameras, such that in the recorded video images, the background stands out in a single color. Scene foreground remains conventionally illuminated with bright (white) light sources. Because the retro-reflective background requires only low ring light intensities, color bleeding ef-

Figure 2.9. A recording studio, equipped with black curtains and carpet for robust image segmentation. *(Reprinted from [291], © 2003 Eurographics.)*

(a) (b)

Figure 2.10. Clean-plate segmentation: with the help of pre-acquired background images, (a) the dynamic foreground object can (b) be segmented based on statistical color differences. *(Reprinted from [176], courtesy of Ming Li.)*

fects are avoided while shadows cast on the background from foreground lighting drown in the retro-reflected, uni-color ring light.

If the background cannot, or is not supposed to, be manipulated, segmentation must be based on comparing the recorded images to previously acquired images of the background [17]. These additional *clean plates* depict the static background and are recorded with the same cameras and from the identical positions as the dynamic sequence; see Figure 2.10. Electronic noise causes the background pixel values to vary slightly, especially in low-light conditions. To determine the average color and variance per pixel, a number of background images are recorded. Mean color and variance are then used to compute two threshold values per pixel that are used to decide whether the pixel belongs to the foreground or the background [46]. If the pixel value is between both threshold values, no clear decision can be made, which is still much more useful than a bogus classification.

In the dynamic image sequences, background appearance may not be completely static due to shadows cast by the foreground. From the observation that scene regions do not, in general, change in color appearance when shadowed, pixel classification is based on pixel hue instead of intensity level to obtain more robust segmentation results. Because scene background is not controlled, similar colors can coincide in the foreground and the background, typically causing holes in the silhouettes. The segmented silhouettes are therefore post-processed employing a morphological dilate/erode operation [134]. Suitably implemented, background subtraction and morphological filtering can be done on-the-fly during multi-video acquisition.

Plate V depicts eight segmented reference images for one time frame. This is the input data to all wide-baseline VBR algorithms discussed in Chapters 4 to 6.

2.2   Geometry Reconstruction from Multiple Views

To render a real-world scene from arbitrary perspectives, its three-dimensional structure must be known. Since only image data is available as input, 3D scene geometry must first be reconstructed from the imagery. In the general case, unfortunately, 3D reconstruction is highly ambiguous: given a set of input images, there can be many different scene geometries that are consistent with it. Actually, if surface reflectance (more exactly, the bidirectional reflectance distribution function, BRDF) is left completely arbitrary, a set of images can come from a scene of arbitrary geometry. An example are holograms whose physical geometry (a planar piece of glass or film) can't be recovered from images showing the content of the hologram. Unconstrained multi-view geometry reconstruction is therefore an ill-posed problem.

The vast majority of objects in nature, however, meet certain constraints that allow us to reconstruct geometry that is at least close to their true shape. If the input images can be segmented into object foreground and scene background, *silhouette-based* reconstruction methods yield the object's (approximate) *visual hull*. The visual hull is the 3D shape that results if all the object silhouettes are back-projected into the scene and intersected. The visual hull is *silhouette-consistent* in that all 3D scene points within the visual hull volume project onto the object silhouette, regardless of viewing direction. While the visual hull always envelops the object's true geometry, it cannot recover local concavities because concave regions do not affect the object silhouette.

Another constraint that is crucial for all but silhouette-based reconstruction approaches is diffuse reflectance. Diffusely reflecting, i.e., Lambertian, surfaces exhibit the beneficial property that their appearance remains constant when viewed under arbitrary orientation, as long as the illumination is static. This appearance invariance allows the establishing of correspondences between different views. Fortunately, most materials in nature exhibit predominantly diffuse reflectance properties. *Photo-consistent* reconstruction approaches are based on the assumption of inter-image similarity in pixel color and intensity. To decrease the probability of false matches, color similarity is frequently measured not per pixel but for a small patch of pixels. As similarity measures, the sum of absolute differences (SAD), the sum of squared differences (SSD), or the normalized cross-correlation (NCC) between rectangular image patches are commonly used. The NCC measure (see Equation (3.2)) is the most robust, as it is invariant to differences in overall brightness. However, none of these low-level similarity measures are invariant to projective transformation or rotation [109].

From known image recording positions, pixel correspondences directly yield the 3D positions of scene surface points. But even for diffusely reflecting objects, photo-consistency remains ambiguous if surfaces show no color variation. Reliable correspondences can be established only at discontinuities. For uniform image regions, use can be made of the regularizing observation that constant image regions typically also correspond to smooth object surfaces. The flat-shaded regions are then plausibly interpolated from reliably established 3D points.

While silhouette-based approaches inherently yield only approximations to the true geometry of general 3D shapes, photo-consistent approaches assume diffuse reflectance and must rely on regularization. Accordingly, reconstructed geometry cannot be expected to be exact. When considering a reconstruction technique for a given camera set-up, two scenarios must be distinguished. If the input images are recorded from nearby viewpoints such that they exhibit high similarity, *depth-from-stereo* algorithms that aim at assigning a depth value to each image pixel are applicable. For images recorded from widely spaced positions, *shape-from-silhouette* techniques as well as *photo-hull reconstruction* methods, both of which recover a full 3D model, can be applied. In the following, the different reconstruction approaches will be described in more detail.

2.2.1   Depth from Stereo

Depth-from-stereo reconstruction from two or more images has been at the core of computer vision research for decades. As input, two or more images are available that depict the scene from similar perspectives, such that any point in the scene is ideally visible in two or more images. For metric reconstruction, the recording cameras must be calibrated so that the images can be related geometrically [109]. Figure 2.11(a) illustrates the *epipolar* recording geometry for a pair of stereo cameras $C_{1,2}$. A 3D scene point P visible in both images $I_{1,2}$ establishes a correspondence between two pixels $P_{1,2}$ from either image. In reverse, a correspondence between two pixels from both images determines the 3D position of the scene point. A pixel P_1 in image I_1 can have a corresponding pixel in image I_2 only along the respective *epipolar line* l_2, and vice versa. The epipolar line l_2 is the projection of the viewing ray from the center of projection of camera C_1 through P into image I_2, so the search space for pixel correspondences is confined to the respective one-dimensional epipolar line.

To establish correspondence between pixels, image regions around the pixels are commonly compared using sum of squared differences (SSD), sum of absolute differences (SAD), or normalized cross-correlation (NCC) as similarity measures. The normalized cross-correlation is generally more robust than SSD or SAD. The NCC between two image regions $I_1(C_\mathbf{p})$ and $I_2(C_\mathbf{q})$ is defined by

$$C(\mathbf{p}, \mathbf{q}) \;=\; \frac{\sum_i \left[I_1(p_i) - \bar{I}_1(C_\mathbf{p})\right]\left[I_2(q_i) - \bar{I}_2(C_\mathbf{q})\right]}{\sqrt{\sum_i \left[I_1(p_i) - \bar{I}_1(C_\mathbf{p})\right]^2 \sum_i \left[I_2(q_i) - \bar{I}_2(C_\mathbf{q})\right]^2}}, \qquad (2.4)$$

where p_i, q_i denote region pixels, and $\bar{I}_1(C_\mathbf{p})$, $\bar{I}_2(C_\mathbf{q})$ are the mean pixel values of each region.

For accelerated performance, stereo image pairs can be *rectified* prior to image region comparison; see Figure 2.11(b). A projective transform takes both stereo images $I_{1,2}$ to a common image plane and aligns epipolar lines in parallel to image

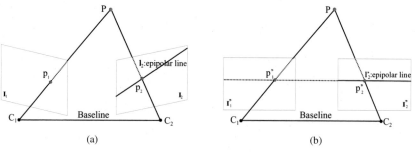

Figure 2.11. Stereo reconstruction: (a) The 3D coordinates of a scene point P can be triangulated from its 2D projection coordinates $P_{1,2}$ in two non-parallel image planes $I_{1,2}$. (b) For faster block-matching, stereo image pairs can be rectified such that epipolar lines correspond to image scanlines. *(Reprinted from [176], courtesy of Ming Li.)*

scanlines. This way, the search for corresponding pixels between I_1' and I_2' can be carried out by evaluating the similarity measure for rectangular image blocks around each pixel. The minimum distance from the scene to the cameras limits the search range.

Stereo reconstruction is typically approached by defining an energy functional over the images that incorporates image formation constraints (visibility, similarity, consistency) and regularizing characteristics (smoothness). The global minimum of the functional is expected to correspond to the true 3D scene depth. Unfortunately, any useful energy functional for stereo reconstruction is necessarily non-convex, and finding the global minimum of such a functional is known to be NP-hard. Nevertheless, by cleverly choosing the energy functional, there exist stereo algorithms that do find good minima such that useful dense depth can be estimated for a wide range of real-world input images.

One approach to formulate the correspondence problem is in terms of level sets and solving it by numerical techniques to obtain a local minimum as the solution of a set of partial differential equations (PDEs) [6, 75]. Alternatively, the stereo reconstruction problem can be discretized first by considering only a finite number of different depth layers. It can then be attacked by combinatorial optimization methods. A large class of energy functionals can be minimized this way using graph cuts [153]. The graph cut approach has been successfully applied to a number of vision problems, including stereo and motion [18, 28, 133, 253, 252] and voxel occupancy [279]. Experimental evaluations of different stereo algorithms using real images with known ground-truth dense depth show that depth-from-stereo approaches based on combinatorial optimization yield very robust results [257, 284]. An additional advantage of the graph cut minimization approach is that it can be directly extended to multi-view scene reconstruction [152]. As an example for a multi-view stereo reconstruction approach, and to demonstrate what can be expected from state-of-the-art depth-from-stereo methods, a graph cut–based reconstruction algorithm is described in Section 3.2.1.

2.2.2 Shape from Silhouette

To reconstruct 3D geometry from wide-baseline imagery, most time-critical systems rely on the shape-from-silhouette approach [160]. These algorithms make use of the very efficiently reconstructible, yet only approximate, *visual hull representation* of actual object geometry.

The visual hull of an object is obtained by finding the 3D shape that is consistent with all object silhouettes that can possibly be recorded from any possible viewing direction. In practice, a close approximation to the true visual hull is reconstructed: by using only a handful of silhouette images recorded from widely

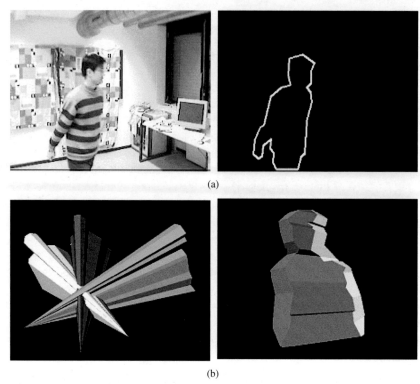

Figure 2.12. Shape-from-silhouette reconstruction: the object foreground is segmented from the scene background. The object silhouettes as seen from different viewpoints are back-projected into the scene. The intersection of these silhouette cones is the object's *visual hull. (Reprinted from [192], © 2003 IEEE.)*

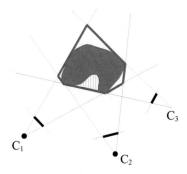

Figure 2.13. Fundamental limitation of visual hull reconstruction: concavities (hatched area) cannot be recovered, regardless of the number of reference views. *(Reprinted from [176], courtesy of Ming Li.)*

separated viewpoints, the visual hull is typically well approximated. Commonly, the visual hull approximation resulting from a finite set of silhouettes is abbreviatedly referred to as *the* visual hull.

As described in Section 2.1.7, foreground object pixels are segmented from the image background; see Figure 2.12. Each object silhouette is projected back into 3D scene space, forming a generalized cone with the camera's center of projection at its tip. The object's visual hull is then the intersection of all silhouette cones. Different techniques have been devised to reconstruct the visual hull at interactive frame rates; see Chapter 4. In volumetric visual hull recovery, the scene volume is subdivided into small volume elements, or *voxels* [242, 285, 225, 218, 143, 221, 24, 309, 46, 183, 287]. Each voxel is projected into all reference images to check whether its projection coordinates lie inside all images' silhouettes. Polyhedral visual hull reconstruction consists of approximating the silhouette outlines as polygons that are back-projected into scene space to determine their intersecting surface represented as a polygon mesh [161, 209, 86, 170]. Alternatively, novel views can also be rendered directly from the segmented imagery by implicitly making use of the visual hull concept [208].

For an object surface point to lie on the visual hull, it must project to the silhouette outline from at least one perspective (in which case the point is also on the silhouette outline from the opposite direction). Accordingly, for general object shapes, the visual hull is only an approximation of the true geometry: Object surface regions that are locally concave in all directions cannot be reconstructed. For illustration, Figure 2.13 depicts a 2D slice through the centers of projection of three cameras $C_{1,2,3}$. In visual hull reconstruction, the concave region of the object (hatched) is approximated as a planar surface. The visual hull, on the other hand, always envelops the true geometry, as no part of the object can "stick out" of the visual hull without affecting the silhouettes.

Well calibrated cameras and robustly segmented images of the object are necessary prerequisites for visual hull reconstruction. Inaccuracies in camera calibration parameters cause the extruded silhouette cones to intersect with slight mismatch. As a result, the visual hull shrinks. Segmentation errors either amputate or inflate the visual hull, depending on whether object pixels are wrongly classified as background, or background pixels are erroneously associated with the object, respectively.

2.2.3   Shape from Photo-Consistency

In order to obtain more accurate 3D geometry, besides silhouette information, photo consistency can also be taken into account to reconstruct geometry from wide-baseline imagery. Such a photo-consistent model can be reconstructed by subdividing the scene volume into discrete volume elements (voxels); see Figure 2.14(a). Each voxel is projected into all images, and the color similarity of the projected image regions is determined. If the reference image regions are similar (see Figure 2.14(b)), the voxel is considered photo-consistent and, thus, likely to coincide with the object's surface. Dissimilar voxel projections, on the other hand, indicate that the voxel is not located on the scene surface. A photo-consistent voxel is assigned the mean color of its image projections, while inconsistent voxels are set to be transparent. Similarity is typically determined by comparing differences in pixel color value to a preset threshold value. For specific camera recording arrangements, each voxel must be checked only once [264]. For a general recording configuration, however, the voxels must be repeatedly tested to ensure correct visibility [157, 64]. The voxels are considered from the outside of the volume inward, so that the model is "carved out" of the solid scene volume. By testing all voxels in this order, the obtained *photo hull* is the union of all possible shapes that are photo-consistent with the recorded images. The resulting photo hull geometry consists of many small voxel cubes, somewhat reminiscent of a LEGO® model; see Figure 2.15.

When projecting the input images onto the photo hull, they ideally line up such that each surface point is assigned similar color values from different images. This obviously requires that the surface of the recorded scene object is diffuse. For object surfaces featuring specular highlights, however, no photo-consistent surface can be found, and the geometry model gets hollowed out at the highlight. As photo-consistency measure, only per-pixel color values are typically being compared, because region-based measures would have to correct for perspective projection and image plane rotation, which additionally requires knowing the local surface normal direction. Accordingly, a voxel is erroneously identified as photo-consistent if its projections from the camera centers happen to fall onto similarly colored object regions. Such spurious voxels are typically eliminated in a post-processing step by deleting any cluster of contiguous voxels smaller than a preset threshold. The ensemble of voxels remaining after this operation, however, may not be truly photo-consistent anymore.

A more sophisticated similarity measure is described by Ruigang Yang and his coworkers [331]. It can handle structureless surfaces as well as specular highlights by enforcing the reconstruction of only locally smooth surfaces. Generally, photo-hull reconstruction is a time-consuming approach since each voxel has to be repeatedly checked for photo-consistency. This is due to the non-local effect on overall visibility when changing a single voxel's classification from opaque to transparent, or vice versa.

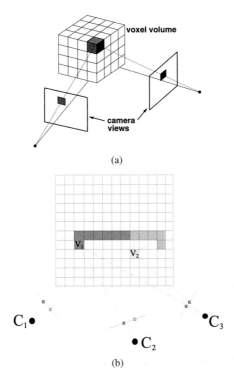

(a)

(b)

Figure 2.14. Volumetric photo hull reconstruction: (a) the scene volume is discretized into volume elements (voxels). Each voxel is projected into all visible reference images. (b) A voxel is photo-consistent if its corresponding pixels are similar in color (V_1). It is set transparent if pixel colors differ (V_2). *((a) Reprinted from [189], © 2000 SPIE. (b) Reprinted from [176], courtesy of Ming Li.)*

Figure 2.15. Reconstructed volumetric photo hull model. *(Reprinted from [194], © 2000 IEEE.)*

2.3   Image-Based Rendering

Image-based rendering evolved in the 1990s with the goal of achieving truly photorealistic rendering results of real-world (still) objects at interactive frame rates.
Instead of model geometry, textures, and shaders, conventional photographs of
actual objects are used in IBR to capture the visual appearance, the *light field*
of an object. The underlying observation is that, given sufficiently many images
from different directions, any view of the object from outside its convex hull can
be reconstructed. The light field is a digital approximation of the scene's *plenoptic function*. The notion of the plenoptic function forms the theoretical basis of
IBR. Over the years, a multitude of different IBR schemes have been proposed,
differing with respect to viewpoint constraints, use of geometry information, and
the amount of image data necessary. The following section first addresses the theoretical concept behind image-based rendering, and then several IBR techniques
are reviewed that form the basis of many VBR approaches described later in the
book.

2.3.1   The Plenoptic Function

The space around an illuminated object is filled with light (radiance) reflected off
the object's surface. If the distribution of radiance with respect to spatial position,
direction, and wavelength,

$$\Phi \;\; = \;\; \Phi(x, y, z, \theta, \phi, \lambda), \tag{2.5}$$

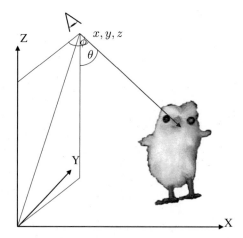

Figure 2.16.   The *plenoptic function* describes radiance distribution at any position
(x, y, z) and viewing direction (θ, ϕ) in space. *(Reprinted from [196].)*

were known (see Figure 2.16), ray optics–based image formation would consist of simply sampling the *plenoptic function*; see Equation (2.5). For a static scene, Φ expresses light power per unit area per unit solid angle per unit wavelength, i.e., spectral radiance, received at location x, y, z from direction θ, ϕ. The plenoptic function contains all information about a scene that can be gathered by our sense of vision [1]. Correspondingly, any view of a scene can be accurately reconstructed if its plenoptic function is known. The continuously varying plenoptic function cannot be acquired exactly by digital means, unfortunately, but must be sampled with appropriate recording devices. In the following, the term *light field* is used to denote a sampled and quantized representation $\hat{\Phi}$ of some scene's plenoptic function Φ [91]. Light fields can be digitally acquired, processed, and rendered [168]. A light field represents a database of radiance samples that can be queried to determine the radiance value corresponding to a specific viewpoint and viewing direction. Suitably parameterized, light-field dimensionality can be reduced and radiance querying accelerated.

2.3.2 Light-Field Rendering

To use the plenoptic function concept for computer graphics rendering, Equation (2.5) must first be suitably parameterized, sampled, and quantized. One challenge is to break the "curse of dimensionality" [16] by reducing the plenoptic function's number of dimensions. In a first step, the human visual system's (HVS) color perception characteristics are exploited, and the wavelength dependence is substituted by tristimulus values:

$$\Phi_{R,G,B} \;=\; \Phi_{R,G,B}(x, y, z, \theta, \phi) \tag{2.6}$$

The RGB-valued plenoptic function, Equation (2.6), now depends on three spatial and two directional degrees of freedom.

To reduce the plenoptic function's dimensionality further, the assumption can be made that scene illumination is incoherent and unpolarized, and that the object is surrounded by completely transparent space. In this case, no interference effects need to be taken into account, so in free space, the plenoptic function is constant along any line of sight, up to the point where the viewing ray intersects an opaque object surface. This redundancy in the five-dimensional light-field representation, Equation (2.6), can be eliminated by parameterizing the plenoptic function in ray space. Different parameterizations have been proposed in the literature, jointly expressing viewpoint position (x, y, z) and viewing direction (θ, ϕ) as oriented lines in space. In the direction-and-point representation [34], rays are parameterized by intersection coordinates with a plane and a sphere. A different spherical light-field representation is employed in [123], and other polar parame-

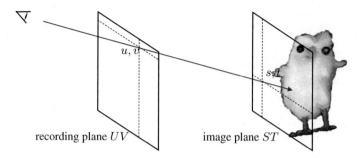

Figure 2.17. Two-plane light-field parameterization: a viewing ray is parameterized by its intersection coordinates (u, v, s, t) with the recording plane UV and the parallel image plane ST. *(Reprinted from [196].)*

terizations are proposed in [319, 299]. The effects of different parameterizations on rendering artifacts have been investigated in [33].

Despite these parameterization alternatives, the most convenient and widely used ray parameterization is still the original two-plane parameterization proposed by Marc Levoy and Pat Hanrahan [168] as well as by Steve Gortler and his coworkers [104]. In the two-plane parameterization, arbitrary viewing rays can be very efficiently converted to light-field coordinates, while intermediate radiance values can be linearly interpolated in light-field space. Adopting Marc Levoy's notation [168], a viewing ray is parameterized by its intersection coordinates (u, v) and (s, t) with a recording plane UV and a parallel image plane ST, respectively, shown in Figure 2.17,

$$\Phi_{R,G,B} = \Phi_{R,G,B}(u, v, s, t), \qquad (2.7)$$

and the plenoptic function Equation (2.6) is reduced to four dimensions. Given Equation (2.7), the scene can be faithfully rendered from any viewpoint on the near side of the recording plane. By arranging six pairs of planes in a cube enclosing the object, any view from outside the cube can be rendered. Since no information is available about ray intersection with the actual object surface, viewpoints within the cube are undetermined. Without visibility information, rendered views remain accurate as long as the viewpoint is located outside the object's convex hull.

Another advantage of the two-plane parameterization is that light fields can be directly acquired in the representation of Equation (2.7). The set-up is shown in Figure 2.18. Conventional photographs are recorded from the positions in the recording plane UV, with the optical axis of the camera always pointing always in a direction normal to the plane. This way, the image plane ST is automatically

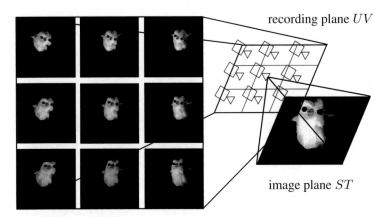

Figure 2.18. Recording the light field of an object in the two-plane parameterization is done by taking conventional images from regularly spaced positions on the recording plane UV. The image plane ST is aligned in parallel to the recording plane UV. *(Reprinted from [187], © 1999 IEEE.)*

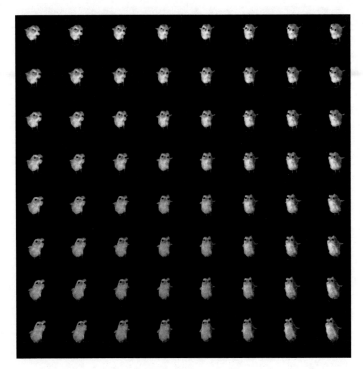

Figure 2.19. The two-plane parameterized light field resembles a 2D array of images. *(Reprinted from [196].)*

recording plane UV

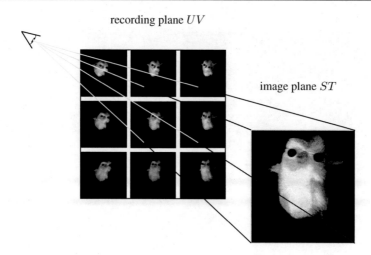

image plane ST

Figure 2.20. Light-field rendering consists of resampling the recorded image array. *(Reprinted from [187], © 1999 IEEE.)*

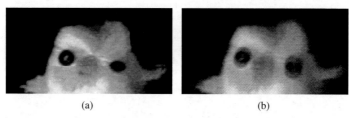

(a)   (b)

Figure 2.21. Rendering results from subsampled light-field data: (a) nearest neighbor interpolation. (b) quadra-linear interpolation. *(Reprinted from [196].)*

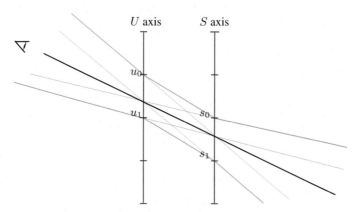

Figure 2.22. Quadra-linear interpolation, depicted in 2D: because viewing rays generally do not intersect recording and image plane at exact sampling positions, the four nearest pixels in each of the four closest images are weighted and averaged.

aligned parallel to the recording plane UV. By arranging image recording positions in a regular grid, the plenoptic function is directly captured in the form of Equation (2.7) at regular sampling points. A light field $\hat{\Phi}_{R,G,B}$ is obtained that can be quickly queried. The four-dimensional light-field data structure $\hat{\Phi}$ resembles a 2D array of 2D images (Figure 2.19), which is also referred to as a *light-field slab* [168]. By recording six light-field slabs arranged in a cube enclosing the scene, the scene's entire light field is captured.

Rendering. Light-field rendering is equivalent to resampling the 4D light field database $\hat{\Phi}$, i.e., the array of recorded images shown in Figure 2.19. For every output image pixel, a ray is traced from the viewpoint location, and the intersection coordinates (u, v, s, t) with the recording plane and the image plane are calculated; see Figure 2.20. In general, the rays' intersection coordinates will not coincide with exact image recording positions and pixel coordinates. By rounding intersection coordinates to the nearest recorded positions, ghosting artifacts due to aliasing occur if image recording positions are spaced too far apart; see Figure 2.21. Instead, pixels from adjoining images can be weighted and averaged to low-pass filter the sampled data. Commonly, *quadra-linear interpolation* is applied [168, 104], as shown in Figure 2.22. The sought-after radiance value is linearly interpolated from 16 pixels, corresponding to the four pixel coordinates closest to the ray's image plane intersection coordinates (s, t) in each one of the four light-field images nearest the ray's recording plane intersection coordinates (u, v). For subsampled light-field representations that consist of too few images for the image resolution, the rendering results are blurred; see Figure 2.21.

Ghosting artifacts or image blur occur if light-field image recording positions are spaced too far apart such that adjacent images differ by more than one pixel due to parallax. The number of light-field images needed to ensure aliasing-free yet pixel-sharp rendering results depends on light-field image resolution. A criterion stating how many images have to be acquired to achieve optimal light field rendering quality can be derived by relating light-field image resolution to maximally tolerable disparity.

Light-Field Sampling. Let's assume the plenoptic function Equation (2.7) is critically sampled if the maximum disparity between adjacent light-field images is smaller than one pixel. This way, views of the scene can be rendered at the resolution of the original light-field images without loss in quality. The resolution of the light-field images then determines the maximum allowable distance between image recording positions.

In the following, the relation between image resolution and the necessary number of light-field images is derived first for a spherical light-field parameterization. The sampling criterion is then extended to the two-parallel-plane parameterization. As it turns out, matching the image resolution according to the light-field sampling criterion is shown to be equivalent to aperture prefiltering [168].

Figure 2.23 illustrates camera recording parameters. The scene is enclosed by a minimum sphere of radius r. Camera resolution is fixed by the number of pixels along one row, N_S, each spanning a length of Δs. To make full use of

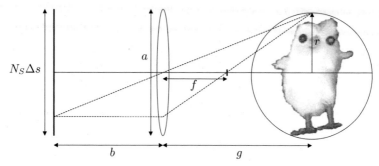

Figure 2.23. Recording parameters: the focal length f, maximum object radius r, the number of pixels along one side N_S, and pixel size Δs determine optimal recording distance g and image-plane distance b. *(Reprinted from [196].)*

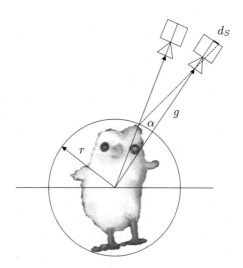

Figure 2.24. Recording geometry: a sphere of radius r encloses the object, g denotes the distance between the object's center and the camera, and d_S is the maximum disparity caused by moving the camera by an angle α. *(Reprinted from [196].)*

available camera resolution, the projected image must fill the entire recording area without being clipped at the edges. Given a fixed focal length f, the optimal object distance g is then

$$g = f\left(1 + \frac{2r}{N_S \Delta s}\right). \tag{2.8}$$

Bringing the object center into focus, the distance between the camera lens and image plane b is

$$b = \frac{fg}{g - f}. \tag{2.9}$$

To record sharp images of the entire object, the camera's depth of field must be considered. From the minimum distance of an object point to the camera lens, $g - r$, the maximum image plane distance b' follows:

$$b' = \frac{f(g - r)}{(g - r) - f}.$$

As image distance is kept fixed at b, a finite-sized spot results in the image plane. The circle of confusion has a maximum diameter of Δe and depends on the clear aperture a of the camera lens

$$\Delta e = \left| a\left(1 - \frac{b}{b'}\right) \right|. \tag{2.10}$$

The same argument applies to points on the far side of the object. Any object point outside the focal plane is imaged as a spot of finite extent. Assuming that out-of-focus regions become apparent only if the circle of confusion Δe grows larger than the size of one pixel, Δs, sharp images are recorded as long as

$$\Delta e < \Delta s.$$

By solving Equation (2.10) for the lens diameter a, it follows that

$$a < \frac{\Delta s}{f}(g - f)\left(\frac{g}{r} - 1\right). \tag{2.11}$$

Optimal imaging distance g and maximum lens aperture a can now be determined from Equations (2.8) and (2.11).

From Figure 2.24, it is apparent that to avoid aliasing effects during light-field rendering, maximum disparity d_s between neighboring images must not be larger than one pixel,

$$d_s \leq \Delta s. \tag{2.12}$$

If camera position changes by an angle α, a 3D point on the sphere enclosing the scene is projected to different positions in the image plane. For small angles α, this disparity is approximated by

$$d_s \approx \frac{b}{g-r}\, r\alpha \leq \Delta s. \tag{2.13}$$

Solving Equation (2.13) for α by using Equations (2.8), (2.9), and (2.12) yields

$$\alpha \leq \frac{\Delta s}{fg}\,(g-f)\left(\frac{g}{r}-1\right).$$

At distance g, the angular camera displacement α results in a translatory motion of

$$\alpha\, g \leq \frac{\Delta s}{f}\,(g-f)\left(\frac{g}{r}-1\right). \tag{2.14}$$

Note that the maximum amount of shift between two recording positions, Equation (2.14), coincides with the maximum lens diameter to record sharp images, Equation (2.11).

If image recording positions are spaced farther apart than Equation (2.14) suggests, the images need to be *prefiltered* prior to rendering [168]. This effectively increases pixel size Δs, i.e., image resolution is reduced until Equation (2.14) is met. The overall number of images N_{img} needed to cover the entire sphere around an object can now be estimated by

$$N_{\text{img}} \approx \frac{4\pi}{\alpha^2} = \frac{4\pi g^2}{\left(\frac{2}{N_S}\left(f + \frac{2rf}{N_S \Delta s} - r\right)\right)^2}. \tag{2.15}$$

The same line of argument can be applied to light fields recorded in the two-plane parameterization. Focal length is normalized to $f = 1$ in the following, and camera distance is assumed to be large compared to object size, $g \gg r$. To determine the number of images to cover a 90° angle from the object, imaging parameters must be chosen such that the object with radius r in Figure 2.25 fills the image plane of side length $N_S \Delta s$ without being clipped at the edges:

$$N_S \Delta s = 2\sqrt{2}r. \tag{2.16}$$

Setting maximum disparity between neighboring image recordings equal to pixel size Δs, the angle α between adjacent cameras must not exceed

$$\alpha \approx \frac{\Delta s}{r} = \frac{2\sqrt{2}}{N_S}. \tag{2.17}$$

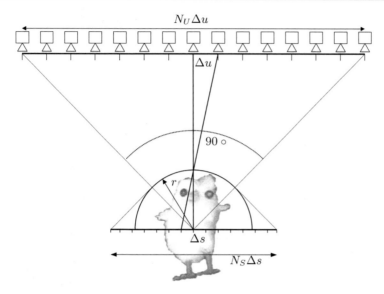

Figure 2.25. Two-plane recording geometry: A row of N_U cameras aligned in parallel and equally spaced by Δu record an object of maximum radius r from far away. Camera resolution is N_S pixels along one side. Pixel size is Δs. *(Reprinted from [196].)*

As one light-field slab covers an angle of $\pi/2$ along one side, the number of light-field images N_U along one side of the light-field slab is determined by

$$N_U = \frac{\pi/2}{\alpha} = N_S \frac{\pi}{4\sqrt{2}}. \tag{2.18}$$

The same argument applies to the other slab direction with N_V images and N_T pixels. To capture the light field from all directions, six slabs need to be combined to enclose the scene. The total number of images N_{img} is then

$$N_{\mathrm{img}} = 6N_U N_V = 6\left(\frac{\pi}{4\sqrt{2}}\right)^2 N_S N_T \approx 1.85\, N_S N_T. \tag{2.19}$$

It follows from Equations (2.15) and (2.19) that, for critical light-field sampling, huge numbers of images are required. For example, if a light field is to be recorded with $N_S \times N_T = 256^2$-pixel resolution per image, Equation (2.19) yields that more than 120,000 images are necessary to render arbitrary views of the scene at the same resolution without loss of detail. For 24-bit color images, this is equivalent to 22 GB of data that would have to be acquired, stored, and queried at interactive rates. Realistically, light fields are always subsampled representations of the plenoptic information that would be necessary for aliasing-free rendering.

2.3.3 Unstructured Lumigraph Rendering

Light-field rendering relies on a regular, planar grid of recording positions in order to be able to query the light-field database fast enough for interactive rendering frame rates. This requires either a very well controlled (and constrained) acquisition procedure, in which the recording camera is moved precisely to the grid point locations [168], or the acquired light field must be resampled prior to rendering, which leads to a loss in achievable rendering quality [104].

Chris Buehler and his coworkers have devised an *unstructured lumigraph rendering* algorithm that can render novel views in real time from light-field images that have been acquired from irregularly spaced camera positions in 3D [31]. In contrast to lumigraph rendering, however, the recorded light-field images do not have to be rebinned, preserving original image fidelity for rendering. Real-time rendering frame rates are achieved by making use of standard graphics hardware texturing capabilities. The output image is rendered directly from the unstructured collection of light-field images recorded. Besides the image data, the algorithm requires as input the camera calibration parameters of each image. As in lumigraph rendering [104], available scene geometry information can be utilized to improve rendering quality. The geometric proxy compensates for disparity and takes visibility into account. If no scene geometry information is available, a simple plane serves as geometry proxy.

Unstructured lumigraph rendering preserves epipole consistency, i.e., for each pixel of the rendered output view, the best possible samples are selected from the available light field data; see Figure 2.26(a). In contrast, view-dependent texture

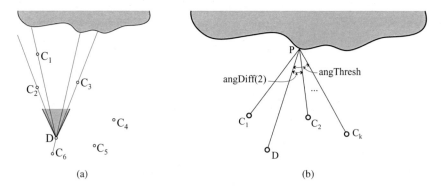

(a)   (b)

Figure 2.26. Unstructured lumigraph rendering: (a) for each viewing ray from viewpoint D, the best-matching reference image C_i is individually selected. (b) Several reference images are weightedly blended according to angular distance. *(Reprinted from [31], courtesy of Chris Buehler, © 2001 ACM.)*

mapping (VDTM), in Section 2.3.4, reconstructs all pixels of a polygon of the geometric proxy from the same three light-field images. To render each pixel, unstructured lumigraph rendering selects those light-field ray samples whose directions deviate least from the desired viewing ray. A light-field sample contributing to one viewing ray also influences nearby viewing rays. This ensures spatial continuity over the desired image plane and avoids rendering artifacts.

Unstructured lumigraph rendering allows for arbitrary camera positions, orientations, and focal lengths during light-field acquisition. As a consequence, different light-field images depict scene regions at different resolutions, and pixels from different images may span different solid angles. For best rendering results, light-field images with resolutions similar to the desired output image should be selected. Finally, when moving the desired viewpoint along a viewing ray, the same light-field samples should be selected to determine the color of the ray, regardless of proximity to one camera or another. All these aspects are taken into account by the camera blending field.

Camera Blending Field. The heart of the algorithm consists of determining a dense *camera blending field*. For each pixel in the output image, the blending field indicates which pixels from which light-field images contribute how much to the final pixel color. Because several light-field image pixels typically contribute to one output image pixel, the blending field stores for each output image pixel several references to source images with accompanying pixel coordinates and contributing weights.

Figure 2.26(b) depicts the derivation of camera blending field weights. First, for each viewing ray, the intersection point P with the geometry proxy is determined. From point P, those k camera positions are selected whose angular distances α_i from the desired viewing ray are smaller than some angle threshold α_{max}. In the reference implementation [31], the $k = 4$ best matching cameras are taken into account. The ray direction from point P to each reference camera position also determines which pixel p_i from light-field image i contributes to the desired viewing ray. In addition to the difference in ray direction, difference in image resolution between source image and desired view are taken into account by another factor

$$\beta_i \quad = \quad \max\left(0, \|P - C_i\| - \|P - D\|\right) . \tag{2.20}$$

$\|P - C_i\|$ denotes the distance from the intersection point P of the viewing ray with the geometry proxy to the image recording position C_i, and $\|P - D\|$ is the distance along the ray from the viewpoint to the geometry proxy. Note that this relationship does not take into account surface orientation or differences in focal length among cameras. For a more exact evaluation, the normal in point P

must be known, in which case the Jacobian of the planar homography relating the desired view to a reference camera can be evaluated. A third factor γ_i takes into consideration the field of view of reference camera i: γ_i is set to zero if P lies within the field of view of camera i. It steeply but smoothly increases towards the boundary of image i. If a detailed geometry proxy is available, visibility between P and C_i can be determined, and γ_i is set to a very large value if point P is not visible in the view from C_i. From these three factors, the blending weight $\bar{w}_i$ of pixel p_i in reference image i is determined via a smooth, linear falloff relationship,

$$w_i \;=\; 1 - \frac{a\alpha_i + b\beta_i + c\gamma_i}{\alpha_{\max}} \;, \tag{2.21}$$

followed by normalization over all k contributing light-field images,

$$\bar{w}_i \;=\; \frac{w_i}{\sum_{j=1}^{k} w_i} \;. \tag{2.22}$$

The constants a, b, and c control the influence of the different factors. Typical values used so far are $a = 1$, $b = 0.05$, and $c = 1$ [31].

The blending field weights must be computed for all pixels in the output image. Unfortunately, these weights cannot be precomputed, as they depend on the (varying) viewpoint and viewing direction. To still achieve real-time rendering performance, the blending field is evaluated only at a sparse set of points. Plate VII illustrates the construction of the camera blending field. The algorithm implicitly assumes that the blending field is sufficiently smooth so that it can be interpolated from the values at the sample positions. The rendering algorithm runs on standard graphics hardware.

- After clearing the frame buffer, appropriate blending field sampling locations in the output image are determined. These are: the target image projections of all vertices of the geometry proxy, as well as the projection coordinates of all reference cameras. Additionally, a regular grid of sample points is added to obtain a dense set of samples. Typical sizes are 16×16 or 32×32 samples covering the entire output image.

- For each sampling location, the contributing light-field image pixels p_i and associated blending weights $\hat{w}_i$ (see Equation (2.22)) are calculated and stored. The sampling positions are triangulated using a constrained Delaunay triangulator [271]. The projected edges of the geometry proxy as well as the edges of the regular grid serve as triangulation constraints. These prevent the triangles from spanning two different proxy surfaces, or triangulation from flipping as the viewpoint moves. The triangulation algorithm automatically inserts new vertices at edge-edge intersections.

- Finally, the output image is hardware-rendered as a set of projectively textured triangles. Each triangle is rendered as many times as there are different light-field images contributing at its three vertices. During each pass, each vertex of the triangle is assigned an alpha value equal to the blending field weight $\bar{w}_i$ of the current input image i. The rasterization engine automatically interpolates the weight, which is multiplied by the texture value looked up from the current input image. Since the interpolated weight values add to one, the accumulation result of all rendering passes yields the final result.

Rendering Results. Plate VII(d) depicts an unstructured lumigraph-rendered view. Using structure-from-motion techniques to recover camera calibration parameters, unstructured lumigraph rendering can also render new views of a scene from reference images captured with a hand-held camera. By making use of graphics hardware programmability, the blending field can be computed completely on the graphics board. Unstructured lumigraph rendering is a very general light-field rendering approach. One bottleneck, however, is the limited memory capacity of graphics hardware that allows only a limited number of input light-field images to be stored on the graphics board.

2.3.4   View-Dependent Texture Mapping

To increase light-field rendering quality, the light field must be sampled more densely, i.e., more light-field images must be recorded. For very sparsely sampled light fields that are acquired by recording only a few images from widely spaced viewpoints all around the scene, novel views can be rendered in real time using view-dependent texture mapping [58] as long as a complete, if approximate, 3D geometry model of the scene is available. The original implementation by Paul Debevec and his coworkers described in the following does not yet make use of modern graphics hardware programmability. Projective texture mapping and shadow mapping on modern graphics boards realize in real time today what still had to be precalculated in 1998. The original approach, nevertheless, includes many ideas that are valuable for IBR in general.

As the name already suggests, the notion of VDTM consists of applying to the geometric proxy a texture that varies with viewpoint position. The geometry proxy is a triangle mesh representing (approximate) 3D scene geometry, while the calibrated input images serve as texture. In the reference implementation [58], the geometry model is preprocessed offline prior to real-time rendering. Preprocessing consists of three steps:

- Visibility computation: determine for each polygon in which input image it is visible; polygons that are only partially visible in an image are split such that one part is entirely visible and the other part is completely occluded.

- Hole-filling: for polygons that are not depicted in any image, determine appropriate vertex colors; during rendering, Gouraud shading is used to mask the missing texture information.

- View-map generation: for each polygon and for a set of viewing directions distributed regularly over the viewing hemisphere of the polygon, store which reference image is closest in angle.

Preprocessing is possible because of the fixed geometric relationship between image recording positions and proxy polygons. If scene geometry was changing, as in VBR, the preprocessing steps had to be repeated for each time frame, so VDTM in its original form cannot real-time render dynamic scene content. Today, programmable graphics hardware has made the first and third preprocessing steps obsolete, enabling on-the-fly view-dependent texture mapping as demonstrated, e.g., by the free-viewpoint video system in Section 6.1. Nevertheless, all three preprocessing steps are discussed here, as they help clarify all issues that need to be taken into account in VDTM.

Visibility Computation. To determine whether an individual mesh polygon is entirely visible, partially visible, or completely occluded in one reference image, a hybrid object space-image space approach is pursued. First, an ID number is assigned to all polygons. The geometric proxy is depth-test rendered from the source image's recording position, using the color-encoded ID number to flat-shade each polygon. Each front-facing polygon is uniformly sampled, and all sample points are projected onto the reference image plane. In the case where the color-encoded, rendered ID number at any projected point position is different from the ID number of the currently considered polygon, the polygon is clipped against the occluder(s) in object space [310]. If parts of the polygon remain visible in the source image, the polygon is split along the visibility boundary by inserting new vertices, defining two subpolygons and eliminating the original polygon from the polygon list. To both subpolygons, the ID number of their predecessor is assigned, since in the following those two new polygons cannot occlude each other. While looping over all polygons, each polygon is stored whether it is visible in the current source image or not. The routine is repeated for all source images. In the end, mesh topology has been altered such that each polygon is either completely visible in one or more light-field images or it is entirely occluded in all source images.

Hole-Filling.   Some polygons may not be visible in any recorded light-field image. During rendering, such regions would show up as holes in the scene; see Plate VIII(a). To mask the absence of genuine texture information, plausible textures are "hallucinated" for such invisible polygons. An elegant solution is to make use of the human visual system's reduced acuity to image regions exhibiting low spatial variation. Plate VIII(b) shows the result. Instead of defining texture patches that are as detailed as the image texture in visible regions, invisible polygons are simply Gouraud-shaded using suitable color values for the polygon vertices. In contrast to interpolation in image space that may result in flickering artifacts, object-space hole-filling yields consistent polygon appearance with changing viewpoint.

The vertices of invisible polygons are assigned color values from the texture of adjacent visible polygons. For each shared vertex, the average color is computed by projecting the centroid of each linked polygon into all visible light-field images and sampling the texture at the projected image coordinates. Because the vertices of some invisible polygons may not be shared by visible polygons, the routine is iterated until all invisible polygon vertices are assigned a color value.

Because the assigned vertex color is an average of samples from possibly different input images, the invisible polygons do not show any variation with viewing direction. Interestingly enough, though, the Gouraud-shaded image regions remain almost imperceptible during animated rendering [58].

View-Map Construction.   To minimize the projection error due to incorrect geometry, as well as to reproduce specular reflections most faithfully, those reference images, closest in angle to the viewing direction, are applied as texture to each polygon. As different visible polygons may have different "best views," a *polygon view map* is precomputed for each polygon visible in more than one view. Figure 2.27 illustrates the approach. A polygon view map stores for one polygon that reference image which is closest in angle to a number of preset viewing directions. The viewing directions are sampled in a regular triangular grid over the hemisphere above the polygon. All sampled viewing directions are considered, and for each viewing direction the light-field image closest in direction is determined. If the polygon is visible in the determined source image, its image ID is stored in the polygon's view map as entry for the considered viewing direction. If it is invisible, this is also stored. It should be noted that, by assigning the closest reference image to the predefined sampling directions, image recording positions are not preserved exactly. The polygon view map indicates which input image to use as texture for all sampled viewing directions.

During rendering, viewing direction, in general, does not coincide with the sampled directions of the view map. Therefore, each polygon is textured by

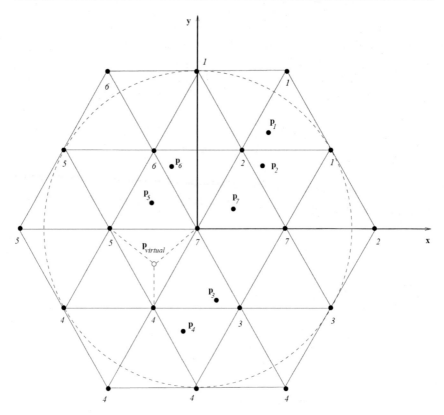

Figure 2.27. Polygon view map: the hemisphere above each polygon is regularly sampled. For each sampled viewing direction, the closest reference camera P_i is determined (numbers next to vertices). During rendering, the polygon is textured using those three reference images that are assigned to the vertices of the grid triangle in which the target view direction $P_{virtual}$ currently resides. The respective barycentric coordinates of the target view direction serve as blending weights. *(Reprinted from [58], courtesy of Paul Debevec, http://www.debevec.org, © 1998 Eurographics.)*

weightedly blending up to three input images that correspond to the three view-map directions that are closest to the desired viewing direction. Blending the light-field images also avoids the perceptually distracting effect of sudden switching between polygon texture. As blending weights, the barycentric coordinates of the desired viewing direction within the triangle of viewing direction samples are used. This guarantees smooth image-weight transitions as the viewpoint changes. To texture a visible polygon, its view map is queried for the desired viewing direction. The view-map look-up returns the index numbers of up to three light-field images, with the barycentric coordinates corresponding to the individual blending weights. Note that the view map must be queried with viewing direction expressed in the local coordinate system of each polygon, requiring multiplying the global viewing direction by the appropriate matrix.

Rendering. Actual view-dependent rendering consists of passing over the geometric proxy multiple times. First, all invisible polygons are rendered using Gouraud shading by applying the vertex colors that were determined in the second preprocessing step. Also, all polygons are drawn that are visible in only one light-field image. Figure 2.28(a) shows the result after rendering invisible polygons and polygons that are seen in only one reference image.

Then, all polygons are rendered that are visible in two or more reference images, making use of each polygon's view map to determine which input images to use as texture. Only these polygons can be view-dependently texture mapped. In three passes, each polygon is textured using up to three contributing light-field images. Texture mapping is performed in the OpenGL *modulate mode* to weightedly average the textures. The Z-buffer test is set to *less than or equal to* to blend each polygon with itself as it is drawn multiple times. For the first pass, one best-matching source image is selected as texture. Its texture matrix is loaded to the texture matrix stack, and all polygons are rendered for which the selected light-field image is the best match. The weight is determined individually for each polygon by applying the viewing direction's individual barycentric coordinates as modulation color. These steps are repeated for all source images that represent the best match for any polygon. After the first pass, the depth buffer is filled with the scene's local depth values. For the second and third pass, frame

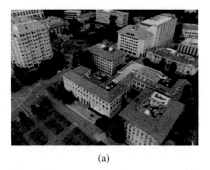

(a)   (b)

Figure 2.28. View-dependent texture mapping: (a) background buildings and terrain are visible in only one reference image and are rendered including hole-filling prior to the VDTM passes. (b) The polygons of the foreground model are rendered on top of the background and are view-dependently textured from three reference images. *(Reprinted from [58], courtesy of Paul Debevec, http://www.debevec.org, © 1998 Eurographics.)*

buffer blending is enabled to add the following fragment values to the pixel values that are already rendered. During both passes, again all second- and third-best reference images are considered, and affected polygons are rendered with the corresponding barycentric weights as modulation color. Figure 2.28(b) shows the view-dependently-texture-mapped foreground tower.

Summary. Excluding preprocessing, the described reference VDTM implemention runs at 20 frames per second on SGI's InfiniteReality hardware [58]. Because neighboring proxy polygons are textured using different input images, seam artifacts can occur along polygon edges. Also, spatial resolution of the original images is ignored when selecting the best input images per polygon.

2.4   Rendering on Graphics Hardware

Most early IBR techniques were implemented almost entirely in software [42, 45, 212, 168, 104] because the fixed-function rendering pipeline of earlier graphics boards did not allow for much hardware acceleration of non-polygon-based IBR methods. Today, modern graphics hardware offers much more flexible programmability, which IBR algorithms can exploit to accelerate rendering performance as well as to free the CPU for additional computations. Within the fixed-flow rendering pipeline (Figure 2.29), geometry processing as well as per-fragment computations can be customized to accommodate a large range of algorithms. With Cg ("C for graphics"), NVIDIA was among the first to develop a high-level language to program consumer graphics hardware [81]. Alternatively, a vendor-independent approach to graphics hardware programming has been created with the finalization of the *GLSL* standard ("OpenGL Shading Language") [250], which is going to be a vital part of the forthcoming OpenGL2.0 standard.

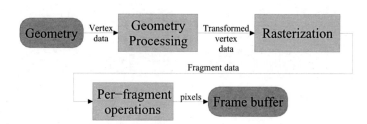

Figure 2.29.   OpenGL rendering pipeline: on modern graphics hardware, geometry processing and per-fragment operations can be individually programmed with considerable flexibility. *(Reprinted from [176], courtesy of Ming Li.)*

2.4.1   3D Image Warping

Given a set of images with dense, pairwise pixel correspondence information, in-between viewpoints along camera baselines are interpolated by *flowing/warping/morphing* pixels from both endpoint images towards their respective correspondents [42, 212, 213, 263]. In conjunction with calibrated recording cameras, inter-image pixel correspondences yield global scene depth; see Section 2.2.1. From per-pixel 3D scene information, visibility can be taken into account to accurately render in-between views.

Three-dimensional image warping from imagery with accompanying dense depth maps can be implemented very efficiently on programmable graphics hardware. A nice, step-by-step description of performing the 3D warping calculations in the OpenGL graphics pipeline framework is given by Zhongding Jiang [137]. For each pixel, a vertex is sent through the pipeline whose 3D coordinates are determined by the 2D image pixel coordinates and the associated depth. A small vertex program multiplies homogeneous vertex coordinates by a warping matrix. The 4×4 warping matrix is the same for all pixels. It is composed of the relative model-view and projection matrices between reference image and output view, and the view port transform to the output image. By enabling the Z-buffer test, visibility is automatically taken into account. However, this point-based warping approach leads to gaps in the output image as adjacent vertices get warped to non-adjacent pixels. Also, regions becoming unoccluded show up as holes in the rendering result. To avoid such artifacts, several reference images can be warped

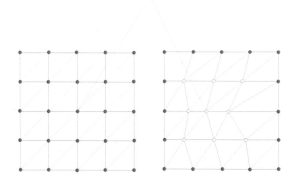

Figure 2.30. 3D image warping on graphics hardware: a regular mesh is laid over the image. To each mesh vertex, local scene depth as well as 2D texture coordinates are attributed. When the viewpoint moves, 2D vertex positions shift depending on viewpoint movement and local scene depth. Gap-free warping is accomplished by texture-mapping the shifted mesh using the vertices' original 2D image coordinates as texture coordinates.

and blended. At the same time, use can be made of the rasterization stage for interpolation between vertices. Figure 2.30 illustrates the concept. An implementation of multi-view warping is described in Section 3.2.2.

A special case occurs if the viewpoint moves parallel to the image plane and the direction of the optical axis does not change. In that case, all vertices shift in parallel in the opposite direction of the movement of the viewpoint. The amount of vertex shift d is known as *disparity*. Disparity is proportional to viewpoint movement b and reciprocal to local scene depth z: $d \propto b/z$.

While 3D warping can be performed very efficiently, it must be noted that only viewpoint positions lying in the plane of image recording positions are accurately interpolated. In contrast to light-field rendering or unstructured lumigraph rendering (Sections 2.3.2 and 2.3.3), the available set of images is not resampled on a per-pixel basis to determine the individually best match per viewing ray. For many VBR applications, however, restricting the point of view to the recording hull that is spanned by camera positions does not seriously impede overall usability [103, 345].

2.4.2 Projective Texture Mapping

In conventional texture mapping, texture coordinates are assigned explicitly to each geometry vertex. *Projective texturing*, in contrast, applies texture as if an image was projected from a slide projector onto the geometry model. This approach is especially useful in image-based rendering, because light-field images are related to the geometry proxy by projective transformations anyway. For projective texture mapping, besides object geometry, the image projection parameters must be specified: the center of projection, projection direction, and the focal length of the projector lens. If these parameters are chosen identical to the camera parameters during image recording, projective texturing constitutes, in a sense, the *reverse* of the acquisition step in that it recreates scene appearance from the image.

A hardware-accelerated projective texturing algorithm was proposed by Mark Segal and his collaborators to determine shadowed regions and lighting effects in image space [261]. It can be easily implemented on graphics hardware using the OpenGL graphics programming standard. The user specifies the position and orientation of the virtual camera as well as the virtual image plane of image texture. The texture is then cast onto the geometry model using the camera position as the center of projection. An easy-to-follow implementation of projective texture mapping on programmable graphics hardware is described in Randima Fernando and Mark Kilgard's book on Cg programming [81]. The algorithm can also be translated into OpenGL commands. On programmable graphics hardware, the vertex program takes care of calculating the projective texture coordinates for each vertex, while the fragment program performs the projective texture look-up. Thus, the per-vertex calculations are highly similar to the vertex transformations of the standard graphics pipeline. Per-vertex texture coordinates are computed from the vertex coordinates in object space using the appropriate projective transformation matrix. In order of application to a vertex, the projective texturing matrix is the concatenation of

- the *modeling matrix*, which applies any necessary modeling transformations irrespective of projective texturing,

- the *virtual-camera (look-at) matrix*, which rotates and translates the vertices into the virtual camera's frame of reference,

- the *projection matrix*, which defines the field of view of the image to be projected, and

- the *scale/bias matrix*, which is necessary for non–power-of-two textures to rescale the range of coordinates to the valid texture index range from 0 to 1.

The model matrix and the virtual-camera matrix are typically combined to form the equivalent to the model-view matrix in conventional rendering. Projective texturing is simply the reverse of image recording: the third dimension lost during imaging is re-inserted by the geometry model. During polygon rasterization, which generates pixels on the screen, a fragment program simply queries the projective texture image at the texture coordinates interpolated by the rasterization engine.

Standard projective texturing has one severe limitation: it does not take visibility into account. The described algorithm applies the image texture not only to the visible geometry surface, but the texture is also projected onto polygons that are occluded. To avoid such unnatural rendering artifacts, visibility must be determined prior to projective texture mapping using, e.g., a *shadow-mapping* algorithm.

2.4.3   Shadow Mapping

Different algorithms exist to compute local visibility either in object space or in image space. In conjunction with projective texture mapping, one convenient approach consists of using *shadow mapping* to determine visibility in image space. Lance Williams described shadow mapping as casting shadows on arbitrary surfaces [315]. A modern implementation of the basic algorithm using programmable graphics hardware can be found in Fernando and Kilgard's book [81]. The

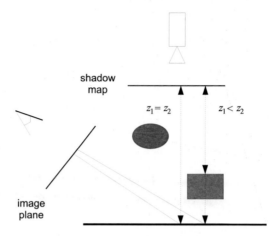

Figure 2.31. Shadow mapping for image-space visibility determination: the scene is rendered twice, first from the light source (or the texture projector) to store the depth map z_1, and a second time from the desired target viewpoint. During the second rendering pass, the scene is projectively textured with the depth map z_1 of the first pass. Each fragment's distance z_2 to the light source is tested against its texture-projected value z_1. If z_1 is smaller than z_2, the fragment must be in shadow. Only if z_1 is equal to z_2 is the fragment visible from the light source.

underlying idea is to render the scene *twice*: once as it appears from the light source, and in a second pass as seen from the desired viewpoint. Figure 2.31 illustrates the approach. During the first pass, the scene is rendered from the position of the light source with the Z-buffer test enabled. For each pixel of the resulting image, the distance from the light source to the closest model surface is recorded in a depth texture, or *shadow map*. In the second pass, the scene is rendered from the desired viewpoint while projective texturing is applied to project the shadow map from the light-source position onto the scene. For each fragment, the depth sample from the projected shadow map is compared to the actual distance from the light source. If the light is farther away than the shadow-map value, the current fragment is not the closest one to the light source, so it must be occluded.

To use shadow mapping for visibility-correct projective texturing, the geometry proxy is rendered first from the texture image's center of projection. The resulting depth map is then used as the shadow map during the second rendering pass. The second rendering pass casts the shadow map onto the geometry. Because visibility can vary from pixel to pixel, shadow mapping must be done on a per-fragment basis. The fragment program looks up the projective texture map value and compares it to the fragment's distance to the light source to determine its visibility. On modern graphics hardware, per-pixel depth comparison and visibility determination is a hard-wired feature of the fragment processor, and by varying a fragment's alpha value with visibility, zero-visibility fragments (occluded fragments) are not drawn to the frame buffer.

Chapter 3

Dynamic Light Fields

All VBR algorithms are generally concerned with representing and querying the time-varying plenoptic function arising from an animated scene. *Dynamic light fields* (DLF) extend the light-field notion outlined in Section 2.3.2 to time-varying content. Dynamic light fields exhibit a five-dimensional data structure, encompassing the four light-field dimensions that apply to transparent empty space, plus an additional dimension to capture the scene's temporal evolution.

In theory, the most straightforward way of capturing dynamic light fields and visualizing a time-varying scene from arbitrary viewpoints is to place video cameras *everywhere*. By "hopping" from camera to camera, the scene can then be viewed from any viewpoint. This brute-force approach is, of course, not practically possible, as each camera would only see other cameras obstructing the view onto the actual scene. As a compromise, cameras can be distributed sparsely around the circumference of the scene. Sill, each camera would be within other cameras' fields of view. To appear small enough so as not to be recognizable, the cameras must be placed far away from the action. *Camera hopping* is feasible only for outdoor scenes, e.g., large-scale sports events.

Because the acquisition cameras must be positioned along the circumference of the scene, hopping between camera views can only provide the visual sensation of virtually moving *around* the scene, not through it. To achieve seemingly smooth motion, the cameras must be spaced close enough such that parallax between adjacent camera images remains unnoticed when switching from one camera to the next. In addition, the optical axes of all cameras must converge on a common point in the scene. Otherwise, scene content jumps annoyingly around in the output image while hopping from one camera to the next. This requires precisely aligned and/or calibrated cameras.

The action in large-scale, outdoor environments is typically localized within a small region of interest that, however, moves around over time. Given limited camera resolution, only the region of interest should be recorded with high detail. To enable camera hopping, all cameras must then concertedly follow the region of interest, e.g., by mounting all cameras on servo-driven pan-tilt units. Because the action must be captured from a distance, cameras must be equipped with tele-lenses, resulting in subarc minute angular resolution. Keeping all cameras homed in on a common scene point with such accuracy is a challenging task, both in mechanical and calibrational terms.

Despite these challenges, the *EyeVision* system demonstrates that such a camera-hopping system is feasible [72]. It was first employed during the US-wide television coverage of the American football Super Bowl in 2001 [72]. The system was originally developed by CBS in partnership with Core Digital Technologies and PVI. More recently, the German cable company Sat.1 joined the consortium, which employs the system for soccer broadcasts. At the Super Bowl in 2001, the system consisted of 30 television-grade cameras with computer-controlled zoom lenses mounted on robotic pan-tilt tripods. The cameras were placed at equal intervals along a $210°$ arc on the stadium roof, some 25 meters above the playing field. All camera units are connected via control cables to one master camera that is equipped with sensors to measure pan and tilt angle. All slave camera units automatically follow the motion and zoom of the master camera that is controlled by a human operator. The scene is captured by all 30 cameras in sync at 30 frames per second. The live streams are fed via cable to digital tape decks for recording. For playback, the TV director can freeze the frame and rotate the viewpoint around the stadium to show critical situations from different vantage points. Because the cameras were spaced approximately $7°$ apart, however, the freeze-and-rotate sequence must be played at a swift angular rate of about $200°$/second, or else the discontinuous camera hops become noticeable.

With the successful deployment of the *EyeVision* system in a live TV broadcast, camera hopping can currently be considered the most advanced, if most basic, VBR technique to create the illusion of a freely navigable viewpoint on a dynamic scene. The technique's potential is hampered mostly by the considerable hardware effort necessary. While the system was used again during the NCAA basketball finals in 2001 [71], and once again for the Super Bowl in 2004 [73], hopes that a number of stadiums and sports arenas would be permanently equipped with the expensive acquisition gear have not yet materialized.

3.1 3D TV

Instead of simply switching between different cameras, views from arbitrary vantage points between and behind recording cameras can be interpolated using light-field rendering; see Section 2.3.2. By arranging multiple synchronized video cameras in a dense, regular 2D grid, time-varying scenes can be captured in the two-plane light-field parameterization; see Section 3.1. The matrix of cameras can be thought of as spanning a virtual window onto the scene. The *3D TV* system by Wojciech Matusik and Hanspeter Pfister allows the user to view the recorded event online from any position behind this virtual window [207].

While the feasibility of online dynamic light-field processing on commodity hardware has been demonstrated previously by Jason Yang and his collaborators [329], the 3D TV system is a complete end-to-end installation. It is intended to be a realization of Gavin Miller's *hyper display* concept [217]. The underlying idea is to capture the time-varying plenoptic function in one surface and to reconstruct the same plenoptic function over another surface someplace else.

In the 3D TV system, dynamic light fields are acquired as well as rendered at interactive frames rates. Given sufficient bandwidth for transmission, live 3D broadcasting can be realized. Sixteen video cameras capture the dynamic light field, and 16 video projectors, in conjunction with a lenticular projection screen, recreate the recorded light field [207]. Due to the auto-stereoscopic display design, several users can simultaneously view the scene in true color and full 3D, including binocular and motion parallax, without the need to wear special glasses or to track the users. By relying on a distributed architecture, the entire system scales with the number of cameras and projectors. This way, the same system can easily incorporate more cameras and/or projectors, depending on available funds.

3.1.1 Acquisition

The 3D TV system uses a small-baseline camera acquisition set-up, a conventional communication channel for broadcast to an arbitrary number of receiving parties, and special hardware at the receiver side for auto-stereoscopic 3D display. Figure 3.1 depicts the complete end-to-end processing pipeline of the 3D TV system. A distributed, scalable architecture is employed at the sender as well as at the receiving end to meet the high computational and bandwidth demands of real-time performance. On the acquisition side, eight 3 GHz Pentium 4 *producer PCs* each control two Basler A101fc cameras via an IEEE1394 (FireWire™) bus. These Bayer-mosaic CCD cameras feature 12 fps, 1300 × 1030-pixel images at 8 bits per pixel. The cameras are externally triggered via a control signal sent out by one of the PCs.

The 16 video cameras are set up next to each other in a straight line, with optical axes aligned roughly in parallel. The linear arrangement allows for horizontal parallax only, but 16 cameras are not sufficient to densely sample a sizable portion of the dynamic light field along two dimensions. The intrinsic

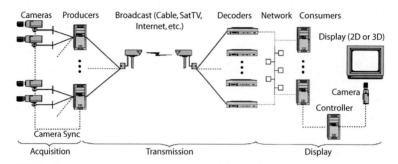

Figure 3.1. 3D TV infrastructure: a hierarchical processing architecture on the acquisition side as well as at the receiving end yield a scalable end-to-end system. *(Reprinted from [207], courtesy of Wojciech Matusik and Hanspeter Pfister, © 2004 ACM.)*

and extrinsic camera parameters are determined using standard calibration approaches [297, 298, 339].

3.1.2 Transmission

Each producer PC separately encodes the video stream of each connected camera using standard MPEG-2 compression. While this approach does not exploit redundancy between different camera streams, it does avoid having to process all video data on one machine, which would corrupt the system's scalability. The encoded bitstreams are then transmitted to all receivers using conventional television broadcast infrastructure, e.g., via fiber cable, terrestrial, or satellite transmission. In contrast to conventional television programs, 3D TV requires broadcasting as many bitstreams as there are acquisition cameras. As a consequence, fewer 3D TV programs can be delivered over the same channel capacity. At the receiver, as many decoding units as video bitstreams recover the dynamic light field on the fly.

The 3D TV reference implementation omits actual data transmission [207]. Instead, the encoded bitstreams are decoded again right away on the producer PCs.

3.1.3 Rendering

At the receiving end, the entire dynamic light-field data must be available for display. In the full-fledged broadcast scenario, a bank of commercial MPEG decoders would decompress all bitstreams simultaneously. From the decoded dynamic light-field data, a cluster of eight *consumer PCs* drives the autostereoscopic display. Each consumer PC is connected via gigabit Ethernet™ to all decoders/producer PCs, providing all-to-all connectivity for distributed rendering. A dual-output graphics card per computer allows connecting two NEC LT-170 projectors to each consumer PC, totaling 16 projectors of 1024×768-pixel resolution each.

Ideally, dynamic light-field acquisition and 3D display constitutes a one-to-one mapping between video camera pixels and projector pixels. In practice, however, it is not possible to match camera and projector position and orientation with sufficient accuracy, and camera and projector resolution differ as well. The decoded dynamic light field must therefore be "reshuffled" for 3D display. Since the cameras and projectors are not necessarily arranged in a regular grid, unstructured lumigraph rendering provides an elegant approach to resampling the dynamic light field in software; see Section 2.3.3. The plane serving as geometric proxy is thereby set to the center of the display's depth of field, while the virtual viewpoints for the projected images are chosen at even spacings.

As cameras and projector locations are static, the contribution of each camera to each projector pixel remains constant and can be determined in advance. Each output pixel is a linear combination of several acquisition camera pixels (i.e., dynamic light-field rays), blended by constant, precalculated weights. Thus, to generate the output images, each consumer PC requires only a small part of the complete light field. Which parts are needed, and with which weight each camera pixel contributes, is computed in advance and stored in a look-up table. This greatly reduces the amount of data that must be transferred between the decoders and the consumer PCs, and it preserves system scalability.

Because the light field is resampled in software, no computation must be performed on the graphics cards. Inexpensive graphics boards with standard output resolution and frame rate suffice. However, since graphics cards and projectors are not synchronized to the acquisition cameras, extended motion blur occurs for fast moving objects. Genlock-capable graphics cards and projectors that are driven by the acquisition side's synchronization signal are needed to overcome this limitation.

3.1.4 3D Display

The projectors are mounted along three rows to approximately match projector spacing to the arrangement of recording cameras. Each projector is focused onto a screen of cylindrical lenses. Figure 3.2 illustrates the principle of an auto-stereoscopic display. For a rear-projection screen, two lenslet sheets are glued together back-to-back with an optical diffuser material sandwiched in between. Both lens arrays have the same resolution. The projector-side lenses image each pixel to distinct positional coordinates in the focal plane. The diffuser in the focal

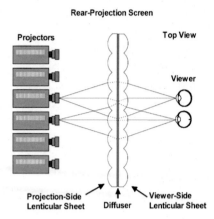

Figure 3.2. Auto-stereoscopic display: two lens arrays are used to recreate the plenoptic function in front of the screen. Multiple projectors illuminate the lenticular screen from the back. The rear lenticular sheet focuses each projector pixel to a distinct spatial location in the focal plane. A diffuser in the focal plane scatters projected pixel intensity evenly in all directions. Each lenslet in the front array transforms a range of spatial coordinates in the focal plane to a range of ray directions in front of the screen. *(Reprinted from [207], courtesy of Wojciech Matusik and Hanspeter Pfister, © 2004 ACM.)*

plane scatters the light evenly in all directions. The viewer-side lenslets serve as a demultiplexer by transforming each 2D point in the focal plane to a ray traveling in a different direction. Spatial screen resolution is determined by the number of lenses in the array, while directional resolution depends on the number of projector pixels falling onto each lenslet. Directional resolution denotes the number of different images projected over the display's total angle-of-view. The sum of projected pixels is allocated between spatial and directional resolution. By using cylindrical lenses, vertical directional resolution is sacrificed for the sake of improved spatial resolution in the vertical direction, so only horizontal parallax can be reproduced.

3.1.5 Results

Plate VI shows two views of a moving scene as it appears on the auto-stereoscopic display from different directions. Between the images, the jumping person shows noticeable parallax with respect to the background. The motion blur is mainly due to the missing synchronization between image acquisition and display while almost no ghosting artifacts are visible.

Aligning the projector-lens sheet system is not trivial. An automated calibration procedure makes use of a video camera in front of the display. From its viewpoint, the camera records the image on the display and feeds it back to the controller PC. Geometric as well as photometric calibration can be done automatically using this camera-in-the-loop approach. If the two lenticular sheets are not glued together in exact alignment, moiré patterns degrade the output image.

The lenticular lens sheets are 1.8×1.2 meters in size and span a field of view of about $30°$. To avoid aliasing effects, the viewer must stand at least three meters from the 3D display. Spatial resolution of the screen, which is determined by the number of lenses per unit length, has been matched to the horizontal projector resolution (approximately 1,080 lenses). With 16 projectors and $30°$ field of view, the angular (directional) resolution is then approximately $2°$. At a viewing distance of 3 meters, this corresponds to about 10 cm, which is slightly larger than the typical space between the eyes, so the viewer does not experience full binocular parallax. With more projectors (and cameras), however, true 3D is well within reach of this technique.

3.1.6 Summary

The 3D TV approach is a real-time, end-to-end VBR system featuring, in addition, an auto-stereoscopic 3D display as an output device. The complete pipeline performs at the acquisition camera frame rate of 12 frames per second. The approach relies entirely on dense dynamic light-field information. No depth estimation or disparity compensation is involved. To obtain convincing visualization results, the acquisition cameras must be very closely spaced for sufficiently densely sampled dynamic light-field data. Consequently, only a fraction of the entire omnidirectional light field can be captured with moderate numbers of cameras, and the viewing experience resembles looking at the scene through a window rather than a feeling of true immersion.

Video conferencing is another potential, yet even more demanding, application for this VBR technique. The overall temporal delay between acquisition and display of currently almost one second must be reduced to offer a natural communication atmosphere. With two-way communication, data compression and bandwidth become truly critical, in addition to quality of service and other network-related challenges.

3.2 Dynamic Light-Field Warping

To achieve convincing rendering results using the 3D TV system, dynamic light fields must be captured in a very-small-baseline camera configuration, which necessitates either large numbers of video cameras or restricts the viewing angle to a very small range. To cover a useful viewing range with a limited number of acquisition cameras, the camera must be spaced so far apart that adjacent camera images depict noticeable parallax; see Section 2.3.2. Smooth view interpolation results can still be obtained, however, if image disparity can be compensated for. To do so, dense depth maps must be reconstructed for all video images prior to rendering.

The idea to apply disparity compensation between several video streams for view interpolation was first considered in the context of video conferencing applications [74, 9]. In visual communications, the goal is to enable users to change, within limits, their individual viewing perspective on their partner, to achieve a more natural, immersive experience. For offline VBR applications, it suffices that the user can play back a dynamic scene from different viewpoints. The *video view interpolation* approach by Larry Zitnick et al. is a realization of such a system [345]. By combining sophisticated depth estimation with boundary matting to mask segmentation errors, video view interpolation achieves high visual fidelity. Because their acquisition system consists of only eight cameras, the authors decided to arrange the cameras along a 45° arc around the scene.

For true dynamic light-field warping from a comfortably wide range of viewing angles in both dimensions, many more cameras are necessary. This implies not only a quantitative difference but also a qualitative distinction in system design. Systems to acquire many dozens of video streams in sync are not yet commercially available, so suitable recording hardware must be custom-built. A working prototype is the Stanford Multi-Camera Array. It consists of 100 CMOS imagers delivering 640×480-pixel resolution, MPEG-compressed, and synchronized video data over the FireWire^{TM} bus [312]. The VBR system that serves as reference for the following description has been designed to be able to cope with the large amount of input streams from the Stanford array [103]. Similar to the video view interpolation system [345], depth is reconstructed offline while making additional use of background information. For rendering, intermediate views are warped and blended from nearby video images on graphics hardware; see Section 2.4.1. Real-time rendering performance is achieved by restricting the viewpoint to the plane spanned by the camera positions. This way, only the nearest four camera images need to be uploaded to the graphics board and processed for each time frame. Restricting the viewpoint to the camera plane is an acceptable tradeoff in exchange for real-time rendering performance that also applies, e.g., to video view interpolation [345].

3.2.1 Multi-View Depth Estimation and Image Segmentation

To be able to compensate for image disparity during rendering, dense depth maps must be reconstructed from the acquired multi-video first. The scientific literature provides a multitude of different depth-from-stereo algorithms from which to choose; see Section 2.2.1. To illustrate what can be expected from state-of-the-art reconstruction algorithms, an approach based on combinatorial optimization is described [98]. The algorithm is based on Vladimir Kolmogorov's seminal work on graph cut-based stereo [152] and exploits background images for enhanced robustness. Overall, the described reconstruction algorithm combines a number of advantageous characteristics:

- All input images are regarded symmetrically.

- Visibility is handled properly.

- Spatial smoothness is imposed while discontinuities are preserved.

- The images are simultaneously segmented into (static) background and (dynamic) foreground.

The segmentation of video content into foreground and background is an especially important image analysis clue [107, 179], and 3D reconstruction and background separation can symbiotically benefit from each other: if the background of an image can be identified, these pixels must have the same depth as the background, while all foreground pixels must be closer to the camera. Likewise, if the depth of each pixel is known, then only pixels with a depth value smaller than the background are those that belong to the foreground. This interdependency can be efficiently exploited for joint depth estimation and image segmentation, yielding more robust and accurate results.

Joint Depth Estimation and Image Segmentation. The goal is to assign corresponding depth to all pixels in the input images and to classify them correctly as scene fore- or background. As a pre-reconstruction step, images of the static scene background have been captured beforehand, and dense depth maps for these background images have been estimated separately using, e.g., Vladimir Kolmogorov's original graph cut algorithm [152].

Input: The input to the depth reconstruction algorithm is the set of pixels $\mathcal{P}_k$ from each source camera k, together with the following mappings for every pixel $\mathbf{p} \in \mathcal{P} := \bigcup_k \mathcal{P}_k$:

$I(\mathbf{p})$ The color value of the input image at pixel $\mathbf{p}$.
$\Delta I(\mathbf{p})$ The value of the (discretely evaluated) Laplacian of the input image.
$B(\mathbf{p})$ The color value of the background image.

Output: The goal is to find the "best" mapping $\lambda : \mathcal{P} \to \mathfrak{L}$ into a set of labels $\mathfrak{L}$ (the meaning of "best" will be specified later). To each pixel, a label $\mathfrak{l} = (\mathfrak{l}_d, \mathfrak{l}_b)$

is assigned that represents a pair of values. Each label stands for a (discrete) depth layer $\mathfrak{l}_d$ and the pixel classification into foreground or background $\mathfrak{l}_b$. By convention, the Boolean value $\mathfrak{l}_b$ is true if and only if $\mathbf{p}$ is a background pixel, while $\mathfrak{l}_d$ denotes the depth of $\mathbf{p}$.

The notion of "depth" is used here in a somewhat abstract fashion: depth labels correspond to level sets of a function $D : \mathbb{R}^3 \longrightarrow \mathbb{R}$ that satisfy the following property: for all scene points $P, Q \in \mathbb{R}^3$ and all cameras k,

$$P \text{ occludes } Q \text{ in } k \;\Rightarrow\; D(P) < D(Q) \,.$$

This is a natural requirement for a function indicating depth. The existence of such a function D implies that there is a way to define depth globally, i.e., independent of a specific camera. An important special case in which the constraint is automatically satisfied occurs when all cameras are located on one side of a plane P, and all cameras point across the plane. The level sets of D can then be chosen as planes that are parallel to P.

Topology: The definition of the algorithm must include the topological properties of the input images. A set-theoretic description can be given by assigning to every pixel $\mathbf{p} \in \mathcal{P}$ the following sets of pixels:

$\mathcal{N}_{\mathbf{p}}$ A set of neighbors of $\mathbf{p}$ in $\mathcal{P}_k$ *excluding* $\mathbf{p}$ over which the energy functional will encourage continuity.

$\mathcal{C}_{\mathbf{p}}$ A neighborhood of $\mathbf{p}$ *including* $\mathbf{p}$. These regions will later be relevant for the computation of normalized cross-correlations that are used to quantify photo-consistency.

Geometry: The geometric relationship between pixels in different images must be specified with respect to their current labels and the images' respective camera positions. These are encoded in the set $\mathfrak{I}$ denoting pixel interactions. A pixel $\mathbf{p}$ in image k together with its label $\mathfrak{l}$ corresponds to a point in 3D space via the projection parameters of the camera k. Let this 3D point be denoted by $\langle \mathbf{p}, \mathfrak{l} \rangle$. Interactions then represent the notion of "proximity" of two 3D points in the following sense (Figure 3.3): a pair of pixel projections $\{\langle \mathbf{p}, \mathfrak{l} \rangle, \langle \mathbf{q}, \mathfrak{l} \rangle\}$ belongs to $\mathfrak{I}$ if and only if

1. $\mathbf{q} \in \mathcal{P}_k$ and $\mathbf{p} \notin \mathcal{P}_k$, i.e., p and q must come from two different cameras, and

2. $\mathbf{q}$ is the nearest pixel to the projection of $\langle \mathbf{p}, \mathfrak{l} \rangle$ into the image of camera k.

This implies that interacting pixels always share the same label $\mathfrak{l}$. In particular, foreground can only interact with foreground, whereas background pixels only interact with background pixels, and interacting pixels must have the same depth, i.e., belong to the same level set of D.

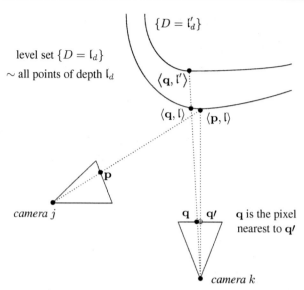

Figure 3.3. Interactions and occlusions: the 3D points $\langle \mathbf{p}, \mathfrak{l} \rangle$ and $\langle \mathbf{q}, \mathfrak{l} \rangle$ interact: $\{\langle \mathbf{p}, \mathfrak{l} \rangle, \langle \mathbf{q}, \mathfrak{l} \rangle\} \in \mathfrak{I}$. On the other hand, $\langle \mathbf{q}, \mathfrak{l}' \rangle$ is occluded by $\langle \mathbf{p}, \mathfrak{l} \rangle$ in camera image k, so $\{\langle \mathbf{p}, \mathfrak{l} \rangle, \langle \mathbf{q}, \mathfrak{l}' \rangle\} \in \mathfrak{O}$. *(Reprinted from [98], © 2003 IEEE.)*

The set $\mathfrak{O}$ of occlusions is used to enforce visibility constraints. It is comprised of the following 3D point pairs:

- A pair $\{\langle \mathbf{p}, \mathfrak{l} \rangle, \langle \mathbf{q}, \mathfrak{l}' \rangle\}$ belongs to $\mathfrak{O}$ if and only if $\{\langle \mathbf{p}, \mathfrak{l} \rangle, \langle \mathbf{q}, \mathfrak{l} \rangle\} \in \mathfrak{I}$ and $\mathfrak{l}_d < \mathfrak{l}'_d$. Geometrically, this means that if $\langle \mathbf{p}, \mathfrak{l} \rangle$ is projected onto q, then it will occlude q if and only if the depth assigned to p is smaller than the depth assigned to q.

The Energy Functional. The goal is to find the "best" label configuration λ of all pixels. Mathematically speaking, the best configuration corresponds to the one that minimizes an energy functional $E(\lambda)$. This functional encodes the high-level knowledge about image formation: unlikely or impossible assignments of labels are penalized, while very likely configurations are encouraged.

A suitable energy functional for depth reconstruction consists of a sum of contributions from every single pixel as well as every possible pixel pair:

$$
E(\lambda) = \sum_{\mathbf{p},\mathbf{q} \in \mathcal{P}} \left[E_{\text{photo}}^{p,q}(\lambda) + \beta E_{\text{smooth}}^{p,q}(\lambda) + E_{\text{vis}}^{p,q}(\lambda) \right]
$$
$$
+ \alpha \sum_{\mathbf{p} \in \mathcal{P}} E_{\text{background}}^{p}(\lambda) . \tag{3.1}
$$

The terms on the right-hand side differ from zero only if $\mathbf{p}$ and $\mathbf{q}$ interact ($E_{\text{photo}}^{p,q}(\lambda)$) or occlude each other ($E_{\text{vis}}^{p,q}(\lambda)$) in a specific configuration, or if $\mathbf{p}$ and $\mathbf{q}$ are neighbors ($E_{\text{smooth}}^{p,q}(\lambda)$). In effect, the sum runs only over relatively few pairs of points. The positive weights α and β are free parameters to weigh background/foreground similarity and local smoothness regularization against photo-consistency, respectively. Values of $\alpha = 0.6$ and $\beta = 0.4$ have been found to work well.

To find an assignment λ of labels to all pixels such that $E(\lambda)$ (Equation (3.1)) is at least locally minimal [153], a technique from combinatorial optimization is used. The approach is known to converge to a local minimum that is at most a multiplicative factor larger than the global minimum, where the factor is determined by the structure of the graph [153]. The four contributing energy functional terms are the photo-consistency term, the smoothness term, the visibility constraints, and the background term.

Photo-Consistency Term. For interacting pixels sharing a similar color, a photo-consistency bonus is issued. This rule is derived from the assumption of Lambertian surface reflectance characteristics: if a 3D scene point is projected to pixel $\mathbf{p}$ in one image and to pixel $\mathbf{q}$ in another image, and if the 3D point is visible in both images, then the pixels and their respective neighborhoods $\mathcal{C}_{\mathbf{p}}$ and $\mathcal{C}_{\mathbf{q}}$ should be similar:

$$E_{\text{photo}}^{p,q}(\lambda) := \begin{cases} -C(\mathbf{p}, \mathbf{q}) & \text{if } \{\langle \mathbf{p}, \lambda(\mathbf{p}) \rangle, \langle \mathbf{q}, \lambda(\mathbf{q}) \rangle\} \in \mathfrak{I}, \\ 0 & \text{otherwise.} \end{cases}$$

The correlation term $C(\mathbf{p}, \mathbf{q}) \in [0, 1]$ must be small if $\mathcal{C}_{\mathbf{p}}$ differs from $\mathcal{C}_{\mathbf{q}}$, and large if the local pixel neighborhoods are very similar. A quite reliable photo-consistency criterion has been found to be

- the normalized cross-correlation (NCC) between the sets of color values $I(\mathcal{C}_{\mathbf{p}})$ and $I(\mathcal{C}_{\mathbf{q}})$, taking always the minimal correlation of the three color channels, and

- the normalized cross-correlation between the sets of Laplacians $\Delta I(\mathcal{C}_{\mathbf{p}})$ and $\Delta I(\mathcal{C}_{\mathbf{q}})$, again computing the three color channels separately and taking the minimum.

A weighted average of these two values is then assigned to $C(\mathbf{p}, \mathbf{q})$. For the local neighborhood of each pixel, a small square region of 3×3 pixels has been found to work well. The normalized cross-correlation between two image patches $I(\mathcal{C}_{\mathbf{p}})$ and $I(\mathcal{C}_{\mathbf{q}})$ is defined as

$$C(\mathbf{p}, \mathbf{q}) \quad = \quad \frac{\sum_i \left[I(p_i) - \bar{I}(\mathcal{C}_{\mathbf{p}}) \right] \left[I(q_i) - \bar{I}(\mathcal{C}_{\mathbf{q}}) \right]}{\sqrt{\sum_i \left[I(p_i) - \bar{I}(\mathcal{C}_{\mathbf{p}}) \right]^2 \sum_i \left[I(q_i) - \bar{I}(\mathcal{C}_{\mathbf{q}}) \right]^2}} , \qquad (3.2)$$

where p_i, q_i denote patch pixels, and $\bar{I}(\mathcal{C}_\mathbf{p})$, $\bar{I}(\mathcal{C}_\mathbf{q})$ are the mean pixel values of each patch. Especially for real-world images, the NCC is a much more robust similarity measure than other kinds of distance measure between color values. This is because different cameras typically output slightly different signals for the same scene point, so stereo images taken simultaneously by different cameras often exhibit different color values even for corresponding pixels. While this effect can be reduced by careful calibration, it remains a potential source of error. Since the NCC measures statistical similarity and not absolute similarity in pixel value, it yields more reliable results and is also applicable to photometrically uncalibrated images, as long as camera response is approximately linear.

The normalized cross-correlation of the Laplacians is calculated equivalent to Equation (3.2). This high-frequency-sensitive operator is included in $C(\mathbf{p}, \mathbf{q})$ to give more weight to matches between image features like edges and corners. Small additional improvements in quality can be achieved by matching other characteristics like partial derivatives or even the coefficients of local Fourier expansions. In general, however, the obtained results do not justify the considerable increase in computational complexity.

Smoothness Term. Drastic changes in image depth, such as transitions from background to foreground, are typically accompanied by color discontinuities. This regularizing observation is expressed by the smoothness energy

$$E_{\text{smooth}}^{p,q}(\lambda) := V^{p,q}\big(\lambda(\mathbf{p}), \lambda(\mathbf{q})\big) , \quad \text{where}$$

$$V^{p,q}(\mathfrak{l}, \mathfrak{l}') := \begin{cases} 0 & \text{if } \mathbf{q} \notin \mathcal{N}_\mathbf{p} \text{ or } \mathfrak{l} = \mathfrak{l}' , \\ 2L_{\max} - \|\Delta I(\mathbf{p})\|_\infty - \|\Delta I(\mathbf{q})\|_\infty & \text{otherwise.} \end{cases}$$

This expression penalizes differences in depth or "backgroundness" if two pixels are neighbors in the same image but the color in their respective neighborhoods $\mathbf{p}$, $\mathbf{q}$ is varying smoothly. To keep the smoothness measure locally confined, smoothness is enforced only over the four nearest neighbors making up the set $\mathcal{N}_\mathbf{p}$. The Laplacian of the image is used here as a simple edge detector. If desired, it can be substituted for a more sophisticated local discontinuity measure. The maximum norm in the above definition denotes the maximum of all color channels, so a change in value in any channel is sufficient to indicate the presence of a discontinuity, which is a natural assumption. $L_{\max}$ is the largest possible absolute value for the Laplacian, which depends on color encoding and level of discretization. It assures that $E_{\text{smooth}}^{p,q}(\lambda) \geq 0$, since discontinuities should not result in an energy bonus.

Visibility Constraints. Certain label configurations are impossible because of occlusions. In Figure 3.3, for example, if pixel $\mathbf{p}$ in camera j is assigned a depth label $\mathfrak{l}$, and the projection of $\langle \mathbf{p}, \mathfrak{l} \rangle$ into another camera k is pixel $\mathbf{q}$, then it is not possible for $\mathbf{q}$ to have a larger depth than $\mathbf{p}$. Such illegal configurations are taken into account by the set of occlusions, which are penalized by assigning

$$E_{\text{vis}}^{p,q}(\lambda) := \begin{cases} \infty & \text{if } \{\langle \mathbf{p}, \lambda(\mathbf{p}) \rangle, \langle \mathbf{q}, \lambda(\mathbf{q}) \rangle\} \in \mathfrak{O}, \\ 0 & \text{otherwise.} \end{cases}$$

The visibility term is either zero or infinity to distinguish legal from illegal configurations, respectively.

Background Term. To classify pixels as belonging to the foreground or the background, the normalized cross-correlation $C_b(\mathbf{p})$ (Equation (3.2)) is used again. This time, it is computed between the ordered sets of neighboring image pixel colors $I(\mathcal{N}_{\mathbf{p}})$ and background image colors $B(\mathcal{N}_{\mathbf{p}})$. A high correlation between the local image patch and the corresponding background patch is penalized if λ does not classify $\mathbf{p}$ as a background pixel. A second clue is background depth: if $\lambda_b(\mathbf{p}) = \text{true}$, i.e., if $\mathbf{p}$ belongs to the background, then $\mathbf{p}$ must have the same depth $\mathfrak{b}_d(\mathbf{p})$ as the background. This results in the following background energy expression:

$$E_{\text{background}}^{p}(\lambda) := \begin{cases} C_b(\mathbf{p}) & \text{if } \lambda(\mathbf{p})_b = \text{false}, \\ \infty & \text{if } \lambda(\mathbf{p})_b = \text{true} \\ & \text{and } \lambda(\mathbf{p})_d \neq \mathfrak{b}_d(\mathbf{p}), \\ 0 & \text{otherwise.} \end{cases}$$

In image areas with little texture variation, it can happen that image noise causes the correlation value $C_b(\mathbf{p})$ to be low even if $\mathbf{p}$ is actually a background pixel. For this reason, low-correlation regions are not penalized even if the current labeling λ classifies $\mathbf{p}$ as background.

Energy Minimization via Graph Cuts. In the context of discrete labels, joint depth estimation and image segmentation is equivalent to finding the configuration of labels that minimizes the energy functional, Equation 3.1. A standard technique from combinatorial optimization offers an elegant approach to determine a label configuration that represents a strong local minimum [153]. The idea is to construct a graph whose nodes correspond to the image pixels and whose weighted edges are derived from the energy functional. A (binary) minimum graph cut then separates the graph into two disjoint parts such that the sum of weights of the cut edges is minimal, while each pixel node remains connected to one of two special nodes, the *source* node or the *sink* node of the graph; see Figure 3.4. The problem is equivalent to finding the maximum flow through the

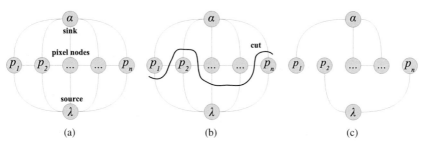

Figure 3.4. Binary minimum graph cut: (a) each image pixel is represented by a pixel node. Weighted edges connect nodes of pixels that jointly contribute to the energy sum. Edge weights are determined by the energy functional. Two special nodes, the source node λ and the sink node α, are connected to all pixel nodes. (b) The minimum graph cut separates the graph into two disjoint parts such that the sum of all cut edges is minimal. (c) Pixels remaining connected to the sink node are assigned the label α, while pixels connected to the source node keep their label.

network from the source to the sink. A real-world example could be the maximal amount of water flowing from a source inlet through a maze of pipes to a sink/drain, where each pipe has a different, finite diameter/flow capacity. For this binary problem, algorithms have been devised that find the minimum cut in polynomial time [84, 97].

In stereo reconstruction, unfortunately, it is not a binary decision (between source or sink) that has to be made for each pixel, but each pixel must be assigned one out of multiple possible pixel labels, one possible label for each depth layer times foreground/background classification. Correspondingly, the graph has multiple sinks (or sources). This *multi-way graph cut problem*, however, is NP-hard.

Fortunately, the α-expansion algorithm [28] enables the use of the graph cut technique to find a strong local minimum of the energy functional (Equation (3.1)). Instead of optimizing over all labels at once, α-expansion considers each label at a time, breaking down the multi-way problem into computing multiple binary graph cuts.

The algorithm repeatedly iterates over all possible labels. At each iteration step, a binary graph is constructed. The source node always represents the current label configuration λ. It is connected to all pixel nodes $\mathcal{P}$. The sink node is the label α currently under scrutiny. It is also connected to all pixel nodes. The edge weights must be derived from the energy functional (Equation (3.1)). An elegant way to determine suitable edge weights for a general class of energy functionals has been described by Vladimir Kolmogorov and Ramin Zabih [153, 154].

For the constructed binary graph, the minimum cut is determined using a standard graph-cut algorithm [84, 97]. The pixels whose corresponding nodes remain connected to the sink node are assigned the new label α, while all other pixels still connected to the source node keep their previous labels λ. Formally, the new label configuration $\lambda_{\mathcal{A},\alpha}$ for every $p \in \mathcal{P}$ follows from

$$\lambda_{\mathcal{A},\alpha}(p) := \begin{cases} \alpha & \text{if } p \in \mathcal{A}, \\ \lambda(p) & \text{otherwise}, \end{cases}$$

where $\mathcal{A} \subset \mathcal{P}$ is the set of pixels that should be relabeled as α to reduce the total energy (Equation (3.1)). If $\mathcal{A}$ is empty, the label configuration remains unchanged to always satisfy $E(\lambda_{\mathcal{A},\alpha}) \leq E(\lambda)$. The α-expansion algorithm terminates if no further energy-reducing cuts can be found for any label.

In the beginning, the α-expansion algorithm must be initialized with a valid label configuration. Any valid starting configuration λ_0 with $E(\lambda_0) < \infty$ is permissible. A straightforward, valid initialization consists of setting each pixel to the maximum possible depth and tagging it as foreground. Since energy is always reduced, and impossible configurations are assigned infinite energy, only valid configurations can result.

Depth and Segmentation Results.   For a quantitative verification of the described joint depth estimation and image segmentation algorithm, a synthetic scene was rendered from four different viewpoints; see Figure 3.5(a). The scene was rendered once without the chessmen on the board, representing the background images, and another time with the foreground. Disparity between the images ranges from 2 to 20 pixels. For each image, the graphics card's Z-buffer was read out to have available true per-pixel depth information. The stereo algorithm was then applied to the four images. Figures 3.5(b), 3.5(c), and 3.5(d) depict the segmented foreground pixels, the recovered depth map, and the residual error for one of the test images. The results were obtained from input images that were artificially corrupted by adding Gaussian noise to all color channels. This was done to validate the algorithm's robustness against additive noise. Prior to depth-map estimation, random, Gaussian-distributed noise with standard deviation σ, stated in pixel intensity units, was added to all image pixels. Figure 3.6 depicts the percentage of pixels that were assigned a wrong depth or segmentation label. Results are shown with and without simultaneous image segmentation. Even in the absence of image noise, depth estimation in conjunction with image segmentation reduces the number of spurious depth labels by almost 50% when compared to the case without exploiting background information. When noise is deliberately added to the images, the increased robustness of the joint approach becomes even more evident. The percentage of erroneous pixels remains below 5% even at significant noise levels.

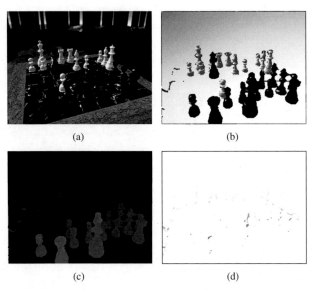

(a) (b)

(c) (d)

Figure 3.5. Joint depth estimation and image segmentation: (a) one source image of a synthetic test scene, (b) segmented foreground, (c) reconstructed pixel depth, and (d) wrong depth label assignments as compared to the known ground truth. Gaussian noise of $\sigma = 5$ pixel intensity values was added to the source images. *(Reprinted from [98], © 2003 IEEE.)*

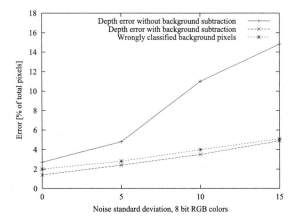

Figure 3.6. Depth/segmentation reconstruction robustness: the plot depicts the percentage of wrongly labeled image pixels with respect to the amount of Gaussian noise added to the input images. Results of the joint depth estimation and segmentation algorithm are the dotted line; results for the original graph cut algorithm are the solid line [152]. Segmentation error, the dashed line, is almost coincidental with depth error. *(Reprinted from [98], © 2003 IEEE.)*

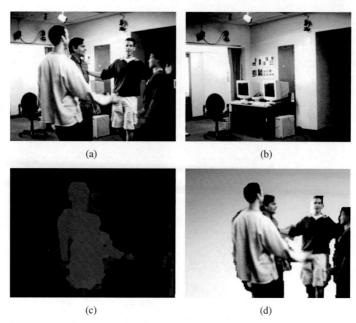

(a)   (b)

(c)   (d)

Figure 3.7. Reconstruction results for real-world imagery: (a) one image of the dynamic scene, (b) recording of the static background, (c) estimated depth map, and (d) segmented foreground. *(Reprinted from [98], © 2003 IEEE.)*

Joint depth estimation and image segmentation also performs very well on real-world imagery [103]. Dynamic light fields recorded with the Stanford Multi-Camera Array were available for evaluation [312]. During acquisition, the cameras were spaced relatively far apart, resulting in a disparity range of up to 34 pixel units in images of 320×240-pixel resolution. Images from different cameras also varied considerably due to missing photometric calibration and MPEG compression artifacts, challenging the depth reconstruction algorithm. Figures 3.7(a) and 3.7(b) depict one image of the dynamic light field and the corresponding static background image. Figures 3.7(c) and 3.7(d) show the reconstructed depth map and segmented foreground. Despite motion blur and compression artifacts, the foreground is segmented cleanly, and the depth map is of sufficient quality to yield convincing rendering results.

Optimization-based approaches to depth reconstruction typically trade robustness and accuracy for offline performance. For the described algorithm, one full iteration over 65 labels for four 320×240-pixel images takes approximately 65 seconds on a 1.7 GHz Pentium III Xeon PC. Typically, four iterations are necessary to converge to the final result. Note that, without image segmentation, the number of labels that need to be considered, and therefore the time per iteration, is cut in half.

3.2.2   Rendering

In light-field rendering (see Section 2.3.2), the target image is constructed by resampling from all light-field images. Pursuing an equivalent approach for time-varying scenes would imply that for each time step, all dynamic light-field images of that time frame including respective depth maps must be available in local memory. Transfer bandwidth very quickly limits the amount of light-field data that can be continuously updated. Instead, the target viewpoint is commonly restricted to lie within the plane of cameras [103, 345]. In that case, 3D image warping can be applied (see Section 2.4.1) to interpolate the target image from only three or four reference images. The cameras recording the dynamic light field span a recording hull around the scene. To render a view of the dynamic scene from any viewpoint C situated on the recording hull, the reference images $\{I_{k=1,...,m}\}$ nearby the desired viewpoint need to be 3D-warped to the intermediate position C and blended [103]. The warping and blending computations can be executed very efficiently on graphics hardware.

To avoid holes between warped pixels as well as to accelerate rendering performance and reduce transfer rate to the graphics board, the graphics hardware's rasterization engine can be exploited by considering each reference image's depth map λ_k as a polygonal *warping mesh*. A regular triangle mesh is laid over each source image $\{I_k\}$. To each vertex $\mathbf{v}$ of the mesh, a depth value $\lambda(\mathbf{v})$ is assigned that is computed, e.g., to be the mean depth of surrounding pixels in λ_k. By varying the number of vertices in the warping mesh, effective depth-map resolution is varied continuously, controlling also the number of warping transformation calculations. Coarse meshes also reduce the amount of data that has to be transferred to the graphics card. Different-sized warping meshes can be precomputed for each reference image and stored on hard drive.

Prior to hardware-supported multi-texturing and fragment shaders, warping and blending m images on the graphics board implied that the output image is composited in multiple rendering passes. During the kth pass, the warp matrix from reference camera position C_k to the desired viewpoint C as well as the image's blending weight ω_k are passed on to the GPU. Then, the source image I_k is uploaded to the texture memory on the graphics card. Finally, the warping mesh is sent through the rendering pipeline as a sequence of triangle strips. A small vertex program assigns texture coordinates to each vertex v and computes its warped coordinates. The blending weight should decrease with increasing

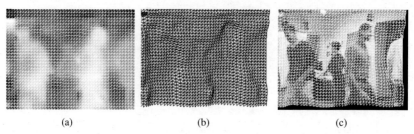

(a)   (b)   (c)

Figure 3.8. 3D warping on GPU: (a) depth map with superimposed warping mesh, (b) warped mesh, and (c) warped reference image with superimposed mesh. *(Reprinted from [103].)*

distance $\mathbf{d}_k$ between reference image and target image, e.g.,

$$\omega_k := \exp(-c\,\mathbf{d}_k \cdot \mathbf{d}_k). \tag{3.3}$$

Using a Gaussian weight function is not mandatory, but the weight function should be unity for $\mathbf{d}_k = 0$ and fall off smoothly. To accelerate rendering performance, images with a weight value below some threshold $\epsilon > 0$ can be neglected since their contribution is too small to have a visible impact on the target image. In Equation (3.3), the constant c can be chosen so that ω_k falls below ϵ just when $\mathbf{d}_k$ equals the minimum distance between two cameras. This way, a reference image is reproduced exactly, without interference from other source images, if the desired viewing position coincides with one of the source cameras.

From the reference images' individual weights, the final blending weight w_k, as can be used in the OpenGL blend equation, is computed via cumulative normalization,

$$w_k = \frac{\omega_k}{\sum_{i=1}^{k} \omega_i}.$$

The stencil buffer can be used to ensure that full weight is used in areas to which no image data has yet been written. This guarantees that all pixels are blended with the correct weight relative to the images already considered, and that for each pixel all weights sum to one after each pass. By enabling the Z-buffer test, occlusions due to overlapping triangles are automatically handled correctly. Back-facing triangles are culled during rendering, as their pixels are obscured from the current view.

Figure 3.8(a) shows the warping mesh superimposed on a reference image's reconstructed dense depth map. The mesh is then warped according to the desired viewpoint and vertex depth; see Figure 3.8(b). The warped image in Figure 3.8(c) is obtained by simple texturing, using the vertices' original 2D image coordinates as texture coordinates. The final output image is constructed by weightedly blending several warped reference images; see Plate IX.

If, in addition to depth maps, image segmentation information is also available, e.g., by employing the algorithm described in Section 3.2.1, enhanced results can be obtained by rendering the foreground and the background layer separately before combining them into the final output image [268]. By rendering the foreground and background individually and then compositing the resulting image, visibility along the foreground outline is treated correctly. To avoid unnaturally crisp contours across the foreground/background boundary, alpha matting can be additionally applied in a strip along the outline, yielding perceptually very convincing results [345].

Rendering Performance. The above-described GPU-accelerated warping algorithm has been evaluated on a 1.8 GHz Pentium Xeon with an NVIDIA GeForce4^{TM} graphics card. The output image is rendered from $m = 4$ source images that have been recorded from the corners of a square with optical axes aligned in parallel; see Plate IX(a). Disparity ranges from 0 to 34 pixel units. The source images exhibit 320×240-pixel RGB resolution while the target view is rendered at an output resolution of 640×480 pixels.

Plate IX(b) displays the rendering result for a viewpoint located at the center of the square spanned by the cameras, at equal distance to all four source images. Blurring artifacts are apparent (red circles). No depth information is available for the upper right corner because this region is visible in only one image. In general, depth information near the boundary is not as accurate as in the center, a common problem in dense depth estimation [6]. The blurred region around the person's legs, on the other hand, is due to motion blur that is already present in the source images; see Plate IX(a). Regions around image features, such as the wall corner or the computer monitor, encircled green, are rendered accurately.

Table 3.1 lists measured rendering frame rates for different warping mesh resolutions. The mesh size corresponds to the horizontal and vertical edge length

triangle size [pixel]	mesh res.	triangles [#]	frame rate [Hz]	PSNR [dB]
8	40x30	9600	72.99	28.55
4	80x60	38400	32.15	28.65
2	160x120	145200	10.87	28.67

Table 3.1. GPU-accelerated warping from four reference images on an NVIDIA GeForce4^{TM} graphics board. The table depicts rendering frame rates and reconstruction accuracy for different warping mesh sizes. *(Reprinted from [103].)*

triangle size	time per frame for		
	rendering	loading images	loading warping meshes
8	13.7 ms 26.4 %	36.8 ms 70.8 %	1.5 ms 2.8 %
4	31.1 ms 42.0 %	36.8 ms 49.7 %	6.1 ms 8.3 %
2	99.8 ms 61.9 %	36.8 ms 22.8 %	24.5 ms 15.3 %

Table 3.2. Dynamic light-field warping: timings for different mesh sizes for continuous upload from hard drive and rendering. *(Reprinted from [103].)*

of one triangle in pixels. To exclude the time overhead for continuously uploading the time-varying images and meshes to the graphics card, the measurements are taken for a static set of reference images and warping meshes. Four source images can be warped and blended at real-time frame rates down to mesh sizes of 4×4 pixels. By selecting different warping mesh resolutions, the rendering algorithm can adapt to the processing power of the system it runs on. Rendering on graphics hardware has the additional advantage that the output image can be scaled to almost arbitrary size without significant impact on rendering performance.

Table 3.2 depicts timing measurements when continuously updating the four reference images plus warping meshes from hard drive, as is necessary to display the scene in motion. Hard drive transfer bandwidth limits attainable rendering frame rate considerably. At 320×240-pixel source image resolution, roughly 1 MB of image data and depth information must be transferred per time step from hard drive to the graphics card. At advertised uploading rates of 25 MB per second for standard IDE drives, frame rates of 25 Hz should be attainable. Measurements, however, rarely yield transfer rates exceeding 15 MB/s, presumably because the data is not stored linearly on the drive. This has to be taken into consideration when rendering from large dynamic light fields, as reference images and warping meshes must be accessed randomly depending on viewpoint position.

Intuitively, output image quality is expected to increase with the number of warping mesh vertices. To evaluate rendering accuracy, one of the four reference images is predicted by rendering its view using the other three source images. The rendered result is then compared to the ground truth from the reference image using as error measure the peak signal-to-noise ratio (PSNR). Table 3.1 lists in the last column the PSNR values for different triangle sizes. Prediction quality appears to be largely independent of warping-mesh resolution, indicating that interpolating local scene depth via the rasterization engine is by and large adequate. The limited overall prediction quality is due to the fact that the source images are

Figure 3.9. Residual error between reference image and rendered view prediction: prediction errors are concentrated along depth discontinuities where large differences in color result from only small calibration inaccuracies. *(Reprinted from [103].)*

not radiometrically calibrated and have been MPEG-compressed during acquisition [312]. Figure 3.9 illustrates the difference between the warped estimate and the original image. Errors occur predominantly along depth discontinuities where small inaccuracies in camera calibration result in potentially large color differences. To minimize these errors, subpixel-accurate camera calibration would be necessary. Alternatively, the error can be visually masked by blurring the image locally across known depth discontinuities [49, 111, 345]; per-pixel transparency can also be reconstructed [282, 210].

3.2.3 Summary

Dynamic light-field warping achieves convincing rendering results at real-time frame rates on commodity hardware. The dynamic light field must be acquired in a small-baseline camera set-up, but images may exhibit noticeable disparity. This allows it to cover substantially larger viewing angles than in the 3D TV system; see Section 3.1. However, reliable depth maps and segmentation information can typically be reconstructed only offline. Image segmentation information enables masking the artifact-prone regions along the boundary between image foreground and background to render depth or segmentation errors perceptionally unnoticeable. By making use of graphics hardware, output image size doesn't affect rendering performance, and rendering frame rates can be adapted to computational resources. The main drawback of dynamic light-field warping is that the viewpoint is constrained to lie on the recording hull spanned by the recording camera positions.

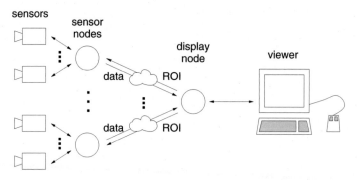

Figure 3.10. Distributed processing of generalized lumigraphs: the display host is connected to all camera client PCs, from which it requests image and depth data for specific regions of interest (ROI). *(Reprinted from [259], courtesy of Hartmut Schirmacher,* © *2001 Eurographics.)*

3.3   Generalized Lumigraphs

The 3D TV system of Section 3.1 is capable of rendering online views from arbitrary viewpoints, yet it requires a lot of input images from acquisition cameras very close together. Dynamic light-field warping (see Section 3.2) yields convincing rendering results from more widely spaced camera arrangements, yet the viewpoint must lie on the recording hull, and it requires offline processing. In Hartmut Schirmacher and his coworkers' *generalized lumigraph* system, the advantages of both approaches are combined to overcome their respective drawbacks [259]. The approach hinges on the display host's ability to control the acquisition network (see Figure 3.10), so one limitation remaining is that remote rendering, as in the 3D TV system, is not possible.

3.3.1   Acquisition

For generalized lumigraph rendering, the recording cameras must be arranged in a convex configuration, with roughly equal distances to the scene. The original implementation uses a bookshelf to mount the video cameras [259]; see Figure 3.11. This *Lumi-Shelf* consists of six calibrated Sony DFW-V500 cameras that are arranged in three pairs. Each camera pair is connected to one client PC via the IEEE1394 (FireWire™) bus. The three client PCs are, in turn, connected via 100-Mb Ethernet™ LAN to the display host; see Figure 3.10. Over the network, the display host is able to request image and depth data for only a specific region of interest (ROI) from each camera client PC. The ROIs for each camera client are determined on the fly during rendering. They represent the part of each

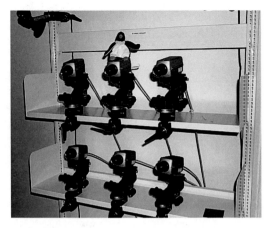

Figure 3.11. The generalized lumigraph system uses light-field data recorded with a *Lumi-Shelf*, i.e., a bookshelf equipped with three synchronized camera pairs. *(Reprinted from [259], courtesy of Hartmut Schirmacher, © 2001 Eurographics.)*

light-field image that is needed to render the current target view. Depth-map estimation is carried out on the client PCs only for those image pixels within the specified region of interest. This approach keeps network traffic constant and typically reduces depth-map computation times significantly.

3.3.2 On-the-Fly Depth Estimation

Each client PC performs conventional depth-from-stereo estimation on the stereo image pair provided by its two connected video cameras. Since, in the worst case, a client PC has to estimate dense depth for all image pixels, a fast stereo estimation algorithm must be employed to guarantee online performance. There exist, indeed, some CPU implementations of fast stereo estimation algorithms that are capable of achieving interactive frame rates [116, 52]. In the generalized lumigraph system, a more conventional correlation-based stereo estimation is used. All camera images are first rectified to coincide with a common image plane. The images are then divided into square blocks. For each image block, the position of the best-matching block situated on the same scan line but in the other image is sought. To save time, the entire scan line is not considered during block matching search. Instead, only a range of *disparity values* from the block's original position are tested. As a similarity measure between image blocks, the sum of squared differences (SSD), the sum of absolute differences (SAD), or the normalized cross-correlation (NCC) over all pixels of the block can be employed. The disparity value corresponding to the highest NCC value, or the smallest SSD or

SAD value, is selected as the most probable block disparity. From known camera calibration, the found disparity value can be immediately converted to scene depth.

The depth maps are refined hierarchically by considering different image block sizes in descending order. This way, depth-map resolution can be traded for reconstruction frame rate. On an 800-MHz Intel III machine, the proposed stereo reconstruction algorithm achieves 0.5–3 frames per second for 320×240-pixel depth maps [259].

Depth-from-Stereo on Graphics Hardware. Today, state-of-the-art stereo algorithms based on CPU [52] or GPU [328] implementations are fast enough to let a current implementation of the system attain truly interactive frame rates. Ruigang Yang and Marc Pollefeys describe an implementation to perform real-time stereo estimation on graphics hardware [328]. The approach is based on a multi-resolution (mip-map) representation of the stereo images and does not require rectified input images. Using multiple rendering passes, an imaginary plane is swept through the scene volume, and the two stereo images are projected onto the plane. To determine mutual color similarity, the sum of squared differences is computed by exploiting the mip-map representation of the images. For each pixel, the depth layer resulting in the minimal SSD value is selected, neglecting occlusion effects. A similar approach that also takes visibility issues into account has been proposed by Jan Woetzel and Reinhard Koch [318]. Their algorithm has also been demonstrated to work for more than two camera images, and better preserves depth discontinuities by using a different SSD computation approach than Yang and Pollefeys.

3.3.3   Rendering

For rendering, RGB color values and associated depth are transmitted for all pixels within the respective ROIs from the camera clients to the display host. The actual rendering algorithm is similar to unstructured lumigraph rendering (see Section 2.3.3) and the plenoptic rendering approach described by Benno Heigl and his collaborators [114].

During stereo estimation, the recorded images have been rectified to lie in one common image plane. Now, camera recording positions are projected from the desired viewpoint onto the common image plane. From a predetermined triangulation of camera positions, the image plane is now partitioned into triangles. Each triangular region will be textured by the three cameras corresponding to its vertices. Each camera thereby contributes only to the triangle fan around its projected vertex. The ROI of a camera is determined by its vertex's triangle fan, plus a preset safety margin that is necessary because the following forward disparity compensation potentially shifts some pixels from outside the fan into view. The pixels and depth values within the ROI are transferred back to the display server, where they are projected onto the common image plane as seen from the target viewpoint. The triangle texture contributions from all three cameras are then composited using the Z-buffer test to take mutual occlusions into account. Regions visible in more than one camera pair are smoothly blended applying the barycentric coordinates as weights. Rendering frame rates of 9 frames/sec are achieved at 256×256-pixel output resolution.

3.3.4 Summary

Generalized lumigraph rendering is an on-site, online VBR approach for small-baseline, convex acquisition set-ups. The viewpoint can leave the recording hull surface as defined by the camera positions. It yields disparity-compensated rendering results at interactive frame rates. In comparison to dynamic light-field warping, however, sacrifices have to be made with respect to rendering quality. Because dense depth is reconstructed from only two images, the error percentage is much higher than that which is achievable with sophisticated multi-view stereo reconstruction algorithms; see Section 3.2.1.

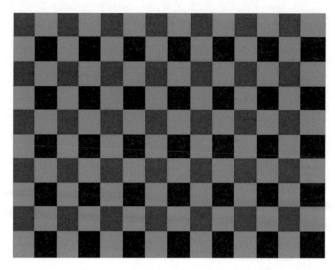

Plate I. Bayer mosaic (Section 2.1.1). In front of each CCD pixel, a green, blue, or red color filter is placed. A 2 × 2-pixel block represents one color unit that consists of two green-filtered pixels, one blue-filtered pixel, and one red-filtered pixel. CCD chip resolution is divided among the color channels. *(Reprinted from [141], courtesy of Neel Joshi, © 2004 N. Joshi.)*

Plate II. (Section 2.1.2) Mobile VBR acquisition set-up in a workshop. *(Reprinted from [3], © 2004 IEE.)*

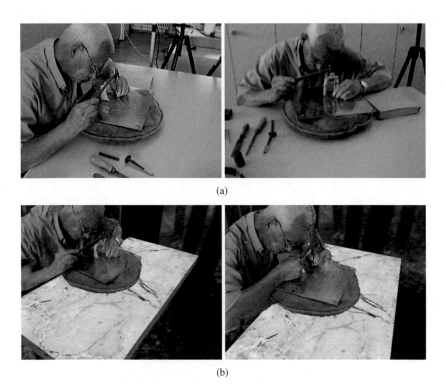

(a)

(b)

Plate III. (Section 2.1.2) (a) Two of eight input views from the *Craftsman* sequence recorded with the mobile acquisition set-up; (b) results for volumetric visual-hull rendering (Section 4.1) in a virtual backdrop. *(Reprinted from [3], © 2004 IEE.)*

(a)   (b)

Plate IV. Color calibration (Section 2.1.6). Both images of the same scene are taken under identical illumination conditions but with different cameras. For color calibration, the 24-patch Macbeth ColorChecker^{TM} is placed into the scene. *(Reprinted from [141], courtesy of Neel Joshi, © 2004 N. Joshi.)*

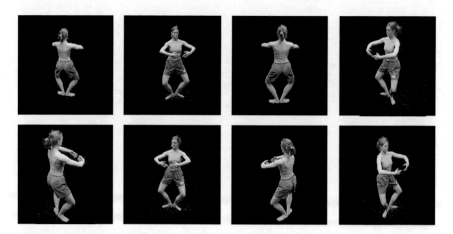

Plate V. Segmented multi-video images serve as input to most VBR algorithms (Section 2.1.7). These eight segmented reference images correspond to one time frame. *(Reprinted from [191], © 2004 IEEE.)*

(a)

(b)

Plate VI. 3D TV (Section 3.1). Views of a dynamic scene on the autostereoscopic display from two different directions. *(Reprinted from [207], courtesy of Wojciech Matusik and Hanspeter Pfister, © 2004 ACM.)*

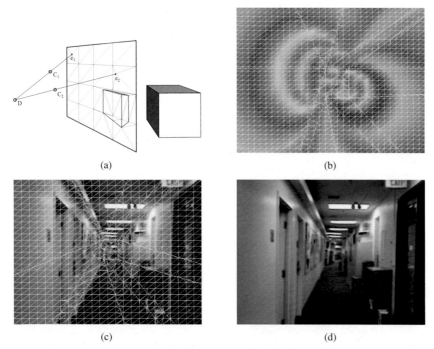

(a)

(b)

(c)

(d)

Plate VII. Camera blending field for unstructured lumigraph rendering (Section 2.3.3). (a) Available scene-geometry vertices as well as reference-view positions C_i are projected from the current viewpoint D onto the target view's image plane. Regular grid points are added. The resulting image-space vertices are triangulated; (b) For each image-plane vertex, the contributing reference views with corresponding weights are determined (color-coded). On graphics hardware, the blending field is interpolated from the image-space vertices; (c) Per pixel, the reference images designated in the blending field are weightedly blended; (d) The rendering result takes into account visibility, view dependency, and image resolution. *((a) and (b) Reprinted from [31], courtesy of Chris Buehler, © 2001 C. Buehler. (c) and (d) reprinted from [32], courtesy of Chris Buehler, © 2002 C. Buehler.)*

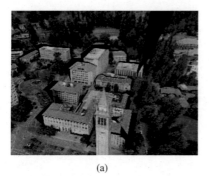 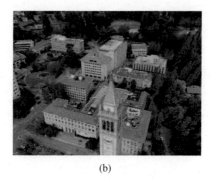

(a)   (b)

Plate VIII. Hole-filling in view-dependent texture mapping (Section 2.3.4). (a) A general problem in image-based rendering is to fill scene regions that were not acquired by any reference image (black gaps); (b) By interpolating holes via low-pass filtering, the human eye's reduced acuity to smooth image regions is elegantly exploited to mask missing image information. *(Reprinted from [58], courtesy of Paul Debevec, http://www.debevec.org,* © *1998 Eurographics.)*

 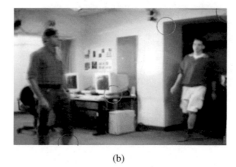

(a)   (b)

Plate IX. Dynamic light-field warping (Section 3.2). (a) Four input images serve as input to render (b) the target view whose viewpoint is located in the middle between the four camera positions. Sharp features are reproduced without blurring (green circles). Blurred regions (red) are due to motion blur in the source images (leg), or the region being visible in only one camera (ceiling).

(a)   (b)

Plate X. Image-based visual-hull rendering (Section 4.3). The images show a recorded person in a virtual backdrop. *(Reprinted from [211], courtesy of Wojciech Matusik, © 2001 W. Matusik.)*

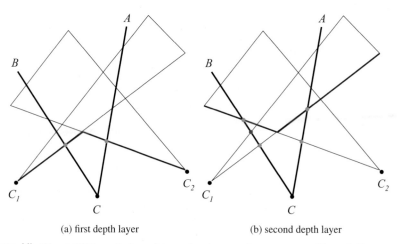

(a) first depth layer   (b) second depth layer

Plate XI. Direct CSG rendering of two visual cones from cameras C_1 and C_2 as seen from viewpoint C (Section 4.4). (a) From the first depth layer (blue) to the viewpoint C, both exemplary lines of sight CA and CB encounter one front-facing fragment (green). (b) On or in front of the second depth layer (blue), two front-facing fragments (green) are encountered along CA, while two front-facing and one back-facing fragment (red) are encountered along CB. Since the number of intersecting visual cones in this example is two, CA intersects the visual hull at the second depth layer, whereas CB does not.

| (a) colored voxel model | (b) ray casting with cubic voxels | (c) ray casting with surface fit |

Plate XII. Spatiotemporal view interpolation (Section 5.1). (a) Rendering the model as a collection of cubic voxels; each voxel is assigned the average color of its reference image projections. (b) Spatiotemporal ray casting of the cubic model surface; the limited resolution of the volumetric model limits attainable rendering quality. (c) Rendering result when intersecting viewing rays with a smooth surface fitted through the centers of adjacent surface voxels. *(Reprinted from [308], courtesy of Sundar Vedula, © 2001 S. Vedula.)*

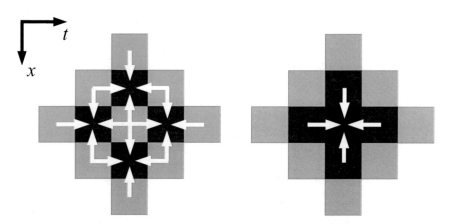

Plate XIII. Spacetime-coherent reconstruction (Section 5.2). Evaluation of the differential operator via finite differences. In the first step, the values of u_q in the green cells are used to compute the level-set normals $\mathbf{n} \in \mathbb{R}^4$ of the blue cells by central differences. In the second step, the red center cell is evaluated from the blue cells. For illustrative purposes, the three spatial dimensions are represented as one. *(Reprinted from [101], © 2004 IEEE.)*

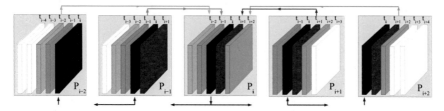

Plate XIV. Spacetime-coherent reconstruction (Section 5.2). Data distribution and communication. Each process stores five slices $\Sigma_t(t_{i,i\pm1,i\pm2})$ corresponding to five consecutive time steps. The process P_i is responsible for computing the central slice corresponding to time t_i. Before the next iteration step, the previous iteration result of P_i is transmitted over the network. Simultaneously, P_i receives the temporally adjacent slices from other processes. Slices of the same color denote the same information after data transfer.

$\alpha = 0$ $\alpha = 3$ $\alpha = 15$

Plate XV. Free-viewpoint video (Section 6.1). Reference image blending. Because model geometry can locally deviate from the actual object surface, projecting multiple reference images onto the model leads to blurriness and ghosting artifacts ($\alpha = 0$). By taking into account relative triangle orientation with respect to the reference cameras, aliasing artifacts can be reduced ($\alpha = 3$) or even completely eliminated ($\alpha = 15$), at the expense of view-independent texturing results.

Chapter 4

Visual- and Photo-Hull Rendering

Depth-from-stereo algorithms are applicable to light-field images with largely overlapping fields of view. If only a handful of cameras are spaced far apart to capture the scene from all around, different reconstruction techniques must be applied in order to recover dynamic 3D geometry.

The *visual hull* has been widely used as a 3D geometry proxy because it can be computed very efficiently from wide-baseline images. The visual hull represents a conservative approximation of true object geometry; see Section 2.2.2. Research on visual-hull reconstruction from real images dates back to the mid-1970s [13]. Since then, a variety of algorithms have been proposed to accelerate reconstruction as well as to improve visual-hull geometry. All algorithms discussed in the following allow for online processing. Another advantage of visual-hull–based VBR algorithms is that reconstruction robustness and rendering quality are unaffected by surface properties. As long as object foreground can be reliably segmented from image background, surface glossiness and reflections do not impede visual-hull rendering.

4.1 Volumetric Visual Hulls

The most straightforward approach to fast visual hull reconstruction consists of computing the silhouette intersection volume by discretizing scene space. The scene volume that is visible in all camera views is subdivided into cubic volume elements (voxels); see Figure 4.1. Each voxel is tested for silhouette consistency. Each volume element is projected into all camera views. The projection coordi-

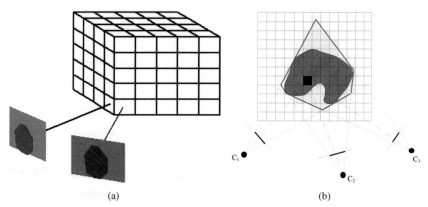

(a)   (b)

Figure 4.1. Volumetric visual-hull reconstruction: (a) the scene volume is discretized into volume elements (voxels). (b) Each voxel is reprojected into all reference views. Voxels falling inside all image silhouettes belong to the visual hull. *(Reprinted from [176], courtesy of Ming Li.)*

nates are looked up in the respective segmented image to see whether the projected voxel lies within the object's silhouette. Only voxels that consistently fall within the silhouettes in all images belong to the visual hull. All other volume elements must be located outside the visual hull and are set transparent. This way, a binary-valued visual-hull model is reconstructed that consists of many small voxels; see Figure 4.2.

Many different implementations of volumetric visual-hull reconstruction are described in the literature [242, 285, 225, 218, 143, 221, 24, 309, 46, 183]. The main challenge consists of building a distributed computer network to achieve on-line performance. One realization based on commodity PC hardware shall serve as an example [291].

Figure 4.2. Volumetric visual-hull model.

4.1.1   Online Reconstruction

Based on a distributed client-server architecture (see Section 2.1.4), one client PC controls two synchronized video cameras; see Figure 4.3. The client PC performs on-the-fly background subtraction on both incoming video streams to obtain the segmented object foreground; see Section 2.1.7. From both silhouette images, the client PC then reconstructs a coarse volumetric visual-hull approximation; see Figure 4.3. Because the known camera calibration parameters allow it to precompute voxel projection coordinates in both images, the volumetric reconstruction runs at interactive frame rates. Finally, the client PCs run-length-encode their respective partial binary visual-hull volumes and transmit the data over the network to the server. Here, the intersection volume is determined by combining the partial volumes and applying a simple AND operation to each voxel. On a network of 1 GHz Athlon PCs, a $64 \times 64 \times 64$-voxel volume can be reconstructed at 8 fps [291].

In order to accommodate arbitrary numbers of cameras in a time-critical system, the infrastructure layout must be scalable. Instead of merging all partial visual hulls on the server, additional layers of processing nodes can be inserted between the camera clients and the display host of Figure 4.3. In a binary tree-hierarchical network architecture, for example, each computer node receives two partial volumes, determines the intersection, and passes it on to the next layer. For

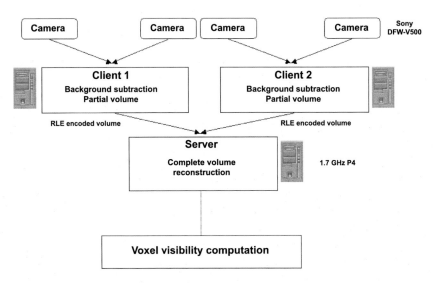

Figure 4.3. Volumetric visual-hull reconstruction can be realized in real-time by distributed computing. *(Reprinted from [192], © 2003 IEEE.)*

n video cameras, a binary-tree structured network requires $n - 1$ PCs. The final visual hull is reconstructed and rendered on the server PC representing the tree root. This way, network traffic and computational load remains constant, which allows for including almost arbitrarily many cameras. To also limit network traffic for video texture transfer, the display server requests only those images from the respective camera clients that contribute to the target view.

4.1.2   Billboard Rendering

The surface of the obtained volumetric visual hull is composed of numerous cube-shaped voxels; see Figure 4.2. For realistic rendering, the surface has to be textured using the recorded video images. Commodity graphics hardware, however, cannot directly render textured voxels.

One solution is to convert the voxel surface to a triangle mesh. Unfortunately, volume triangulation algorithms such the *marching cubes* method [180] do not perform at interactive frame rates. Instead, each surface voxel can be point-based rendered [325]. This requires assigning one color to each voxel, excluding view-dependent effects.

Alternatively, *billboard rendering* can be employed to synthesize view-dependently textured views directly from the volumetric visual hull [100]. The approach is based on Shuntaro Yamazaki and his coworkers' work on *microfacet billboarding* [327]. In contrast to microfacet billboard rendering, however, only the voxel model plus reference images are used as rendering input.

Each voxel is represented as a small, planar rectangle. The billboard is centered on the position of its corresponding voxel. It is always oriented in parallel to the current output image plane. During rendering, each billboard is projected into the cameras' image planes, and texture coordinates are obtained from the projected footprint.

Since the cameras are at fixed locations, the projection Π_k of the voxel center into camera k can be precomputed. During rendering, these projective texture coordinates are used for hardware-accelerated dependent texturing; see Figure 4.4. In a preprocessing step, the projections between all voxels and camera images are precomputed. A 3D texture T_k^Π is initialized for each camera k. For each voxel center, its Π_k-projected homogeneous 2D texture coordinates in camera k are color-coded and stored in the 3D texture map T_k^Π.

During rendering, several video images I_i^t of the current time frame are uploaded as texture images T_i^I to the graphics card. To use only those image pixels inside the silhouettes for texturing, an alpha value of one is assigned to all silhouette pixels, while zero is assigned to all outside pixels. By assigning an alpha value of 0.5 to pixels along the boundary of the silhouettes, the silhouette outlines of two camera images are smoothly blended.

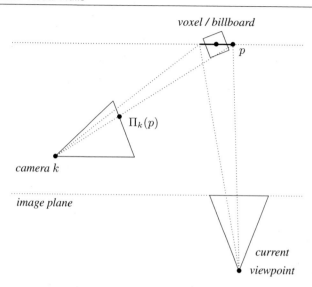

Figure 4.4. Billboard rendering: the billboard associated with each voxel is oriented parallel to the target view's image plane. The billboard is then projectively textured from several camera images. *(Reprinted from [99], © 2003 SPIE.)*

For rendering the level set via projective billboard texturing, two cameras i and j are selected for each voxel according to the following criteria.

- The voxel is visible in I_i^t and I_j^t, as already determined during reconstruction, i.e., $\nu_{i,j}(u_q^{xyzt}) = 1$.

- Those two cameras i and j are selected whose optical axes form the smallest angles α_i and α_j with the viewing direction.

Both image contributions are weighted depending on the angle of the respective camera's optical axis with the current viewing direction. The blending weights ω_i and ω_j for the cameras are

$$\omega_{i,j} := 1 - \frac{\alpha_{i,j}}{\alpha_i + \alpha_j}.$$

If the viewing direction coincides with the optical axis of a camera, the image is reproduced exactly, while transitions between images are blended smoothly. For each time frame, the display server determines which two cameras i and j are closest in angle. The display server then requests these two images to be transferred via the network from the respective camera clients to the display server.

For each surface voxel, a single rectangular billboard, centered on the voxel and aligned in parallel to the current target image plane, is rendered. The billboard is slightly larger than the voxel size so it entirely covers the voxel's footprint from any viewing direction. To correctly blend all voxel billboards onto each other, the surface voxels are rendered in back-to-front order.

Rendering a voxel billboard via dependent texturing requires two passes and makes use of at least two hardware texture units. During the first pass, the 3D texture T_i^{Π} is uploaded to texture unit 1. Unit 1 computes the texture coordinates for texture unit 2, to which the camera image T_i^I has been assigned. Blending is enabled to ensure that background pixels are transparent. The fragment program looks up the first billboard texture from T_i^I, interpolating the projection coordinates from the voxel center projection coordinates stored in the 3D texture map T_i^{Π}. A second rendering pass is necessary to apply billboard texture from the second image texture T_j^I using its projective texture coordinates stored in T_j^{Π}. To blend the second texture correctly with the first texture, the blending weight ω_j of the second texture relative to the first one is stored in the alpha channel, and the second pass's output color values are modulated by the alpha channel prior to average blending. The enabled depth test ensures that only visible billboards are blended.

Besides the (negligible) amount of geometry information, data transfer from memory to the graphics card consists of continuously updating the image textures per time frame. Considering the AGP 4x peak bandwidth between CPU and GPU of about 1 GB/s, multi-video transfer from local memory to the graphics card is not a problem. Instead, sustaining sufficient network bandwidth to transfer multiple reference images per time step from camera clients to the display host is much more critical. By selecting only those cameras that are able to contribute to the target view, the amount of transferred data can be reduced. To guarantee overall online performance, only two reference images are used to texture the entire visual hull. If sufficient bandwidth is available, billboard rendering can also be applied with many reference images. This way, each voxel billboard can be textured individually with the best-matching images.

To optimize caching, frequent changes between different textures can be avoided by tiling all image textures into one single texture. After initialization, the billboard algorithm is capable of rendering a $64 \times 64 \times 64$-voxel volume from arbitrary perspective at 30 fps on a 1.8 GHz Pentium IV Xeon and an NVIDIA GeForce^{TM} 4 Ti 4600 graphics card.

It should be noted that, on the latest graphics hardware, the dependent-texture look-up yields no acceleration anymore over transforming billboard vertex coordinates directly. The mapping from 3D space to image coordinates for texturing can be equivalently computed per billboard corner vertex by a vertex program.

4.1.3 Summary

The described billboard rendering approach exhibits two distinct limitations. By color-coding the precalculated voxel projection coordinates, strictly speaking only input images no larger than 256×256 pixels could be used. Fortunately today's graphics hardware also provides more elegant ways to store 16-bit–valued and even floating-point textures. More serious is the negligence of voxel visibility with respect to the selected two cameras' viewpoints. Volumetric visual-hull reconstruction itself does not provide information on which visual-hull voxels are or are not visible in any camera view. If the display server has sufficient computational power, per-voxel visibility can be determined prior to rendering. Only those cameras that can possibly contribute to the target view need to be considered, i.e., cameras whose viewing direction is at most $90°$ from the target view direction. A number of voxel visibility algorithms and other volume-based reconstruction methods can be found in Greg Slabaugh's paper [275]. Given per-voxel visibility, the display server requests multiple camera images over the network and renders each billboard by applying only image textures from unoccluded camera views.

4.2 Polyhedral Visual Hulls

Volumetric visual-hull reconstruction does not provide a triangle mesh of the visual-hull surface that could be rendered right away. Alternatively, a polyhedral approach towards real-time visual-hull rendering can be pursued by describing silhouette contours as polygons [161, 209, 86]. The extruded contour polygons' intersection can be determined, e.g., using constructive solid geometry (CSG) algorithms, which directly yield a polyhedral representation of the visual hull [170].

4.2.1 Online Reconstruction

For online polygonal visual-hull recovery, the same acquisition set-up and processing network as for volumetric visual-hull reconstruction can be used; see Section 4.1. The client PCs segment the incoming video images, and the contours of the segmented silhouettes are automatically approximated as 2D polygons using readily available routines from the OpenCV library [270]. By varying the contour polygons' number of vertices, reconstructed visual-hull accuracy can be traded for reconstruction frame rate. All silhouette polygons are transmitted to the server PC, where they are extruded into scene space from their respective cameras' center of projection to form visual cones; see Figure 4.5(a). The polyhedral intersection of the silhouette cones are determined on the fly using the open-source Boundary Representation software library (BREP) [15]. The result

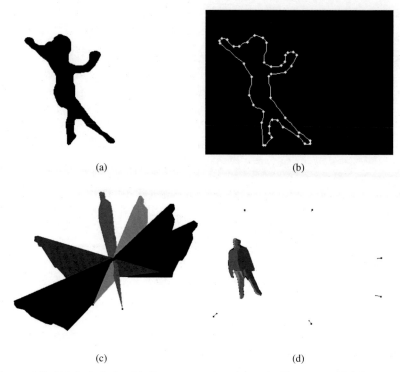

(a)   (b)

(c)   (d)

Figure 4.5. Polyhedral visual hull reconstruction: (a) each silhouette outline is approximated (b) as a polygon. (c) From the cameras' center of projection, the silhouette polygons are back-projected into the scene to form visual cones. (d) The intersection of all cones is calculated and represented as a polygonal mesh. *(Reprinted from [176], courtesy of Ming Li.)*

is an approximation of the segmented object's visual hull in the form of a polygon mesh; see Figure 4.5(b). Special care must be taken to ensure that the acquisition set-up is well calibrated. To account for inevitable small calibration inaccuracies, a minimum-distance measure is applied during visual-cone intersection computation to ensure robust mesh reconstruction. For a visual-hull approximation consisting of approximately 500 triangle faces, the acquisition system described in Section 4.1 accomplishes foreground segmentation, polygonal silhouette approximation, and visual-cone intersection computation faster than the synchronized cameras' acquisition frame rate of 13 frames per second [170].

4.2.2   Opaque Projective Texture Mapping

Alongside the polygonal silhouette contour data, the segmented image foreground is sent to the server PC for textured rendering. As in Section 4.1.2, the alpha

(a) projective texturing   (b) opaque projective tex-turing   (c) two-pass shadow-map rendering

Figure 4.6. Opaque projective texture mapping of the visual hull for one camera image: (a) conventional projective texturing does not take visibility into account, so the hands' texture through-projects onto the shoulders. (b) Opaque texture mapping takes visibility into account and prevents through-projection. However, texture-leak artifacts occur along the contour. (c) Two-pass shadow map rendering eliminates texture leaks. *(Reprinted from [170].)*

channel of each reference image is used to signal whether a pixel resides inside ($\alpha = 1$) or outside ($\alpha = 0$) the object silhouette. To apply an image as texture to a visual-hull polyhedron, each image is projected onto those surfaces that face the respective camera. Figure 4.6(a) shows, however, that projective texturing by itself does not take visibility into account; see Section 2.4.2. If all visual cones were convex, the surfaces' normals could be used to compute visibility. But since the visual hull is, in general, a better geometry approximation than the object's convex hull, self-occlusion and partially visible faces can occur. This visibility problem can be solved either by clipping the silhouette faces in a preprocessing step [58] or by using a shadow-mapping approach [256]. Harpreet Sawhney and his collaborators' *opaque projective texture mapping* approach is a graphics hardware algorithm that makes use of the availability of multiple texture units. While one reference image resides in the first texture unit, its corresponding shadow map is generated in the second texture unit using the offscreen P-buffer for shadow-map generation. During texturing, each shadow map texel is modulated with the alpha value in the first texture unit, which signifies whether a pixel lies inside or outside the silhouette. The enabled alpha test ensures that occluded object regions are not textured. Only camera-facing triangles are rendered to avoid artifacts on visual-hull surfaces that are tangent to the camera direction.

By applying opaque projective texture mapping directly to visual-hull rendering, texture-leak artifacts still occur along the contours; see Figure 4.6(b). This is because front surfaces may not occlude the back part completely due to finite resolution of the shadow map, so the silhouette contour leaks onto occluded surfaces. Increasing the shadow-map resolution, however, results in decreased rendering performance, while even high-resolution depth maps are not guaranteed to eliminate texture leakage completely. One naive way to avoid this artifact is to shrink image silhouette contours, e.g., by a morphological erosion operation, such that boundary pixels do not project onto the object anymore. An erosion operation, however, also removes detail along the object's silhouette.

Alternatively, shadow leaks can be eliminated by *extending* the silhouettes for shadow-map generation [170]. Simply rendering a scaled-up version of the silhouettes, however, does not suffice, because a mismatch between shadow-map and projective-texture coordinates would result. The interior of the silhouette must be kept unchanged, while expanding only the contour of the object. This can be accomplished by *two-pass shadow-map rendering*. During the first pass, the visual-hull polyhedron is rendered in line-drawing mode by employing a thick line width. In the second pass, the visual hull is rendered in normal fill mode. This way, object contour is expanded while the interior region is at the correct original depth; see Figure 4.6(c). This approach of considering the foreground/background boundary separately is similar to boundary matting in small-baseline VBR [345, 111].

Because of perspective projection, effective shadow-map resolution varies non-uniformly over the scene. To optimize shadow-map accuracy, the depth range between the near and far rendering planes is kept minimal. The employed polyhedral 3D intersection algorithm [15] conveniently also computes the bounding box of the visual hull, so its minimum and maximum Z-values are readily available to set the near and far planes. The computational overhead is negligible since only the eight corner vertices of the bounding box need to be considered.

Projective texturing using multiple images typically requires uploading the images to the graphics card one by one. Switching between different textures, however, is a time-consuming operation. Packing all video images into one texture map prior to sending the data over the bus to the graphics card reduces the number of texture-switching operations and improves rendering performance.

The rectangular silhouette bounding box for each reference image is determined automatically on the client PCs. The foreground image regions are transmitted to the server where the rectangular patches are assembled into one texture map prior to uploading the data to the graphics card.

4.2.3 Results

Figure 4.7 illustrates the two-pass opaque projective texture mapping algorithm. Programmed as separate threads, network handling, polyhedral visual-hull reconstruction, and rendering are decoupled to perform at individual frame rates. From six 320×240-pixel reference image streams, the polyhedral visual hull consisting of about 500 triangles is reconstructed at about 15 fps, which is faster than the camera acquisition frame rate of 13 fps. Rendering frame rates of 23 fps are achieved on an NVIDIA GeForce3™ graphics card. This way, real-time view interactivity is ensured despite lower reconstruction and acquisition frame rates.

   (a) line mode   (b) fill mode   (c) opaque pro-   (d) multiple dynamic ob-
                                          jective texture   jects
                                          mapping

Figure 4.7. Polyhedral visual-hull rendering results from six input video streams. *(Reprinted from [170].)*

4.2.4 Joint Stereo and Visual-Hull Reconstruction

While the visual hull of an object can be robustly reconstructed in real-time from a handful of silhouette images, estimating robust dense depth in real-time, as described in Section 3.3, is a demanding computational challenge. Depth maps, on the other hand, represent photo-consistent geometry information, whereas the visual hull is, in general, only a coarse approximation of the object's actual shape; see Figure 4.8. By suitably combining visual-hull reconstruction with depth-map estimation, the beneficial properties of both approaches can be preserved to obtain superior reconstruction results [172].

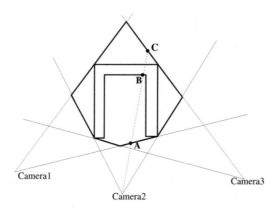

Figure 4.8. Joint stereo and visual-hull reconstruction: object concavities cannot be re-constructed by shape-from-silhouette algorithms (point **B**). The visual hull, however, can be used to constrain the depth search range for stereo reconstruction (from point **A** to point **C**).

Distributed Processing.   Figure 4.9 depicts a hybrid acquisition configuration to simultaneously benefit from wide-baseline visual-hull recovery and small-baseline depth-from-stereo reconstruction. Six video cameras are grouped into three pairs of two. From the center of the stage area, each camera pair is about $5°$ apart, while the camera pairs are equidistantly distributed along a horizontal $90°$-wide arc. The client PCs, each operating one camera pair, rectify the stereo image pairs, segment the object, and approximate the silhouettes as polygons.

Figure 4.9. Joint stereo and visual-hull reconstruction: The scene is captured in a hybrid small-baseline, wide-baseline camera configuration. Six cameras are arranged in three pairs along a $90°$ arc. *(Reprinted from [172], © 2002 IEEE.)*

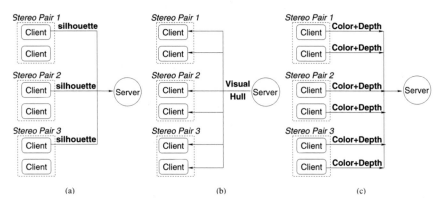

Figure 4.10. Distributed computing for joint stereo and visual-hull reconstruction: (a) foreground segmentation and silhouette contour approximation are performed on the client PCs. (b) On the server, the polyhedral visual hull is reconstructed and broadcast back to all client PCs. (c) The clients estimate depth from stereo by using the visual hull to restrict depth search range. Depth maps and foreground image regions are then sent back to the server for rendering. *(Reprinted from [172], © 2002 IEEE.)*

For distributed processing (Figure 4.10), first the silhouettes are transmitted to the server. The polyhedral visual hull is reconstructed on the server and sent back to the client PCs. On each client PC, the visual hull is then used to determine the minimum and maximum possible depth value for each object pixel. The limited search range accelerates depth estimation and decreases the probability of false matches; see Figure 4.8. Minimum depth is obtained by making use of the client PC's graphics board. The visual hull is rendered from the respective camera pair's viewpoint, and the Z-buffer is read back into memory. Front and back surface depth are determined in two separate rendering passes. The visual-hull–derived maximum depth value is frequently much too conservative, since most natural objects exhibit only moderate concavities. Instead of rendering the visual hull two times, the depth range can be alternatively determined by simply adding a preset maximum range value to the minimum depth. This speeds up depth-map estimation considerably and has been found to give good results in practice. To estimate dense depth from stereo, each image pair is rectified on the client PC prior to depth-map estimation. For each silhouette pixel, the corresponding pixel in the other image is sought by considering a small block of neighboring pixels, as described in Section 3.3. The sum of absolute differences is used as a similarity measure because it can be efficiently implemented [78]. To improve depth-map accuracy, neighboring SAD scores are compared, and pairwise consistency is checked to remove false matches [87].

Rendering. For rendering, the estimated depth maps and segmented image foreground are transferred to the server; see Figure 4.9(c). The depth maps could be merged into one single polygonal model to be rendered using texture mapping. Unfortunately, mesh reconstruction from multiple depth maps cannot yet be done at interactive frame rates. Instead, 3D image warping is employed to render novel views directly from the images and accompanying depth maps; see Section 2.4.1. The four stereo-pair images that are closest to the target view direction are used for rendering, making use of incremental computations to speed up the warping calculations [268]. Rendering is decoupled from reconstruction so that interactive rendering frame rates can be ensured regardless of reconstruction performance.

Results. At 320×240-pixel reference image resolution, the distributed processing system is capable of reconstructing depth maps at a rate of 3–4 fps [172]. Besides stereo reconstruction, the network transmission times for the silhouettes and visual-hull data limit reconstruction performance. In contrast, rendering frame rates of 10 fps and more are achieved on a GeForce2^{TM} graphics card.

4.3   Image-Based Visual-Hull Rendering

Instead of reconstructing 3D visual hull geometry explicitly, either as a voxel volume or a polygonal mesh, new views of the textured visual hull can also be rendered by operating solely in 2D image space. Working in 2D image space is guaranteed to perform robustly, which can be an issue with the CSG algorithms in polygonal visual hull reconstruction. At the same time, image-based visual-hull rendering requires no data resampling, which avoids any quantization errors. Rendering quality is therefore equivalent to rendering results achievable otherwise only from an exact representation of the 3D silhouette cone intersection, given the finite resolution of the input images.

The key idea behind image-based visual-hull rendering is that any CSG object can be ray traced without the need for an explicit 3D geometry model [251]. The reference algorithm described in the following was proposed by Wojciech Matusik [208]. It renders view-dependent visual hulls by making use of epipolar geometry to speed up the intersection calculations in the images. The complete system consists of four synchronized video cameras and five PCs and is capable of generating image-based models in real-time.

4.3.1   Online Rendering

Image-based visual-hull rendering is essentially a ray-tracing technique. To generate the target view image, each pixel in the output image is considered indi-

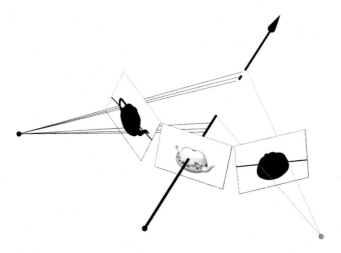

Figure 4.11. Image-based visual-hull rendering: for each pixel of the desired view, its viewing ray is projected into all reference images, yielding the respective epipolar line. In each reference view, the intersection intervals of the epipolar line with the object's silhouette are determined. The intervals are back-projected onto the viewing ray where they are intersected to determine which point lies closest to the rendered viewpoint. *(Reprinted from [211], courtesy of Wojciech Matusik, © 2001 W. Matusik.)*

vidually. For each output pixel, the corresponding pixels in the input images are considered assuming that the visual hull represents the object surface. Figure 4.11 depicts the approach.

1. Each viewing ray is projected into all reference images. The projected line segment in each input image is the pixel's epipolar line between the desired view and the input view; see Section 2.2.1.

2. In each input image, the 2D intersection coordinates of the epipolar line with the object silhouette are determined.

3. From all reference images, the individual silhouette-intersection intervals are back-projected onto the viewing ray. On the viewing ray, the intervals are intersected to determine that part of the viewing ray that is consistent with all reference image silhouettes. Its endpoints define the intersections of the viewing ray with the object's visual hull. The frontal endpoint closest to the desired view is the 3D point on the visual hull. Its projection onto the closest unoccluded reference image determines the color of the pixel under consideration.

To efficiently compute the intersections of the reference-image–projected viewing ray with the object silhouette, the silhouette contour is represented as a list of edges enclosing the silhouette boundary pixels. The silhouette edges are generated on the fly by a 2D variant of the marching cubes algorithm [180]. For k input images and n^2 pixels in the output image, a straightforward implementation of the above-described algorithm has computational complexity $O(lkn^3)$ if the number of edges in the silhouette edge list is of order nl, where l is the average number of intersections of a projected viewing ray with the silhouette contour [208].

To achieve faster performance, computational complexity can be reduced by making use of epipolar coherence. When the output image pixels along a scan line are traversed in sequential order, the slope of the projected viewing rays in any reference image increases or decreases monotonically, depending on traversal direction. Taking advantage of this monotonicity, silhouette intersections for an entire scan line can be determined incrementally. First, the $O(nl)$ contour vertices in the silhouette edge list of each input image are sorted with respect to the slope of the line connecting each vertex to the image's epipole. The sorted vertex slopes divide each input image into $O(nl)$ bins. To each bin are assigned those silhouette edges that are intersected by epipolar lines with a slope falling within the bin's extent. Since typically many more pixels per scan line n must be considered than there are average intersections l, the computational overhead for sorting and binning is negligible.

When traversing the scan lines of the output image, the projected viewing ray monotonically sweeps over the reference view. The slope determines the correct bin, and the projected viewing ray is intersected only with the edges associated with this bin. Each bin contains, on average, $O(l)$ edges, so computing a scan line of n pixels takes $O(nl)$ intersection calculations per reference view. Considering all n scan lines of the output image, and taking all k input images into account, total algorithmic complexity amounts to $O(lkn^2)$.

The need to sort, bin, and suitably traverse the silhouette edge lists can be avoided by rectifying the input images with respect to the desired output view. Image rectification, however, requires resampling of the original image data, which compromises optimal rendering quality, especially for wide-baseline recording scenarios. In the worst case, rectification becomes degenerate, i.e., the epipole of a reference image falls within the field of view of the target image.

4.3.2   Joint Shading and Visibility

When shading the visual-hull surface using the video images as texture, view-dependent effects are to be preserved. For each output pixel, therefore, the ref-

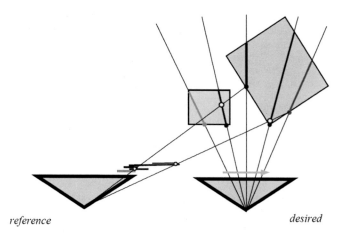

reference   *desired*

Figure 4.12. Visibility: to account for visibility, the viewing-ray intervals are projected into each reference image in occlusion-compatible order. The front-most point of a viewing-ray interval is visible in a specific reference image if no previous interval has yet been mapped onto its image projection coordinates. *(Reprinted from [211], courtesy of Wojciech Matusik, © 2001 W. Matusik.)*

erence images are ranked according to the angle between the viewing ray and camera directions. While the reference image with the smallest angle yields the most truthful view-dependent color, it must be assured that the line of sight to the camera is not blocked by any other part of the visual hull. Because the visual hull always encloses the true geometry (see Section 2.2), checking for visibility using the visual hull instead of true geometry is conservative: all invisible points are identified as being invisible, while potentially some visible points may erroneously get marked as being invisible. Figure 4.12 depicts how visibility is taken into account during image-based visual-hull shading. The target image's pixels are considered in front-to-back order with respect to the reference view. The correct order is determined by the epipolar geometry between target and reference image; see Section 2.2.1. For each viewing ray, the visual-hull intersection interval is projected into the reference view, and coverage intervals are subsequently accumulated. To determine its visibility, each viewing ray's front-most visual-hull interval boundary is projected into the reference view and checked against the accumulated coverage. If the projected point is already covered, the point is declared not visible from this reference view, and another camera must be used to color the pixel. Otherwise, the point is visible in the reference image, and the pixel color at the projection coordinates is used as the color for the target image pixel.

Considering the target image pixels in front-to-back order with respect to a reference image implies stepping along epipolar lines. On the discrete pixel raster of the output image, however, many pixels do not share the exact same epipolar plane. To solve this problem, visibility is computed only along those epipolar lines that correspond to the pixels along the target image's boundary. Every pixel in the image plane is then touched by one or more of these epipolar lines. Because typically more than one epipolar line touches a pixel, for every target pixel the visibility results are combined using the Boolean *OR* operation.

4.3.3   Results

The reference system renders live image-based visual hulls from four input video streams [208]. It consists of four synchronized Sony DFW500 cameras recording at $256 \ times \ 256$-pixel RGB resolution. Four 600-MHz PCs control the cameras, correct for radial lens distortion, and perform image segmentation via background subtraction; see Section 2.1.7. Silhouette and texture information is then encoded and sent over a 100-Mb Ethernet^{TM} link to a quad-processor, 550-MHz PC server. The server executes the image-based visual-hull rendering algorithm and interactively displays the result. Plate X illustrates the shaded rendering result. Depth-buffer compositing allows rendering of the foreground object into arbitrary virtual surroundings.

Rendering quality depends on camera separation as well as segmentation accuracy. Image-based visual-hull rendering is very sensitive to inaccuracies in foreground segmentation. Chroma keying can be used to achieve optimal rendering results. The system achieves rendering frame rates of about 8 fps. With modern hardware, real-time frame rates are also achievable for higher reference image resolution.

4.3.4   Summary

Image-based visual-hull rendering is an elegant technique that combines live processing with interactive rendering frame rates at acceptable output quality. One drawback of the described reference implementation is that pixel color is determined from one input image only, instead of weightedly blending output pixel color from different input images. This causes the textured visual hull to vary discontinuously in appearance when the viewpoint moves. Because visual-hull geometry is not reconstructed explicitly, the image-based visual-hull rendering approach cannot be easily extended, e.g., to attain photo-consistent rendering results.

4.4   Visual-Hull Rendering on Graphics Hardware

Instead of performing visual hull reconstruction and rendering separately, both steps can be incorporated into one algorithm that runs on modern graphics hardware. The server CPU is freed up for other computations, and the only remaining tasks to be done in software, image segmentation and polygonal silhouette approximation, are performed on the client PCs. In the following, two different GPU-based algorithms are described. Both approaches have their inherent drawbacks. By appropriately combining both methods, however, a hybrid visual-hull rendering algorithm can be devised that eliminates the respective limitations while preserving the advantages.

4.4.1   Projection-Based Rendering

The visual-hull surfaces can be determined on graphics hardware if projective texturing is exploited in conjunction with alpha blending [173]. The approach is depicted in Figure 4.13. As in previous visual-hull rendering approaches, the alpha channel value of each reference image pixel is set to one in the image foreground and to zero in the background (see Section 4.1.2), and the silhouettes are approximated as polygons; see Section 4.2.1. From each camera's center of projection, the visual cone is then extruded. It is rendered as seen from the target viewpoint. Employing projective texturing (see Section 2.4.2), the silhouettes from

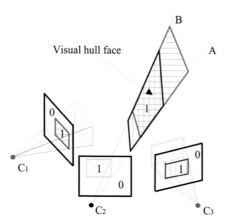

Figure 4.13. Projection-based cone cropping: the triangle C_2AB represents one face of the visual cone extruded from the silhouette in camera C_2 (hatched area). It is projectively textured with the images from cameras C_1 and C_3. By multiplying each fragment's alpha channel value (1: inside, 0: outside the silhouette), only the visual-hull surface is assigned an alpha value of one (cross-hatched area). *(Reprinted from [173].)*

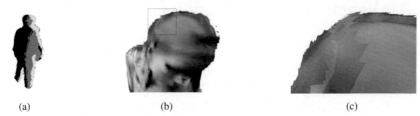

(a)   (b)   (c)

Figure 4.14. Visual-hull rendering using projection-based cone cropping causes aliasing artifacts due to the pixel-rasterized silhouette representation. *(Reprinted from [175].)*

all other camera viewpoints are projected onto the rendered visual-cone triangles. By making use of all available texture units, multiple images can be projected in one rendering pass. During projection, the alpha-channel values are multiplied, and the rendering pipeline's alpha test is enabled so that only those fragments are drawn into the frame buffer that lie within the intersection area of all silhouettes; see Figure 4.13. This way, only the visual-hull surface is drawn.

The advantage of this algorithm is its rendering efficiency. Since each visual cone must be rendered only once, and multiple image silhouettes can be projected simultaneously with modern graphics boards, time complexity is $O(n)$, where n corresponds to the number of camera images. Unfortunately, the method also exhibits a severe limitation, as obvious from Figure 4.14. Because silhouettes are represented on the discrete pixel raster of the camera images, their 3D projections cause jaggy boundaries on the visual-cone surfaces. This aliasing artifact arises whenever rendered output image resolution does not match camera recording resolution. It becomes more pronounced for close-up views and for oblique camera projection angles.

4.4.2   CSG-Based Rendering

A different rendering approach can be pursued if the visual hull is regarded in the context of constructive solid geometry. In contrast to determining the visual hull via silhouette projection, CSG rendering is not plagued by aliasing artifacts by reconstructing the intersection volume of the visual cones, similar to polyhedral visual reconstruction on the CPU as described in Section 4.2. Again, the visual cones are extruded from the camera viewpoints based on the polygonal silhouette approximations determined on the client PCs. But instead of calculating the intersection volume in software, CSG rendering is now accomplished entirely on the graphics board by making use of the stencil buffer.

All visual cones are rendered as seen from the target viewpoint. For each output pixel, the number of rendered front faces and back faces are counted separately. It turns out that, for a fragment belonging to the visual hull, the difference between front-facing and back-facing surfaces encountered along the way from the fragment's 3D position to the viewpoint must be equal to the total number of visual cones [108]. Plate XI illustrates the direct CSG rendering algorithm in two dimensions. In this example, the intersecting region of two visual cones, extruded from cameras C_1 and C_2, is rendered from viewpoint C. In the beginning, all front-facing cone faces are depth-test rendered, yielding the front-most depth layer; see Plate XI(a). The following steps are now repeatedly executed.

1. The stencil buffer is set to zero.

2. While rendering both cones, any fragment lying on or in front of the current depth layer either increments (front face) or decrements (back face) the local stencil buffer value by one. Fragments behind the current depth layer have no effect.

3. If the stencil buffer value equals the number of intersecting objects (here: two visual cones), the local depth value is frozen.

4. The next depth layer, Plate XI(b), is determined by rendering all front faces and comparing the depth to the previous depth layer via depth peeling [69]. Depth values frozen during Step 3 remain unchanged. The algorithm terminates if no front face remains to be drawn, e.g., in this example after the second pass.

In the depicted example, the stencil buffer value for direction CA is 1 after the first pass and 2 after the second pass. Since the count 2 is equal to the number of intersecting objects (2 visual cones), CA intersects the visual hull at the second depth layer. The stencil buffer value for direction CB is 1 after the first pass and also 1 after the second pass (two front-facing and one back-facing fragment), signifying no intersection with the visual hull. The CSG rendering algorithm returns the depth map of the visual hull as seen from the target viewpoint C.

Because the algorithm performs entirely in target image space, no aliasing artifacts occur. Figure 4.15 depicts the CSG-rendered results equivalent to Figure 4.14. The CSG approach achieves significantly better rendering quality without aliasing artifacts.

Earlier direct CSG rendering methods [311, 280] relied on expensive depth-buffer–readback operations to determine the depth layers. By utilizing the depth-peeling technique [69], this readback operation is circumvented [108]. Unfortunately, depth peeling still requires as many rendering passes as there are depth layers. For visual hull-reconstruction, the minimum number of depth layers is equal to the number of visual cones n. As the described CSG rendering algorithm

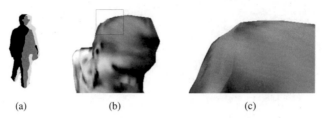

(a)   (b)   (c)

Figure 4.15. CSG-based rendering of visual hulls on graphics hardware. Compare to
Figure 4.14: no aliasing artifacts occur; however, rendering complexity is $O(n^2)$ in the
number of reference images n. *(Reprinted from [175].)*

loops over all depth layers, the computational complexity of CSG rendering is
$O(n^2)$, in contrast to $O(n)$ for texture-projection–based visual-hull rendering.

4.4.3   Hybrid Visual-Hull Rendering

To improve the rendering quality of projection-based visual-hull rendering, or to
accelerate the performance of direct CSG rendering, both methods can be combined to form a hybrid algorithm that preserves the strengths of both, offering
several advantages over either rendering approach [175].

In direct CSG rendering for visual hull-reconstruction, each visual-cone polygon is sent through the graphics pipeline multiple times. The polygons can be
very large and consume considerable fill-rate capacity. In practice, however, the
intersection result of the visual hull will yield only a small part of the output viewport. This region is denoted the *valid region*. If this region was known a priori,
fill rate could be significantly reduced by making use of the graphics pipeline's
scissor test. Another operation to benefit from knowing the valid region is depth
peeling. The depth-peeling technique requires frame-buffer-to-texture copying or
rendering-to-texture operations when sweeping through all depth layers. Given
the valid region, the copying or rendering operations can be carried out for the
affected pixels only instead of for the entire window.

The hybrid approach consists of exploiting projection-based visual-cone cropping to determine the valid region prior to CSG rendering. Towards this end, the
visual hull is rendered in a small offscreen window. The rendered buffer is read
back to main memory, and the rectangular bounding box enclosing the visual hull
is determined. This region is expanded somewhat to account for rounding errors
due to the low-resolution version of the visual hull. The rectangular region is then
scaled up to correspond to the actual target viewport size. Note that for determining the valid region, aliasing artifacts introduced by the projection-based cone
trimming method do not matter. Instead, the ability to restrict CSG visual-hull

rendering to the valid region only overcompensates for the additional computational cost.

Target-View Depth-Map Rendering. Once the valid region has been identified, the visual cones are CSG-rendered within the valid region only to obtain the target image's depth map. Because the depth map is constructed at the target viewport's resolution, no aliasing artifacts occur.

To render the visual hull, the original CSG method can be used as long as the target viewpoint is not situated inside a visual cone [108]. In that case, however, parts of the cone's faces are clipped by the near plane of the view volume. Clipped cone faces lead to erroneous face counting and subsequently to incorrect rendering results. To overcome this problem, the *zfail* shadow volume algorithm is applied [37]. Instead of counting front and back faces from the fragment to the viewpoint, the *zfail* algorithm considers front and back faces between infinity and the front-most rasterized fragment. The updating strategy for the stencil buffer must be altered accordingly. A stencil buffer value is now decreased for front faces and increased for back faces if the depth test *fails*. This way, correct counting results are obtained without interference from the near clipping plane. By applying two-sided stencil operations [226], the number of rendering passes can be additionally reduced, and hardware-accelerated occlusion testing allows it to determine when to terminate depth layer traversal [115].

Reference-View Depth-Map Rendering. One critical issue in multi-view texturing is how to determine local visibility. For surface regions that are occluded from one reference camera, the corresponding image color information must be ignored during texturing. In view-dependent texture mapping, the problem is solved in object space by splitting object triangles such that they are either fully visible or completely invisible from any source view; see Section 2.3.4. For real-time applications, however, this preprocessing step is not appropriate. Instead, visibility can be determined in image space using hardware-accelerated shadow mapping; see Section 2.4.3. Shadow mapping requires rendering the visual hull's depth map as seen for each reference view. While depth maps of the visual hull can be generated by either projection-based or CSG rendering, the projection-based method is considerably faster. Because multiple textures will later get smoothly blended, aliasing artifacts in the depth maps caused by projection-based visual-hull rendering are unnoticeable in the final rendering result. Note that the target view depth map that is necessary for shadow mapping is already available from the previous step.

Textured Visual-Hull Rendering. The reference images can now be applied as texture to the visual hull. The depth test is enabled as *equal*, and all visual cones are rasterized again. Each visual cone is textured from all reference images except for the image whose silhouette provides the current visual cone. Trivially, a reference image cannot contribute to its own visual cone's texture because, by definition, its cone surface normals are oriented at 90° from the camera's viewing direction.

For smooth transitions across views, fragment color c is calculated as a convex combination of all texture values in the reference views,

$$c = \frac{\sum_{k=1}^{N} w_k \cdot i_k}{\sum_{k=1}^{N} w_k} , \qquad (4.1)$$

where N is the number of reference views, and i_k and w_k are the texture color and weight factor from the kth input image, respectively. The weight w_k consists of four components

$$w_k = v_k \cdot w_{kf} \cdot w_{ks} \cdot w_{kd} . \qquad (4.2)$$

The variable v_k denotes visibility with respect to reference image k. Local visibility is determined via shadow mapping using the per-camera depth maps created previously. The variable w_{kf} is a feathering weight. Its effect is to eliminate seams that arise from sampling different reference views along silhouette boundaries [57, 283, 246]. Figure 4.16 shows that the feathering weight assumes one at the center of the silhouette and falls smoothly to zero towards the silhouette outline. The feathering weight map is calculated on the client PCs by applying a distance transformation to the binary silhouette masks [23]. For transfer to the rendering server, the feathering weight maps are embedded in the alpha channel of the silhouette images. The variable w_{ks} is the surface obliqueness weight.

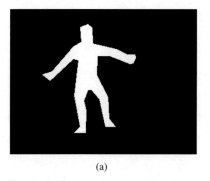 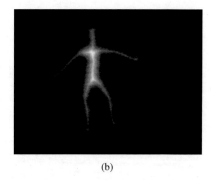

(a)   (b)

Figure 4.16. Feathering weight derivation: (a) to the object silhouette, (b) a distance transformation is applied that smoothly ramps down to zero towards the edges. *(Reprinted from [176], courtesy of Ming Li.)*

It penalizes surfaces that are oriented at a slanted angle with respect to the kth camera direction:

$$w_{ks} = \max(\mathbf{d}_k \cdot \mathbf{n}, 0)^\alpha. \tag{4.3}$$

For each rasterized fragment, the vector $\mathbf{d}_k$ represents the viewing direction from the current fragment position towards the kth reference camera, whereas $\mathbf{n}$ denotes the polygon normal at the current point. The parameter α controls the falloff slope of the weight function with angular difference. The last weighting factor w_{kd} varies with target viewpoint. It emphasizes reference cameras whose viewing directions $\mathbf{d}_k$ are close to the target view's direction $\mathbf{d}_t$,

$$w_{kd} = (\mathbf{d_k} \cdot \mathbf{d_t} + 1)^\beta. \tag{4.4}$$

The parameter β controls the weight's directional sensitivity. The offset ensures that w_{kd} is always non-negative, which is necessary to obtain a convex weight combination for the final pixel color.

Per-Fragment View-Dependent Texturing. View-dependent texture mapping customarily relies on computing weight factors per vertex, which are then linearly interpolated across polygons [246, 58, 234, 31]. In CSG rendering, however, no vertex information is available about the polygons making up the visual-hull surface. The only geometry entities are the visual cones whose vertices are located in one camera's center of projection as well as far behind the scene volume. Per-vertex weight computations on the elongated visual-cone triangles would therefore result in large errors and noticeable rendering artifacts.

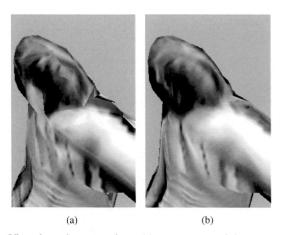

(a)   (b)

Figure 4.17. View-dependent texturing: (a) per-vertex weight computation, and (b) per-fragment weight computation. Both images are rendered from the same viewpoint. *(Reprinted from [175].)*

Instead, the weight factors are determined per-fragment to achieve high rendering quality [8, 7]. For per-fragment view-dependent texture mapping, the 3D coordinates of visual-cone vertices and the normal vectors of visual-cone polygons are passed on from the vertex program to the rasterization stage. The rasterization engine interpolates the 3D coordinates per-fragment, which a fragment program uses to compute w_{ks} and w_{kd}. For acceleration, viewing vector normalization in Equations (4.3) and (4.4) is implemented as a look-up into a normalization cube map [326]. The binary value of v_k is determined via a look-up into the corresponding shadow map, while w_{kf} and i_k are obtained from the alpha and color channel values of the projective silhouette textures, respectively. The fragment color is then determined according to Equation (4.1)).

Figure 4.17 depicts the difference in rendering quality if blending weights are computed per-vertex or per-fragment. Per-fragment view-dependent texture mapping is not restricted to visual-hull rendering alone. Thanks to the locally determined accurate weight values, better rendering results can be achieved whenever explicit 3D geometry is projectively textured by multiple images.

4.4.4   Results

The rendering algorithm has been evaluated using the distributed online acquisition and processing system described in Section 4.1.1. The hybrid visual-hull rendering algorithm accepts eight reference images as input, each acquired at 320×240-pixel RGB resolution at 13 fps. The cameras are arranged at about equal distance all along the perimeter of the scene. Rendering performance is measured for an NVIDIA GeForce^{TM} FX 5800 Ultra graphics card, with target

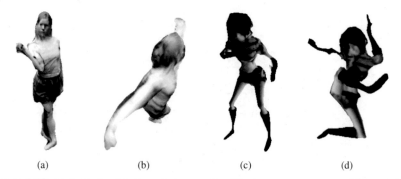

(a)   (b)   (c)   (d)

Figure 4.18. Hybrid visual-hull rendering results. The images are generated from eight reference views. The depicted images correspond to target view positions between camera locations. (a) and (b) are rendered from real-world multi-video data, whereas (c) and (d) show results for a synthetic multi-video animation sequence. *(Reprinted from [175].)*

image resolution set to 640×480 pixels. Each reference image's visual cone is approximated by approximately 50 line segments, so that in turn each visual cone consists of about 50 very long and narrow triangles. The valid region typically occupies about one third of the viewport area.

For eight reference views, the attainable rendering frame rate is about 4 fps. In comparison, CSG rendering achieves only 2.9 fps, whereas projection-based visual-hull rendering performs at about 7.5 fps, albeit producing rendering artifacts. Detailed measurements show that the fragment processing stage of the rendering pipeline is the computationally most expensive part, suggesting that geometry complexity of the visual cones is not a limiting factor. If the number of polygons for the visual cones is increased by a factor of two, the rendering frame rate decreases by only about 10%.

Snapshots of online rendering results for both real-world data as well as synthetic animation sequences are depicted in Figure 4.18. No aliasing artifacts are apparent, while overall rendering quality is clearly better than projection-based visual-hull rendering.

4.4.5 Summary

Hybrid visual-hull rendering on graphics hardware yields rendering results that are close to the limit of what can be expected from visual-hull rendering. The algorithm performs at interactive frame rates and works robustly for arbitrarily complex objects, since all intersection computations are done in target image space. By merging projection-based visual-cone cropping with direct CSG rendering, the inherent aliasing problem plaguing the former method is avoided, while the latter method's performance is accelerated. Per-fragment view-dependent texture mapping additionally improves rendering quality.

The maximum number of input silhouette images that can be accommodated in a single rendering pass is determined by the number of texture units available on the graphics hardware. The latest generation of graphics cards, however, currently features 16 texture units, which is more than the number of video cameras available in most existing wide-baseline acquisition systems.

4.5 Photo-Hull Rendering on Graphics Hardware

Using the visual hull as the geometry proxy for time-critical VBR applications offers the advantage that it can be reconstructed and rendered very efficiently. Its approximate nature, however, inevitably limits attainable rendering quality.

To achieve better rendering results, object geometry must be reconstructed more accurately.

More accurate 3D geometry can be reconstructed from wide-baseline recordings if photo-consistency is taken into account in addition to silhouette information; see Section 2.2.3. Unfortunately, shape-from-photo-consistency approaches are computationally much more expensive than visual-hull reconstruction. To accelerate photo-hull reconstruction, Andrew Prock and Charles Dyer [245] as well as Miguel Sainz and his coworkers [255] suggest using texture mapping to project input images onto the voxel model in order to obtain corresponding voxel color more quickly. Similarly, Bruce Culbertson and his collaborators use graphics hardware to determine voxel visibility [53]. Alternatively, Gregory Slabaugh and his coworkers describe a photo-hull rendering algorithm in software that works without explicitly reconstructing object geometry [276]. To achieve faster performance, Ruigang Yang and his coworkers sacrifice visibility consistency to implement a photo-hull rendering approach entirely on graphics hardware [330]. If visibility is additionally taken into account, the photo hull can still be rendered entirely on the graphics board at near-interactive frame rates [174].

4.5.1   Time-Critical Photo-Hull Rendering

In contrast to volumetric photo-hull reconstruction (see Section 2.2.3), photo-hull rendering on graphics hardware recovers 3D object geometry implicitly during the rendering process. The scene volume occupied by the object is stepped through by rendering a set of *slicing planes* parallel to the image plane of the output target view. These slicing planes are processed in front-to-back order. While each plane is rendered, all visible (active) reference images are projected onto the plane. During rasterization, each fragment is checked for photo-consistency, i.e., the unoccluded pixels from all active reference images that project onto the fragment are compared in color. For visibility, a mask is associated with each active image that is continuously updated after each slicing plane has been rendered. Photo-consistent fragments are drawn to the output frame buffer, while photo-inconsistent fragments are discarded. For display, the color of a photo-consistent fragment is determined as the weighted average of the corresponding pixel values in the reference images.

Slicing-Plane Generation.   A priori, the location of the object of interest within the recorded scene volume is unknown. Using the silhouette information, first, the bounding box of the object is determined, so the rendered region can be constrained to the bounding volume of the object. As the object moves around, the bounding volume must be continuously updated. Because the visual hull completely encloses the photo hull (see Section 2.2), the silhouette-derived bounding box does not clip the true object geometry.

To find the bounding volume, the depth map of the visual hull as seen from the target viewpoint is generated. This can be easily accomplished, e.g., by employing the projection-based rendering approach (see Section 4.4.1) and rendering the visual hull to a small offscreen window. The depth buffer is read back to main memory, and the axis-aligned rectangular region enclosing the visual-hull area is determined. To account for rounding errors introduced by rendering a down-sampled visual hull, the bounding rectangle is expanded before it is scaled up to actual target view resolution. In addition, the minimum and maximum depth values of the depth map are extracted to determine visible depth range along the viewing direction. The depth values are converted from window space to eye space via

$$z_e = \frac{z_n \cdot z_f}{z_f - z_w \cdot (z_f - z_n)} \, ,$$

where z_w and z_e are the depth values in window space and eye space, respectively, and z_n and z_f define the near and far clipping planes of the target viewing volume. By utilizing minimum and maximum depth map values, the depth range does not enclose the entire visual hull but covers only the visible part. Since the excluded far side of the visual hull does not contribute to the target view, this accelerates rendering performance.

Knowing the bounding rectangle as well as the depth range of the visual hull in the target view, the visible visual-hull volume is now stepped through by rendering slicing planes that are oriented parallel to the target view; see Figure 4.19. To

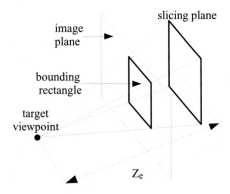

Figure 4.19. Slicing-plane generation: through the rectangular bounding volume that encloses the object, slicing planes are rendered perpendicular to the image plane at various depths z_e covering the entire depth range of the object's visible visual hull. *(Reprinted from [174], © 2004 Eurographics.)*

tighten the bounding volume further, the complete depth range can be divided into several subranges to define smaller bounding rectangles for each subrange. Visual-hull rendering and depth-buffer read-back account for only about 2% of total rendering time.

Slicing-Plane Rendering. Traditionally, photo-hull-based approaches consider reconstruction and rendering separately, and photo-consistency is checked in object space (see Section 2.2.3). In photo-hull rendering on graphics hardware, in contrast, the reconstruction step is embedded in the rendering algorithm. The slicing planes are sequentially sent through the graphics pipeline in front-to-back order. They are transformed to the target viewport and rasterized into fragments. For each fragment, a fragment program checks photo-consistency on the fly to evaluate whether or not the current fragment is to be drawn to the output frame buffer. To test fragment photo-consistency, all reference image pixels that project to the fragment's 3D position need to be found first. Because cameras oriented at a slanted angle to the slicing plane cause oblique-angle texturing artifacts, reference cameras behind the front-most slicing plane are excluded from the photo-consistency check. The remaining images are *active reference images*.

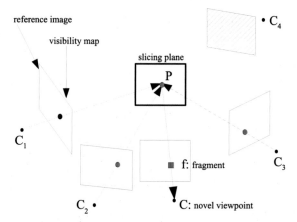

Figure 4.20. Photo-consistency check of a fragment f: cameras C_1, C_2, C_3 contribute active reference images to the target view C, whereas C_4 lies behind the front-most slicing plane and is not considered. The dotted frames next to each active reference image represent the associated visibility maps. From camera C_1, the fragment's 3D position P is occluded according to its visibility map, so its pixel does not partake in the fragment's photo-consistency check. The pixels in the active reference images C_2 and C_3 are both visible and similar in color, so fragment f is photo-consistent and drawn to the output frame buffer. Finally, the visibility maps for C_2 and C_3 are updated to indicate that the two pixels have been drawn to the frame buffer already and are occluded from now on while rendering all remaining slicing planes. *(Reprinted from [174], © 2004 Eurographics.)*

The per-fragment photo-consistency check is illustrated in Figure 4.20. Projective texture mapping is employed to find the fragment's corresponding reference image pixels. To take self-occlusions into account, a visibility map is kept for each active reference image. The visibility map keeps track of which pixels in its corresponding reference image still remain to participate in upcoming photo-consistency checks. Each visibility map coincides with its associated reference image and shares the same texture coordinates.

Photo-consistency is measured using the variance of the projected reference image pixels' color values. Instead of approximating the variance using the sum of squared differences [330], the true variance σ^2 is computed in the fragment program by

$$\sigma^2 = \left[\sum_{i=1}^{N}(r_i - \bar{r})^2 + \sum_{i=1}^{N}(g_i - \bar{g})^2 + \sum_{i=1}^{N}(b_i - \bar{b})^2 \right] / N \ .$$

N denotes the number of active reference images in which the 3D point associated with the fragment is visible, (r_i, g_i, b_i) is the sampled pixel color from the ith reference image, and $(\bar{r}, \bar{g}, \bar{b})$ is the mean color of the corresponding pixels in all N images. The numerical value of σ^2 is thresholded to decide whether a fragment is photo-consistent or not.

Attention must be paid to pixels close to the silhouette contours in the reference images, as these pixels frequently represent a mixture of foreground and background color [282]. These pixels are ignored during the photo-consistency check. Instead, a feathering map is computed for each reference image on the client PCs and encoded in the alpha channel, equivalent to Section 4.4.3. The feathering maps have a value of one in the central parts of the foreground object that drops gradually to zero towards the silhouette outlines, while zero-value entries in the feathering maps represent scene background. Thresholding prevents pixels near the boundary from contributing to the photo-consistency check. A fragment is silhouette-consistent only if the alpha values sampled from all active reference images are greater than zero [178]. Thus, the feathering maps additionally allow for checking of silhouette consistency in the fragment program prior to the photo-consistency check.

If a fragment passes both the silhouette-consistency and the photo-consistency check, a composite color is assigned to the fragment,

$$(r, g, b) = \frac{\sum_{i=1}^{N} a_i \cdot (r_i, g_i, b_i)}{\sum_{i=1}^{N} a_i} \ ,$$

where a_i is the alpha value in the ith reference image's feathering map. The feathering weight eliminates seam artifacts along silhouette boundaries on the photo hull. During color processing, the alpha channel of the frame buffer is set to one for fragments passing the photo-consistency test. This information is then used to update the visibility maps.

Updating the Visibility Maps. Taking local camera visibility and self-occlusion into account is necessary to obtain correct rendering results; see Figure 4.21. Initially, all visibility maps are set to zero, signifying that the front-most slicing plane is entirely visible from all active reference images. In the following, the slicing planes are regarded successively from front to back. During slicing-plane rendering, implicit geometric information about the object is accumulated in the rendered image's alpha map. This information is used to update the active reference images' visibility maps after each slicing plane.

The algorithm for updating the visibility maps proceeds as follows.

- Having photo-consistently rendered the current slicing plane, the alpha channel of the target view is copied to a texture T_a. The copying operation must be carried out only for the area of the object's bounding rectangle, which can be considerably smaller than the entire viewport.

- Using T_a, the current slicing plane is rendered as seen from the active reference cameras. These back-projections are rendered to an offscreen buffer so as not to interfere with the output frame buffer of the target view. Because T_a represents per-pixel occlusion as accumulated over all slicing planes rendered so far, the rendered alpha-channel maps represent the reference images' updated visibility maps. These are copied to be available for visibility-compliant photo-consistency checking of the next slicing plane.

(a)   (b)

Figure 4.21. Visibility-consistent photo-hull rendering: (a) without local visibility information, the black color from the raised right boot participates in the color-consistency check on the left thigh to cause holes. (b) Visibility-consistent photo-hull rendering avoids such artifacts. *(Reprinted from [174], © 2004 Eurographics.)*

- Before rendering the next slicing plane, the target image's alpha channel is cleared. It will be reconstructed again from the reference images' visibility maps during the next photo-consistent rendering pass.

Because all steps are executed on the graphics card, no copy operations between frame buffer and main memory are necessary.

4.5.2 Results

For experimental evaluation, a GeForce™ FX 5800 Ultra graphics card is installed on the display server of the distributed acquisition system; see Section 2.1.4. The eight video cameras record the scene at 320×240-pixel resolution. Rendered target image resolution is also set to 320×240 pixels. The bounding rectangle enclosing the photo hull occupies about one third of the entire

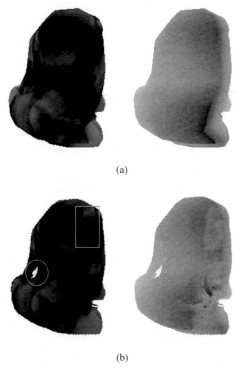

(a)

(b)

Figure 4.22. (a) Visual-hull versus (b) photo-hull rendering on graphics hardware: photo-hull rendering is able to recover object concavities (circle). More accurate geometry also reduces texture blur (box). *(Reprinted from [174], © 2004 Eurographics.)*

(a)   (b)

Figure 4.23. Photo-hull rendering on graphics hardware: results from eight input images (a) of a synthetic sequence and (b) of real-world multi-video footage. *(Reprinted from [174], © 2004 Eurographics.)*

viewport. The depth range of the visible visual hull is discretized into 60 slicing planes orthogonal to the target viewing direction.

Experiments are carried out on three data sets. The first test image set consists of real image data of a toy puppy. Eight reference cameras are placed around the stuffed animal at equal distances, spanning an arc of about $120°$. Figure 4.22 depicts rendering results for hybrid visual-hull rendering (see Section 4.4), and photo-hull rendering on graphics hardware. The comparison makes evident that photo-hull–based rendering achieves superior rendering results. For eight active views, photo-hull rendering performs at about 1.7 fps on an NVIDIA GeForce FX 5800 Ultra graphics card.

The second test data set is a synthetic animation sequence of a girl performing kung fu. Eight virtual cameras are distributed evenly around the scene. The third data set again consists of a real-world sequence recorded with the distributed acquisition system; see Section 2.1.4. Figure 4.23 depicts photo-hull–rendered novel views of both scenes. All eight reference views are used for rendering. On average, three cameras provide active reference images to render the target image. Rendering frame rates of about 2 fps are achieved on a GeForce™ FX 5800 Ultra graphics card.

4.5.3 Summary

Joint photo-hull reconstruction and rendering on graphics hardware achieves superior rendering results when compared to visual-hull rendering. Several of the limitations encountered in the described implementation have already been rendered obsolete by the progress in graphics hardware capabilities. For one thing, the number of reference images is restricted by the maximum number of texture units available on the graphics hardware. While the graphics card used in the reported experiments has eight texture units, current-generation graphics hardware can already accommodate twice as many reference images. Another factor limiting performance of the described implementation is the lack of conditional branching instructions on graphics hardware. This inability forces the fragment program to perform weighted color averaging not only for photo-consistent fragments but also for fragments already known to be rejected. This waste of computational resources can be avoided on latest-generation graphics hardware. As potential acceleration depends on the ratio of accepted and rejected fragments, interactive frame rates should be within reach on latest-generation graphics hardware.

The photo-consistency check is currently based on a single sample from each active reference view, which makes the photo-consistency test vulnerable to calibration errors, image noise, and coincidental matches. Incorporating local neighborhood information will provide more robust reconstruction and rendering results. Mipmapping, as utilized for stereo-based depth estimation on graphics hardware [328], may be adopted for more robust photo-consistent reconstruction.

Chapter 5

Utilizing Temporal Coherence

The VBR approaches described so far consider each time frame separately, independent of image content at preceding or following time frames. The fundamental physical property of inertia, however, causes all macroscopic objects to evolve continuously over time. By ignoring temporal coherence during geometry reconstruction, no use is made of this regularizing property. What's more, if temporal coherence is not observed, reconstruction errors at one time step are independent of reconstruction errors at the next time step. The resulting dynamic geometry is temporally inconsistent, which shows up as motion jitter and jumping artifacts during rendering. In contrast, by capitalizing on the fact that motion is continuous, object geometry is recovered more robustly, temporarily occluded regions are plausibly interpolated, and the animated object is rendered coherently.

5.1 Spatiotemporal View Interpolation

Sundar Vedula and his coworkers propose *spatiotemporal view interpolation* to incorporate temporal coherence into video-based rendering [306]. Figure 5.1 illustrates the goal: the recorded scene is to be rendered not only from intermediate viewpoints, but also for moments in time in-between recorded time frames. By interpolating scene motion in between recorded time frames, retimed, slow-motion fly-by movies become possible. The spatiotemporal view interpolation requires reconstructing an explicit, volumetric 3D geometry model for each time step separately. In a second, separate step, the 3D motion of each surface voxel is estimated. The motion field of the set of surface voxels is the object's three-dimensional *scene flow* [304]. It is estimated locally between two 3D volume models at consecutive time frames. Dense 3D scene-flow fields are able to de-

Figure 5.1. Spatiotemporal view interpolation: for a viewpoint in between cameras at a point in time in between time frames, 3D geometry and surface texture is interpolated from reference images adjacent in space and time. *(Reprinted from [308], courtesy of Sundar Vedula, © 2001 S. Vedula.)*

scribe the motion of any rigid or non-rigid object surface. The scene is rendered from an intermediate viewpoint and in between two time frames. To render the scene from an intermediate viewpoint and in between two time frames, the surface is interpolated across time, and offline ray casting is employed to color the surface voxels [303]. Spatiotemporal scene interpolation differs from all other VBR approaches presented in this book in that it is not interactive.

5.1.1 Geometry Reconstruction

For spatiotemporal view interpolation, explicit 3D scene geometry must be available. For each time frame, the volumetric photo hull is reconstructed separately from the segmented reference images; see Section 2.2.3. The volumetric model provides dense geometry information, in the sense that any reference image pixel projects onto some voxel. Photo-hull reconstruction assumes that object surfaces are approximately Lambertian. The 3D sceneflow estimation algorithm described in the following is also based on diffuse reflectance.

5.1.2 Scene-Flow Recovery

Having reconstructed a separate volume model per time frame, correspondences are sought between each surface voxel at time step t and a surface voxel at $t +$

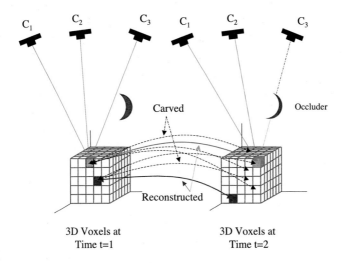

Figure 5.2. 3D scene flow: A volumetric model is reconstructed for each time frame. To relate scene geometry over time, dense correspondences are sought among surface voxels of adjacent time frames. *(reprinted from [308], courtesy of Sundar Vedula, © 2001 S. Vedula.)*

1. The surface voxel correspondences describe the potentially non-rigid motion of the object surface. This dense motion vector field is also referred to as the *3D scene flow*. Figure 5.2 illustrates the idea. The scene flow assigns to each surface voxel at position $\mathbf{x}$ a 3D motion vector $\dot{\mathbf{x}} = d\mathbf{x}dt$ that points towards the voxel's position in the next time frame, $\mathbf{x}+x\vec{v}ec$. Given known camera calibration parameters, the scene flow also relates 2D image pixels $\mathbf{u}$ across time:

$$\frac{d\mathbf{u}_i}{dt} = \frac{\partial \mathbf{u}_i}{\partial \mathbf{x}} \frac{d\mathbf{x}}{dt} , \qquad (5.1)$$

where the term $\partial \mathbf{u}_i/\partial \mathbf{x}$ is the 2×3 Jacobian matrix. It describes how the projected 2D image coordinates $\mathbf{u}$ in camera i change if the corresponding 3D scene point $\mathbf{x}$ is shifted by an infinitesimal amount from its original position. The Jacobian matrix elements are computed from the known camera calibration parameters and are constant for each voxel [304].

From the reconstructed voxel models and the reference images, the 3D scene flow, Equation (5.1), is computed separately for each time frame. First, the 2D optical flow is calculated between successive frames in each video stream. The optical flow assigns a 2D vector $\mathbf{u}_i = d\mathbf{u}/dt$ to each pixel $\mathbf{u}_i$ in image I_i^t of camera i. The optical flow vector of a pixel points to the pixel's corresponding position in the next frame I_i^{t+1}:

$$\frac{d\mathbf{u}_i}{dt} = -\frac{1}{|\nabla I_i^t|} \frac{\partial I_i^t}{\partial t} . \tag{5.2}$$

To recover the optical flow from a sequence of images, scene reflectance must be assumed to be diffuse and scene illumination to be constant [307]. In addition, some form of regularization must be applied since Equation (5.2) yields only one equation per pixel that applies to the local image gradient (normal direction) only. To estimate a complete 2D vector for each pixel, optical-flow reconstruction is typically based on least-squares regularization [182, 12].

The reconstructed 2D optical flow of a camera pixel $\dot{\mathbf{u}}_i$ provides only two linear constraints on the three components of the corresponding scene point's $\dot{\mathbf{x}}$ 3D scene-flow vector $\dot{\mathbf{x}}_i$; see Equation (5.1). However, if a 3D scene point is visible in two or more cameras, its scene flow is over-constrained. To reconstruct 3D scene flow, each surface voxel at time t is projected into all visible reference images. If a voxel is visible in $n \geq 2$ cameras, the corresponding optical flow vectors are used to determine the voxel's 3D scene flow $\dot{\mathbf{x}}_j = d\mathbf{x}_j/dt$ via

$$\mathbf{B}\frac{d\mathbf{x}_j}{dt} = \mathbf{U}, \tag{5.3}$$

with

$$\mathbf{B} = \begin{bmatrix} \frac{\partial u_1}{\partial x} & \frac{\partial u_1}{\partial y} & \frac{\partial u_1}{\partial z} \\ \frac{\partial v_1}{\partial x} & \frac{\partial v_1}{\partial y} & \frac{\partial v_1}{\partial z} \\ & \cdot & \cdot \\ \frac{\partial u_n}{\partial x} & \frac{\partial u_n}{\partial y} & \frac{\partial u_n}{\partial z} \\ \frac{\partial v_n}{\partial x} & \frac{\partial v_n}{\partial y} & \frac{\partial v_n}{\partial z} \end{bmatrix}, \quad \mathbf{U} = \begin{bmatrix} u_1 \\ v_1 \\ \cdot \\ \cdot \\ u_n \\ v_n \end{bmatrix}. \tag{5.4}$$

Equation (5.3) is solved for the scene flow in a least-squares sense by applying singular-value decomposition (SVD) to $\mathbf{B}$ [244]. This minimizes the average reprojection error between the reconstructed scene-flow vector and the optical flow in the reference images. By having available multiple camera views for scene-flow reconstruction, the resulting scene flow is typically much smoother than the input optical-flow fields from the camera streams, which can be rather noisy. For scene-flow reconstruction, only unoccluded camera views must be taken into account, i.e., the linear system of equations, Equation (5.3), must be inverted for each surface voxel individually while observing its visibility from each camera. In the end, each surface voxel at time t is assigned a 3D vector that points towards the voxel's position at time $t + 1$.

The described scheme for scene-flow reconstruction is asymmetric because, while the optical flow has been computed between frame t and $t + 1$, it is only applied to the voxel model at time t. This can lead to (small) inconsistencies, as interpolating voxel motion backward from time frame $t + 1$ does not necessarily coincide with forward interpolation from frame t. Ideally, every voxel at time t should flow to a corresponding voxel at time $t + 1$ (*inclusion*), and every voxel at $t + 1$ should have a voxel at t that flows to it (*onto*). This would guarantee that the voxel model of frame t flows forward to exactly the voxel model at $t + 1$, and vice versa. Unfortunately, such a one-to-one mapping cannot be enforced, because the number of reconstructed surface voxels is allowed to vary over time. To deal with this kind of model expansion and contraction, first, the scene-flow vectors at frame t are "grid-snapped" to the nearest surface voxel at $t + 1$. Each voxel at time t now has a correspondence at $t + 1$. To satisfy the *onto* condition as well, *duplicate voxels* are introduced [306]. Duplicate voxels are inserted at time frame t for those voxels at $t + 1$ that were not assigned a correspondence. The duplicates are inserted by inverting the average scene flow in the vicinity of the free voxel at $t + 1$. Duplicate voxels enable inverting the flow direction such that forward interpolation from t and backward interpolation from $t + 1$ give identical results. Without this trick, holes result during spatiotemporal view interpolation.

Instead of reconstructing 3D scene flow from 2D optical flow, scene flow can also be estimated directly. In their *surfel* approach, Rodrigo Carceroni and Kyros Kutulakos generalize the brightness constancy equation of the optical-flow constraint to the temporal domain [36]. Here, the motion of 3D patches (surfels) is determined directly from the input images by regularizing over the 3D object surface implicitly. Similarly, the shape and motion carving approach described by Sundar Vedula also computes voxel model and scene flow simultaneously [305].

5.1.3   Rendering

As input to spatiotemporal view-interpolated rendering, the reference images, voxel models, and scene flows of the two nearest time frames are needed. Figure 5.3 illustrates the processing steps. To render the object at a time instance in between frames, first, an estimate of momentary scene shape is generated by flowing the two voxel models from the previous and the next time frame to the intermediate moment in time. This interpolated voxel model is then rendered by ray casting each pixel in the target view. During ray casting, the 3D model surface is implicitly smoothed to avoid artifacts due to the voxels' cubic shape. The 3D intersection coordinates of the viewing ray with the voxel model are stored for each target image pixel. Then the three intersection coordinate components are 2D low-pass filtered over the target image plane using a small Gaussian kernel. The filtered intersection coordinate values are then used to determine the reprojection coordinates of each intersection point into the reference images. To do so requires following the scene flow forward and backward to the two adjacent time

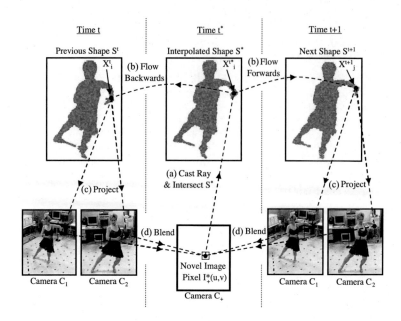

Figure 5.3. Spatiotemporal ray casting: the geometry model is "flowed" to the current intermediate moment in time t^*. (a) For each target image pixel, its viewing ray is intersected with the model. (b) The scene flow is followed from the intersection point forwards and backwards in time to the adjacent recorded time frames. (c) The corresponding voxels are projected into the reference images. (d) The pixel values are weighted and blended and assigned to the target image pixel. *(Reprinted from [308], courtesy of Sundar Vedula,* © *2001 S. Vedula.)*

frames recorded, and projecting the resulting 3D positions into all unoccluded cameras. The forward/backward flow is done by linear interpolation, which implicitly assumes that each voxel travels along a straight line at constant velocity. The pixel color values from different cameras are weighted according to the angle between the viewing ray and the reference camera $\theta_i(u, v)$:

$$\frac{1/\left(1 - \cos\theta_i(u, v)\right)}{\sum_{j=1}^{vis(t,u,v)} 1/\left(1 - \cos\theta_i(u, v)\right)} ,$$

where $vis(t, u, v)$ denotes the set of cameras for which the flowed 3D point corresponding to target image pixel (u, v) is visible at time t. Finally, all contributing pixel colors are blended according to their weight.

Plate XII depicts the differences in rendering quality if the volumetric model is (a) simply flowed to the intermediate point in time and rendered as a collection of cubic voxels, is (b) ray-cast rendered using the cubic voxel surface, or is (c) ray-cast rendered using a smooth surface interpolation through the center of adjacent voxels.

5.1.4 Summary

In contrast to all other VBR approaches described in this book, the ray-casting approach used for spatiotemporal view interpolation does not achieve interactive frame rates. Spatiotemporal view interpolation results are instead rendered offline at high quality. The results demonstrate that a volume resolution of $80 \times 80 \times 120$ voxels suffices to render convincing slow-motion movies from $17\,320 \times 240$-pixel input video streams.

5.2 Spacetime-Coherent Reconstruction

Spatiotemporal view interpolation establishes local correspondences between voxels of adjacent time frames. The geometry itself, however, is reconstructed individually per time frame. If use is to be made of the continuous nature of any macroscopic motion to recover time-consistent, more robust, and more accurate geometry, it is helpful to consider geometry evolution in the context of 4D spacetime, where the fourth dimension represents the continuous flow of time. When regarded in 4D spacetime, dynamic object surfaces describe 3D hypersurfaces that vary smoothly over time. The goal in spacetime-coherent reconstruction is then to find the continuous 3D hypersurface that is photo-consistent with all images recorded by all cameras over the entire time span of the sequence.

It turns out this approach can be elegantly described as a minimization problem. Formulating the solution to computer vision problems implicitly in the form of weighted minimal hypersurfaces is actually a common approach. The desired hypersurface is defined as minimizing an energy functional that has the form of a weighted area integral over the hypersurface domain. One well known technique that utilizes minimal surfaces are *geodesic active contours*, or *snakes* [39]. Originally designed for segmentation in 2D [144], the approach can be generalized to three dimensions [39] and is particularly attractive for modeling surfaces from point clouds [341, 342]. Geodesic contours have also been employed for 2D detection and tracking of moving objects [231]. Minimal surfaces are also being employed for 3D reconstruction of static scenes from multiple views [76], and even to simultaneously estimate geometry and surface reflectance [138].

The VBR reconstruction approach presented in the following is based on an energy functional whose minimal 3D hypersurface in 4D spacetime coincides with the time-varying surface of a dynamic object. From investigations of the mathematical foundations of weighted minimal hypersurfaces, this implicit definition can be reformulated as a Euler-Lagrange equation that represents a necessary minimum criterion for the solution [102]. The Euler-Lagrange reformulation applies to a general class of weight functions in arbitrary dimension, which makes it applicable to many different variational approaches in computer vision. Spacetime-coherent surface reconstruction is just one specific application of this approach [101].

5.2.1   4D Surfaces in Spacetime

To derive the mathematics of spacetime hypersurface reconstruction, first, continuous signals over space and time are assumed. The obtained expressions are then discretized in a second step to formulate the numerical reconstruction algorithm. As input data, only multi-video imagery is available, along with extrinsic and intrinsic camera calibration data. Several dynamic objects may be present in the scene, and the objects' topology may change over the sequence. The goal is to obtain smooth surfaces Σ_t for each time instant t that coincide with the geometry of the dynamic scene objects. As constraints, all object surfaces are to evolve continuously over time, and the reconstructed object surfaces are to be as photo-consistent as possible with the recorded video data.

To ensure temporal coherence, individual time frames cannot be considered separately. Instead, the 2D object surface Σ_t must be regarded as the cross section of one smooth, 3D hypersurface $\mathfrak{H}$, which itself is embedded in 4D spacetime. From this viewpoint, the reconstructed 2D object surface

$$\Sigma_t = \mathfrak{H} \cap \left(\mathbb{R}^3, t\right) \subset \mathbb{R}^3$$

is the intersection of $\mathfrak{H}$ with 3D hyperplanes of constant time. Because $\mathfrak{H}$ is continuous and encompasses all time steps, temporal coherence is guaranteed.

To enforce photo-consistency of the reconstructed geometry, an energy functional

$$\mathcal{A}\left(\mathfrak{H}\right) := \int_{\mathfrak{H}} \Phi\left(s, \mathbf{n}\left(s\right)\right) \, dA\left(s\right) \tag{5.5}$$

is defined as the integral of a scalar-valued weight function Φ over the hypersurface domain $\mathfrak{H}$. The function Φ expresses photo-consistency error density. It depends on the four-dimensional position s, and optionally also the local normal direction $\mathbf{n}$ in s. The higher the value of Φ, the larger the photo-consistency error. The goal is to find the hypersurface $\mathfrak{H}$ that minimizes $\mathcal{A}\left(\mathfrak{H}\right)$ (Equation (5.5)). The weight function Φ expresses photo-consistency, while temporal smoothness is ensured because the sought-after minimal hypersurface $\mathfrak{H}$ minimizes the integral of the weight function over a closed domain.

While Equation (5.5) is a mathematically elegant description of the notion of spacetime-coherent reconstruction, the algorithmic problem remains how to actually find the minimal hypersurface $\mathfrak{H}$. Fortunately, it can be shown [102] that an n-dimensional surface $\mathfrak{H} \subset \mathbb{R}^{n+1}$ which minimizes the functional $\mathcal{A}(\mathfrak{H}) := \int_{\mathfrak{H}} \Phi(s, \mathbf{n}(s)) \, dA(s)$ satisfies the Euler-Lagrange equation

$$\langle \Phi_s, \mathbf{n} \rangle - \text{Tr}(\mathbf{S}) \Phi + \text{div}_{\mathfrak{H}}(\Phi_{\mathbf{n}}) = 0, \tag{5.6}$$

where $\mathbf{S}$ is the shape operator of the surface, also referred to as the Weingarten map or the second fundamental tensor, and Φ_s and $\Phi_{\mathbf{n}}$ denote the error measure's $n+1$-dimensional gradient vectors with respect to spacetime position and normal orientation, respectively. The theorem has been proven to hold for arbitrary dimensionality n [102]. In the form of the Euler-Lagrange equation, Equation (5.6), a minimal surface of Equation (5.5) can be found explicitly using a surface evolution approach.

Spacetime Continuity. At time t, acquisition camera k records image I_k^t. The camera lens projects the scene surface onto the image plane via a fixed projection $\pi_k : \mathbb{R}^3 \to \mathbb{R}^2$. The color c_k^t of a hypersurface point $s = (x, t)$, as observed by camera k, is then

$$c_k^t(x) = I_k^t \circ \pi_k(x). \tag{5.7}$$

Assuming Lambertian surface reflectance characteristics, a suitable photo-consistency error measure is defined by

$$\Phi^S(x, t) := \frac{1}{V_{x,t}} \sum_{i,j=1}^{l} \nu_i^t(x) \nu_j^t(x) \cdot \left\| c_i^t(x) - c_j^t(x) \right\|. \tag{5.8}$$

The double sum extends over all cameras l. $\nu_i^t(x)$ denotes whether the 3D point (x) on the 2D object surface Σ_t is currently visible from camera i or not. $\nu_i^t(x)$ is one if x is visible and zero if the point is occluded. $V_{x,t}$ normalizes the function value and denotes the number of camera pairs that are able to see the point x at time t. Equation (5.8) is the weight function introduced by Olivier Faugeras and Renaud Keriven to reconstruct regular surfaces in $\mathbb{R}^3$, i.e., for static scene recovery [76]. When inserted into Equation (5.6) for $\mathbb{R}^3$, Φ^S yields a continuous form of voxel coloring or space carving by regarding each time step separately [264, 156].

Normal Optimization. Because Equation (5.6) also holds for error functions that depend on local surface normals, normal orientation can simultaneously be taken into account. Because the presented approach makes use of spatiotemporal coherence, the error measure may also be a function of normal direction $\mathbf{n}$ in

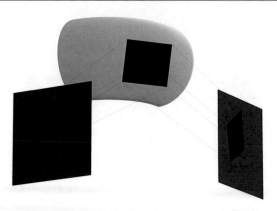

Figure 5.4. Practical computation of the photo-consistency measure for two cameras: a small grid in the tangent plane of the object's surface Σ_t at time instant t is projected into both reference images. The normalized cross-correlation of the corresponding pixels' color values yields a measure of photo-consistency. *(Reprinted from [191], © 2004 IEEE.)*

4D spacetime [101]. Instead, the photo-consistency measure makes use only of normal direction in the three spatial dimensions, $\mathbf{n}^t$: it is used here to determine the correct projection footprint of a surface patch into the reference images; see Figure 5.4.

An appropriate photo-consistency error measure has to quantify how well a hypersurface point at time t, 3D spatial coordinates x, and 4D normal $\mathbf{n}$ brings all unoccluded camera images I_k^t into agreement. A small patch $\square_{x,\mathbf{n}^t}$ around x is considered whose plane is orthogonal to $\mathbf{n}^t$; see Figure 5.4. $\mathbf{n}^t$ corresponds to the normal of Σ_t at (x) and denotes the projection of $\mathbf{n}$ into the three spatial dimensions. The tangential surface patch $\square_{x,\mathbf{n}^t}$ is a rectangular region; the patch shape does not noticeably influence reconstruction performance.

To quantify how well a surface patch $\square_{s,\mathbf{n}^t}$ matches to all visible reference images I_k^t, normalized cross-correlation is used. The resulting photo-consistency error function for a point $s = (x, t) \in \mathbb{R}^4$ with normal direction $\mathbf{n}$ is defined as follows:

$$\Phi^G(s, \mathbf{n}) := -\frac{1}{V_{x,t}} \sum_{i,j=1}^{l} \nu_i^t(x)\nu_j^t(x) \cdot \frac{\chi_{i,j}^t(x, \mathbf{n}^t)}{A\left(\square_{x,\mathbf{n}^t}\right)} , \qquad (5.9)$$

with zero-mean cross-correlation

$$\chi_{i,j}^t(x, \mathbf{n}^t) := \int_{\square_{x,\mathbf{n}^t}} \left(c_i^t(x) - \overline{I}_i^{t,x,\mathbf{n}^t}\right) \left(c_j^t(x) - \overline{I}_j^{t,x,\mathbf{n}^t}\right) \, dA(x) ,$$

and the mean color value of the projected patch in the images computed according to

$$\overline{I}_i^{t,x,\mathbf{n}^t} := \frac{1}{A\left(\square_{x,\mathbf{n}^t}\right)} \int_{\square_{x,\mathbf{n}^t}} c_i^t(x) \, dA(x).$$

The variable $c_{i,j}^t(x)$ in Equation (5.7) denotes reference image pixel color at the projection coordinates of (x) in camera i, j, respectively. The correlation measure $\chi_{i,j}^t$ for a pair of cameras is normalized by the area $A\left(\square_{x,\mathbf{n}^t}\right)$ of the patch. The patch $\square_{x,\mathbf{n}^t}$ lies in the tangential plane of Σ_t. The patch $\square_{x,\mathbf{n}^t}$ must be chosen sufficiently large so that it is projected onto several pixels. On the other hand, it should not be too large, otherwise only parts of it may be visible in the images. As a compromise, the patch diameter is set equal to the cell diameter of the underlying computation grid. The mean patch values $\overline{I}_i^{t,x,\mathbf{n}^t}$ are determined from the image I_i^t.

While the error measure Φ^G can depend on the 4D normal $\mathbf{n}$ of $\mathfrak{H}$ (Equation (5.6)), the photo-consistency expression, Equation (5.9), depends only on the 3D normal $\mathbf{n}^t$ to the surface Σ_t. In practice, $\mathbf{n}^t$ is composed of the three spatial coordinates of $\mathbf{n}$.

By minimizing the weight function, Equation (5.9), using Equation (5.6)), two constraints are simultaneously taken into account: each surface Σ_t, together with its normal field, is determined such that it matches best the images at time t, and a smooth change of Σ_t along the temporal dimension is encouraged by the curvature term $\mathrm{Tr}\,(\mathbf{S})\,\Phi$ in the Euler-Lagrange equation, Equation (5.6).

5.2.2 Numerical Evaluation

In order to obtain an explicit representation of the minimal surface defined implicitly by Equation (5.5), the Euler-Lagrange equation, Equation (5.6), must be solved numerically. To do so, the problem is expressed in the form of a surface evolution equation. Defining the left-hand side in Equation (5.6) as

$$\Psi := \langle \Phi_s, \mathbf{n} \rangle \; - \; \mathrm{Tr}\,(\mathbf{S})\,\Phi \; + \; \mathrm{div}_{\mathfrak{H}}(\Phi_{\mathbf{n}}), \tag{5.10}$$

a surface $\mathfrak{H}$ that is a solution to the Euler-Lagrange equation $\Psi = 0$ is also a stationary solution to the surface evolution equation

$$\frac{\partial}{\partial \tau}\mathfrak{H}_\tau \; = \; \Psi\mathbf{n}, \tag{5.11}$$

where Ψ describes a generalized force along surface normal direction. By starting with an initial surface $\mathfrak{H}_0$ and letting the surface iteratively evolve via Equation (5.11), the surface converges to a local minimum of Equation (5.5). The variable τ denotes the iteration parameter.

Level-Set Evolution Equation.   Instead of implementing the surface evolution directly, a level-set approach is pursued [229, 48]. This numerical evaluation technique for multidimensional PDEs has become well established for a wide range of applications [266]. The surface $\mathfrak{H}_\tau$ is expressed for each iteration parameter value $\tau \geq 0$ as the zero level set of a regular function

$$u : \mathbb{R}^4 \times \mathbb{R}^{\geq 0} \to \mathbb{R}, \quad u(x, \tau) = 0 \iff x \in \mathfrak{H}_\tau , \qquad (5.12)$$

where $u(x, \tau)$ is positive inside the volume enclosed by $\mathfrak{H}_\tau$ and negative outside. With ∇ denoting the gradient operator, the outer normal can be rewritten as

$$\mathbf{n} = -\frac{\nabla u}{|\nabla u|} \quad \Longrightarrow \quad |\nabla u| = - \langle \nabla u, \mathbf{n} \rangle .$$

By taking the derivative of $u(x, \tau)$ on $\mathfrak{H}_\tau$ with respect to τ, making use of the chain rule, and using Equation (5.11), the evolution equation for u becomes

$$\frac{\partial}{\partial \tau} u \Big|_{\mathfrak{H}_\tau} = - \left\langle \nabla u, \frac{\partial}{\partial \tau} \mathfrak{H}_\tau \right\rangle = - \langle \nabla u, \mathbf{n} \rangle \Psi = \Psi |\nabla u| . \qquad (5.13)$$

Into the definition of Ψ, Equation (5.10), the identity for the curvature of the level sets of u is substituted, yielding

$$\mathrm{Tr}\,(\mathbf{S}) = \mathrm{div}\left(\frac{\nabla u}{|\nabla u|}\right).$$

The first and second term of Equation (5.10) can now be integrated by parts (i.e., the product rule is applied in reverse), to take on the form

$$\frac{\partial}{\partial \tau} u = \left[- \mathrm{div}\left(\Phi \cdot \frac{\nabla u}{|\nabla u|} \right) + \mathrm{div}_{\mathfrak{H}}(\Phi_\mathbf{n}) \right] |\nabla u| . \qquad (5.14)$$

This is the reformulation of Equation (5.6) in terms of a level-set evolution equation.

To determine u numerically, Equation (5.14) must be discretized in space and time. The equation is solved on a regular 4D lattice, and the derivatives of Φ are evaluated using finite differences. The large size of the lattice, however, requires a parallel processing approach.

In order to solve the level-set evolution equation, Equation (5.14), the volume surrounding the hypersurface $\mathfrak{H}$ is discretized into a regular, 4D grid of evenly spaced cells. On commodity PC hardware, a spatial resolution of 128^3 cells is manageable, while temporal resolution must be kept equal to the number of time frames in the input sequence which can consist of many hundreds to thousands of frames. For any sequence of reasonable length, massive amounts of data are involved. As the entire data set cannot be stored in main memory of a standard PC, a parallel processing approach, which distributes the computational load and data over several computers, is inevitable.

Numerical Solution of the Surface Evolution. The discretized version of the evolution equation, Equation (5.14), is solved using the narrow-band level-set method [266]. The narrow-band method has the advantage that it evaluates only grid cells next to the zero level set, and it is straightforward to parallelize. The algorithm is initialized with a starting surface $\mathfrak{H}_0$ and the values u_0^{xyzt} of the corresponding level-set function u_0 at the center of the grid cells. A suitable initialization is, for example, the volumetric visual hull of the object; see Section 4.1.

The values of the level-set function are iteratively updated using the upwind scheme [266]. At iteration $q+1$, the new grid cell values u_{q+1}^{xyzt} are obtained from the previous values u_q^{xyzt} by employing an explicit time step:

$$u_{q+1}^{xyzt} = u_q^{xyzt} + \Psi\left(u_q^{xyzt}\right)\left|\nabla u_q^{xyzt}\right| \cdot \Delta\tau. \tag{5.15}$$

The time step $\Delta\tau$ is the iteration step size. The norm of the discretized gradient $\left|\nabla u_q\right|$ is also determined via the upwind scheme [266]; $\Psi\left(u_q^{xyzt}\right)$ is the result of the discretized version of the differential operator, Equation (5.14) acting on u_i and evaluated at (x,y,z,t).

The partial derivatives occuring in Equation (5.14) are numerically evaluated using central differences on the 4D grid; see Plate XIII.

- Using central differences, the values of u_q in the green cells allow the computation of the level-set normals $\mathbf{n} \in \mathbb{R}^4$ in the blue cells. Given $\mathbf{n}$, Φ^G can be computed for the blue cells; see Equation (5.9).

- In a second step, the red center pixel is evaluated. The discrete formula for $\mathrm{div}(\Phi \cdot \mathbf{n})$ at position $s = (x,y,z,t)$ is

$$\sum_{i=1}^{4} \frac{\Phi^{s+e_i}n_i^{s+e_i} - \Phi^{s-e_i}n_i^{s-e_i}}{2},$$

where e_i denotes the unit index vector along the ith dimension. Though not necessary for evaluating Equation (5.14), the curvature term $\mathrm{Tr}\,(\mathbf{S})$ can be computed likewise by omitting Φ in the above formula.

- The expression $\mathrm{div}_{\mathfrak{H}}(\Phi_{\mathbf{n}})$, which must be evaluated for the center cell, is equivalent to the trace of $\Phi_{\mathbf{n}s}$, restricted to the tangent plane Π that is orthogonal to the normal $\mathbf{n}$ in s. First, $\Phi_{\mathbf{n}}$ is computed for the adjacent blue cells using finite differences. From these values, the 4×4 matrix $\mathbf{U} := \Phi_{\mathbf{n}s}$ is set up for the center cell. By choosing an arbitrary orthonormal base $\{\mathbf{b}_0, \mathbf{b}_1, \mathbf{b}_2\}$ of the tangent plane Π in s, the mapping $\Phi_{\mathbf{n}s}|_{\Pi}$ can be represented by a 3×3 matrix $\mathbf{V}$ whose elements are

$$\mathbf{V}_{ij} = \mathbf{b}_i^T \mathbf{U} \mathbf{b}_j, 1 \leq i,j \leq 3,$$

and whose trace is equal to $\mathrm{div}_{\mathfrak{H}}(\Phi_{\mathbf{n}})$ of the center cell.

Grid cell visibility $\nu_i(u_q^{xyzt})$ in reference image i as well as the normalization factor $V_{x,t}$ (see Equations (5.8) and (5.9)) are determined via ray casting.

The numerical evaluation of the term $\mathrm{div}_{\mathfrak{H}}(\Phi_\mathbf{n})$ is computationally expensive. However, it is zero if the photo-consistency measure does not depend on $\mathbf{n}$, as, for example, Equation (5.8). The term must be evaluated only if Equation (5.9) is used as a photo-consistency measure.

Time-Step Size Determination. The differential operator is evaluated for grid cells close to the zero level set. To ensure numerical stability, the step size $\Delta\tau$ is chosen such that the level sets of u_i do not cross more than one cell diameter per iteration step, corresponding to the Courant-Friedrichs-Levy (CFL) condition

$$\Delta\tau \leq \max_{(x,y,z,t)} \left(\frac{\mathrm{diam\ cell}(x,y,z,t)}{\left| \Psi\left(u_q^{xyzt}\right) \cdot \nabla u_q^{xyzt} \right|} \right). \tag{5.16}$$

To adapt step size, the maximum value of $\left| \Psi\left(u_q^{xyzt}\right) \cdot \nabla u_q^{xyzt} \right|$ must be determined over all grid cells for each iteration.

5.2.3   Distributed Implementation

Because the calculations necessary for each grid cell depend only on each cell's local neighborhood, the computations can be easily divided into separate processes. To keep network traffic low, each process computes complete scene geometry for a fixed time instant t_i. The result from each process is a discrete version of $\Sigma_t(t_i)$, i.e., a time slice of $\mathfrak{H}$. Each slice contains grid cell values around the zero level set.

In order to evaluate the differential operator $\Psi\left(u_q^{xyzt}\right)$, Equation (5.14), grid cell values are needed up to two cells away from (x,y,z,t) along all four dimensions; see Plate XIII. Each process P_i must therefore access the time slices of four other processes, $P_{i\pm1,i\pm2}$. These have to be communicated over the network. Plate XIV depicts the data exchange between processes of adjacent time frames $t_{i\pm1,2}$. In addition to grid-cell information, each process must have access to the reference images of its own time step t_i to perform the photo-consistency check. Each process may run on a separate PC or a cluster node. In summary, one iteration consists of the following four steps.

- Each process evolves its assigned grid slice $u_q^{xyzt_i}$ by one step size $\Delta\tau$ according to Equation (5.15).

- Each process transmits its evolved geometry slice $u_q^{xyzt_i}$ to the adjacent processes and receives the other evolved slices $u_q^{xyzt_{i\pm1,i\pm2}}$ from its four neighbors; see Plate XIV.

- Each process keeps track of $\Psi\left(u_q^{xyzt}\right)$ for all cells near the zero level set of u_q and transmits the maximum value to a special server process.

- From the maxima of $\Psi\left(u_q^{xyzt}\right)$, the server process calculates the next step size $\Delta\tau$ according to Equation (5.16) and broadcasts it to all processes.

During surface evolution, the server polls the current version of the level set to evaluate convergence status. The algorithm stops when the flow field is zero everywhere. Alternatively, it terminates after a maximum number of iteration steps.

Initialization. The visual hull is a suitable initial surface $\mathfrak{H}_0$ to start the iteration process; see Figure 5.5(a). By definition, it represents a superset of the correct scene geometry and encloses it; see Section 2.2. For initializing the 4D grid structure, volumetric visual hulls are determined for all time steps from the segmented reference images; see Section 4.1. To represent the visual hulls as level sets, for each grid cell, a number of evenly distributed sample points within the voxel are selected. These points are projected into all source images. The percentage $p \in [0, 1]$ of projected points that fall into the object silhouettes is computed, and the value $2p - 1$ is assigned to the initial level set function u_0. This way, all cells inside the silhouettes are assigned value 1, while cells outside the silhouettes have value -1. Cells on the border have intermediate values. The projection of the zero level set of u_0 into the source images very closely matches object silhouette. Using the visual hull as an initialization surface has been found to yield excellent convergence results in practice; see Figure 5.5(b).

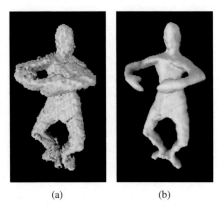

(a)   (b)

Figure 5.5. Spacetime-coherent reconstruction initialization: (a) the visual hull at each time instant is used to initialize the 4D computation grid, yielding (b) robust PDE evolution results. *(Reprinted from [101], © 2004 IEEE.)*

5.2.4   Rendering

Solving the evolution equation, Equation (5.14), using the level-set approach
yields the reconstruction result in the form of scalar-valued regular grid cells,
or voxels, that line the actual surface represented by the zero level set. To obtain
a conventional triangle-mesh representation of the zero level set, it has to be triangulated and resampled. Alternatively, the level-set representation is rendered
directly using billboard rendering; see Section 4.1.2.

Because spacetime-coherent reconstruction is an offline VBR approach, the
input data can be preprocessed prior to rendering to obtain the best rendering
results. During preprocessing, the voxels bordering the zero level set are determined, and their visibility is checked in all reference images. While in volumetric
visual-hull rendering (see Section 4.1), each voxel takes on a binary value indicating whether the voxel lies inside or outside the visual hull, the level-set method
assigns to each voxel a floating-point value that signifies how close the voxel center actually lies to the zero level-set surface. By appropriately scaling the level-
set values and adding an offset of 0.5, an alpha value between zero and one is
assigned to each voxel adjacent to the zero level set. These alpha values are later
used to weightedly blend billboards, as opposed to rendering opaque billboards
on top of each other as is done for online performance; see Section 4.1. For each
time frame, all surface voxels are stored alongside the respective list of visible
reference images and alpha values.

Real-time rendering frame rates are achieved by balancing computational load
between CPU, vertex program, and fragment shader. For each time frame, the reference images are uploaded to graphics texture memory, and the surface voxels'
alpha values are uploaded as a 3D texture map. For each surface voxel in the
precomputed list, the CPU determines which two visible reference images are
closest to the current target view direction and calculates their individual blending weights. The voxel's 3D world coordinates are then sent to the graphics board,
and the display list is invoked to render a unit square. In the vertex program, the
unit square is translated, scaled, and rotated to face the target view at the correct
viewport coordinates, and its corner vertex coordinates are projected into the two
reference views to determine the texture coordinates. The fragment program, in
turn, takes the texture coordinates and weights to composite the billboard square
texture from both reference images. The billboard is rendered to the frame buffer
by assigning to the alpha channel the voxel's alpha value looked up in the 3D
texture map.

5.2.5   Results

To illustrate spacetime-coherent reconstruction quality, results for a real-world
human dance sequence are shown in Plate V. The input images are automatically

segmented into foreground and background [17], and a level-set representation of the visual hull is used to initialize the voxel volume. The cameras are arranged along the perimeter of the scene at about eye level, so some body regions are temporarily not visible from any cameras, e.g., when the arms are in front of the chest. In such cases, the visual-hull approximation is only a crude approximation of actual geometry; see Figure 5.6(a). For invisible regions, photo-hull reconstruction cannot improve the result, either; see Figure 5.6(b). Spacetime-coherent reconstruction, on the other hand, is able to plausibly interpolate intermittently invisible regions; see Figure 5.6(c): by enforcing temporal coherence, occluded regions are automatically interpolated from previous and future time frames.

Figure 5.7(a) depicts reconstructed geometry from eight wide-baseline video streams. Billboard rendering results of the model are shown in Figure 5.7(b). Sustainable rendering frame rates of 30 fps are achieved on a GeForce4™ Ti 4600 if the data is stored in local memory.

Spacetime-coherent reconstruction is an offline algorithm. Table 5.1 lists the memory requirements of a single process and computation times for one iteration, evaluated on a Sun Fire 15K with 75 UltraSPARC III+ processors at 900 MHz, featuring in total 176 GB of main memory. Evaluating the photo-consistency term, Equation (5.9), requires substantially more computation time than computing Equation (5.8). Because taking normal information into account has an impact

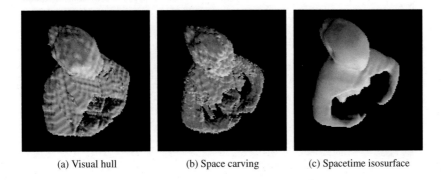

(a) Visual hull	(b) Space carving	(c) Spacetime isosurface

Figure 5.6. Comparison of different reconstruction algorithms: the dancer is rendered from above with eight recording cameras arranged in the horizontal plane. Grid resolution is 128^3 cells. Since there is no camera to capture the scene from above, (a) visual-hull reconstruction does not delete voxels in the occluded region between arms and chest. (b) As this region is currently not visible from any two cameras, photo-hull reconstruction shows little improvement. (c) Spacetime-coherent reconstruction, on the other hand, plausibly interpolates the intermittently invisible region between the arms from previous and future time steps, making implicit use of temporal coherence. *(Reprinted from [101], © 2004 IEEE.)*

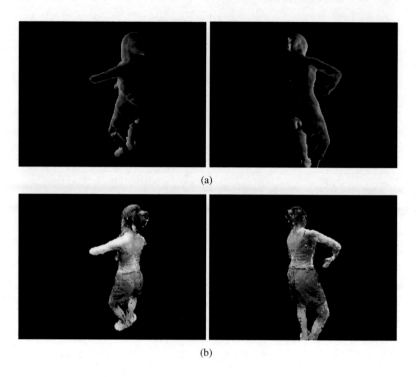

(a)

(b)

Figure 5.7. (a) Spacetime-coherently reconstructed geometry and (b) billboard-rendered views of the dancer. *((a) Reprinted from [101], © 2004 IEEE.)*

grid res.	time per iteration Φ^S (5.8) Φ^G (5.9)		memory per proc.
32^3	2.5 s	60 s	80 MB
64^3	17 s	360 s	120 MB
128^3	102 s	1200 s	535 MB

Table 5.1. Computation time of a single iteration step, depending on the resolution of the grid lattice. Each process computes one time slice. Measurements are listed for photo-consistency measures with (see Equation (5.9)) and without (see Equation (5.8)) surface-normal dependence. *(Reprinted from [101], © 2004 IEEE.)*

mainly on the reconstruction of small surface details, object geometry is recon-structed first using Equation (5.8) as a photo-consistency measure. On average, convergence is reached after about 100 iteration steps. The reconstruction result is then refined by employing Equation (5.9) as a photo-consistency measure. After about 20 more iteration steps, the surface converges to the final result.

5.2.6 Summary

Spacetime-coherent reconstruction is a wide-baseline algorithm that takes global temporal coherence into account. It achieves more accurate and robust results than conventional, per-time-frame photo-hull reconstruction. By considering all reference images of all time frames simultaneously, a photo-consistent and tempo-rally smoothly varying geometry surface is recovered. In addition, scene regions that are temporarily not visible in any reference view are plausibly interpolated by preserving temporal coherence to previous and future time frames.

As with any iterative method attempting to optimize a non-convex energy functional, spacetime-coherent reconstruction can potentially converge to local minima. Visual-hull initialization, however, appears to be a robust starting point to achieve good convergence results.

Chapter 6

Model-Based Analysis and Synthesis

The VBR methods described in the preceding chapter all reconstruct dynamic scene geometry from scratch. In contrast, for many VBR scenarios it is known in advance what kind of object is being recorded. Suitably implemented, such a priori knowledge can be exploited to bias the reconstruction outcome towards plausible results only. To do so, a suitable model of the recorded object must be available. A model also enables the enforcing of low-level as well as high-level constraints about the object's motion, from temporally coherent movement to anatomically consistent motion. Model geometry can be highly detailed, which facilitates high-quality rendering results and circumvents rendering inaccuracies due to poorly resolved geometry. In summary, model-based VBR has the potential to attain more robust and accurate rendering results than VBR methods ignorant of recorded scene content.

One crucial component in model-based VBR is evidently an appropriate model representation of a priori scene knowledge. The approach described in the following relies on an adaptable 3D geometry model description of the dynamic object(s) in the scene. The model is adaptable in the sense that it features a number of free parameters that can be varied to match model appearance to its recorded real-world counterpart. A parameterized geometry model ensures temporal coherence by enforcing model parameter values to vary smoothly over time. In addition, any kinematic constraints set by the nature of the object are met by restricting the permissible range of parameter values.

145

6.1 Free-Viewpoint Video

Methods making use of a priori 3D geometry information for static-image analysis have been investigated predominantly in the context of object recognition [181, 30, 239]. Matching 2D image contours to a projected object geometry outline has been proven useful for estimating object pose and camera orientation [132, 223, 205, 197]. Using a geometry model of the calibration object, automated camera calibration via analysis-by-synthesis has been demonstrated [67]. In a similar manner, silhouette information has been used to register still photographs of an object to laser-scanned 3D object geometry [163, 164].

Algorithms that make use of parameterized geometry models to analyze time-varying scene content have been investigated in conjunction with low-bit-rate video coding [151]. Given suitably parameterized models, linearized reconstruction from optical flow has been shown to work well to determine facial animation parameters [66] as well as body pose [29]. Similarly, kinematic body representations have been matched to reconstructed 3D object geometry models for optical motion capture [25, 46, 215]. Alternatively, the kinematic skeleton can also be adapted to the recorded subject using dense depth maps and silhouettes [235].

While for motion-capture purposes it is sufficient to recover model animation parameters, VBR imposes the additional demand that the resulting model must be able to produce convincing rendering results. The challenge in model-based VBR is how to automatically, robustly, and visually consistently match a parameterized 3D geometry model to reference image content. In the following, a model-based VBR method is described that is based on matching object and model silhouettes using an analysis-by-synthesis approach [38]. For accelerated processing, the method can be parallelized and implemented on a distributed system [290]. Besides silhouette information, additional object texture can be made use of to refine the model match [293].

6.1.1 Silhouette-Based Optical Motion Capture

Model-based VBR starts with devising a suitable model of the object in the scene. To capture the time-varying shape of the object, the model must consist of 3D geometry as well as a description of the object's kinematic structure. While 3D object geometry can be represented in various ways, a triangle mesh representation is especially useful for VBR, as it can be rendered directly on graphics hardware. In order to be able to take on any pose that its real-world counterpart is capable of, the model is composed of multiple rigid-body parts that are linked by a hierarchical kinematic chain. The kinematic chain describes connectivity of different rigid-body parts. It also defines the types of rotations as well as permissible rotation ranges for each joint between segments. The number of independent joint parameters reflects the model's kinematic degrees of freedom. To match the model to a person's individual stature, in addition to body pose, the shape and dimension of each body part must also be individually adaptable, within reasonable bounds.

Throughout the remainder of the chapter, image footage of a human jazz dance performance is used to demonstrate model-based VBR performance. Free-viewpoint video, however, is much more general: not only can human motion be analyzed, but the movements of any animal or object can be captured, as long as its movements can be modeled by a number of rigid-body parts that are interconnected to form a kinematic chain [193].

Parameterized Object Model.   As the geometry model, a publicly available VRML geometry model of a human body is used; see Figure 6.1. The model consists of 16 rigid-body segments, one for the upper and lower torso, neck, and head, and pairs for the upper arms, lower arms, hands, upper legs, lower legs, and feet. In total, more than 21,000 triangles make up the human body model. A hierarchical kinematic chain connects all body segments, resembling the human skeleton. Seventeen joints are controlled by 35 joint parameters that define the pose of the model. The root node at the pelvis represents three separate joints. Model joints are parameterized based on human anatomy, incorporating high-level knowledge about what a human can and cannot do. For example, the elbow joints cannot be extended beyond $180°$. This way, the outcome of the model-based analysis is constrained to only anatomically plausible results.

Figure 6.1. To demonstrate model-based VBR, a human body model is used that consists of 16 rigid-body parts. The model can be adapted to a person's individual proportions by independently scaling and deforming each body part. Human motion is captured by 17 body joints that are controlled by 35 pose parameters.

Because the generic body model will, in general, not have the same proportions as its human counterpart, each segment can be individually scaled and its surface deformed to adapt model size and proportions. The parameters controlling model stature and build need to be set only once during initialization and are kept fixed during actual motion capture.

Silhouette Matching.   One challenge in model-based VBR is to find a way to automatically and robustly adapt the geometry model to the subject's appearance as recorded by the video cameras. Since the geometry model is suitably parameterized to alter, within anatomically plausible limits, its shape and pose, the problem consists of finding those parameter values that achieve the best match between the model and the video images. In the following, this task is regarded as a non-linear optimization problem.

Etienne de Silhouette, Louis XV's financial minister, realized that the outline of a man's head, while inexpensive to acquire, contains enough information about the depicted subject to allow one to recognize the person. To save money, he ordered *silhouette* cuts to be made for the court's ministerial gallery, instead of oil paintings as was customary before his time.

Some 250 years later, silhouettes are still cheap to render on graphics hardware. The subject's silhouettes, as seen from the different camera viewpoints,

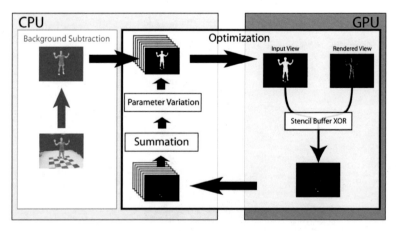

Figure 6.2.   Analysis-by-synthesis: to match the geometry model to the multi-video recordings, the reference images are segmented and binarized, and the model is rendered from all camera viewpoints. The boolean XOR operation is executed between the reference images and the corresponding model renderings. The number of remaining pixels serves as the matching score. Model parameter values are varied via numerical optimization until the matching score is minimal.

are used to match the model to the reference images: the model is rendered from all camera viewpoints, and the rendered images are thresholded to yield binary masks of the model's silhouettes. At the same time, the foreground in all video images is segmented and binarized; see Section 2.1.7. The rendered model silhouettes are then compared to the corresponding image silhouettes. The number of silhouette pixels that do not overlap when putting the rendered silhouette on top of the recorded silhouette is used as a comparison measure; see Figure 6.2. Conveniently, the logical exclusive-or (XOR) operation between the rendered image and the recorded image yields those silhouette pixels that are not overlapping. By summing up the non-overlapping pixels for all reference images, the matching score is obtained. A matching score of zero denotes an exact match. The matching score can be evaluated very efficiently on graphics hardware; see Figure 6.2: using the graphics card's stencil buffer, up to eight binary foreground masks from the segmented reference images can be XOR-ed with the corresponding model renderings simultaneously. The sum of set pixels that remain after the operation constitutes the matching score. On a GeForce3^{TM} graphics card, more than 100 matching function evaluations are performed per second.

To adapt model parameter values such that the matching score becomes minimal, a standard numerical non-linear optimization algorithm, such as Powell's method [244], runs on the CPU. For each new set of model parameter values, the optimization routine evokes the matching score evaluation routine on the graphics card.

One advantage of model-based analysis is the low-dimensional parameter space when compared to general reconstruction methods: the parameterized model provides only a few dozen degrees of freedom that need to be determined, which greatly reduces the number of potential local minima. Many high-level constraints are already implicitly incorporated into the model, such as kinematic capabilities. Additional constraints can be easily enforced by making sure that all parameter values stay within their anatomically plausible range during optimization. Finally, temporal coherence is straightforwardly maintained by allowing only some maximal rate of change in parameter value from one time step to the next.

Initialization. Prior to motion capture, the generic geometry model's proportions are adapted to the subject in front of the cameras in an initialization step. The model segments are appropriately parameterized: each segment can be scaled individually along the direction of its underlying bone structure. In addition, the surface of each segment is locally scalable via 16 Bézier curve parameters. This way, all segment surfaces can be deformed until they closely match the dancer's stature.

During model initialization, the actor stands still in a predefined pose for a brief moment to have his silhouettes recorded from all cameras. To adapt model proportions automatically to the individual's recorded silhouettes, the silhouette-matching routine is invoked. Segment parameters and joint parameters are optimized in tandem. First, only the torso is considered. Its position and orientation are determined approximately by maximizing the overlap of the rendered model images with the segmented image silhouettes. Then the pose of arms, legs, and head are recovered by rendering each limb in a number of orientations close to the initialization pose and selecting the best match as the starting point for refined optimization. After the model has been coarsely adapted, the uniform scaling parameters of all body segments are adjusted. The algorithm then alternates between optimizing joint parameters and segment scaling parameters until it has converged to the error function's minimum. Now that body pose and proportions have been established, the Bézier control parameters of all body segments are optimized in order to fine-tune each segment's outline to the recorded silhouettes.

Evidently, an exact match between model outline and image silhouettes cannot be attained because the parameterized model has far too few degrees of freedom. As a non-rigidly moving garment causes silhouette outlines to be inconsistent with the body model, it turns out that attempting to match the model exactly to the images is often not even desirable. On the contrary, by not being dependent on exact image silhouette information, model-based motion analysis is capable of robustly handling non-rigidly varying object surfaces. Still, high-quality rendering results can be achieved from non-exact geometry by devising suitable rendering techniques; see Section 6.1.4.

The initialization procedure takes only a few seconds, after which the segments' scaling parameter values and Bézier surface deformation values are known and kept fixed from then on. During motion capture, only the 35 joint parameters are optimized to capture the motion.

Model-Pose Analysis.   The human body is capable of a large range of complex motions. Given the relatively small set of 35 joint parameters, the model can only reproduce a subset of all possible body poses. Fortunately, modeling the 17 most important joints of human anatomy suffices to capture gross motor skills faithfully and to realistically reproduce even such expressive movements as jazz dancing. After initialization, the individualized geometry model is used to automatically track the motion of the human dancer by optimizing at each time frame all 35 joint parameter values.

The numerical optimization of the multidimensional, non-convex matching score functional can potentially converge in suboptimal fitting results. To efficiently avoid local minima in order to obtain reliable model-pose parameter val-

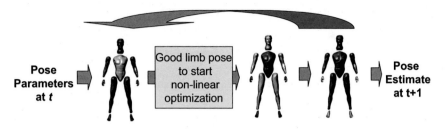

Figure 6.3. During motion-pose analysis, the body parts are matched to the reference images in hierarchical order: the torso first, then arms, legs and head, finally hands and feet. To avoid local minima, for some parameters the optimization is initialized with the result of a limited regular grid search.

ues, the model parameters are not all optimized simultaneously. Instead, model parameter estimation is performed in descending order with respect to the individual segments' impact on silhouette appearance as well as position along the model's kinematic chain; see Figure 6.3. First, position and orientation of the torso are varied to find its 3D location. Next, arms, legs, and head are considered. Finally, hands and feet are regarded.

To initialize the optimization search for each time frame, joint parameter values are predicted from their respective rates of change during previous time steps. To avoid local, suboptimal error minima, for some parameters a limited regular-grid search precedes parameter optimization. During regular-grid search, the matching score is evaluated for a small number of candidate parameter values in the vicinity of the predicted parameter value. The optimization routine is then initialized with the parameter value that resulted in the smallest matching score. This grid-search initialization procedure accelerates convergence and effectively avoids local minima.

A high-level constraint that must be enforced explicitly is the avoidance of inter-penetrations of any two body segments. For example, the hand segments are not allowed to penetrate into the torso segment. This is ensured by testing the segments' bounding boxes during grid search. This way, parameter values always correspond to plausible, non-inter-penetrating body model poses.

Results.   By matching model silhouettes to the segmented reference images, the model faithfully follows even complex movements of the dancer; see Figure 6.4. In contrast to many commercial optical motion tracking systems, the person does not have to wear any markers or specialized hardware, nor is scene content or illumination altered in any way. This is a necessary precondition for model-based VBR since only if motion is captured completely passively can the multi-video imagery be used for photorealistic rendering.

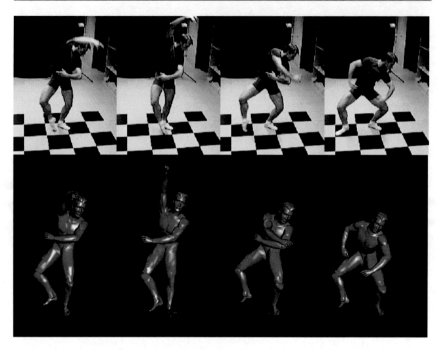

Figure 6.4. Model-based VBR is capable of automatically capturing the complex motion of a jazz dance performance using eight reference images per time frame. *(Reprinted from [38], © 2003 ACM.)*

Silhouette-based pose estimation is robust against glossy highlights and specular reflections on the object's surface as well as local image segmentation errors. The described model-based motion analysis approach is an iterative algorithm that converges towards the best set of joint parameter values. By running Powell optimization on a 1.8 GHz PC and using a GeForce3^{TM} graphics card to evaluate the matching score, human pose analysis takes between 8 and 14 seconds per time frame. To accelerate matching performance, the algorithm can be parallelized such that several computers with graphics cards work simultaneously, each estimating a different set of joint parameter values [290].

6.1.2 Distributed Implementation

Because the root node of the human body's kinematic chain branches into five separate body parts, the pose parameters of all four extremities and the head can be determined independently once torso position and orientation have been established; see Figure 6.5(a). This way, five PCs with graphics cards can work in

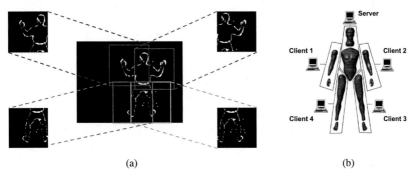

(a)   (b)

Figure 6.5. Distributed model-based motion analysis: after torso position and orientation have been determined, each extremity is evaluated on a separate PC with a graphics card. *((b) Reprinted from [290].)*

parallel on analyzing body pose; see Section 2.1.4. After the server PC has determined the six degrees of freedom of torso position and orientation, each of the four client PCs and the server optimize separately one arm, leg, and the head; see Figure 6.5(b). The reference images are clipped around each body part's approximate position and transferred via the network from the server to the corresponding client. To reduce the influence of other body parts during separate body limb optimization, the client PC renders the entire geometry model once *without* the body segment under scrutiny. This "amputated" silhouette is used as a mask to identify all pixels that are to be ignored. While the masking operation cannot eliminate all silhouette pixels belonging to other body parts, it still efficiently reduces the number of pixels that are not involved in the optimization of the considered limb. This increases the influence of those pixels that do belong to the body part whose pose is being optimized by the client PC. During optimization, only the body segment under scrutiny needs to be rendered, and it is compared only to the non-masked image silhouette pixels. This also reduces the number of rendered geometry triangles and boosts performance. Parallel model-based analysis using five 1.8 GHz PCs reduces the time it takes to estimate full body pose to less than two seconds per frame.

6.1.3   Texture-Based Pose Re nement

So far, only silhouette information has been exploited to match the geometry model to the reference images. While silhouette-based analysis robustly captures large-scale movements, some body part poses may not be unambiguously recoverable from object silhouettes alone. Silhouettes of cylindrically symmetric body parts, especially, are invariant under rotation about the respective axis of symmetry. Small protruding features that break the symmetry, such as the nose or ears for the head, may not be discernible in the silhouettes due to limited image resolution.

In addition to silhouette information, the object's surface texture can be drawn on to resolve ambiguities as well as to fine-tune the silhouette-estimated model pose [289]. Object texture information allows one to reconstruct the *3D motion field* of time-varying surfaces; see Section 5.1. Ideally, ground-truth object texture is available as part of the a priori model description. Unfortunately, a priori object texture may be hard to acquire. Instead, the difference between the reference images of the current time frame and predicted object appearance based on the previous time frame is used to construct a *correction-vector field* of the model. For each model surface point, the 3D correction vector represents the displacement between the silhouette-based reconstruction and its texture-derived 3D position. In hierarchical order, each rigid-body segment is then updated according to the correction vectors of its vertices to arrive at improved pose parameter values.

Correction-Vector Field Estimation. After silhouette-based pose estimation for the time frame $t+1$ (Section 6.1.1), the model is rendered for all camera views using the reference image of time frame t as texture; see Section 6.1.4. Next, the optical flow between the predicted images and the reference images for time frame $t+1$ is computed [182]. From all camera viewpoints i, the 2D optical-flow field $\mathbf{u}_i = (u_i, v_i)$ is projected onto the silhouette-estimated 3D model surface; see Figure 6.6. For each model vertex, a 3D correction vector $\mathbf{x}$ is reconstructed via

$$\mathbf{u}_i = J_i \frac{d\mathbf{x}}{dt}, \tag{6.1}$$

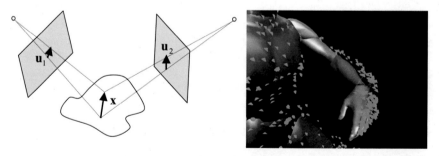

Figure 6.6. Texture-based pose refinement: the 3D correction-vector field on the object surface is reconstructed from the optical flow between the rendered model and the video images. By projecting the 2D optical-flow vectors $\vec{u}_i$ onto the silhouette-derived model surface, each model vertex is assigned a 3D correction vector $\vec{x}$ towards its texture-consistent position.

where $J_i = \partial \mathbf{u}_i / \partial(x, y, z)$ is the Jacobian matrix that has been derived from the camera calibration parameters; see Section 5.1. For a model surface point $\mathbf{x} = (x, y, z)$ that is visible in n reference images, Equation (6.1) reads

$$
\begin{bmatrix}
\frac{\partial u_1}{\partial x} & \frac{\partial u_1}{\partial y} & \frac{\partial u_1}{\partial z} \\
\frac{\partial v_1}{\partial x} & \frac{\partial v_1}{\partial y} & \frac{\partial v_1}{\partial z} \\
 & \cdot & \\
 & \cdot & \\
\frac{\partial u_n}{\partial x} & \frac{\partial u_n}{\partial y} & \frac{\partial u_n}{\partial z} \\
\frac{\partial v_n}{\partial x} & \frac{\partial v_n}{\partial y} & \frac{\partial v_n}{\partial z}
\end{bmatrix}
\cdot
\begin{bmatrix}
\frac{dx}{dt} \\
\frac{dy}{dt} \\
\frac{dz}{dt}
\end{bmatrix}
=
\begin{bmatrix}
u_1 \\
v_1 \\
\cdot \\
\cdot \\
u_n \\
v_n.
\end{bmatrix}
. \tag{6.2}
$$

For $n > 2$, the linear system of equations is over-determined and can be solved for dx/dt using singular-value decomposition [244].

In summary, estimating the correction vector field proceeds as follows.

- Model pose P^{t+1} for time frame $t + 1$ is estimated using the silhouette-based analysis-by-synthesis technique described in Section 6.1.1.

- For each camera perspective k, the geometry model P^{t+1} is rendered (see Section 6.1) using as texture the images I_k^t from the previous time step t. This way, the prediction images $\hat{I}_k^{t+1}$ are obtained.

- The optical flow between each predicted image $\hat{I}_k^{t+1}$ and the corresponding recorded reference image I_k^{t+1} is determined.

- The visibility of each vertex in all reference images is established.

- For each vertex that is visible in at least three cameras, its 3D correction vector is computed; see Equation (6.1). If the vertex is already in the correct position, its correction vector is zero. The correction vector points towards the point to where the vertex should be moved to achieve texture consistency; see Figure 6.6.

It should be noted that optical-flow reconstruction presumes that object reflectance characteristics are by and large Lambertian. In surface regions showing specular highlights, the reconstructed correction-vector field is not reliable. To also apply texture-based pose refinement to surfaces exhibiting specular reflectance, such regions must be detected and excluded during pose-update computation.

Model-Parameter Refinement. The correction vector is added to the 3D coordinates of each vertex to obtain texture-corrected vertex positions in global coordinates. From the corrected 3D coordinates of all vertices of a body segment, the differential pose update for that rigid-body segment is calculated. The solution

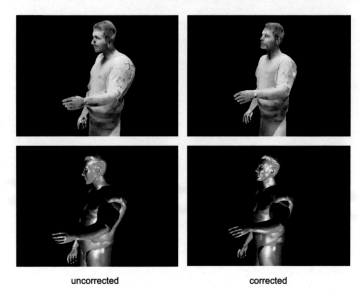

uncorrected   corrected

Figure 6.7. Texture-based pose refinement is able to refine head orientation such that facial details from different reference images match up on the model surface.

to this registration problem between model pose and the vertices' goal coordinates can be formulated in closed form using quaternion notation [120]. Again, the model is hierarchically updated: based on the respective vertices' correction vectors, torso position and orientation are refined first, followed by upper arms, thighs, neck and head, before lower arms and legs as well as hands and feet are corrected. By expressing vertex positions in the global coordinate frame, sequentially updating separate body parts does not alter goal coordinates.

Results. Because projective texturing is used for free-viewpoint video rendering (see Section 6.1.4), inaccuracies in body pose become visible only when the textured model is rendered from an intermediate viewpoint between camera positions. Figure 6.7 depicts the difference between purely silhouette-based motion capture and texture-based pose refinement. By making use of texture information, head pose is corrected so that texture details are projected onto the corresponding geometric details.

6.1.4   Rendering

After model-based analysis, a high-quality 3D geometry model is available that closely, but not exactly, matches the dynamic object in the scene. The model is photo-realistically rendered using the reference images as texture. By making efficient use of multi-video footage, time-varying cloth folds and creases, shadows, and facial expressions can be faithfully reproduced to lend a very natural, dynamic appearance to the rendered object.

Projective texturing on graphics hardware is used to apply the reference images as texture to the triangle-mesh model; see Section 2.4.2. To achieve optimal rendering quality, however, it is necessary to process the video textures offline prior to real-time rendering. Local visibility must be considered correctly to avoid any rendering artifacts due to the inevitable small differences between model geometry and the true 3D object surface. The reference images, which are taken from different viewpoints, must also be blended appropriately to achieve the impression of one consistent object surface texture.

Visibility. Per-vertex visibility v_i from each camera viewpoint i is easily determined by rendering the model and comparing the resulting depth map against the computed vertex depth. However, using this visibility information to determine which reference view to use to texture a triangle leads to rendering artifacts; see Figure 6.8(a). Because model geometry is not exact, the reference image silhouettes do not correspond exactly to rendered model silhouettes. When projecting the reference images onto the model, texture belonging to some frontal body segment potentially leaks onto other segments farther back. To avoid such artifacts, each reference view's *penumbral region* is excluded from texturing. To determine the penumbral region of a camera, vertices of zero visibility are determined not only from the camera's actual position, but also from a few slightly displaced vir-

(a) (b)

Figure 6.8. Penumbral region determination: (a) small differences between object silhouette and model outline can cause the texture of frontal model segments to leak onto segments farther back. (b) By also projecting each reference image onto the model from slightly displaced camera positions, regions of dubious visibility are determined. These are excluded from texturing by the respective reference image. *((a) Reprinted from [38], © 2003 ACM.)*

tual camera positions; see Figure 6.8(b). For each reference view, each vertex is checked to see whether it is visible from all camera positions, actual as well as virtual. A triangle is projectively textured with a reference image only if all of its three vertices are completely visible from that camera, $\nu_i = 1$.

While silhouettes that are too large do not affect rendering quality, outlines that are too small can give rise to untextured model regions. To counter such rendering artifacts, all image silhouettes are expanded by a couple of pixels prior to rendering. Using a morphological filter operation, the object outlines of all reference images are dilated, copying silhouette boundary pixel color values to adjacent background pixel positions.

Reference-Image Blending. Most surface areas of the model are seen from more than one camera. If the model geometry corresponded exactly to that of the recorded object, all camera views could be weighted according to their proximity to the desired viewing direction and blended without loss of detail. However, model geometry has been adapted to the recorded person by optimizing only a comparatively small number of free parameters. The model is also composed of rigid-body elements, which is clearly an approximation whose validity varies, e.g., with the person's apparel. In summary, the available model surface can be expected to locally deviate from true object geometry. Accordingly, projectively texturing the model by simply blending multiple reference images causes blurred rendering results, and model texture varies discontinuously when the viewpoint is moving. If surface reflectance is approximately Lambertian, so that view-dependent reflection effects do not play a significant role, high-quality rendering results can still be obtained by taking into account triangle orientation with respect to camera direction; see Plate XV. For each model triangle, θ_i denotes the positive-valued angle between the triangle normal and the optical axis of camera i. By emphasizing for each triangle individually the camera view with the smallest angle θ_i, i.e., the camera that views the triangle most head-on, a detail-preserving texture is obtained. For each triangle, one viable weight assignment among all visible reference images i is, for example,

$$\omega_i \;=\; \frac{1}{(1 + \max_j(\frac{1}{\theta_j+\epsilon}) - \frac{1}{\theta_i+\epsilon})^\alpha} \;. \tag{6.3}$$

Singularities are avoided by adding a small, non-negative ϵ to the denominators. The parameter α determines the influence of triangle orientation with respect to camera viewing direction and the impact of the most head-on camera view per triangle. Prior to rendering, the weights ω_i still need to be normalized to sum up to unity.

Interactive Display. Having determined vertex visibility ν_i as well as per-triangle reference image weights ω_i for each time frame, the animated model is ready to be interactively rendered. Prior to model-based VBR, the model segment's triangle meshes as well as the reference views' projection matrices are transferred to graphics memory. During rendering, model parameter values, reference images I_i, vertex visibility $\nu_i = \{0, 1\}$, and triangle blending coefficients ω_i are updated per time frame on the graphics card. For each vertex, view-dependent texture weights ρ_i are determined, taking into account the angle ϕ_i between target view and reference view i,

$$\rho_i = \frac{1}{\phi_i + \epsilon},$$

and the view-dependent texture weights ρ_i are normalized over all visible reference views. Pixel color $c(j)$ is then determined by blending all reference images I_i according to

$$c(j) = \sum_i \nu_i(j) \cdot \omega_i(j) \cdot \rho(j) \cdot I_i(j). \tag{6.4}$$

The product $\nu_i(j)\omega_i(j)$ is normalized during texture preprocessing to ensure energy conservation. In practice, the rasterization engine interpolates the product of blending weights per triangle vertex.

6.1.5 Results

Model-based VBR analysis is an iterative algorithm that converges towards the best set of joint parameter values. At 320×240-pixel resolution, the matching score between eight rendered and recorded images can be evaluated at 100 times per second on an NVIDIA GeForce3™. Employing Powell optimization on a single 1.8 GHz Pentium IV Xeon PC, human pose analysis takes between 8 and 14 seconds per time step. Parallel model-based analysis on five PCs reduces that time to less than two seconds per frame. Texture-based refinement takes substantially longer, depending on the optical-flow reconstruction algorithm used. From eight 320×240-pixel images, pose refinement takes approximately 50 seconds. On a conventional PC equipped with an NVIDIA GeForce4™ graphics card, the animated dancer is rendered at 30 fps. Views from arbitrary perspectives are possible, as well as freeze-and-rotate shots, fly-around sequences, close-ups, slow motion, fast forward, or reverse play; see Figure 6.9.

Figure 6.9. Free-viewpoint video rendering: the user can move freely around the dynamic object. A conventional NVIDIA GeForce3^{TM} graphics card achieves continuous rendering rates of 30 frames per second.

6.1.6   Summary

Free-viewpoint video enables one to watch dynamic, real-world objects from arbitrary perspectives in photorealistic quality. While achievable rendering quality is excellent, model-based VBR inherently exhibits two undesired limitations: a suitable parameterized geometry model must be available, and view-dependent reflectance effects cannot be faithfully reproduced without degrading rendering quality. To overcome the former limitation, a parameterized 3D geometry model must be reconstructed from the multi-video sequence, and the underlying kinematic structure must be inferred from the dynamic geometry [55]. To enable view-dependent rendering, the 3D model geometry must be locally refined to account for differences between model and actual 3D surface position and orientation. The texture-derived 3D correction vector field may assist in estimating refinement maps of model geometry. Finally, average object texture, reconstructed globally from all reference images, may be applied to object regions temporarily not visible from any camera.

The analysis-by-synthesis strategy employed to match the model to the input multi-video data solves a traditional computer vision problem by computer graphics means. From a computer graphics point of view, instead of synthesizing a novel view given model parameter values, the inverse problem is solved: determining model parameter values such that the model's rendition is maximally similar to the images. This approach becomes feasible and turns out to be robust and versatile because of the large number of silhouette pixels and texture correspondences that over-constrain the much lower-dimensional model parameter space.

Chapter 7

Outlook

Video-based rendering has only recently become possible due to technological advances and mass-market pricing of video imaging devices and graphics hardware. With these trends almost certain to continue, multi-video acquisition will become easier and cheaper, while rendering performance can be expected to improve further. New research and a variety of novel application scenarios may hatch from video-based rendering in the coming years.

Real-Time 2D Range Sensors. VBR research receives additional stimulus from the advent of reliable, passive video-rate depth cameras [130, 281]. By combining non-intrusive 2D range sensors with conventional color video cameras, true scene geometry will be available in real time along with multi-video footage. The ability to acquire the 3D shape of dynamic objects in real time will also accelerate the development of commercial 3D TV broadcast applications.

Compression. Currently, the amount of VBR raw multi-video data is prohibitively large for convenient distribution. Neither today's standard storage media (CD, DVD) nor online distribution channels (Internet, cable network) provide sufficient capacity or bandwidth. For commercial products, suitable VBR data compression techniques are in dire need. Fortunately, multi-video recordings are highly redundant, and suitable coding schemes for VBR data are already being investigated [343, 344].

Volumetric Phenomena. All VBR methods described in this book are based on the assumption that the dynamic scene consists of opaque object surfaces. Fire, smoke, and running water are examples of dynamic natural phenomena that require alternative representations for video-based rendering. While the first VBR

methods for non-tangible phenomena are being explored [110, 124], adequate
models, temporal coherence, and editing techniques remain to be investigated.

Video-Based Modeling.   To display dynamic scenes from arbitrary perspectives, it is sufficient to recover time-varying scene geometry. Algorithms towards
this goal have been presented in this book. To incorporate a VBR object into
surroundings different from the recording environment, however, scene illumination and local surface reflectance characteristics must also be known. While both
illumination and reflectance can, in theory, be measured offline, reflectance characteristics may be recovered more conveniently from multi-video data directly.
Video-based modeling algorithms have the advantage that any surface point is
generally recorded for many different normal orientations. By considering dynamic geometry and static reflectance characteristics collectively, more accurate,
robust, and versatile BRDF reconstruction algorithms are conceivable.

Example-Based Modeling.   Video-based rendering provides digital models of
recorded real-world events. By suitable (model-driven) abstraction based on a
number of digitized samples of the same or similar events, realistic visualizations
may be interpolated from the recorded instances [19]. The goal in example-based
VBR modeling will be to enable the manipulation of real-world recorded scenes
with a degree of flexibility akin to that of virtual scene descriptions. A recorded
real-world event could then be edited while preserving its visual realism. This
would put animators in a position to edit VBR content to create new, realistically animated and visually authentic content without having to record the desired
event.

Reality-Augmented Virtual Worlds.   Virtual reality applications such as training simulators for aviation, military, or medical training benefit directly from the
ability of VBR technology to import visual realism into virtual environments.

Besides conveying objective information, visual impressions also have a sub-
conscious, emotional-level effect. The merits of virtual reality technology for
treating specific phobias and psychological conditions following traumatic expe-
riences are just starting to be explored [117]. Video-based rendering techniques
may prove to be of valuable help in psychotherapy

Psychophysical Research.   The ultimate benchmark for any VBR algorithm
is the degree of visual realism it is able to create. So far, much is still unknown
about what makes images and video sequences appear realistic. VBR may assist
psychovisual research in developing a theoretical understanding of and quantitative measures for visual realism.

Video-based rendering has the potential to tear down the walls between the virtual world of computer games and training simulators, and the real world as depicted on TV and in movies. Its contributions go both ways: VBR enables the importing of visual realism of natural events into virtual worlds, while future VBR research may allow the editing of real scenes with the same ease and flexibility as virtual environments.

As with any new technological capability, the beneficial prospects of video-based rendering are accompanied by the potential risk of misuse. By offering new, unprecedented ways to work with and manipulate visual information, the advent of VBR suggests that we won't be able to unconditionally trust the content of images and video material anymore. On the other hand, this may also be considered a desirable side effect of video-based rendering.

Appendix A

De nition of Terms

Throughout VBR literature, different technical terms are used to refer to the same things; see Figure A.1. Multiple *video streams* represent the input data to all video-based rendering algorithms. These video streams are recorded simultaneously by several *acquisition/recording cameras* placed around the dynamic scene. A single image recorded by one camera is referred to as a *light-field image, source image, input image,* or *reference image.* Typically, position, orientation, and internal imaging characteristics of the acquisition cameras have been determined beforehand, so the recorded footage consists of *calibrated image data.* The acquisition cameras are synchronized, so a *time frame* corresponds to all images recorded at the same time instant. The rendered new image is the *output image, desired view,* or *target view.* A *viewing ray* is the ray from the viewpoint's center of projection through one pixel of the output image into the 3D scene. Finally, *object space* or *scene space* refers to the 3D space of the recorded scene, as opposed to the 2D *image space.*

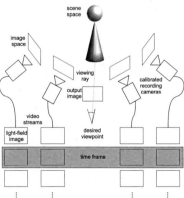

Figure A.1. Definition of frequently used terms in this book.

Appendix B

Algorithm Overview

What follows are brief characterizations of the VBR algorithms covered in this book. The summaries are intended to aid in quickly deciding whether one technique or another is suitable for a given application scenario. Table B.1 compares different VBR approaches with respect to a number of performance features.

Additional information on all VBR approaches, links to project pages, demo videos, and downloads can be found at http://www.video-based-rendering.org. This site is frequently updated to reflect the latest advances in VBR research.

Dynamic Light Fields

All VBR approaches discussed in Chapter 3 require as input synchronized multi-video footage that is captured by many closely-spaced video cameras, i.e., in a small-baseline acquisition set-up.

3D TV

The video streams are processed online by a bank of PCs. After transmission, another bank of PCs at the receiving end drives an autostereoscopic screen for real-time display. Several users can simultaneously observe the recorded scene live and in 3D from arbitrary viewpoints.

Dynamic Light-Field Warping

Prior to rendering, the recorded multi-video data is processed offline to segment the foreground and to estimate dense depth maps. Images of the static background are used to enhance depth-estimation robustness as well as to enhance rendering quality. Novel views are rendered at an interactive frame rate on graphics hardware by warping and blending up to four images from the cameras closest to the desired viewpoint. The viewpoint is restricted to lie on the recording hull, i.e., the polyhedron spanned by reference camera positions.

Generalized Lumigraphs

Dense depth maps are estimated online. The video cameras are arranged in a hybrid set-up: every two cameras form a small-baseline pair for depth-from-stereo estimation, while individual camera pairs are spaced farther apart to cover a larger viewing angle on the scene. In contrast to dynamic light-field warping, views can also be rendered for viewpoints outside the recording hull.

Visual and Photo-Hull Rendering

Chapter 4 presents VBR techniques that are capable of processing wide-baseline–captured multi-video footage on the fly for live display applications. All algorithms require a distributed processing system of networked PCs.

Volumetric Visual Hulls

The visual hull is reconstructed as a voxel model. Billboard rendering facilitates rendering directly from the volume model while reproducing view-dependent effects. Voxel visibility must be determined.

Polyhedral Visual Hulls

Object silhouettes are approximated as polygons and projected into scene space to form visual cones. The intersection of the visual cones is determined as a polygonal mesh. For artifact-free rendering, the polygon mesh is projectively textured in two passes.

Improved object geometry is obtained in joint stereo and visual-hull reconstruction. The visual hull is used to limit the search range during depth-map estimation to accelerate performance and to avoid mismatches.

Image-Based Visual Hulls

The visual hull is rendered directly in the image space of the target view, avoiding explicit geometry reconstruction as well as reference image resampling. Image-based visual-hull rendering does not require graphics hardware acceleration.

Visual-Hull Rendering on Graphics Hardware

Projective texturing and CSG-based rendering on graphics hardware are combined to form a hybrid visual-hull rendering method that overcomes the limitations of either individual approach. The visual hull is reconstructed implicitly during target view rendering. Real-time rendering quality is comparable to offline visual hull rendering in software.

Photo-Hull Rendering on Graphics Hardware

Besides silhouette information, use is made of object texture to reconstruct more accurate geometry. Photo-consistency is checked per fragment, taking visibility into account. Photo-hull information is gathered implicitly during rendering. The algorithm runs entirely on the GPU.

Utilizing Temporal Coherence

Chapter 5 presents two advanced video-based reconstruction and rendering approaches for wide-baseline imagery. Both methods make use of the continuous nature of motion.

Spatiotemporal View Interpolation

The volumetric photo hull is reconstructed per time frame. For each surface voxel, corresponding voxels are found in the preceding and the following time frame. The dense correspondence field is used to continuously interpolate between time frames.

Spacetime-Coherent Reconstruction

Based on variational calculus, object geometry is reconstructed as a weighted minimal surface in space and time. Photo-consistency and continuous surface evolution are taken into account. Due to its global reconstruction characteristic, intermittently invisible object regions are automatically and plausibly interpolated.

Model-Based Analysis and Synthesis

A priori knowledge about scene content is exploited to constrain motion capture and to achieve high-quality rendering results. A suitably parameterized geometry model of what is being recorded must be available.

	3D TV	Dynamic Light Field Warping	Generalized Lumigraph	Volume-based VH	Polygon-based VH	Image-based VH	VH on Graphics Hardware	Photo Hull on GPU	Spatiotemporal View Interpolation	Spacetime Coherence	Free-Viewpoint Video
Section	3.1	3.2	3.3	4.1	4.2	4.3	4.4	4.5	5.1	5.2	6.1
live processing	X		X	X	X	X	X	X			
explicit geometry		X	X	X	X				X	X	X
wide-baseline acquisition				X	X	X	X	X	X	X	X
specular surfaces	X			X	X	X	X				X
photo consistency		X	X					X	X	X	X
reference implementation	[207]	[103]	[259]	[99]	[209]	[208]	[173]	[174]	[306]	[101]	[38]
additional references		[345]	[328] [318]					[330]			

Table B.1. VBR algorithm classification.

Free-Viewpoint Video

The geometry model of a human is used to automatically track the motion of a person. Object silhouettes are used to match the model to the images. For authentic rendering, the animated model is projectively video-textured using the camera images.

Bibliography

[1] E. H. Adelson and J. R. Bergen. "The Plenoptic Function and the Elements of Early Vision." In *Computational Models of Visual Processing*, edited by M. Landy and J. A. Movshon, pp. 3–20. Cambridge, MA: MIT Press, 1991.

[2] A. Agarwala, M. Dontcheva, M. Agrawala, S. Drucker, A. Colburn, B. Curless, D. Salesin, and M. Cohen. "Interactive Digital Photomontage." *ACM Transactions on Graphics (Proc. SIGGRAPH'04)* 23: 3 (2004), 294–302.

[3] L. Ahrenberg, I. Ihrke, and M. Magnor. "A Mobile System for Multi-Video Recording." In *Proc. IEE Conference on Visual Media Production (CVMP'04)*, pp. 127–132. London: IEE, 2004.

[4] B. Allen, B. Curless, and Z. Popovic. "Articulated Body Deformations from Range Scan Data." *ACM Transactions on Graphics (Proc. SIGGRAPH '02)* 21:3 (2002), 612–619.

[5] H.W. Alt. *Analysis III*. Available from World Wide Web (http://www.iam.uni-bonn. de/~alt/ws2001/analysis3.html), 2002.

[6] L. Alvarez, R. Deriche, J. Sánchez, and J. Weickert. "Dense Disparity Map Estimation Respecting Image Discontinuities: A PDE and Scale-Space Based Approach." Technical Report RR-3874, INRIA, 2000.

[7] OpenGL ARB. *ARB_fragment_program OpenGL Extension*. Available from World Wide Web (http://oss.sgi.com/projects/ogl-sample/registry/ARB/fragment_ program.txt).

[8] OpenGL ARB. *ARB_vertex_program OpenGL Extension*. Available from World Wide Web (http://oss.sgi.com/projects/ogl-sample/registry/ARB/vertex_program. txt).

[9] N. Atzpadin, P. Kauff, and O. Schreer. "Stereo Analysis by Hybrid Recursive Matching for Real-Time Immersive Video Conferencing." *IEEE Trans. Circuits and Systems for Video Technology, Special Issue on Immersive Telecommunications* 14:3 (2004), 321–334.

[10] H. Aydinoglu and M. Hayes. "Performance Analysis of Stereo Coding Algorithms." In *Proc. IEEE International Conference on Acoustics, Speech, and Signal*

Processing (ICASSP'96), Atlanta, USA, Vol. 4, pp. 2191–2194.Los Alamitos, CA: IEEE Press, 1996.

[11] A. Azarbayejani and A. Pentland. "Camera Self-Calibration from One Point Correspondence." Technical Report 341, MIT Media Lab, 1995.

[12] J. Barron, D. Fleet, and S. Beauchemin. "Performance of Optical Flow Techniques." *International Journal of Computer Vision* 12:1 (1994), 43–77.

[13] B. Baumgart. "Geometric Modeling for Computer Vision." PhD diss., Stanford University, 1974.

[14] B. Bayer. "Color Imaging Array." US Patent 3,971,065, 1976.

[15] Phillipe Bekaert. *Boundary Representation Library (now: GNU Triangle Surface (GTS) Library).* Available from World Wide Web (http://breplibrary.sourceforge. net/, now: http://gts.sourceforge.net/).

[16] R. Bellmann. *Adaptive Control Processes: A Guided Tour.* Princeton, NJ: Princeton University Press, 1961.

[17] M. Bichsel. "Segmenting Simply Connected Moving Objects in a Static Scene." *IEEE Trans. Pattern Analysis and Machine Intelligence* 16:11 (1994), 1138–1142.

[18] S. Birchfield and C. Tomasi. "Multiway Cut for Stereo and Motion with Slanted Surfaces." In *Proc. International Conference on Computer Vision (ICCV'99),* pp. 489–495. Los Alamitos, CA: IEEE Press, 1999.

[19] V. Blanz and T. Vetter. "A Morphable Model for the Synthesis of 3D Faces." In *Proceedings of SIGGRAPH 99, Computer Graphics Proceedings, Annual Conference Series,* edited by Alyn Rockwood, pp. 187–194. Reading, MA: Addison-Wesley Longman, 1999.

[20] J. Blinn and M. Newell. "Texture and Reflection in Computer Generated Images." *Communications of the ACM* 19:10 (1976), 542–547.

[21] S. Boivin and A. Gagalowicz. "Image-Based Rendering of Diffuse, Specular and Glossy Surfaces from a Single Image." In *Proceedings of SIGGRAPH 2001, Computer Graphics Proceedings, Annual Conference Series,* edited by E. Fiume, pp. 107–116. Reading, MA: Addison-Wesley, 2001.

[22] J. De Bonet and P. Viola. "Roxels:Responsibility Weighted 3D Volume Reconstruction." In *Proc. International Conference on Computer Vision (ICCV'99),* pp. 418–425. Los Alamitos, CA: IEEE Press, 1999.

[23] G. Borgefors. "Distance Transformations in Digital Images." *Computer Vision, Graphics, and Image Processing* 34:3 (1986), 344–371.

[24] E. Borovikov and L. Davis. "A Distributed System for Real-Time Volume Reconstruction." In *Proceedings of Intl. Workshop on Computer Architectures for Machine Perception 2000,* pp. 183–189. Los Alamitos, CA: IEEE Press, 2000.

[25] A. Bottino and A. Laurentini. "A Silhouette Based Technique for the Reconstruction of Human Movement." *Journal of Computer Vision and Image Understanding* 83 (2001), 79–95.

[26] J.-Y. Bouguet. *Camera Calibration Toolbx for Matlab.* Available from World Wide Web (http://www.vision.caltech.edu/bouguetj/calib_doc/), 2004.

[27] Y. Boykov, O. Veksler, and R. Zabih. "Markov Random Fields with Efficient Approximations." In *Proc. IEEE Computer Vision and Pattern Recognition (CVPR'98)*, pp. 648–655. Los Alamitos, CA: IEEE Press, 1998

[28] Y. Boykov, O. Veksler, and R. Zabih. "Fast Approximate Energy Minimization via Graph Cuts." *IEEE Trans. Pattern Analysis and Machine Intelligence* 23:11 (2001), 1222–1239.

[29] C. Bregler and J. Malik. "Tracking People with Twists and Exponential Maps." In *Proc. IEEE Computer Vision and Pattern Recognition (CVPR'98)*, pp. 8–15. Los Alamitos, CA: IEEE Press, 1998.

[30] L. Brunie, S. Lavallée, and R. Szeliski. "Using Force Fields Derived from 3D Distance Maps for Inferring the Attitude of a 3D Rigid Object." In *Proc. European Conference on Computer Vision (ECCV'92)*, pp. 670–675. Berlin: Springer-Verlag, 1992.

[31] C. Buehler, M. Bosse, L. McMillan, S. Gortler, and M. Cohen. "Unstructured Lumigraph Rendering." In *Proceedings of SIGGRAPH 2000, Computer Graphics Proceedings, Annual Conference Series*, edited by E. Fiume, pp. 425–432. Reading, MA: Addison-Wesley, 2001.

[32] C. Buehler. "Rendering from Unstructured Collections of Images." PhD diss., Massachusetts Institute of Technology, 2002.

[33] E. Camahort and D. Fussell. "A Geometric Study of Light Field Representations." Technical report, University of Texas at Austin, Dept. of Computer Sciences, 2000.

[34] E. Camahort, A. Lerios, and D. Fussell. "Uniformly Sampled Light Fields." In *Proc. Eurographics Rendering Workshop (EGRW'97)*, pp. 117–130. Berlin: Springer-Verlag, 1997.

[35] S. Campagna and H.-P. Seidel. "Parameterizing Meshes with Arbitrary Topology." In *Proc. IEEE Workshop on Image and Multidimensional Digital Signal Processing (IMDSP'98)*, Alpbach, Austria, pp. 287–290.Los Alamitos, CA: IEEE Press.

[36] R. Carceroni and K. Kutulakos. "Multi-View Scene Capture by Surfel Sampling: From Video Streams to Non-Rigid 3D Motion, Shape, and Reflectance." In *Proc. International Conference on Computer Vision (ICCV'01)*, pp. 60–67. Los Alamitos, CA: IEEE Press, 2001.

[37] J. Carmack. *Zfail Stenciled Shadow Volume Rendering*. Available from World Wide Web (http://developer.nvidia.com/object/robust_shadow_volumes.html), 2000.

[38] J. Carranza, C. Theobalt, M Magnor, and H.-P. Seidel. "Free-Viewpoint Video of Human Actors." *Proc. SIGGRAPH '03, Transactions on Graphics* 22:3 (2003), 569–577.

[39] V. Caselles, R. Kimmel, G. Sapiro, and C. Sbert. "Three Dimensional Object Modeling via Minimal Surfaces." In *Proc. European Conference on Computer Vision (ECCV'96)*, pp. 97–106. Berlin: Springer-Verlag, 1996.

[40] E. Catmull. "A Subdivision Algorithm for Computer Display of Curved Surfaces." PhD diss., University of Utah, 1974.

[41] J.-X. Chai, X. Tong, S.-C. Chan, and H.-Y. Shum. "Plenoptic Sampling." In *Proceedings of SIGGRAPH '00, Computer Graphics Proceedings, Annual Conference Series*, edited by K. Akeley, pp. 307–318. Reading, MA: Addison-Wesley, 2000.

[42] S. Chen and L. Williams. "View Interpolation for Image Synthesis." In *Proceedings of SIGGRAPH 93, Computer Graphics Proceedings, Annual Conference Series*, edited by James T. Kajiya, pp. 279–288. New York: ACM Press, 1993.

[43] Y.G. Chen, Y. Giga, and S. Goto. "Uniqueness and Existence of Viscosity Solutions of Generalized Mean Curvature Flow." *Journal of Differential Geometry* 33 (1991), 749–786.

[44] X. Chen, J. Davis, and P. Slusallek. "Wide Area Camera Calibration Using Virtual Calibration Objects." In *Proc. IEEE Computer Vision and Pattern Recognition (CVPR'00)*, pp. 520–527. Los Alamitos, CA: IEEE Press, 2000.

[45] S. E. Chen. "Quicktime VR—An Image-Based Approach to Virtual Environment Navigation." In *Proceedings of SIGGRAPH 95, Computer Graphics Proceedings, Annual Conference Series*, edited by Robert Cook, pp. 29–38. Reading, MA: Addison-Wesley, 1995.

[46] K. Cheung, T. Kanade, J.-Y. Bouguet, and M. Holler. "A Real Time System for Robust 3D Voxel Reconstruction of Human Motions." In *Proc. IEEE Computer Vision and Pattern Recognition (CVPR'00)*, pp. 714–720. Los Alamitos, CA: IEEE Press, 2000.

[47] K. Cheung, S. Baker, and T. Kanade. "Visual Hull Alignment and Refinement Across Time: A 3D Reconstruction Algorithm Combining Shape-From-Silhouette with Stereo." In *Proc. IEEE Computer Vision and Pattern Recognition (CVPR'03)*, Volume 2, pp. 375–382. Los Alamitos, CA: IEEE Press, 2003.

[48] D. Chop. "Computing Minimal Surfaces via Level Set Curvature Flow." *Journal of Computational Physics* 106 (1993), 77–91.

[49] Y.-Y. Chuang, A. Agarwala, B. Curless, D. Salesin, and R. Szeliski. "Video Matting of Complex Scenes." *Proc. SIGGRAPH '02, Transactions on Graphics* 21:3 (2002), 243–248.

[50] J.N. Clelland. *MSRI Workshop on Lie Groups and the Method of Moving Frames.* Available from World Wide Web (http://spot.Colorado.EDU/~jnc/MSRI.html), 1999.

[51] D. Cohen-Or, Y. Mann, and S. Fleishman. "Deep Compression for Streaming Texture Intensive Animations." In *Proceedings of SIGGRAPH 99, Computer Graphics Proceedings, Annual Conference Series*, edited by Alyn Rockwood, pp. 261–268, Reading, MA: Addison-Wesley Longman, 1999.

[52] A. Criminisi and A. Blake. "The SPS Algorithm: Patching Figural Continuity and Transparency by Split-Patch Search." In *Proc. IEEE Conference on Computer Vision and Pattern Recognition (CVPR'04)*, pp. 342–349. Los Alamitos, CA: IEEE Press, 2004.

[53] W. Culbertson, T. Malzbender, and G. Slabaugh. "Generalized Voxel Coloring." In *Proceedings of the International Workshop on Vision Algorithms*, Lecture Notes in Computer Science Vol. 1883, pp. 100–115. Berlin: Springer-Verlag, 1999.

[54] J. Davis, R. Ramamoorthi, and S. Rusinkiewicz. "Spacetime Stereo: A Unifying Framework for Depth from Triangulation." In *Proc. IEEE Computer Vision and Pattern Recognition (CVPR'03)*, Vol. 2, pp. 359–366. Los Alamitos, CA: IEEE Press, 2003.

[55] E. de Aguiar, C. Theobalt, M. Magnor, H. Theisel, and H.-P. Seidel. "Marker-Free Model Reconstruction and Motion Tracking from 3D Voxel Data." In *Proc. IEEE Pacific Graphics 2004 (PG'04)*, pp. 101–110. Los Alamitos, CA: IEEE Press, 2004.

[56] M. Op de Beeck and A. Redert. "Three Dimensional Video for the Home." In *Proc. EUROIMAGE International Conference on Augmented, Virtual Environments and Three-Dimensional Imaging (ICAV3D'01)*, Mykonos, Greece, pp. 188–191, 2001.

[57] P. Debevec, C. Taylor, and J. Malik. "Modeling and Rendering Architecture from Photographs: A Hybrid Geometry- and Image-Based Approach." In *Proceedings of SIGGRAPH 96, Computer Graphics Proceedings, Annual Conference Series*, edited by Holly Rushmeier, pp. 11–20. Reading, MA: Addison-Wesley, 1996.

[58] P. Debevec, G. Borshukov, and Y. Yu. "Efficient View-Dependent Image-Based Rendering with Projective Texture-Mapping." In *Proc. Eurographics Rendering Workshop (EGRW'98)*, pp. 105–116. Berlin: Springer-Verlag, 1998.

[59] P. Debevec, Yizhou Yu, and G. Boshokov. "Efficient View-Dependent Image-Based Rendering with Projective Texture-Mapping." Technical Report CSD-98-1003, UC Berkeley, 1998.

[60] P. Debevec, T. Hawkins, C. Tchou, H.-P. Duiker, W. Sarokin, and M. Sagar. "Acquiring the Reflectance Field of a Human Face."In *Proceedings of SIGGRAPH 2000, Computer Graphics Proceedings, Annual Conference Series*, edited by Kurt Akeley, pp. 145–156.Reading, MA: Addison-Wesley, 2000.

[61] Q. Delamarre and O. Faugeras. "3D Articulated Models and Multi-View Tracking with Silhouettes." In *Proc. International Conference on Computer Vision (ICCV'99)*, pp. 716–721. Los Alamitos, CA: IEEE Press, 1999.

[62] I. Dinstein, G. Guy, and J. Rabany. "On the Compression of Stereo Images: Preliminary Results." *IEEE Signal Processing Magazine* 17:4 (1989), 373–381.

[63] C. Dyer. "Volumetric Scene Reconstruction from Multiple Views." In *Foundations of Image Understanding*, pp. 469–489. Hingham, MA: Kluwer, 2001.

[64] P. Eisert, E. Steinbach, and B. Girod. "Multi-Hypothesis, Volumetric Reconstruction of 3-D Objects from Multiple Calibrated Camera Views." In *International Conference on Acoustics Speech and Signal Processing, ICASSP '99*, pp. 3509–3512. Los Alamitos, CA: IEEE Press, 1999.

[65] P. Eisert, E. Steinbach, and B. Girod. "Automatic Reconstruction of Stationary 3-D Objects from Multiple Uncalibrated Camera Views." *IEEE Trans. Circuits and Systems for Video Technology: Special Issue on 3D Video Technology* 10:2 (2000), 261–277.

[66] P. Eisert, T. Wiegand, and B. Girod. "Model-Aided Coding : A New Approach to Incorporate Facial Animation into Motion-Compensated Video Coding." *IEEE Trans. Circuits and Systems for Video Technology* 10:3 (2000), 244–258.

[67] P. Eisert. "Model-Based Camera Calibration Using Analysis by Synthesis Techniques." In *Proc. Vision, Modeling, and Visualization (VMV'02)*, pp. 307–314. Berlin: Akademische Verlagsgesellschaft, 2002.

[68] J. Elson, L. Girod, and D. Estrin. "Fine-Grained Network Time Synchronization using Reference Broadcasts." In *Proc. Operating Systems Design and Implementation (OSDI'02)*, pp. 147–163, 2002. Berkeley, CA: USENIX, 2002.

[69] C. Everitt. "Interactive Order-Independent Transparency." Technical report, Nvidia Corporation, 2002. Available from World Wide Web (http://developer.nvidia.com/ Interactive_Order_Transparency.html).

[70] J. Evers-Senne and R. Koch. "Image Based Rendering from Handheld Cameras Using Quad Primitives." *Proc. VMV 2003*, Munich, Germany, pp. 11–20. Amsterdam: IOS Press, 2003.

[71] EyeVision. *NCAA Basketball Final Four, Minneapolis, Minnesota*. Available from World Wide Web (http://www.buftek.com/eye21.htm), 2001.

[72] EyeVision. *Superbowl XXXV, Tampa, Florida*. Available from World Wide Web (http://www.ri.cmu.edu/events/sb35/tksuperbowl.html and http://www. howstuffworks.com/eyevision.htm), 2001.

[73] EyeVision. *Superbowl XXXVIII, Houston, Texas*. Available from World Wide Web (http://www.tvtechnology.com/features/news/n_CBS_Primed_for_Super. shtml), 2004.

[74] L. Falkenhagen. "Depth Estimation from Stereoscopic Image Pairs Assuming Piecewise Continuous Surfaces." In *Image Processing for Broadcast and Video Production, Springer Series on Workshops in Computing*, edited by Y. Paker and S. Wilbur, pp. 115–127. London: Springer Great Britain, 1994.

[75] O. Faugeras and R. Keriven. "Complete Dense Stereovision Using Level Set Methods." In *Proc. European Conference on Computer Vision (ECCV'98)*, pp. 379–393. Berlin: Springer-Verlag, 1998.

[76] O. Faugeras and R. Keriven. "Variational Principles, Surface Evolution, PDE's, Level Set Methods and the Stereo Problem." *IEEE Trans. Image Processing* 3:7 (1998), 336–344.

[77] Olivier Faugeras and Quang-Tuan Luong. *The Geometry of Multiple Images*. Cambridge, MA: The MIT Press, 2001.

[78] O. Faugeras, B. Hotz, H. Mathieu, T. Vieville, Zhang Z., P. Fua, E. Theron, M. Laurent, G. Berry, J. Vuillemin, P. Bertin, and C. Proy. "Real Time Correlation Based Stereo: Algorithm Implementations and Applications." Technical Report 2013, INRIA, 1993.

[79] O. Faugeras. *Three-Dimensional Computer Vision*. Cambridge, MA: MIT Press, 1993.

[80] C. Fehn, P. Kauff, M. Op de Beeck, F. Ernst, W. Ijsselsteijn, M. Pollefeys, E. Ofek L. Van Gool, and Sexton I. "An Evolutionary and Optimised Approach on 3D-TV." *Proc. International Broadcast Conference (IBC'02)*, pp. 357–365. Amsterdam: RAI, 2002.

[81] R. Fernando and M. Kilgard. *The Cg Tutorial*. Reading, MA: Addison-Wesley, 2003.

[82] R. Fernando. *GPU Gems*. Reading, MA: Addison-Wesley, 2004.

[83] M. Fischler and R. Bolles. "Random Sample Consensus: A Paradigm for Model Fitting with Applications to Image Analysis and Automated Cartography." *Communications of the ACM* 24:6. (1981), 381–395.

[84] L. Ford and D. Fulkerson. *Flows in Networks*. Princeton, NJ: Princeton University Press, 1962.

[85] D. Forsyth and J. Ponce. *Computer Vision: A Modern Approach*. Englewood Cliffs, NJ: Prentice Hall, 2002.

[86] J.-S. Franco and E. Boyer. "Exact Polyhedral Visual Hulls." In *British Machine Vision Conference (BMVC'03)*, pp. 329–338. Malvern, UK: BMVA, 2003.

[87] A. Fusiello, V. Roberto, and E. Trucco. "Efficient Stereo with Multiple Windowing." In *Proc. IEEE Computer Vision and Pattern Recognition (CVPR'97)*, pp. 858–863. Los Alamitos, CA: IEEE Press, 1997.

[88] J. Gaudiosi. *Games, Movies tie the Knot*. Available from World Wide Web (http://www.wired.com/news/games/0,2101,61358,00.html), 2003.

[89] D. Gavrila and L. Davis. "3D Model-Based Tracking of Humans in Action: A Multi-View Approach." In *Proc. IEEE Computer Vision and Pattern Recognition (CVPR'96)*, pp. 73–80. Los Alamitos, CA:, 1996.

[90] D. Gavrila. "The Visual Analysis of Human Movement." *Journal of Computer Vision and Image Understanding* 73:1 (1999), 82–98.

[91] A. Gershun. "The Light Field." *J. Math. Phys.* 18 (1939), 51–151. Original publication in Russian *Svetovoe pole*, Moscow, 1936.

[92] B. Girod and M. Magnor. "Two Approaches to Incorporate Approximate Geometry into Multi-View Image Coding." In *Proc. IEEE International Conference on Image Processing (ICIP-2000)*, Vancouver, Canada, Vol. 2, pp. 5–8. Los Alamitos, CA: IEEE Press, 2000.

[93] B. Girod, P. Eisert, M. Magnor, E. Steinbach, and T. Wiegand. "3-D Image Models and Compression - Synthetic Hybrid or Natural Fit ?" In *Proc. IEEE International Conference on Image Processing (ICIP-99)*, Kobe, Japan, Vol. 2, pp. 525–529. Los Alamitos, CA: IEEE Press, 1999.

[94] B. Girod. "The Efficiency of Motion-Compensating Prediction For Hybrid Coding of Video Sequences." *IEEE J. Select. Areas Commun.* SAC-5 (1987), 1140–1154.

[95] B. Girod. "Efficiency Analysis of Multihypothesis Motion-Compensated Prediction for Video Coding." *IEEE Trans. on Image Processing* 9 (2000), 173–183.

[96] Siteco Beleuchtungstechnik GmbH. Available from World Wide Web (http://www.siteco.de).

[97] A. Goldberg and R. Tarjan. "A New Approach to the Maximum Flow Problem." *Journal of the ACM* 35:4 (1988), 921–940.

[98] B. Goldlücke and M Magnor. "Joint 3-D Reconstruction and Background Separation in Multiple Views using Graph Cuts." In *Proc. IEEE Computer Vision and Pattern Recognition (CVPR'03)*, pp. 683–694. Los Alamitos, CA: IEEE Press, 2003.

[99] B. Goldlücke and M. Magnor. "Real-Time, Free-Viewpoint Video Rendering from Volumetric Geometry." In *Proc. SPIE Visual Communications and Image Processing (VCIP'03)*, edited by Touradj Ebrahimi and Thomas Sikora, pp. 1152–1158. Bellingham, WA: SPIE, 2003.

[100] B. Goldlücke and M. Magnor. "Real-Time Microfacet Billboarding for Free-Viewpoint Video Rendering." In *Proc. IEEE International Conference on Image Processing*, pp. 713–716. Los Alamitos, CA: IEEE Press, 2003.

[101] B. Goldlücke and M. Magnor. "Space-Time Isosurface Evolution for Temporally Coherent 3D Reconstruction." In *Proc. IEEE Computer Vision and Pattern Recognition (CVPR'04)*, Washington, USA, pp. 350–357. Los Alamitos, CA: IEEE Press, 2004.

[102] B. Goldlücke and M Magnor. "Weighted Minimal Hypersurfaces and Their Applications in Computer Vision." In *Proc. European Conference on Computer Vision (ECCV'04)*, pp. 366–378. Berlin: Springer-Verlag, 2004.

[103] B. Goldlücke, M. Magnor, and B. Wilburn. "Hardware-Accelerated Dynamic Light Field Rendering." In *Proceedings of VMV 2002*, edited by Günther Greiner, pp. 455–462. Berlin: Akademische Verlagsgesellschaft, 2002.

[104] S. Gortler, R. Grzeszczuk, R. Szeliski, and M. Cohen. "The Lumigraph." In *Proceedings of SIGGRAPH 96, Computer Graphics Proceedings, Annual Conference Series*, edited by Holly Rushmeier, pp. 43–54. Reading, MA: Addison-Wesley, 1996.

[105] N. Grammalidis and M.G. Strintzis. "Disparity and Occlusion Estimation in Multiocular Systems and Their Coding for the Communication of Multiview Image Sequences." *IEEE Trans. Circuits and Systems for Video Technology* 8:3 (1998), 328–344.

[106] M. Gross, S. Wuermlin, M. Naef, E. Lamboray, C. Spagno, A. Kunz, E. Koller-Meier, T. Svoboda, L. Van Gool, S. Lang, K. Strehlke, A. Vande Moere, and O. Staadt. "blue-c: A Spatially Immersive Display and 3D Video Portal for Telepresence." *ACM Transactions on Graphics (Proc. SIGGRAPH '03)* 23:3 (2003), 819–827.

[107] C. Gu and M. Lee. "Semiautomatic Segmentation and Tracking of Semantic Video Objects." *IEEE Trans. Circuits and Systems for Video Technology* 8:5 (1998), 572–584.

[108] S. Guha, S. Krishnan, K Munagala, and S. Venkat. "Application of the Two-Sided Depth Test to CSG Rendering." In *Proc. 2003 Symposium on Interactive 3D Rendering*, pp. 177–180. New York: ACM Press, 2003.

[109] Richard Hartley and Andrew Zisserman. *Multiple View Geometry*. Cambridge, UK: Cambridge University Press, 2000.

[110] S. Hasinoff and K. Kutulakos. "Photo-Consistent 3D Fire by Flame-Sheet Decomposition." In *Proc. IEEE International Conference on Computer Vision (ICCV'03)*, pp. 1184–1191. Los Alamitos, CA: IEEE Press, 2003.

[111] S. Hasinoff, S. Kang, and R. Szeliski. "Boundary Matting for View Synthesis." In *Proc. IEEE Computer Vision and Pattern Recognition Workshop (CVPRW'04)*, p. 170. Los Alamitos, CA: IEEE Press, 2004.

[112] P. Heckbert. "Survey of Texture Mapping." *IEEE Computer Graphics and Applications* 6:11 (1986), 56–67.

[113] W. Heidrich, H. Schirmacher, H. Kück, and H.-P. Seidel. "A Warping-Based Refinement of Lumigraphs." *Proc. 6th International Conference in Central Europe on Computer Graphics and Visualization*, pp. 102–109. Plzen: Czech Republic: Center of Computer Graphics and Data Visualisation, 1998.

[114] B. Heigl, R. Koch, M. Pollefeys, J. Denzler, and L. Van Gool. "Plenoptic Modeling and Rendering from Image Sequences Taken by Hand-Held Camera." In *Proc. DAGM '99*, pp. 94–101. Berlin: Springer-Verlag, 1999.

[115] Hewlett-Packard. *HP_occclusion_test OpenGL extension*. Available from World Wide Web (http://oss.sgi.com/projects/ogl-sample/registry/HP/occlusion_test.txt).

[116] H. Hirschmuller. "Improvements in Real-Time Correlation-Based Stereo Vision." In *Proc. IEEE Workshop on Stereo and Multi-Baseline Vision*, pp. 141–148. Los Alamitos, CA: IEEE Press, 2001.

[117] L. Hodges, P. Anderson, G. Burdea, H. Hoffman, and B. Rothbaum. "Treating Psychological and Physical Disorders with VR." *IEEE Computer Graphics and Applications* 21:6 (2001), 25–33.

[118] H. Hoppe. "Progressive Meshes." In *Proceedings of SIGGRAPH 96, Computer Graphics Proceedings, Annual Conference Series*, edited by Holly Rushmeier, pp. 99–108. Reading, MA: Addison-Wesley, 1996.

[119] B. Horn. *Robot Vision*. Cambridge, MA: MIT Press, 1986.

[120] B. K. P. Horn. "Closed-Form Solution of Absolute Orientation Using Unit Quaternions." *Journal of the Optical Society of America* 4:4 (1987), 629–642.

[121] B. Horn. *Recovering Baseline and Orientation from Essential Matrix*. Available from World Wide Web (http://www.ai.mit.edu/people/bkhp/papers/essential.pdf), 1990.

[122] T. Horprasert, I. Haritaoglu, D. Harwood, L. Davis, C. Wren, and A. Pentland. "Real-Time 3D Motion Capture." In *Proc. Workshop on Perceptual Interfaces (PUI'98)*, pp. 87–90, 1998.

[123] I. Ihm, S. Park, and R.K. Lee. "Rendering of Spherical Light Fields." In *Proc. Pacific Conference on Computer Graphics and Applications*, pp. 59–68. Los Alamitos, CA: IEEE Press, 1997.

[124] I. Ihrke and M. Magnor. "Image-Based Tomographic Reconstruction of Flames." In *Proc. ACM/EG Symposium on Animation (SCA'04)*, pp. 367–375. New York: ACM Press, 2004.

[125] I. Ihrke, L. Ahrenberg, and M. Magnor. "External Camera Calibration for Synchronized Multi-Video Systems." In *Proceedings of the 12th International Conference in Central Europe on Computer Graphics, Visualization and Computer Vision (WSCG 2004)*, Volume 12, pp. 537–544, Plzen, Czech Republic: UNION Agency—Science Press, 2004.

[126] GretagMacBeth Inc. *MacBeth ColorChecker Chart*. Available from World Wide Web (http://www.gretagmacbeth.com/).

[127] Princeton Video Imaging (PVI Inc.). *EyeVision*. Available from World Wide Web (http://www.pvi-inc.com).

[128] 80/20 Inc. Available from World Wide Web (http://www.8020.net/), 2005.

[129] Edmund Optics Inc. Available from World Wide Web (http://www.edmundoptics.com/US/index.cfm), 2005.

[130] Point Grey Research Inc. Available from World Wide Web (http://www.ptgrey.com/), 2005.

[131] Intel. *IPL - Intel Image Processing Library*. Available from World Wide Web (http://www.intel.com/support/performancetools/libraries/ipl/).

[132] H. Ip and L. Yin. "Constructing a 3D Individualized Head Model from Two Orthogonal Views." *The Visual Computer* 12:5 (1996), 254–268.

[133] H. Ishikawa and D. Geiger. "Occlusions, Discontinuities, and Epipolar Lines in Stereo." In *Proc. European Conference on Computer Vision (ECCV'98)*, pp. 232–248. Berlin: Springer-Verlag, 1998.

[134] R. Jain, R. Kasturi, and B.G. Schunck. *Machine Vision*. New York: McGraw-Hill, 1995.

[135] J. Janesick. *Scientific Charge-Coupled Devices*. Bellingham, WA: SPIE, 2001.

[136] N.S. Jayant and P. Noll. *Digital Coding of Waveforms*. Englewood Cliffs: Prentice-Hall, 1984.

[137] Z. Jiang. "Three-Dimensional Image Warping on Programmable Graphics Hardware." Technical Report TR-03-01, Zhejiang University, China, 2001.

[138] H. Jin, S. Soatto, and A. J. Yezzi. "Multi-View Stereo Beyond Lambert." In *Proc. IEEE Computer Vision and Pattern Recognition (CVPR'03)*, pp. 171–178. Los Alamitos, CA: IEEE Press, 2003.

[139] F. Jordan, T. Ebrahimi, and M. Kunt. "View-dependent texture coding using the MPEG-4 video coding scheme." In *Proc. IEEE International Symposium on Circuits and Systems (ISCAS'98)*, Monterey, USA, Vol. 5, pp. 498–501. Los Alamitos, IEEE Press, 1998.

[140] N. Joshi, B. Wilburn, V. Vaish, M. Levoy, and M. Horowitz. "Automatic Color Calibration for Large Camera Arrays." Technical Report UCSD CS2005-0821, University of California San Diego, 2005.

[141] N. Joshi. "Color Calibration for Arrays of Inexpensive Image Sensors." Technical Report CSTR 2004-02 3/31/04 4/4/04, Stanford University, 2004.

[142] A. Kale, A. Chowdhury, and R. Chellappa. "Video Based Rendering of Planar Dynamic Scenes."In *Proc. IEEE International Conference on Multimedia and Expo*, Baltimore, USA, Los Alamitos, CA; IEEE Press, 2003.

[143] T. Kanade, H. Saito, and S. Vedula. "The 3D Room : Digitizing Time-Varying 3D Events by Synchronized Multiple Video Streams." Technical Report CMU-RI-TR-98-34, The Robotics Institute at Carnegie Mellon University, 1998.

[144] M. Kass, A. Witkin, and D. Terzopoulos. "Snakes: Active Contour Models." *International Journal of Computer Vision* 1 (1988), 321–331.

[145] M. Kemp. *Leonardo on Painting*. New Haven, CT: Yale University Press, 2001.

[146] E. J. Kim, K. H. Yum, C. R. Das, M. Yousif, and J. Duato. "Performance Enhancement Techniques for InfiniBand^{TM} Architecture." In *Proc. International Symposium on High-Performance Computer Architecture (HPCA'03)*, pp. 253–262. Los Alamitos, CA: IEEE Press, 2003.

[147] K. Klein, W. Cornelius, T. Wiebesiek, and J. Wingbermühle. "Creating a "Personalised, Immersive Sports TV Experience" via 3D Reconstruction of Moving Athletes." In *Proc. Business Information Systems*, edited by Abramowitz and Witold. Poznan, Poland: Pozan University of Economics, 2002.

[148] G. Klinker, S. Shafer, and T. Kanade. "A Physical Approach to Color Image Understanding." *International Journal of Computer Vision* 4:1 (1990), 7–38.

[149] R. Koch and L. Van Gool, editors. *3D Structure from Multiple Images of Large-Scale Environments*. Berlin: Springer-Verlag, 1998.

[150] R. Koch, M. Pollefeys, B. Heigl, L. Van Gool, and H. Niemann. "Calibration of Hand-Held Camera Sequences for Plenoptic Modeling." In *Proc. International Conference on Computer Vision (ICCV'99)*, pp. 585–591. Los Alamitos, CA: IEEE Press, 1999.

[151] R. Koch. "Dynamic 3D Scene Analysis through Synthesis Feedback Control." *IEEE Trans. Pattern Analysis and Machine Intelligence* 15:6 (1993), 556–568.

[152] V. Kolmogorov and R. Zabih. "Multi-Camera Scene Reconstruction via Graph Cuts." In *Proc. European Conference on Computer Vision (ECCV'02)*, pp. 82–96. Berlin: Springer-Verlag, 2002.

[153] V. Kolmogorov and R. Zabih. "What Energy Functions Can Be Minimized via Graph Cuts?" In *Proc. European Conference on Computer Vision (ECCV'02)*, pp. 65–81. Berlin: Springer-Verlag, 2002.

[154] V. Kolmogorov and R. Zabih. "What Energy Functions Can Be Minimized via Graph Cuts?" *IEEE Trans. Pattern Analysis and Machine Intelligence* 26:2 (2004), 147–160.

[155] M. Koudelka, S. Magda, P. Belhumeur, and D. Kriegman. "Image-Based Modeling and Rendering of Surfaces with Arbitrary BRDFs." In *Proc. IEEE Computer Vision and Pattern Recognition (CVPR'01)*, pp. 568–575. Los Alamitos, CA: IEEE Press, 2001.

[156] K. N. Kutukalos and S. M. Seitz. "A Theory of Shape by Space Carving." *International Journal of Computer Vision* 38:3 (2000), 197–216.

[157] K. Kutulakos and S. Seitz. "A Theory of Shape by Space Carving." In *Proc. International Conference on Computer Vision (ICCV'99)*, pp. 307–314. Los Alamitos, CA: IEEE Press, 1999.

[158] K. Kutulakos. "Shape from the Light Field Boundary." *Proc. IEEE Computer Vision and Pattern Recognition (CVPR'97)*, pp. 53–59. Los Alamitos, CA: IEEE Press, 1997.

[159] P. Lalonde and A. Fournier. "Interactive Rendering of Wavelet Projected Light Fields." In *Proc. Graphics Interface'99*, Kingston, Canada, pp. 107–114. Wellesley, MA: A K Peters, 1999.

[160] A. Laurentini. "The Visual Hull Concept for Sihouette-Based Image Understanding." *IEEE Trans. Pattern Analysis and Machine Vision* 16:2 (1994), 150–162.

[161] S. Lazebnik, E. Boyer, and J. Ponce. "On Computing Exact Visual Hulls of Solids Bounded by Smooth Surfaces." In *Proc. IEEE Computer Vision and Pattern Recognition (CVPR'01)*, pp. 156–161. Los Alamitos, CA: IEEE Press, 2001.

[162] J. Lengyel. "The Convergence of Graphics and Vision." *Computer* 31:7 (1998), 46–53.

[163] H. Lensch, W. Heidrich, and H.-P. Seidel. "Automated Texture Registration and Stitching for Real World Models." In *Proc. IEEE Pacific Graphics (PG'00)*, pp. 317–326. Los Alamitos, CA: IEEE Press, 2000.

[164] H. Lensch, W. Heidrich, and H.-P. Seidel. "A Silhouette-Based Algorithm for Texture Registration and Stitching." *Graphical Models* 63:4 (2001), 245–262.

[165] H. Lensch, J. Kautz, M. Gösele, W. Heidrich, and H.-P. Seidel. In "Image-Based Reconstruction of Spatially Varying Materials." *Proc. Eurographics Workshop on Rendering (EGRW'01)*, London, UK, pp. 104–115. Berlin: Springer-Verlag, 2001.

[166] H. Lensch, J. Kautz, M. Goesele, W. Heidrich, and H.-P. Seidel. "Image-Based Reconstruction of Spatial Appearance and Geometric Detail." *ACM Transactions on Graphics (TOG)* 22:2 (2003), 234–257.

[167] M. Leung and Y. Yang. "First Sight : A Human Body Outline Labeling System." *IEEE Trans. Pattern Analysis and Machine Intelligence* 17:4 (1995), 359–379.

[168] M. Levoy and P. Hanrahan. "Light Field Rendering." In *Proceedings of SIGGRAPH 96, Computer Graphics Proceedings, Annual Conference Series*, edited by Holly Rushmeier, pp. 31–42. Reading, MA: Addison-Wesley, 1996.

[169] M. Levoy and J. Shade. *A Light Field of Michelangelo's Statue of Night.* Available from World Wide Web (http://graphics.stanford.edu/projects/mich/lightfield-of-night/lightfield-of-night.html), 1999.

[170] M. Li, M. Magnor, and H.-P. Seidel. "Online Accelerated Rendering of Visual Hulls in Real Scenes." In *Proceedings of the 11th International Conference in Central Europe on Computer Graphics, Visualization and Computer Vision (WSCG 2003)*, Volume 11. Plzen, Czech Republic: UNION Agency—Science Press, 2003.

[171] J. Li, H.Y. Shum, and Y.Q. Zhang. "On the Compression of Image Based Rendering Scene." In *Proc. IEEE International Conference on Image Processing ICIP-00*, Vancouver, Canada, Vol. 2, pp. 21–24. Los Alamitos, CA: IEEE Press, 2000.

[172] M. Li, H. Schirmacher, M. Magnor, and H.-P. Seidel. "Combining Stereo and Visual Hull Information for On-Line Reconstruction and Rendering of Dynamic Scenes." In *Proc. IEEE Multimedia Signal Processing (MMSP'02)*, pp. 9–12. Los Alamitos, CA: IEEE Press, 2002.

[173] M. Li, M. Magnor, and H.-P. Seidel. "Hardware-Accelerated Visual Hull Reconstruction and Rendering." In *Proc. Graphics Interface (GI'03)*, pp. 65–71. Wellesley, MA: A K Peters, 2003.

[174] M. Li, M. Magnor, and H.-P. Seidel. "Hardware-Accelerated Rendering of Photo Hulls." In *Proc. Eurographics (EG'04)*, pp. 635–642. Berlin: Springer-Verlag, 2004.

[175] M. Li, M. Magnor, and H.-P. Seidel. "A Hybrid Hardware-Accelerated Algorithm for High Quality Rendering of Visual Hulls." In *Proc. Graphics Interface (GI'04)*, London, Canada, pp. 41–48. Wellesley, MA: A K Peters, 2004.

[176] M. Li. "Towards Real-Time Novel View Synthesis Using Visual Hulls." PhD diss., MPI Informatik, 2005.

[177] Z.-C. Lin, T.-T. Wong, and H.-Y. Shum. "Relighting with the Reflected Irradiance Field: Representation, Sampling and Reconstruction." *International Journal of Computer Vision* 49:2 (2002), 229–246.

[178] B. Lok. "Online Model Reconstruction for Interactive Virtual Environments." In *Proceedings of the 2001 Symposium on Interactive 3D Graphics*, pp. 69–72. New York: ACM Press, 2001.

[179] S. Loncaric. "A Survey of Shape Analysis Techniques." *Pattern Recognition* 31:8 (1998), 983–1001.

[180] W. E. Lorensen and H. E. Cline. "Marching Cubes: A High Resolution 3D Surface Construction Algorithm." *Proc. SIGGRAPH '87, Computer Graphics* 21:3 (1987), 163–169.

[181] D. Lowe. "Fitting Parameterized Three-Dimensional Models to Images." *IEEE Trans. Pattern Analysis and Machine Intelligence (T-PAMI)* 13:5 (1991), 441–450.

[182] B. Lucas and T. Kanade. "An Iterative Image Registration Technique with an Application to Stereo Vision." In *Proc. DARPA Image Understanding Workshop 1981*, pp. 121–130. San Francisco: Morgan Kaufmann, 1981.

[183] J. Luck and D. Small. "Real-Time Markerless Motion Tracking Using Linked Kinematic Chains." In *Proceedings of CVPRIP '02*. Los Alamitos, CA: IEEE Press, 2002.

[184] M.E. Lukacs. "Predictive Coding of Multi-Viewpoint Image Sets."In *Proc. IEEE International Conference on Acoustics, Speech, and Signal Processing (ICASSP'86)*, Tokyo, Japan, pp. 521–524. Los Alamitos, CA: IEEE Press, 1986.

[185] P. Lyman and H. Varian. *How much Information*. Available from World Wide Web (http://www.sims.berkeley.edu/research/projects/how-much-info-2003/), 2003.

[186] M. Magnor and B. Girod. "Fully Embedded Coding of Triangle Meshes." In *Proc. Vision, Modeling, and Visualization (VMV'99)*, Erlangen, Germany, pp. 253–259. Los Alamitos, CA: IEEE Press, 1999.

[187] M. Magnor and B. Girod. "Hierarchical Coding of Light Fields with Disparity Maps." In *Proc. IEEE International Conference on Image Processing (ICIP'99)*, pp. 334–338. Los Alamitos, CA: IEEE Press, 1999.

[188] M. Magnor and B. Girod. "Data Compression for Light Field Rendering." *IEEE Trans. Circuits and Systems for Video Technology* 10:3 (2000), 338–343.

[189] M. Magnor and B. Girod. "Model-Based Coding of Multi-Viewpoint Imagery." In *Proc. SPIE Visual Communication and Image Processing (VCIP-2000)*, pp. 14–22. Bellingham, WA: SPIE, 2000.

[190] M. Magnor and B. Girod. "Sensitivity of Image-based and Texture-based Multi-View Coding to Model Accuracy." *Proc. IEEE Intl. Conf. on Image Processing* , Vol. 3, pp. 98–101. Los Alamitos, CA: IEEE Press, 2001.

[191] M. Magnor and B. Goldlücke. "Spacetime-Coherent Geometry Reconstruction from Multiple Video Streams." In *Proc. IEEE 3D Data Processing, Visualization, and Transmission (3DPVT'04)*, pp. 365–372. Los Alamitos, CA: IEEE Press, 2004.

[192] M. Magnor and H.-P. Seidel. "Capturing the Shape of a Dynamic World—Fast!" In *Proc. International Conference on Shape Modelling and Applications (SMI'03)*, pp. 3–9. Los Alamitos, CA: IEEE Press, 2003.

[193] M. Magnor and C. Theobalt. "Model-based Analysis of Multi-Video Data." In *Proc. IEEE Southwest Symposium on Image Analysis and Interpretation (SSIAI-2004)*, pp. 41–45. Los Alamitos, CA: IEEE Press, 2004.

[194] M. Magnor, P. Eisert, and B. Girod. "Model-Aided Coding of Multi-Viewpoint Image Data." In *Proc. IEEE International Conference on Image Processing (ICIP-2000)*, pp. 919–922. Los Alamitos, CA: IEEE Press, 2000.

[195] M. Magnor, A. Endmann, and B. Girod. "Progressive Compression and Rendering of Light Fields." *Proc. Vision, Modeling, and Visualization (VMV'00)*, Saarbrücken, Germany, pp. 199–203. Saarbrücken, Germany: Aka GmBH, 2000.

[196] M. Magnor. "Geometry-Adaptive Multi-View Coding Techniques for Image-Based Rendering." PhD diss., University of Erlangen, Germany, 2001.

[197] M. Magnor. "Geometry-Based Automatic Object Localization and 3-D Pose Detection." In *Proc. IEEE Southwest Symposium on Image Analysis and Interpretation (SSIAI-2002)*, pp. 144–147. Los Alamitos, CA: IEEE Press, 2002.

[198] M. Magnor. "3D-TV - The Future of Visual Entertainment." In *Proc. Multimedia Databases and Image Communications (MDIC'04)*, Salerno, Italy. Singapore: World Scientific, 2005.

[199] S. Malassiotis and M.G. Strintzis. "Object-Based Coding of Stereo Image Sequences Using Three-Dimensional Models." *IEEE Trans. Circuits and Systems for Video Technology* 7:6 (1997), 892–905.

[200] Manfrotto. Available from World Wide Web (http://www.manfrotto.com).

[201] W. Mark, L. McMillan, and G. Bishop. "Post-Rendering 3D Warping." In *Proc. Symposium on Interactive 3D Graphics*, pp. 7–16.New York, ACM Press, 1997.

[202] W. Mark, R. Glanville, K. Akeley, and M. Kilgard. "Cg: A System for Programming Graphics Hardware in a C-Like Language." *ACM Transactions on Graphics (Proc. SIGGRAPH'03)*. 22:3 (2003), 896–907.

[203] S. Marschner. "Inverse Rendering for Computer Graphics." PhD diss., Cornell University, 1998.

[204] G. Martinez. "3D Motion Estimation of Articulated Objects for Object-Based Analysis-Synthesis Coding (OBASC)." In *Intern. Workshop on Coding Techniques for Very Low Bit-rate Video (VLBV'95)*, 1995.

[205] K. Matsushita and T. Kaneko. "Efficient and Handy Texture Mapping on 3D Surfaces." *Computer Graphics Forum* 18:3 (1999), 349–358.

[206] T. Matsuyama and T. Takai. "Generation, Visualization, and Editing of 3D Video." In *Proceedings of 3DPVT '02*, pp. 234–240. Los Alamitos, CA: IEEE Press, 2002.

[207] W. Matusik and H. Pfister. "3D TV: A Scalable System for Real-Time Acquisition, Transmission, and Autostereoscopic Display of Dynamic Scenes." *Proc. SIGGRAPH '04, Transactions on Graphics* 23:3 (2004), 814–824.

[208] W. Matusik, C. Buehler, R. Raskar, S. Gortler, and L. McMillan. "Image-Based Visual Hulls." In *Proceedings of SIGGRAPH 2000, Computer Graphics Proceedings, Annual Conference Series*, edited by Kurt Akeley, pp. 369–374. Reading, MA: Addison-Wesley, 2000.

[209] W. Matusik, C. Buehler, and L. McMillan. "Polyhedral Visual Hulls for Real-Time Rendering." In *Proceedings of 12th Eurographics Workshop on Rendering*, pp. 115–126. Berlin-Heidelberg: Springer-Verlag, 2001.

[210] W. Matusik, H. Pfister, A. Ngan, P. Beardsley, R. Ziegler, and L. McMillan. "Image-Based 3D Photography Using Opacity Hulls." *Proc. SIGGRAPH '02, Transactions on Graphics* 21:3 (2002), 427–436.

[211] W. Matusik. "Image-Based Visual Hulls." Master's thesis, Massachusetts Institute of Technology, 2001.

[212] L. McMillan and G. Bishop. "Plenoptic Modeling: An Image-Based Rendering System." In *Proceedings of SIGGRAPH 95, Computer Graphics Proceedings, Annual Conference Series*, edited by Robert Cook, pp. 39–46. Reading, MA: Addison-Wesley, 1995.

[213] L. McMillan. "An Image-Based Approach to Three-Dimensional Computer Graphics." PhD diss., University of North Carolina at Chapel Hill, 1997.

[214] A. Menache. *Understanding Motion Capture for Computer Animation and Video Games*. San Francisco, CA: Morgan Kaufmann, 1995.

[215] I. Mikić, M. Trivedi, E. Hunter, and P. Cosman. "Articulated Body Posture Estimation from Multicamera Voxel Data." In *Proc. IEEE Computer Vision and Pattern Recognition (CVPR'01)*, pp. 455–460. Los Alamitos, CA: IEEE Press, 2001.

[216] G. Miller, S. Rubin, and D. Ponceleon. "Lazy Decompression of Surface Light Fields for Precomputed Global Illumination." *Proc. Eurographics Rendering Workshop'98,* Vienna, Austria, pp. 281–292. Berlin: Springer-Verlag, 1998.

[217] G. Miller. "Volumetric Hyper-Reality, A Computer Graphics Holy Grail for the 21st Century?" *Proc. Graphics Interface (GI'95)*, pp. 56–64. Wellesley, MA: A K peters, 1995.

[218] S. Moezzi, A. Katkere, D. Kuramura, and R. Jain. "Reality Modeling and Visualization from Multiple Video Sequences." *IEEE Computer Graphics and Applications* 16:6 (1996), 58–63.

[219] S. Moezzi, L. Tai, and P. Gerard. "Virtual View Generation for 3D Digital Video." *IEEE Multimedia* 4:1 (1997), 18–26.

[220] T. Naemura, J. Tago, and H. Harashima. "Real-Time Video-Based Modeling and Rendering of 3D Scenes." *IEEE Computer Graphics and Applications* 22:2 (2002), 66–73.

[221] P. Narayanan, P. Rander, and T. Kanade. "Constructing Virtual Worlds Using Dense Stereo." In *Proc. International Conference on Computer Vision (ICCV'98)*, pp. 3–10. Los Alamitos, CA: IEEE Press, 1998.

[222] J. Nelder and R. Mead. "A simplex method for function minimization." *Computer Journal* 7 (1965), 308–313.

[223] P. Neugebauer and K. Klein. "Texturing 3D Models of Real World Objects from Multiple Unregistered Photographic Views." *Computer Graphics Forum* 18:3 (999), 245–256.

[224] J. Neumann and Y. Aloimonos. "Spatio-Temporal Stereo Using Multi-Resolution Subdivision Surfaces." *International Journal of Computer Vision* 47 (2002), 181–193.

[225] W. Niem. "Robust and Fast Modelling of 3D Natural Objects from Multiple Views." In *Proc. SPIE Image and Video Processing*, pp. 388–397. Bellingham, WA: SPIE, 1994.

[226] NVIDIA. *EXT_stencil_two_side OpenGL extension*. Available from World Wide Web (http://oss.sgi.com/projects/ogl-sample/registry/EXT/stencil_two_side.txt).

[227] J.-R. Ohm. "Encoding and Reconstruction of Multiview Video Objects." *IEEE Signal Processing Magazine* 16:3 (1999), 47–54.

[228] R. Ooi, T. Hamamoto, T. Naemura, and K. Aizawa. "Pixel Independent Random Access Image Sensor for Real Time Image-Based Rendering System." In *Proc. International Conference on Image Processing (ICIP'01)*, Thessaloniki, Greece, pp. 193–196. Los Alamitos, CA: IEEE Press, 2001.

[229] S. Osher and J. Sethian. "Fronts Propagating with Curvature Dependent Speed: Algorithms Based on the Hamilton-Jacobi Formulation." *Journal of Computational Physics* 79 (1988), 12–49.

[230] R. Pajarola and J. Rossignac. "Compressed Progressive Meshes." Technical Report GIT-GVU-99-05, Georgia Institute of Technology, 1999.

[231] N. Paragios and R. Deriche. "Geodesic Active Contours and Level Sets for the Detection and Tracking of Moving Objects." *IEEE Trans. Pattern Analysis and Machine Intelligence (T-PAMI)* 22:3 (2000), 266–280.

[232] M.G. Perkins. "Data Compression of Stereopairs." *IEEE Trans. Communications* 40 (1992), 684–696.

[233] I. Peter and W. Strasser. "The Wavelet Stream: Interactive Multi Resolution Light Field Rendering." In *Proc. 12th Eurographics Workshop on Rendering,* London, UK, pp. 262–273. Berlin: Springer-verlag, 2001.

[234] F. Pighin, J. Hecker, D. Lischinski, R. Szeliski, and D. Salesin. "Synthesizing Realistic Facial Expressions from Photographs." In *Proceedings of SIGGRAPH 98, Computer Graphics Proceedings, Annual Conference Series*, edited by Michael Cohen, pp. 75–84. Reading, MA: Addison-Wesley, 1998.

[235] R. Plaenkers and P. Fua. "Tracking and Modeling People in Video Sequences." *Journal of Computer Vision and Image Understanding* 81:3 (2001), 285–302.

[236] M. Pollefeys and L. Van Gool. "From Images to 3D Models." *Communications of the ACM* 45:7 (2002), 50–55.

[237] M. Pollefeys, R. Koch, M. Vergauwen, and L. van Gool. "Metric 3D Surface Reconstruction from Uncalibrated Image Sequences." In *Proc. SMILE Workshop*, Lecture Notes in Computer Science 1506, pp. 139–154. Berlin: Springer-Verlag, 1998.

[238] M. Pollefeys. "Self-Calibration and Metric 3D Reconstruction from Uncalibrated Image Sequences." PhD diss., K.U.Leuven, 1999.

[239] A. Pope. "Model-Based Object Recognition—A Survey of Recent Research." Technical Report TR-94-04, Dept. Computer Science, Univ. British Columbia, 1994.

[240] J. Popović and H. Hoppe. "Progressive Simplicial Complexes." In *Proceedings of SIGGRAPH 97, Computer Graphics Proceedings, Annual Conference Series*, edited by Turner Whitted), pp. 217–224. Reading, MA: Addison-Wesley, 1997.

[241] T. Porter and T. Duff. "Compositing Digital Images." *Computer Graphics (Proc. SIGGRAPH'84)* 18:3 (1984), 253–259.

[242] M. Potmesil. "Generating Octree Models of 3D Objects from Their Silhouettes in a Sequence of Images." *Computer Vision, Graphics, and Image Processing* 40 (1987), 1–20.

[243] P. Poulin, M. Stamminger, F. Duranleau, M.-C. Frasson, and G. Drettakis. "Interactive Point-based Modeling of Complex Objects from Images." In *Graphics Interface 2003*, pp. 11–20. Wellesley, MA: A K Peters, 2003.

[244] W. Press, S. Teukolsky, W. Vetterling, and B. Flannery. *Numerical Recipes in C.* Cambridge, UK: Cambridge University Press, 1992.

[245] A. Prock and C. Dyer. "Towards Real-Time Voxel Coloring." In *Proc. DARPA Image Understanding Workshop 1998*, pp. 315–321. San Francisco: Morgan Kaufmann, 1998.

[246] K. Pulli, M. Cohen, T. Duchamp, H. Hoppe, L. Shapiro, and W. Stuetzle. "View-Based Rendering: Visualizing Real Objects From Scanned Range and Color Data." In *Proc. Eurographics Workshop on Rendering (EGWR'97)*, pp. 23–34. Berlin: Springer-Verlag, 1997.

[247] P. Rander, P.J. Narayanan, and T. Kanade. "Virtualized Reality: Constructing Time-Varying Virtual Worlds from Real Events." In *Proceedings of IEEE VIS '97*, pp. 277–283. Los Alamitos, CA: IEEE Press, 1997.

[248] S. Reichenbach, S. Park, and R. Narayanswamy. "Characterizing Digital Image Acquisition Devices." *Optical Engineering* 30:2 (1991), 170–177.

[249] K. Rohr. "Incremental Recognition of Pedestrians from Image Sequences." In *Proc. IEEE Computer Vision and Pattern Recognition (CVPR'93)*, pp. 8–13. Los Alamitos, CA: IEEE Press, 1993.

[250] R. Rost. *OpenGL Shading Language.* Reading, MA: Addison-Wesley, 2004.

[251] S. Roth. "Ray Casting for Modeling Solids." *Computer Graphics and Image Processing* 18 (1982), 109–144.

[252] S. Roy and I. Cox. "A Maximum-Flow Formulation of the n-Camera Stereo Correspondence Problem." In *Proc. International Conference on Computer Vision (ICCV'98)*, pp. 492–499. Los Alamitos, CA: IEEE Press, 1998.

[253] S. Roy. "Stereo Without Epipolar Lines: A Maximum Flow Formulation." *International Journal of Computer Vision* 1:2 (1999), 1–15.

[254] A. Said and W. Pearlman. "A New, Fast and Efficient Image Codec Based on Set Partitioning in Hierarchical Trees." *IEEE Trans. Circuits and Systems for Video Technology* 6:3 (1996), 243–250.

[255] M. Sainz, N. Bagherzadeh, and A. Susin. "Hardware Accelerated Voxel Carving." In *1st Ibero-American Symposium in Computer Graphics*, pp. 289–297, 2002.

[256] H. Sawhney, A. Arpa, R. Kumar, S. Samarasekera, M. Aggarwal, S. Hsu., D. Nister, and K. Hanna. "Video Flashlights—Real Time Rendering of Multiple Videos for Immersive Model Visualization." In *Proc. Eurographics Rendering Workshop (EGRW'02)*, pp. 163–174. Aire-la-Ville, Switzerland: Eurographics Association, 2002.

[257] D. Scharstein and R. Szeliski. "A Taxonomy and Evaluation of Dense Two-Frame Stereo Correspondence Algorithms." *International Journal of Computer Vision* 47:1-3.

[258] H. Schirmacher, W. Heidrich, and H.-P. Seidel. "High-Quality Interactive Lumigraph Tendering Through Warping." In *Proc. Graphics Interface 2000*, Montreal, Canada, pp. 87–94. Wellesley, MA; A K Peters, 2000.

[259] H. Schirmacher, M. Li, and H.-P. Seidel. "On-the-Fly Processing of Generalized Lumigraphs." In *Proceedings of Eurographics 2001, Computer Graphics Forum*, pp. 165–173. Oxford, UK: Blackwell Publishing, 2001.

[260] A. Schödl, R. Szeliski, D. Salesin, and I. Essa. "Video textures." In *Proceedings of SIGGRAPH 2000, Computer Graphics Proceedings, Annual Conference Series*, edited by Kurt Akeley, pp. 489–498. Reading, MA: Addison-Wesley, 2000.

[261] M. Segal, C. Korobkin, R. van Widenfelt, J. Foran, and P. Haeberli. "Fast Shadows and Lighting Effects Using Texture Mapping." *Proc. SIGGRAPH '92, Computer Graphics* 26:2 (1992), 249–252.

[262] S. M. Seitz and C. M. Dyer. "Toward Image-Based Scene Representation Using View Morphing." In *Proceedings of CVPR '96*, pp. 84–89. Los Alamitos, CA: IEEE Press, 1996.

[263] S. M. Seitz and C. M. Dyer. "View Morphing." In *Proceedings of SIGGRAPH 96, Computer Graphics Proceedings, Annual Conference Series*, edited by Holly Rushmeier, pp. 21–30. Reading, MA: Addison-Wesley, 1996.

[264] S. Seitz and C. Dyer. "Photorealistic Scene Reconstruction by Voxel Voloring." In *Proc. IEEE Computer Vision and Pattern Recognition (CVPR'97)*, pp. 1067–1073. Los Alamitos, CA: IEEE Press, 1997.

[265] S.M. Seitz and C.R. Dyer. "Photorealistic Scene Reconstruction by Voxel Coloring." *International Journal of Computer Vision* 35:2 (1999), 151–173.

[266] J. A. Sethian. *Level Set Methods and Fast Marching Methods*, Second edition. Monographs on Applied and Computational Mathematics, Cambridge, UK: Cambridge University Press, 1999.

[267] Several. *ACE - ADAPTIVE Communication Environment.* Available from World Wide Web (http://www.cs.wustl.edu/~schmidt/ACE.html).

[268] J. Shade, S. Gortler, L.-W. He, and R. Szeliski. "Layered Depth Images." In *Proceedings of SIGGRAPH'98, Computer Graphics Proceedings, Annual Conference Series*, edited by Michael Cohen, pp. 231–242. Reading, MA: Addison-Wesley, 1998.

[269] R.W. Sharpe. *Differential Geometry*, Graduate Texts in Mathematics. New York: Springer-Verlag, 1997.

[270] A. Shavit, A. Kuranov, A. Bov, B. Davies, F. Fritze, M. Asbach, Dr. Neurosurgus, R. Lienhart, V. Eruhimov, S. Molinov, and V. Pisarevsky. *Open Computer Vision Library.* Available from World Wide Web (http://www.sourceforge.net/projects/opencvlibrary), 2001.

[271] J. Shewchuck. "Triangle: Engineering a 2D Quality Mesh Generator and Delaunay Triangulator." In *Proc. First Workshop on Applied Computational Geometry*, pp. 327–334. New York: ACM Press, 1996.

[272] H.-Y. Shum and L.-W. He. "Rendering with concentric mosaics." In *Proceedings of SIGGRAPH 99, Computer Graphics Proceedings, Annual Conference Series*, edited by Alyn Rockwood, pp. 299–306. Reading, MA: Addison-Wesley, 1999.

[273] H.-Y. Shum and S. B. Kang. In "A Review of Image-based Rendering Techniques." *Proc. SPIE Visual Communications and Image Processing (VCIP-2000)*, Perth, Australia, Vol. 1, pp. 2–13. Bellingham, WA: SPIE, 2000.

[274] M.-C. Silaghi, R. Plaenkers, R. Boulic, P. Fua, and D. Thalmann. "Local and Global Skeleton Fitting Techniques for Optical Motion Capture." In *Modeling and Motion Capture Techniques for Virtual Environments*, Lecture Notes in Artificial Intelligence 1537, pp. 26–40. Berlin: Springer-Verlag, 1998.

[275] G. Slabaugh, W. Culbertson, T. Malzbender, and R. Schafer. "A Survey of Volumetric Scene Reconstruction Methods from Photographs." In *Volume Graphics 2001*, pp. 81–100. Berlin: Springer-Verlag, 2001.

[276] G. Slabaugh, R. Schafer, and M. Hans. "Image-Based Photo Hulls." In *Proc. 3D Processing, Visualization, and Transmission (3DPVT'02)*, pp. 704–708. Los Alamitos, CA: IEEE Press, 2002.

[277] P.P. Sloan, M. Cohen, and S. Gortler. "Time Critical Lumigraph Rendering." In *Proc. Symposium on Interactive 3D Graphics*, pp. 17–23, New York: ACM Press, 1997.

[278] A. Smolic and D. McCutchen. "3DAV Exploration of Video-Based Rendering Technology in MPEG." *IEEE Trans. Circuits and Systems for Video Technology, Special Issue on Immersive Communications* 14:9 (2004), 348–356.

[279] D. Snow, P. Viola, and R. Zabih. "Exact Voxel Occupancy with Graph Cuts." In *Proc. IEEE Computer Vision and Pattern Recognition (CVPR'00)*, pp. 345–352. Los Alamitos, CA: IEEE Pres, 2000.

[280] N. Stewart, G. Leach, and S. John. "An Improved Z-Buffer CSG Rendering Algorithm." In *Proc. Graphics Hardware 1998*, pp. 25–30. New York: ACM Press, 1998.

[281] 3DV Systems. *ZCam Range Sensing Video Camera*. Available from World Wide Web (http://www.3dvsystems.com/products/zcam.html), 2004.

[282] R. Szeliski and P. Golland. "Stereo Matching with Transparency and Matting." In *Proc. International Conference on Computer Vision (ICCV'98)*, pp. 517–526. Los Alamitos, CA: IEEE Press, 1998.

[283] R. Szeliski and H.-Y. Shum. "Creating Full View Panoramic Mosaics and Environment Maps." In *Proceedings of SIGGRAPH 97, Computer Graphics Proceedings, Annual Conference Series*, edited by Turner Whitted, pp. 251–258. Reading, MA: Addison-Wesley, 1997.

[284] R. Szeliski and R. Zabih. "An Experimental Comparison of Stereo Algorithms." In *Vision Algorithms: Theory and Practice*, Lecture Notes in Computer Science 1883, pp. 1–19. Berlin: Springer-Verlag, 1999.

[285] Richard Szeliski. "Rapid Octree Construction from Image Sequences." *Computer Vision, Graphics, and Image Processing: Image Understanding* 5:1 (1993), 23–32.

[286] G. Taubin, A. Gueziec, W. Horn, and F. Lazarus. "Progressive Forest Split Compression." In *Proceedings of SIGGRAPH 98, Computer Graphics Proceedings, Annual Conference Series*, edited by Michael Cohen, pp. 123–132. Reading, MA: Addison-Wesley, 1998.

[287] C. Theobalt, M. Magnor, P. Schüler, and H.-P. Seidel. "Combining 2D Feature Tracking and Volume Reconstruction for Online Video-Based Human Motion Capture." In *Proc. IEEE Pacific Graphics (PG'02)*, Beijing, China, pp. 96–103. Los Alamitos, CA: IEEE Press, 2002.

[288] C. Theobalt, M. Magnor, P. Schüler, and H.-P. Seidel. "Multi-Layer Fitting for Online Human Motion Capture." *Proc. Vision, Modeling, and Visualization (VMV-2002)*, Erlangen, Germany, pp. 471–478. Berlin: Akademische Verlagsgesellschaft, 2002

[289] C. Theobalt, J. Carranza, M. Magnor, J. Lang, and H.-P. Seidel. "Enhancing Silhouette-Based Human Motion Capture with 3D Motion Fields." In *Proc. IEEE Pacific Graphics 2003*, Canmore, Canada, pp. 183–193. Los Alamitos, CA: IEEE Press, 2003.

[290] C. Theobalt, J. Carranza, M. Magnor, and H.-P. Seidel. "A Parallel Framework for Silhouette-Based Human Motion Capture." In *Proc. Vision, Modeling, and Visualization (VMV-2003)*, pp. 207–214. Berlin: Akademische Verlagsgesellschaft, 2003.

[291] C. Theobalt, M. Li, M. Magnor, and H.-P. Seidel. "A Flexible and Versatile Studio for Synchronized Multi-View Video Recording." In *Proceedings of VVG '03*, pp. 9–16. Aire-la-Ville, Switzerland: Eurographics Association, 2003.

[292] Christian Theobalt, Ming Li, Marcus Magnor, and Hans-Peter Seidel. "A Flexible and Versatile Studio for Synchronized Multi-view Video Recording." Research Report MPI-I-2003-4-002, Max-Planck-Institut für Informatik, Stuhlsatzenhausweg 85, 66123 Saarbrücken, Germany, 2003.

[293] C. Theobalt, J. Carranza, M. Magnor, J. Lang, and H.-P. Seidel. "Combining 3D Flow Fields with Silhouette-Based Human Motion Capture for Immersive Video." *Graphical Models (Special Issue on Pacific Graphics'03)* 66:6 (2004), 333–351.

[294] X. Tong and R.M. Gray. "Compression of Light Fields Using Disparity Compensation and Vector Quantization." In *Proc. IASTED Conference on Computer Graphics and Imaging,* Palm Springs, USA Calgary: ACTA Press, 1999.

[295] X. Tong and R.M. Gray. "Coding of Multi-View Images for Immersive Viewing." In *Proc. IEEE International Conference on Acoustic, Speech and Signal Processing (ICASSP-2000),* Istanbul, Turkey, Vol. 4, pp. 1879–1882. Los Alamitos, CA: IEEE Press, 2000.

[296] B. Triggs, P. McLauchlan, R. Hartley, and A. Fitzgibbon. "Bundle Adjustment—A Modern Synthesis." In *Vision Algorithms: Theory and Practice,* Lecture Notes in Computer Science 1883, pp. 298–375. New York: Springer-Verlag, 2000.

[297] R. Tsai. "An Efficient and Accurate Camera Calibration Technique for 3D Machine Vision." In *Proc. IEEE Computer Vision and Pattern Recognition (CVPR'86),* pp. 364–374. Los Alamitos, CA: IEEE Press, 1986.

[298] R. Tsai. "A Versatile Camera Calibration Technique for High-Accuracy 3D Machine Vision Metrology Using Off-the-Shelf TV Cameras and Lenses." *IEEE Journal of Robotics and Automation* RA-3:4 (1987), 323–334.

[299] G. Tsang, S. Ghali, E. Fiume, and A. Venetsanopoulos. "A Novel Parameterization of the Light Field." In *Proc. Image and Multidimensional Digital Signal Processing (IMDSP'98),* Alpbach, Austria, pp. 319–322. Los Alamitos, CA: IEEE Press, 1998.

[300] D. Tzovaras, N. Grammalidis, and M. G. Strintzis. "Object-Based Coding of Stereo Image Sequences Using Joint 3-D Motion/Disparity Compensation." *IEEE Trans. Circuits and Systems for Video Technology* 7:2 (1997), 312–327.

[301] I. Ulrich, C. Baker, B. Nabbe, and I. Nourbakhsh. *IEEE-1394 Digital Camera Windows Driver.* Available from World Wide Web (http://www-2.cs.cmu.edu/~iwan/1394/), 2002.

[302] C. Urmson, D. Dennedy, D. Douxchamps, G. Peters, O. Ronneberger, and T. Evers. *libdc1394 - Open Source IEEE1394 Library.* Available from World Wide Web (http://www.sourceforge.net/projects/libdc1394).

[303] S. Vedula, S. Baker, and T. Kanade. "Image Based Spatio-Temporal Modeling and View Interpolation of Dynamic Events." To appear in *ACM Transactions on Graphics,* 2005.

[304] S. Vedula, S. Baker, P. Rander, R. Collins, and T. Kanade. "Three-Dimensional Scene Flow." In *Proc. International Conference on Computer Vision (ICCV'99),* pp. 722–729. Los Alamitos, CA: IEEE Press, 1999.

[305] S. Vedula, S. Baker, S. Seitz, and T. Kanade. "Shape and Motion Carving in 6D." In *Proc. IEEE Computer Vision and Pattern Recognition (CVPR'00),* Vol. 2, pp. 592–598. Los Alamitos, CA: IEEE Press, 2000.

[306] S. Vedula, S. Baker, and T. Kanade. "Spatio-Temporal View Interpolation." In *Proc. Eurographics Workshop on Rendering (EGRW'02),* pp. 65–76. Berlin: Springer-Verlag, 2002.

[307] S. Vedula, S. Baker, P. Rander, R. Collins, and T. Kanade. "Three-Dimensional Scene Flow." *IEEE Trans. Pattern Analysis and Machine Intelligence* 27:3 (2005), 475–480.

[308] S. Vedula. "Image Based Spatio-Temporal Modeling and View Interpolation of Dynamic Events." PhD diss., Carnegie Mellon University, 2001.

[309] S. Weik and C.-E. Liedtke. "Hierarchical 3D Pose Estimation for Articulated Human Body Models from a Sequence of Volume Data." In *Robot Vision*, edited by Reinhard Klette, Shmuel Peleg, and Gerald Sommer, pp. 27–34. New York: Springer-Verlag, 2001.

[310] K. Weiler and P. Atherton. "Hidden Surface Removal Using Polygon Area Sorting." *Proc. SIGGRAPH '77, Computer Graphics* 11:2 (1977), 214–222.

[311] T. Wiegand. "Interactive Rendering of CSG models." *Computer Graphics Forum* 15:4 (1996), 249–261.

[312] B. Wilburn, M. Smulski, K. Lee, and M. Horowitz. "The Light Field Video Camera." In *Proceedings of SPIE Conference on Media Processors 2002*. Bellingham, WA: SPIE, 2002.

[313] B. Wilburn, N. Joshi, V. Vaish, M. Levoy, and M. Horowitz. "High Speed Video Using a Dense Camera Array." *Proc. IEEE Computer Vision and Pattern Recognition (CVPR'04)*, Washington, USA, Vol. 2, pp. 294–301. Los Alamitos, CA: IEEE Press, 2004.

[314] D. Williams and P. Burns. "Diagnostics for Digital Capture Using MTF." In *Proceedings of IS&T PICS 2001*, pp. 227–232. Springfield, VA: IS&T, 2001.

[315] L. Williams. "Casting Curved Shadows on Curved Surfaces." *Proc. SIGGRAPH '78, Computer Graphics* 12:3 (1978), 270–274.

[316] R. Willson. *Tsai Camera Calibration Software*. Available from World Wide Web (http://www-2.cs.cmu.edu/~rgw/TsaiCode.html).

[317] A. Wilson, M. Lin, B.-L. Yeo, M. Yeung, and D. Manocha. In "A Video-Based Rendering Acceleration Algorithm for Interactive Walkthroughs." *Proc. ACM Conference on Multimedia*, pp. 75–83. New York: ACM Press, 2000.

[318] J. Woetzel and R. Koch. "Multi-Camera Real-Time Depth Estimation with Discontinuity Handling on PC Graphics Hardware." In *Proc. IEEE International Conference on Pattern Recognition (ICPR'04)*, pp. 741–744. Los Alamitos, CA: IEEE Press, 2004.

[319] T. Wong, P. Heng, S. Or, and W. Ng. "Image-Based Rendering with Controllable Illumination." *Proc. Eurographics Rendering Workshop (EGRW'97)*, pp. 13–22. Berlin: Springer-Verlag, 1997

[320] T.-T. Wong, C.W. Fu, P.-A. Heng, and C.-S. Leung. "The Plenoptic Illumination Function." *IEEE Trans. Multimedia* 4:3 (2002), 361–371.

[321] W.T. Woo and A. Ortega. "Stereo Image Compression with Disparity Compensation using the MRF Model." In *Proc. SPIE Visual Communications and Image Processing (VCIP-96)*, Orlando, USA, pp. 28–41. Bellingham, WA: SPIE, 1996.

[322] D. Wood, D. Azuma, K. Aldinger, B. Curless, T. Duchamp, D. Salesin, and W. Stuetzle. "Surface Light Fields for 3D Photography." In *Proceedings of SIG-GRAPH 2000, Computer Graphics Proceedings, Annual Conference Series*, edited by Kurt Akeley, pp. 287–296. Reading, MA: Addison-Wesley, 2000.

[323] C. Wren, A. Azarbayejani, T. Darrell, and A. Pentland. "Pfinder: Real-Time Tracking of the Human Body." *IEEE Trans. Pattern Analysis and Machine Intelligence* 19:7 (1997), 780–785.

[324] Y. Wu, L. Luo, J. Li, and Y.-Q. Zhang. "Rendering of 3D Wavelet Compressed Concentric Mosaic Scenery with Progressive Inverse Wavelet Synthesis (PIWS)." In *Proc. SPIE Visual Communications and Image Processing (VCIP-2000)*, Perth, Australia, Vol. 1, pp. 31–42. Bellingham, WA: SPIE, 2000.

[325] S. Wuermlin, E. Lamboray, O.G. Staadt, and M.H. Gross. "3D Video Recorder." In *Proceedings of IEEE Pacific Graphics 2002*, pp. 325–334. Los Alamitos, CA: IEEE Press, 2002.

[326] C. Wynn and S. Dietrich. *Cube Maps*. Available from World Wide Web (http://developer.nvidia.com/object/cube_maps.html).

[327] S. Yamazaki, R. Sagawa, H. Kawasaki, K. Ikeuchi, and M. Sakauchi. "Microfacet Billboarding." In *Proc. 13th Eurographics Workshop on Rendering*, pp. 175–186. Berlin: Springer-Verlag, 2002.

[328] R. Yang and M. Pollefeys. "Multi-Resolution Real-Time Stereo on Commodity Graphics Hardware." In *Proc. IEEE Computer Vision and Pattern Recognition (CVPR'03)*, pp. 211–220. Los Alamitos, CA: IEEE Press, 2003.

[329] J. Yang, M. Everett, C. Buehler, and L. McMillan. "A Real-Time Distributed Light Field Camera." In *Proc. Eurographics Workshop on Rendering (EGWR'02)*, pp. 77–86. Berlin: Springer-Verlag, 2002.

[330] R. Yang, G. Welch, and G. Bishop. "Real-Time Consensus-Based Scene Reconstruction Using Commodity Graphics Hardware." In *Proceedings of IEEE Pacific Graphics 2002*, pp. 225–235. Los Alamitos, CA: IEEE Press, 2002.

[331] R. Yang, M. Pollefeys, and G. Welch. "Dealing with Textureless Regions and Specular Highlight: A Progressive Space Carving Scheme Using a Novel Photo-Consistency Measure." In *Proc. IEEE International Conference on Computer Vision (ICCV'03)*, pp. 576–584. Los Alamitos, CA: IEEE Press, 2003.

[332] R. Yang, M. Pollefeys, H. Yang, and G. Welch. "A Unified Approach to Real-Time, Multi-Resolution, Multi-Baseline 2D View Synthesis and 3D Depth Estimation using Commodity Graphics Hardware." *International Journal of Image and Graphics* 4:4 (2004), 1–25.

[333] S. Yonemot, D. Arita, and R. Taniguchi. "Real-time Human Motion Analysis and IK-based Human Figure Control." In *Proceedings of IEEE Workshop on Human Motion*, pp. 149–154. Los Alamitos, CA: IEEE Press, 2000.

[334] Y. Yu, P. Debevec, J. Malik, and T. Hawkins. "Inverse Global Illumination: Recovering Reflectance Models of Real Scenes From Photographs From." In *Proceedings of SIGGRAPH 99, Computer Graphics Proceedings, Annual Conference Series*, edited by Alyn Rockwood, pp. 215–224. Reading, MA: Addison-Wesley, 1999.

[335] C. Zhang and T. Chen. "A Survey on Image-Based Rendering - Representation, Sampling and Compression." *EURASIP Signal Processing: Image Communication* 19 (2004), 1–28.

[336] C. Zhang and J. Li. "Compression and Rendering of Concentric Mosaics with Reference Block Codec (RBC)." In *Proc. SPIE Visual Communications and Image Processing (VCIP-2000),* Perth, Australia, Vol. 1, pp. 43–54. Bellingham, WA: SPIE, 43–54.

[337] L. Zhang, B. Curless, and S. Seitz. "Spacetime Stereo: Shape Recovery for Dynamic Scenes." In *Proc. IEEE Computer Vision and Pattern Recognition (CVPR'03),* Vol. 2, pp. 367–374. Los Alamitos, CA: IEEE Press, 2003.

[338] Z. Zhang. "A New Multistage Approach to Motion and Structure Estimation: From Essential Parameters to Euclidean Motion Via Fundamental Matrix." Technical Report RR-2910, INRIA, 1996.

[339] Z. Zhang. "A Flexible and New Technique for Camera Calibration." *IEEE Trans. Pattern Analysis and Machine Intelligence* 11:22 (2000), 1330–1334.

[340] Z. Zhang. *Zhang Camera Calibration Software.* Available from World Wide Web (http://research.microsoft.com/~zhang/Calib/), 2002.

[341] H. Zhao, S. Osher, B. Merriman, and M. Kang. "Implicit and Non-Parametric Shape Reconstruction from Unorganized Points Using Variational Level Set Method." In *Proc. Computer Vision and Image Understanding (CVIU'00),* pp. 295–319. Boston: Academic Press, 2000.

[342] H. Zhao, S. Osher, and R. Fedkiw. "Fast Surface Reconstruction Using the Level Set Method." In *Proc. IEEE Workshop on Variational and Level Set Methods,* pp. 194–202. Los Alamitos, CA: IEEE Press, 2001.

[343] G. Ziegler, H. Lensch, N. Ahmed, M. Magnor, and H.-P. Seidel. "Multi-Video Compression in Texture Space." In *Proc. IEEE International Conference on Image Processing (ICIP'04),* pp. 2467–2470. Los Alamitos, CA: IEEE Press, 2004.

[344] G. Ziegler, H. Lensch, M. Magnor, and H.-P. Seidel. "Multi-Video Compression in Texture Space Using 4D SPIHT." In *Proc. IEEE International Workshop on Multimedia Signal Processing (MMSP'04),* pp. 39–42. Los Alamitos, CA: IEEE Press, 2004.

[345] C. Zitnick, S.B. Kang, M. Uyttendaele, S. Winder, and R. Szeliski. "High-Quality Video View Interpolation Using a Layered Representation." *Proc. SIGGRAPH '04, Transactions on Graphics* 23:3 (2004), 600–608.

Index

Environmental Life Cycle Analysis

David F. Ciambrone
Hughes Aircraft Company
Newport Beach, California

CRC Press
Taylor & Francis Group
Boca Raton London New York

CRC Press is an imprint of the
Taylor & Francis Group, an **informa** business

CRC Press
Taylor & Francis Group
6000 Broken Sound Parkway NW, Suite 300
Boca Raton, FL 33487-2742

© 1997 by Taylor & Francis Group, LLC
CRC Press is an imprint of Taylor & Francis Group, an Informa business

First issued in paperback 2019

No claim to original U.S. Government works

ISBN-13: 978-0-367-44813-4 (pbk)
ISBN-13: 978-1-56670-214-0 (hbk)

Visit the Taylor & Francis Web site at
http://www.taylorandfrancis.com

and the CRC Press Web site at
http://www.crcpress.com

Library of Congress Card Number 97-8058

Library of Congress Cataloging-in-Publication Data

Ciambrone, David F.
    Environmental life cycle analysis / David F. Ciambrone.
       p.   cm.
    Includes bibliographical references and index.
    ISBN 1-56670-214-3
    1. Industrial ecology.   2. Product life cycle—Environmental
aspects. 1. Title.
TS161.C497   1997
658.5'752—dc21

                                            97-8058
                                             CIP

Typesetter: Pamela Morrell
Cover design: Denise Craig

PREFACE

This book is designed to assist design/systems engineers and managers in determining how to best design or change a product or set of processes to minimize the impact on the environment over the life cycle of the product or process. The first two chapters provide an introduction and overview of the environmental life cycle analysis process.

Chapter 3 describes the basic framework, definition of boundaries, the use of checklists, data gathering issues, construction of models, and interpretation of results. This chapter establishes the basis and methodologies required.

Chapter 4 defines templates and special cases that may be encountered and concepts for handling them. Chapters 5 through 9 go into detail about the modeling, issues, and data collection for each stage of the product life cycle. Chapter 10 provides a summary of the various steps and ideas on how to present data and reports.

The organization of the book follows a logical path for the user to understand the overall concept of environmental life cycle analysis and to walk through each of the stages. The stages are broken down into individual topics to provide a clearer picture of what is included in each stage and the issues involved. The book tries to provide alternatives to the analysis process, thereby allowing the user greater flexibility while still gaining constructive information.

ABOUT THE AUTHOR

Dr. David Ciambrone is an energetic manager, management and environmental consultant, professor, lecturer, writer, and inventor, with more than 30 years experience in the manufacturing, business, and environmental fields. His main fields of interest include environmental management, manufacturing, waste minimization, and wastewater treatment.

Dr. Ciambrone has been Corporate Director of Environmental Affairs for a Fortune 100 company, Director of Manufacturing Engineering and Acting Vice President of Manufacturing for Fortune 500 companies, as well as Manager of Engineering and Business Development for a major environmental company.

He has designed numerous manufacturing processes used in the electronics and metal finishing fields. Dr. Ciambrone has established and managed surface mount assembly operations, hybrid microelectronics facilities, circuit board fabrication plants, and industrial plating operations. He has extensive experience as a turnaround manager for major companies and has experience in the implementation of ISO 9001. Dr. Ciambrone has also managed facilities engineering organizations for a Fortune 100 company. He has designed water and wastewater systems for use on land and by the marine industry for companies in the U.S. and abroad. Some of the systems used novel approaches to waste treatment. He has been a principal consultant in environmental companies conducting engineering projects and business development in the U.S. and internationally.

Dr. Ciambrone served on the Board of Directors of an international environmental company and served on the Management Oversight Board of the Resolution Trust Corporation (U.S. Treasury). He was also President of the southern California chapter of the National Association of Environmental Managers and is a Fellow of the International Oceanographic Foundation. He is a long-standing member of the American Electroplaters and Surface Finishers Society (past President) and is a past President of a chapter of the

National Management Association. He is a Registered Environmental Assessor in California.

Dr. Ciambrone has numerous publications in the fields of metal finishing, waste treatment, and waste minimization and has published books on waste minimization and life cycle analysis. He has patents in the fields of wastewater treatment, chemical and biological weapon destruction, and industrial processes.

Dr. Ciambrone has taught courses in industrial and manufacturing engineering, materials science, business and operation management, TQM, and Just-in-Time methods at major universities. He has lectured at many technical and business conferences and universities on manufacturing. In addition, he has lectured on environmental subjects nationally and internationally.

Dr. Ciambrone received his Bachelors Degree from San Diego State University and his Doctor of Science from Brantridge College, University of Sussex in England. Sir David is also the Laird of Parton in Scotland.

ACKNOWLEDGMENTS

The author wishes to acknowledge the following individuals for their contributions in the preparation of materials for this book:

Ms. Joan Moscrop, without her kind help, this book would not have happened

Mr. James Waylonis for preparation of figures

Mr. Norm Sealander, Northrop Grumman Corporation, for his support and encouragement

Dr. D. Mehta, Hughes Aircraft, for his support and encouragement

Kathy Ciambrone for her support and encouragement

Ms. Andrea Demby, for her assistance and editorial support

CONTENTS

1   INTRODUCTION

The trend in U.S. industry, and the U.S. EPA, is toward preventing wastes before they are created instead of treating or disposing of them later. An example of the interest by the government is the U.S. Army Strategic Defense Command regulation USASDCR 200-2. This regulation requires an environmental impact analysis of weapon systems from design through use and disposal. The advancement of ISO 14000 is another example of companies, technical associations, and governments trying to organize a voluntary approach to waste prevention, In international markets this is extremely important. European countries have "green" requirements on products and are expanding the requirements at a rapid rate. This is evident in Germany, The Netherlands, Denmark, Scandinavian countries, and Great Britain. Asian countries, such as Singapore, have also initiated a similar set of programs. Part of a green product and green manufacturing is understanding the *total* impact and cost the product has on the environment. This means evaluating the total life cycle of a product from raw materials and manufacturing through distribution, use, and ultimate reuse/disposal (Figure 1-1). That a product has a finite life cycle implies that there are associated costs that go along with it. Examples of these costs are shown below:

- Design costs
- Stocking/handling costs
- User/operating costs
- Disposal costs
- Manufacturing costs
- Shipping/transportation costs
- Reuse/recycle costs
- Compliance/licensing costs

This illustrates that the impact on the environment and life cycle costs are larger than just the manufacturing costs (Figure 1-2). Understanding the life cycle costs will assist the company in finding ways to reduce postmanu-

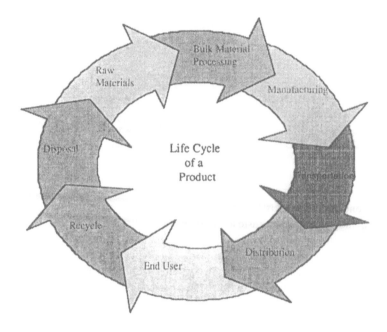

Figure 1-1.   Environmental life cycle analysis stages.

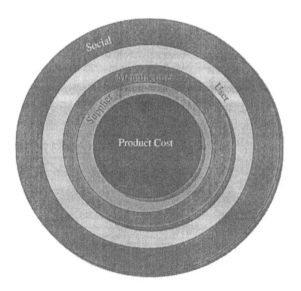

Figure 1-2.   Life cycle cost circle.

Figure 1-3. **Team approach to environmental quality and customer satisfaction. (From *Waste Minimization as a Strategic Weapon*, Ciambrone, D. F., CRC/Lewis Publishers, Boca Raton, FL, 1995.)**

facturing costs. Reducing these costs will also help in reducing the environmental impacts. While the concept of life cycle has existed for more than 20 years, there has been no comprehensive procedure that will facilitate understanding the process and provide the basic tools needed for a company to conduct the analysis in a rigorous yet cost-effective manner. This book would provide the industrial user with the necessary background, simple and effective tools, instruction, and examples to conduct environmental life cycle analysis on their products in a cost-effective manner.

Environmental life cycle analysis is a systematic tool used for assessing the environmental impacts associated with a specific product or service. The application of the process, and associated waste minimization practices by management, design, and manufacturing (Figure 1-3) can also lead to better and less-polluting products that are less expensive and provide a marketing edge over the competition. The importance of the life cycle analysis goes beyond the marketability of the product being studied. In Chapter 10, it will be shown that the outcome of the life cycle analysis can have a positive impact on human health, the ecosystem, and natural resources (Figure 1-4).

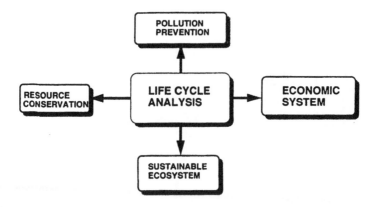

Figure 1-4.   Life cycle goals.

2 OVERVIEW

BRIEF HISTORY

Environmental issues have gained greater public and legal scrutiny in the past 25 years. The public has become more aware and interested in the consumption of goods and services and their impact on the natural resources and the quality of the environment. A nationwide study in 1991 by the *Wall Street Journal*/NBC found that 80% of Americans considered themselves environmentalists. In the past 12 years, an increasing number of firms have been shifting their focus from remediation of pollutants to pollution prevention. This has included "green" design activities and replacing some materials and manufacturing processes with more environmentally friendly ones. These efforts on behalf of the companies involved have drastically reduced the levels of industrial pollution. The impact, or "MANPRINT", on the environment by the products use and disposal has not usually been included in the environmental assessment of the pollution prevention program.

Industry is realizing that the impact their products have on the environment does not start and end with the manufacture of the product. The impact a product has on the world starts with the design and ends at the ultimate disposal of the product after its useful life. What considerations are made during the design phase of a product affects the whole life cycle. It is important to not have solely a means of determining the environmental impacts of the manufacturing process but what impact the product will have on the environment and its ability to be recycled.

While reducing the impact a company and its products make on the environment is a good idea, the costs associated with minimizing these impacts must be considered. Everything a company does has an effect on its bottom line. Environmental compliance has been considered a cost of doing business, and staying out of jail. The increased use of waste minimization programs has not only reduced the costs of compliance (which goes up over time) but has lowered the costs of producing the products. In a number of cases the quality of the product has improved. This in itself reduces costs and improves competitiveness of the products. In the global marketplace, the reduced impact of

5

products on the environment has serious marketing impact. Sound environmental practices will result in designs that meet or exceed the requirements of the countries where they will be sold. This is especially true in Europe where manufacturers retain responsibility for disposal of their products after retired by their users. There are laws on the books in Germany that require the removal of unnecessary packaging from products and lets merchants pay for the disposal of this waste. It is reasonable therefore to consider the total impact on the environment of a product and plan means of reducing that impact during the planning and design phase of the product life cycle.

Life cycle analysis had its beginnings in the 1960s. One of the first publications on the subject was presented at the World Energy Conference in 1963 by Harold Smith. He reported on his calculation of cumulative energy requirements for the production of chemical intermediates and product. Later in the 1960s global modeling studies were published in *The Limits to Growth* (Meadows et al., 1972) and *A Blueprint for Survival* (Club of Rome). These studies involved the demand for finite raw materials and energy resources. In 1969 researchers did a study for The Coca-Cola Company that was to be the foundation for current methods of life cycle analysis. In the early 1970s other companies in the U.S. and Europe performed similar life cycle analyses. The process of quantifying the use of resources and the release of products into the environment in the U.S. became known as Resource and Environmental Profile Analysis (REPA). In Europe it was called Econobalance. During the late 1970s to early 1980s interest in REPA waned in the U.S. However, interest in the process increased in Europe. The Green Movement, especially the formation of Green political parties in Europe, reawakened interest in the subject. When solid waste became an issue worldwide in the late 1980s, the life cycle analysis technique reemerged as a tool for analyzing environmental problems. The Iraqi invasion of Kuwait in 1990 and once again the prospect of oil shortages as well as concerns for solid waste disposal reemphasize the need for environmental life cycle analysis tools.

The concept of a life cycle as used here simply means that the inputs to the "cycle" (energy, materials, etc.) and outputs (energy, waste materials, products, etc.) are evaluated for each step of a product or process life. The cycle begins at conception of the product or process and completes with the recycle/disposal of the product and its constituents (Figure 2-1). In the past, companies have used the "cradle to grave" analysis as indicated. During the 1995 to 1997 time frame, some companies have used the "fence line approach". This approach assesses the impacts associated with the product on site and disregards off-site functions. While this approach does not provide valuable information needed to assess the total impact, it will provide insights into the operations at the site and their impact on the environment. It can also point out areas for environmental and cost improvements. The fence line approach is not a true life cycle analysis but should be considered when determining the exact requirement of the analysis. During a life cycle analysis, the impact on the environment is considered. From this one may be able to ascertain if

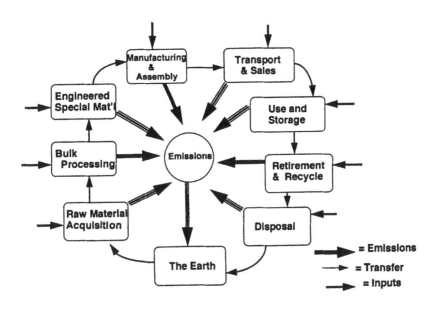

Figure 2-1. Life cycle.

materials or processes may be used to minimize the impact the product has on the environment. This we refer to as the product's MANPRINT.

ASSESSMENT METHODOLOGY OVERVIEW

The environmental life cycle analysis methodology has three basic components. These components overlap and build on each other to develop a life cycle analysis. The three components are

- Inventory analysis
- Impact analysis
- Improvement analysis

It should be noted that the life cycle analysis can be conducted for use both internally to an organization as well as externally. A life cycle analysis that is not properly set up will cost far more than is necessary and be totally impractical. Setting the boundaries for a life cycle analysis is one of the most critical steps in conducting the analysis. Setting the proper boundaries will define what one will obtain from the study and determine the costs associated with the analysis.

A life cycle assessment inventory will provide a quantitative catalog of inputs (materials, energy) and outputs (including environmental releases) for a specific product, activity, or process. Once the inventory analysis has been completed and verified, the results can be used for the impact and improvement analysis phases. The results of a life cycle analysis may also be used to determine the selection of one product or products over another. This could be based on the product's overall impact on the environment. An example of this type of use was illustrated in a California State Polytechnic University at Pomona upper division engineering class. In the class the professor divided the class into groups. Each group of students was to determine which of two choices was the best from an environmental standpoint. The question was, "A checkout lady in a grocery store asks you what type of bag do you want, paper or plastic?" The first three groups of students looked at the problem slightly differently but all three groups came up with the same answer — the plastic bag was best. This was repeated in three different classes and all the results were the same. The students conducted a limited life cycle analysis considering raw materials, raw materials processing, making the bags, energy required, transportation issues, use, recycle, and disposal. The students also considered the chemicals used in processing and recycling and the waste products and their disposal. The overall MANPRINT was reviewed. The plastic won out by a large margin. What the students thought was a silly question (they all thought the answer would be paper because it's natural) but learned through an analysis was that the true solution was plastic. Life cycle analysis can change accepted thought and "truth".

The cataloging of inputs and outputs must have an objective. The specific objectives for conducting an inventory include, but are not limited to, the following:

- Compare inputs and outputs associated with alternative products, materials, or processes
- Determine points within the life cycle or given process where the greatest reduction in resource requirements and fugitive emissions might be achieved
- Assist in guiding the development of new products that reduce the overall MANPRINT
- Establish a comprehensive baseline
- Assist in training personnel responsible for reducing the environmental impact associated with products or processes
- Assist in the substantiation of product claims about reducing their impact on the environment
- Supply information for the evaluation of public policy affecting resource uses, recycling, or releases

LIFE CYCLE INVENTORY CRITERIA

It is recognized that inventories will vary from screening to extremely technical and practical as possible. To be a useful tool, however, a life cycle inventory should meet, as a minimum, the following criteria:

- Quantitative — All data should be quantified and documented with suitable quality control. Any assumptions in the data and methodology must be specified.
- Replicable — The sources of the information and methodology are sufficiently described or referenced so the same results could be obtained by a skilled person and evidence would be available to explain any deviations.
- Scientific — Scientific based analysis is used to obtain and process the data.
- Comprehensive — All significant energy and materials uses and waste releases are included. Any elements missing because of data unavailability or cost and time constraints are clearly documented.
  • Detail — The inventory is conducted in a manner and to a level of detail commensurate with the purpose of the study.
- Peer reviewed — If the study results are to be used in a public manner, they should be peer reviewed using accepted protocols.
- Useful — The users of the study can make appropriate decisions in areas covered by the inventory. Any limitations regarding the utility of the study should be clearly noted.

The meeting of these criteria should make the life cycle inventory report useful, technically supportable, unbiased, and applicable.

EXAMPLES OF APPLICATIONS

In Chapter 1, the study of paper vs. plastic shopping bags was mentioned. In the analysis, conducted by students at the California State Polytechnic University at Pomona, the plastic bag won out over the paper bag as the most environmentally friendly. The studies considered:

- Raw materials processing
- Energy usage
- Bag manufacturing
- Usage
- Disposal and recycling

The students considered the chemicals used in the various processing steps and their MANPRINT. Table 2-1 shows the environmental impact resulting from the manufacture of one air dry ton of wood pulp by wood type. Figure 2-2 illustrates the impact on a landfill of disposal of 1000 paper and plastic bags. Figure 2-3 illustrates the impact of 1 million paper vs. plastic bags on the environment. Table 2-2 provides a summary of the data collected by the students in one of the studies. Before the study, the students did not comprehend the amount of energy and chemicals used in the processing of paper. The

**Table 2-1 Environmental Impacts of Manufacture of
1 Dry Ton of Wood Pulp**

	Kraft		
Item	Unbleached	Bleached	Groundwood
Virgin material (dry, tons)	1.0	1.1	1.1
Wastewater volume (gal)	24×10^3	47×10^3	10×10^3
Energy (BTU)	16×10^6	22×10^6	18×10^6
Solid wastes (lb)	135	225	164
Air emissions (lb)	50	64	65
Waterborne wastes[a] (lb)	46	90	25

[a] Includes BOD.

energy and chemicals involved with recycle of paper bags was seen as something most people would not have considered. The quantities and disposal of the wastes from the processing was a shock to the engineering student. There is no reason to think that a similar study of industrial products would not open the eyes of many senior managers.

Another example is a manufacturer of computer terminals. In this case the study started with the component manufacturing, i.e., semiconductor chips, semiconductor packages, printed wire board fabrication, displays, computer systems and assembly, use, and disposal (Figure 2-4). In each step of the processing, a study was made of all the material and energy inputs and outputs. This was a very large study. The report took multi-three-ring binders. The

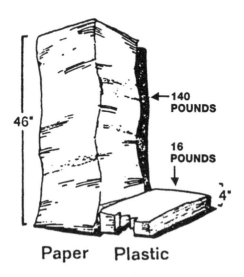

Paper   Plastic

Figure 2-2.   Impact on a landfill of disposal of 1000 paper grocery bags vs. 1000 plastic grocery bags.

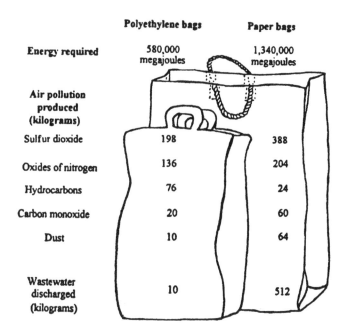

	Polyethylene bags	Paper bags
Energy required	580,000 megajoules	1,340,000 megajoules
Air pollution produced (kilograms)		
Sulfur dioxide	198	388
Oxides of nitrogen	136	204
Hydrocarbons	76	24
Carbon monoxide	20	60
Dust	10	64
Wastewater discharged (kilograms)	10	512

Figure 2-3. The energy dilemma. The environmental burdern per 1 million bags.

report resulted in reductions in chemicals used, changes to chemicals used, and lower energy consumption. Examples of chemicals originally used include

- Sulfuric acid
- Phosphine
- Xylene
- Glycol ethers
- Gold
- Isopropyl alcohol
- Epoxies
- Plastic molding compounds
- Polyethylene glycol
- RMA flux
- Alloy 42
- Nickel salts
- Metal resists
- Terpenes
- Chromic acid
- Yttrium compounds
- Hydrochloric acid
- Arsine

Table 2-2 Paper vs. Plastic Data Sheet

Process	Energy	Environmental impact	Manufacturability	Recyclability	Disposal
Plastic	580,000 megajoules per bag required Can be incinerated to produce energy High internal energy content (BTU/lb) Uses about half the energy it takes to produce an equal number of paper bags	Thermal decomposition produces aldehydes Water wastes produced through production Littering of postconsumer plastic; trash on streets, oceans, and wilderness areas Primary source of raw material is nonrenewable Can use renewable sources but more expensive	Inert final product Low energy consumption Gas blown Water-based inks Polyethylene pellets Uses additives such as oxidizing agents and colorants Easy to produce Raw material is a by-product of refining	Loses some desired properties Contamination issues Chemical additives (minor issue) Readily recyclable Recycle uses less energy than paper Has multiple secondary uses Easy to recycle	Not normally biodegradable; additives required Less volume in landfill than equal number of paper bags Less weight High internal energy content Can be incinerated

Paper				
1,340,000 megajoule per bag required Numerous equipment transfers required to complete a finished product	Odor producing Produces air and water pollutants Inorganic fillers such as ink and adhesives produce large quantities of wastes Deforestation Carcinogenic byproducts produced Not readily biodegradable	Messy manufacturing Numerous operations to finish the product Government rules have increased costs	Low profit margin in recycling Limited degree of reprocessing Secondary fibers are lower quality Very high capital investment	Increases solid wastes Not readily biodegradable Large relative volume

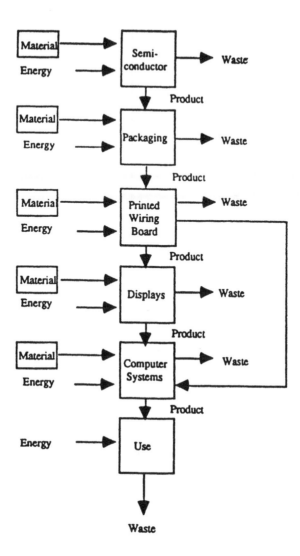

Figure 2-4A. Top level schematic for the manufacture of a computer.

- Acetone
- Diborane
- Cyanide
- Aluminum
- RTV
- Dioctyl phthalate plasticizer
- Tin/lead solder
- Copper compounds
- Sodium hydroxide

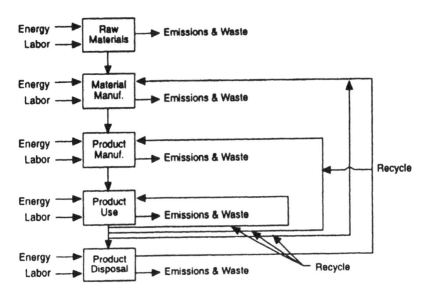

Figure 2-4B.   Basic product flow diagram. (From *Waste Minimization as a Strategic Weapon*, Ciambrone, D. F., CRC/Lewis Publishers, Boca Raton, FL, 1995.)

- Fluoboric acid
- Organic solvents
- Zinc sulfate
- Urethanes

and many others. One can readily see the opportunities for possible savings. This list does not include the use of energy. During the manufacture of the semiconductor chips, energy is used to power evaporators, ion diffusion equipment, and etchers. Plating baths use large quantities of power. For example, when plating printed wire boards with copper, the plating bath required 25 Amps per square foot of area being plated. An 18" × 24" panel, plated on both sides, requires 150 A. If there are eight panels in the tank at a time, this will require 1200 A. The injection molding equipment used to make the plastic housings, keyboard, etc., requires large electric motors. Machining the dies used on the molding equipment requires large motors as well. All of these processes have waste. This waste must be disposed of. Some of the waste or by-products are vapors and fugitive emissions that affect the environment. Reducing/changing the materials and processes can result in savings to the company and the environment.

Some of the savings mentioned resulted by redesign of the product. For example, by redesigning the computer keyboard, multiconfigurations could be built on the same basic base and subcomponents. The display housing would be the same for different configurations. If a different power supply was needed for one configuration and a different one for a second, the power supply went in the same location, fastened to different screw locations in the housing. A new housing was not required. The choice of material of construction was changed to allow for reuse of old housings or recycle of the material into new equipment. These changes had side affects. It now took the manufacturer less time and labor to assemble hardware with a net savings. The changes in processes and chemicals resulted in less material costs, stocking, and handling. The result was a less-expensive computer system and a better strategic advantage. Changes in processing should have a positive effect on the company's bottom line or it isn't worth doing. By reducing waste, however, the company reduced environmental costs and future liability.

3   LIFE CYCLE FRAMEWORK

SCOPE

This chapter discusses the procedural framework for performing a life cycle inventory. While there is agreement on the major elements of an inventory, procedural discussions occur at many phases of the process. To perform a study whose intended use is to evaluate the environmental burden (MANPRINT) associated with a product, process, or activity, the scope of the study must be clearly defined. The following components, at a minimum, should be defined:

- How the results will be used
- The product, process, and activity to be studied
- Reasons for conducting the study
- The elements not to be addressed
- The elements of the analysis

At the onset of the study, the level of detail must be decided. Sometimes it is obvious from the application or intended use. In other circumstances, there will be several options to choose. These will range from generic study to one that is very product or process specific. Most life cycle studies fall between these two extremes. Even at the product-specific study level the company can determine whether their need can be met by one of the following approaches:

- Full scale life cycle
- Partial life cycle
- Individual stages or processes

The partial life cycle approach consists of several stages. This allows for stages to be omitted if they have been studied before and are static for purposes of this study. The life cycle analysis can also be limited to specific stages or processes. This would be the case if a new process is being considered or if the product finds another use or market.

To assist in providing focus and direction, it is extremely important to clearly understand how the results will be used. Management needs to be able to clearly define why the study is being undertaken, who will use the data and why. The potential users need to understand what is being supplied and what they are expected to do with the information. This will help define how the data are taken and formatted for future use.

Probably the most enterprising step is to define what is to be studied. The organization has a reason for wanting to conduct the study. Now the issue is exactly what to study. This sounds ridiculous but, unfortunately, it's true. Here we must not only specifically define which product or process to study but which aspects of it. In some cases, companies have tried to study the "whole" life cycle and it wasn't too difficult. Their product was early in the "food chain." A logging company looking at their impact on the process of logging wouldn't have as large a study as a company making airplanes. Obviously, a study could be made on airplanes, assuming someone wanted to pay for it. A supermarket studying paper or plastic bags would not be focusing on vegetable deliveries or their containers.

The depth of the study is linked to the reason for wanting it. In some cases, certain aspects will be studied in depth and other areas in less depth. It is not unusual to look at certain selected processes or define the major areas of the life cycle of interest and use the data to compare alternative processes or products. In the case of airplanes, a company wanted to look at after-sale service and repair. This was to determine the impacts of the as-designed plane and what improvements could be made in the aircraft to help minimize these impacts. For example, a part of the study found that, during customer maintenance, stripping paint from the planes and repainting created a large amount of hazardous waste. The waste included paint strippers and the dissolved paint. The local air quality management authority would be interested in the impact on air. The airplane manufacturer had the same problem to a lesser degree. The study of the maintenance cycle found that heavy abrasives damaged the aluminum skin of the planes. Sandblasting could also cause damage, depending on the parameters of the setup and where it was used. They found that by blasting with very small carbon dioxide pellets the paint came off with no damage to the airplane's skin. The process did not create air pollution and the only residual was the solid paint. The carbon dioxide sublimated to a gas leaving just the solid paint. The solid paint was not considered a hazardous waste. This saved not just all the paperwork, health, safety, and environmental issues but also the costs of disposing of a hazardous waste.

A summary study could also be made to provide management with areas that would potentially lead to cost or environmental improvements. This approach would provide for future focused studies.

As indicated above, knowing what to study is half the problem. The other half is to define what is *not to be studied.* For example, " This study will not address aesthetic and socioeconomic issues." By understanding the purpose of the study and the system boundaries (what is and isn't included), it will assure a valid interpretation of the results.

To follow the process one needs to understand some basic definitions that will be used in the text and graphics. The following short definitions will provide the reader with the knowledge required.

In life cycle analysis, the "system" refers to a collection of operations that together perform some well-defined function.

Life cycle inventory accounts for every *significant* step in a product system. To assist, system flow diagrams are used. The diagrams assist with necessary calculations.

DEFINING BOUNDARIES

Boundary conditions refer to what is included and excluded from each step in the process. Since various aspects may be bundled, the boundary condition defines what is bundled and not treated independently. For example, a study might include transportation, distribution, and storage as one "operation" because other aspects of the product life cycle are more important at the time.

A complete life cycle inventory includes and quantifies resource and energy use and environmental releases throughout the product life cycle as illustrated in Figure 3-1. The major stages considered include the following activities:

Raw materials acquisition and energy. The boundaries of this element include all activities needed for the acquisition of all raw materials

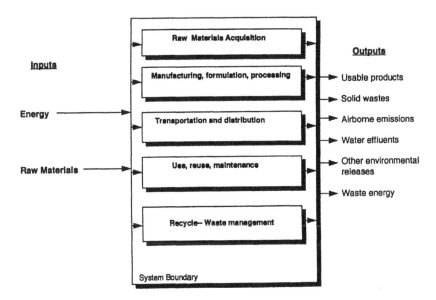

Figure 3-1. Life cycle inventory.

and or ends with the first manufacturing or processing stage that refines the raw materials.

Manufacturing, formulation, and processing. The processing step takes the raw materials and converts them into products.

Transportation and distribution. This aspect of a life cycle analysis is common to almost all such studies. In this stage, the product undergoes a physical change in location or configuration. It does not involve a transformation of materials. Transportation is movement of materials and energy involved. The transportation and distribution stage might involve multiple activities at various times in the life cycle. Transportation during the raw materials and manufacturing stage is usually included in the these stages. The stage for transportation and distribution involves those activities used after manufacturing.

Use, reuse, and maintenance. The boundary condition for this stage begins after the distribution of product or materials and ends at the point where the product or materials are discarded and enter a waste management system. The impact the product has on the environment during use/reuse will vary with each product. If the product uses energy, fuel, or another natural resource, this is an important stage.

Recycle, waste management. The recycle step involves reclaiming materials out of the waste management system and returning them to the manufacturing or processing stage. Waste management is the effective disposal of any material released to any environment — land, air, or water. Waste streams are generated at each phase of the life cycle. Waste management includes any mechanisms for treating, handling, or transportation of wastes prior to their release into the environment.

The obtaining of raw materials and the manufacturing stages can be and usually are complex. Because of this we can establish sub-boundary conditions for these activities. An example is shown in Figure 3-2. In the figure the manufacturing boundary has included three fundamental steps.

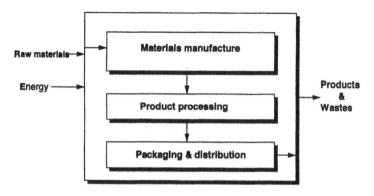

Figure 3-2. Manufacturing stage.

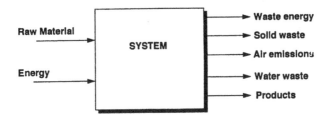

Figure 3-3. Top layer model.

To keep the analysis under control, the mapping of the "processes" to be included needs to be done. This will enable the process to be visualized and facilitate the proper setting of boundaries and depth of analysis. This can be accomplished using a simple method of modeling. In this "systems" model you will start at the *top* layer as shown in Figure 3-3. In Figure 3-3, the whole of what is to be studied is in the box. This is level 1.0. Level 1.0 can be broken down into the next layer. For example, the owner of "Acme Plastics & Plating" does injection molding of plastic parts and chrome plates them. He is interested in the life cycle impact of the plated plastic shower heads on the environment. To do this he will model the life cycle of his product and decide the boundary conditions based on his model. The owner has decided to exclude the processes of making the ABS plastic and the manufacture of the plating solutions he purchases. These will be considered raw materials to him. The top level system diagram (1.0), therefore, is shown in Figure 3-4.

Level 2.0 further breaks the process down as shown in Figure 3-5. Each block on the model has a number assigned based on where it came from. For example, in the level 2.0 model layer, each block has an identification number, such as 2.1 for manufacturing. This allows the user to take each block and systematically break it down as far as he wants to without losing track of where it belongs in the system. This is further illustrated in Figure 3-6. In this figure, block 2.1, manufacturing, was expanded. We further expanded this in Figure 3-7 by breaking down block 2.1.3. Each of the blocks in Figure 3-6

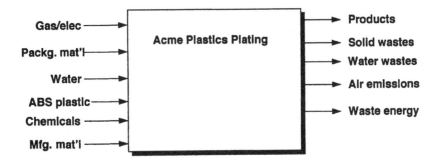

Figure 3-4. Acme level 1.0.

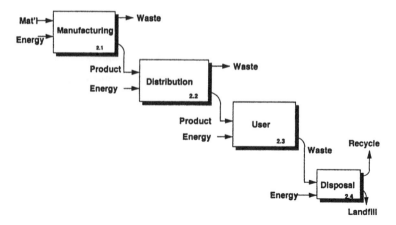

Figure 3-5.   Level 2.0 model.

can and should be further broken down. As a rule, each breakdown should not have more than four to six blocks. In our example, Figure 3-7 is as far as we need to go for this block. Modeling in this fashion provides the following advantages:

- Understand the process flow in detail
- Simple means to verify the flow
- Identify and quantify the wastes and products from each step
- Insure you captured all the required information
- Facilitates trying a "what if" scenario process

The models can actually have quantifiable numbers written in for each arrow on the incoming and outgoing side of each block or allow the use of formal check sheets for each block. If the quantifiable numbers for such things

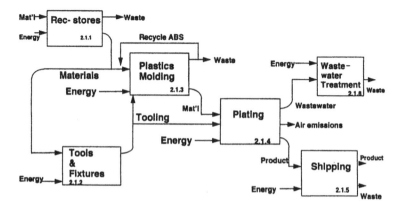

Figure 3-6.   Manufacturing.

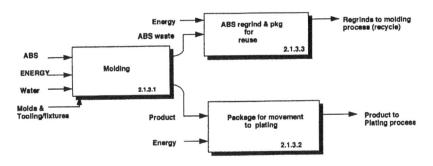

Figure 3-7. Plastics molding.

as energy is not available at each step, the analyst may try to arrange for measurements, calculate the energy based on data about the equipment (HP of motors, etc., for the time of analysis), or find the level where it is available and partition it as best as possible. For example, the user could take the total gas and electric usage for the facility and apportion the approximate amount to the areas under study. Whatever method is used, make special note of it for future reference. Whenever possible, the data describing the performance of the subsystems should be drawn from primary sources. In some cases, the manufacturing subsystem will be unique to the system being studied. When secondary or published data sources are used, the data source should be clearly referenced. Any inherent limitations in the data should be clearly identified.

When conducting the study, it is essential that the operating period chosen be long enough to smooth out any atypical behavior such as machine downtime, setup operations, or changes in flow due to stock/material fluctuations. A period of 9 to 12 months is found to be best. Although it is tempting to use industry averages, it is better to use actual data from the processes being studied whenever possible.

CHECKLISTS AND THEIR APPLICATION AND USE

The use of this type of modeling facilitates both simple and complex processes and systems. The model makes use of data gathering and check sheets for easier understanding and minimizes missed data. A sample check sheet is shown in Figure 3-8. Because the user may want to determine where the MANPRINTS are the largest or where there are opportunities in the product stream to minimize environmental impacts, this method can provide a less-costly means of analysis and data gathering than conventional methods.

When the user actually models the product flow it will become evident that certain processes are interdependent on others. Therefore, a change to one area needs to be analyzed to determine the impact, if any, downstream. In the case of Acme Plastics & Plating, if the engineers changed thermoplastic to improve the molding process and reduce waste, there might be a major impact (positive or negative) on the plating operation.

DATA GATHERING

Many life cycle inventories are conducted for internal use only, where confidentiality is not an issue. All data collected should be considered company private. However, some aspects of the inventory may require outside information. Obtaining accurate data is of concern. This difficulty can be somewhat overcome by the use of outside sources of "standard" data, peer review for external data and inventories be developed to provide for maintenance of the generic information and insure relative accuracy. The acquiring of data from external sources will to some extent rely on the use of confidentiality agreements. There are many sources of public information for use in the life cycle inventory. Examples of these include:

- U.S. Department of Energy (DOE) databases of energy uses by industry aggregate
- U.S. Environmental Protection Agency (EPA) databases include the range of chemical quantities used by site and emissions estimations
- Local/regional gas and electric companies
- Open literature, including journals, patents, trade publications
- Trade/technical associations publications and databases
- U.S. Department of Commerce (DOC) databases
- U.S. Department of Defense (DOD) databases

The use of case-specific and industry average data is an important issue. No requirements exist that define what type of data is to be used for the analysis. The quality of the data can have a drastic affect on the life cycle inventory results. Because of this, it is important to be aware of the source of the data, the type of data (industry average, literature data, specific process data, etc.), worst case or average or best case, and the limitations. Data on specific environmental emissions are preferable in the inventory whenever possible. The data should also be normalized for the actual amount of product being produced, not the plant capacity. There will be sections of the life cycle analysis that can and should use industry data to control cost of the analysis. In all cases, the most recent data should always be used.

When evaluating wastes from any process, all the wastes must be accounted for. Wastes from some processes are easy to quantify. They are solids and can be weighed. In the cases of the injection molding process for Acme Plastics & Plating, the wastes are plastic (weighable), water from the molding die cooling line (measurable — gal/min, heat — temp), and fugitive heat (nonmeasurable to any accuracy). In other cases there are mainstream and fugitive emissions. Both should be used. When an emission is not measurable, a qualitative discussion is required, and conclusions should explicitly reflect this deficiency or condition. There is another release that needs to be considered in the time period being studied: the accidental release. The inclusion of accidental releases should be made based on history of the process. It can be included as a correction factor and added to routine releases.

During the data gathering, it is likely that you will encounter gaps in the data. This will be because the information is not available, is inconsistent, or is reported as nondetectable. It is important to note what data were not available and why. In the case of the not available category, information is sometimes lumped in with other data that the accounting or management uses. Sometimes it is extractable. However, it usually isn't worth the effort or cost to obtain it. In some instances, data are available from the people working on the processes being studied. Their data are usually more accurate and up to date. Some information that management thinks is unavailable is obtainable from the workers in the area in question. Don't forget to talk to the people actually doing the work. Sensitivity analysis will be covered in a later chapter.

CONSTRUCTION OF A CONCEPTUAL MODEL

To construct the basic models the user will make a "flow diagram" of the overall product/process flow to be considered in the study. This can be along the lines of that shown in Figures 3-5 and 3-6. Next the user will make detailed process diagrams as shown in Figure 3-7. If more detail is needed then further refinements at lower levels will need to be made. Consult with process/product experts to insure model and data requirements accuracy. Once the auditor is satisfied that he or she has enough detail in the models to satisfy the audit requirements, then the data gathering will begin. This way the auditor knows exactly what data are required. This saves time collecting useless information. The sample checksheet as shown in Figure 3-8 may be used for each process for information gathering. Next the auditor will assemble the data on each applicable diagram to characterize each individual process (see Figure 3-9). This process allows for the accounting of all the information and identifications of data gaps. The diagrams can now be put together and the data added at each process detail level for inclusion on the next level diagram above them. For example, if Figure 3-9 is one of the elements on Figure 3-7, and all the other "processes" on Figure 3-7 are complete, then their totals would be entered on Figure 3-6 for process block 2.1.3 Likewise, all the data on Figure 3-6 could be totaled and entered in Figure 3-5 for block 2.1, etc.

Starting at the top and breaking everything down to the lowest appropriate level allows for an understanding of the total operation and prevents omissions. By starting at the lowest level and researching/entering the required data, it allows for a systems accounting of all the data and identification of gaps. Spreadsheets can sometimes help (see example in Figure 3-10). This upward linking prevents inadvertent omissions and double counting errors. During this operation the use of standard metrics will be applied. This includes the conversion of energy fuel value into standard energy units, such as million BTU or gigajoule. This principle also allows the user to identify possible reuse or

```
┌─────────────────────────────────────────────────────────────┐
│                   ELCA DATA CHECKSHEET                        │
├─────────────────────────────────────────────────────────────┤
│ ELCA PROJECT NAME:        _____             │
│                                                              │
│ INVESTIGATOR:             _____             │
│                                                              │
│ DATE:                _____                           │
│                                                              │
│ MODEL SUBASSEMBLY BLOCK                                      │
│    REFERENCE NUMBER:      _____                      │
│                                                              │
│ PROJECT ID NUMBER:        _____                      │
│                                                              │
│ COMPANY                                                      │
├─────────────────────────────────────────────────────────────┤
│      INPUT ITEMS          QTY.          UNITS                │
│                                                              │
│      RAW MATERIALS                  Kg/lbs/gal/ltr/cuft      │
│                                                              │
│                                                              │
│                                                              │
│         Energy                      KW/Hp/MJ                 │
│                                                              │
│         OTHER                                                │
│                                                              │
│      OUTPUT ITEMS                                            │
│                                                              │
│      RAW MATERIALS                  Kg/lbs/gal/ltr/cuft      │
│                                                              │
│                                                              │
│         ENERGY                      KW/Hp/MJ                 │
│                                                              │
│                                                              │
│         OTHER                                                │
└─────────────────────────────────────────────────────────────┘
```

Figure 3-8.   Sample checksheet.

recycle applications for wastes from each process. For example, the waste hot water in Figure 3-9 may be able to be used as a final rinse in the plating operation at the plant or to heat a plating tank. This would allow for less energy costs to the plant and dual use for the water. The discharge may be usable for irrigation or other use if not contaminated. One will notice the impact of one area or process on another. It is imperative that the auditor keep track of the interdependencies between processes. It should be clear that an action in the manufacturing can impact something in distribution, use, or disposal.

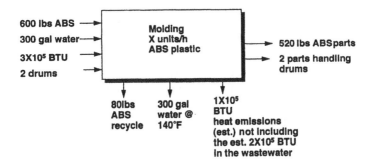

Figure 3-9. Data model example. There are six identical molding machines, each running two 8-hour shifts per 5-day week.

INTERPRETATION AND REPORTING OF RESULTS

When writing a report to present the final results of the life cycle inventory, it is important to consider the following:

- The methodology used
- The *intended use* of the study
- The boundary conditions set
- All assumptions used
- The *intended users* of the study

Life cycle inventories generate a great deal of information. The auditor/analyst needs to select the presentation format and content that are best

Purpose: What is being studied ? Why ?									
Scope / Limitations: What are the boundaries ? Assumptions ?									
	Inputs				Outputs				Other
Process number	Air	Water	Chem./Mat'l	Energy	Air	Water	Chem./Mat'l	Energy	
No.									
Raw materials									
Materials									
Packaging									
Products									
Wastes									
Energy									

Use spreadsheet for each process under study.

Figure 3-10. Sample spreadsheet for data integration.

suited for the intended purpose of the study. It is now that the data collected becomes information. The data will now be analyzed and formatted to provide information the intended user can actually use. It is important to not simplify the information solely for the sake of the presentation. In preparing for the presentation, it is useful to identify the various perspectives embodied in the life cycle information. These include but are not limited to the following:

- Relative contributions of each "process" to the overall system
- Overall system and its subunits
- Temporal issues
- Data parameters groups within each category, e.g., water wastes, air emissions, solid wastes
- Data categories across processes
- Geographic conditions relevant to the study
- Data parameters within groups

The analyst must present the information in a manner that increases the comprehension of the results without oversimplifying them. It is obvious, therefore, that knowing who is going to use the results and for what purpose will simplify the analyst's job of presenting the information. The information can be presented in graphic and tabular formats. The author suggests a combination of both. The following suggestions should be considered when presenting the information.

- Provide total energy results
- Provide energy results broken down by "process" (process is each stage or useful subgroup)
- Present wastes as industrial, package/distribution, consumer, and postconsumer
- Categorize air emissions, waterborne wastes, and industrial solid wastes by process
- Present energy utilization by major category or by process

The use of tabular presentation is very comprehensive. The choice of how the tables are formatted varies based on the scope and use of the study. If the study was to determine what packaging system to use, the overall system results can be used. If it is to compare two competing packaging systems, again the overall system results would be of interest. However, if the study was performed to determine how the packaging could be changed to minimize the impact from its use on the environment, then it is important to not just present the overall results but contributions made by each component of the packaging system. For example, in the case of the plated plastic parts from Acme, it would be necessary to consider the plastic bag each part is placed in, the cardboard box it is placed in, the corrugated box the individual boxes are packaged in, and the stretch wrap around the boxes. If a pallet is used as part of the shipping then it will be included. The user can concentrate improvement efforts on the components that make substantial contributions to minimizing the environmental impact of the packaging.

Graphical presentation of information helps to augment tabular data and aids comprehension. Pie or bar charts or graphics such as drawings, flow charts, photos, or combinations are useful. These types of charts help the user take ownership of the information. When making the report and charts, the analyst needs to ask and answer questions about what each graph is intended to convey. It may be necessary to use multiple charts to convey the intended message. Figures 2-2, 2-3, 10-4, 10-5, 10-8, and Appendix C illustrate the use of multiple format graphics.

As noted earlier, it is imperative that the analyst understand the intended use of the study. It will facilitate determining what type of data is most applicable, for example, industry wide or mostly site specific. It will assist in the preparation and the presenting of the information. Understanding the user and the intended use of the study will prevent misunderstandings and unintended use of the study. The effective communication of the results must include an understanding of the assumptions made and the boundary conditions placed on the study. Careful interpretation is required to avoid making unsupported claims.

An important aspect of the interpretation or understanding of the study is the data accuracy. If the data are "industry wide", the user must be careful in their use. The same process conducted at different plants may use similar but different materials, technologies, equipment, and be of different age and efficiency. The different plant sites may be operating under different government regulations such as environmental. Factors such as these need to be understood before using the industry data. If the data are from industry averages and not heavily weighted in the overall study, use may contribute to the conclusion but, in itself, is not a driving factor. These data are subject to both systematic and random error. Site-specific data are true random error. This type of error can be described in conventional statistical terms using mean and standard deviation of the measured results. However, systematic variation due to feedstock or technology/equipment differences is not random error. These sources of variability are "explainable" by virtue of the conditions, technology, age, or other identifiable factors of the plants used. The analyst should explain the importance of these sources of variability to the user. For example, some plating equipment uses steam for the source of heat while others use electricity.

Boundary conditions and data for many internal life cycle studies may require the interpretation of the results for a particular corporation. The results may be very specific to that particular company. This would preclude the use of industry standards or averages. Therefore, a high degree of accuracy may be assumed.

Most life cycle studies are for the internal use of the company or organization that chartered and funded it. When results of life cycle analysis are released to the public, however, they are usually used to support a specific statement by the company. It is important that the information provided was not selectively derived and that all pertinent information is included

The use of published studies comparing competitive products, processes, materials, or practices must be presented cautiously. The assumptions, boundaries, and data quality should be considered in presenting conclusions. Studies with different boundary conditions may have different results but both may be accurate.

4   GENERAL ISSUES

Before a life cycle inventory is started, it is important that each of the participants understand their respective role. The following summarizes the main role of key participants.

Life cycle participant	Responsibilities
Accounting	Assign environmental costs to products, processes, calculate hidden liabilities, etc.
Marketing/advertising	Give feedback on existing products and demands for alternatives, value of low environmental impact, inform customers of reduced environmental risk and benefits
Distribution/packaging	Provide data requested; provide reduced impact concepts and estimate of cost/environmental impacts-risks
Government regulators Standards organizations	Provide copies of rules/regulations/laws, provide copies of studies/reports, provide environmental impact data previously developed
Design engineers	Provide information on materials and "processes" used in present products and what is being considered on new products; provide data on concepts for reducing environmental impact and any cost studies associated with the concepts
Manufacturing engineers	Provide data on manufacturing processes including inputs and outputs, wastes and pollution prevention activities in place or underway; materials and process inputs and outputs
Management	Establish corporate environmental policy; charter the life cycle inventory and analysis, insure follow up and implementation of proper and cost-effective activities arising from the analysis

Life cycle participant	Responsibilities
Purchasing	Provide the input on products/raw materials including specifications, costs, and known environmental impacts; assist suppliers in reducing environmental impact by sharing company data cleared for release by management
Waste management professionals	Offer information on the fate of industrial wastes and retired consumer products; environmental impacts and risks, alternative waste disposal methods and costs and risks associated with the alternatives, information on recyclability and markets
Service	Provide input on repair and maintenance processes and concepts for improvements

TEMPLATES

During a life cycle analysis there will be issues that are encountered in evaluating and using the information. Most references emphasize the use of templates. The key issues to be discussed in this chapter include

- The use of templates
- Boundary conditions
- Data issues and concerns

A life cycle analysis can become quite complex in a very short time. As illustrated in Chapter 3, the easiest way to map out the product flow and processes involved is to use diagrams or templates. A template is a guide used to aid the analyst in collecting and allocating data. Product flows can start as simply as the one shown in Figures 2-4 and 3-5 and the Appendix. However, it becomes obvious that this level of detail is inadequate. Detail diagrams are required. More detailed process flow charts for the "manufacturing" processes are illustrated in Figures 4-1 and 4-2. Examples are illustrated in Chapter 3. Some texts use the basic template shown in Figure 4-3. The basic templates used must be developed to the lowest level (subsections) necessary to obtain the required data. The diagrams assist in keeping track of the information. Whether the analyst uses the contemporary format, Figure 4-3, or the type illustrated in Chapter 3, they all attempt to do the same thing. Each chart will have

Inputs	Outputs
Raw or intermediate materials	Air emissions
Energy	Waterborne wastes

Inputs	Outputs
Water	Solid wastes
Other inputs	Products

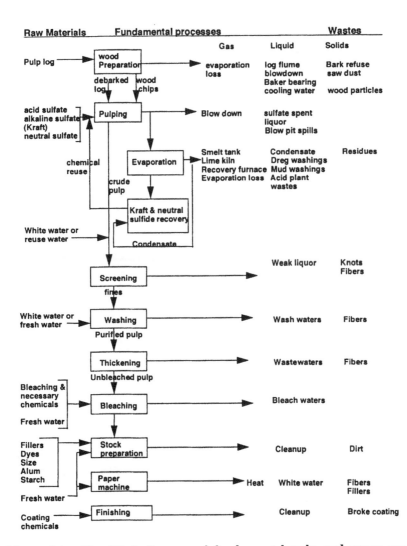

Figure 4-1. Simplified diagram of fundamental pulp and paper processes. (From *Industrial and Hazardous Waste Treatment,* Nemerow, N.L. and Dasgupta, A.D., Van Nostrand Reinhold, New York, 1991, 928. With permission.)

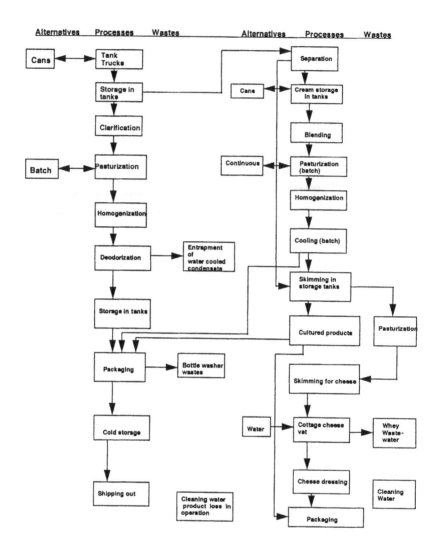

Figure 4-2.   Process flow chart for fluid-milk preparation. (From *Industrial and Hazardous Waste Treatment,* Nemerow, N.L. and Dasgupta, A.D., Van Nostrand Reinhold, New York, 1991, 462. With permission.)

DATA ISSUES

The thing to remember is that in some cases the materials input is actually the product of a previous step. With that product may be packaging materials that will become waste or raw materials. During the analysis, any waste

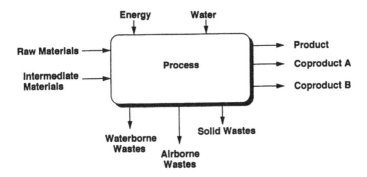

Figure 4-3. Life cycle inventory template.

treatment system used during a process is considered a process and should be modeled as such.

The input materials for each subsection are referred to as raw or intermediate materials. Raw materials are usually materials that have been extracted from the earth but have not been refined or manufactured. Examples include mineral ore, animals, plant products, etc. Intermediate materials are those that have undergone some level of processing. The most complete life cycle inventory will begin at the raw materials level. In the case of the milk in Figure 4-2, it may be considered an intermediate because of the cows. There is an impact on the environment from the raising and keeping of cows. Others may consider the milk a raw material since nothing has happened to it prior to arriving at the milk processing plant. If one considers the milk to be the starting point, then the rationale for the decision must be noted. The same rationale may be applied to the pulp/paper process in Figure 4-1.

Deciding which raw/intermediate materials to include in a life cycle inventory is complex. Several options are available:

- Include all materials no matter how minor.
- Within the scope of the study and boundary conditions set, exclude inputs less than a predetermined and clearly stated threshold.
- Within the boundary and scope of the study, exclude inputs determined to be negligible relative to the intended use of the analysis.
- Within the scope of the study, consistently exclude certain classes or types of inputs. Again, clearly define this exclusion and why the decision was made.

The advantage of the first approach is that the analyst does not have to explain or defend what has been included or excluded. The disadvantage is that the whole study could become a long, expensive exercise. The computational aspect of including everything could be exhaustive.

The second alternative, implemented with full explanation of what the threshold was and why it was selected, would have the advantage of less time, lower cost, consistency, and less cumbersome calculations. An accepted means of accomplishing this is to use the 1% rule. Any contribution considered to be less than 1% to the specified subsystem will be excluded. Care must be used, however. If something in that 1% has a serious affect on the overall MANPRINT, then it can not be excluded.

A life cycle analysis may be used to improve the "GREENNESS" of a product including its processing or its overall MANPRINT on the environment. In cases such as these, the analyst will want to determine and indicate whether the materials/resources used are renewable or nonrenewable. A set of definitions for these two terms are

- Renewable material/resource — A renewable material or resource is one that is being replaced in the environment in a time frame relevant to society.

Examples include certain species of wood, farm crops, kelp, etc. Note that the materials/resources must be renewable and be replenished in a time frame relevant to society. Some materials that would have been renewable have been so overused that they are no longer considered renewable.

- Nonrenewable material/resource — Nonrenewable materials/resource is one that is *not* being replaced in the environment in a time frame relevant to society.

Examples include minerals mined from the land, coal, oil, natural gas, and materials from exhausted supplies.

Energy is shown as an input on templates. The energy shown at higher levels is a composite of those at each subsequent subsystems. There are three classes of energy for use in the analysis: process energy, transportation energy, and energy of material resources.

Process energy is required to operate and run each process in the subsystems. These include electrical power for motors, pumps, reactors, plating cells, etc. and gas for heating. Transportation energy is the energy required for various modes of transportation such as trucks, ships, airplanes, rail carriers, barges, and pipelines. Forklifts and conveyors could be considered either as transportation or as process according to their role in the subsystem. There are alternatives to reporting energy used. One is to report actual energy input such as cubic feet of gas or kilowatt hours of electricity. The second is to report the specific quantities of fuels used to generate the produced energy forms in the subsystem.

The first approach has definite advantages. In this approach, mixed energy sources can be easily handled. For example, if the company wanted to evaluate the use of an electrically heated system compared to a natural gas system, they could evaluate the kilowatt hours to cubic feet of natural gas. Costs could easily be compared. The cubic feet of gas and kilowatt hours could be converted to megajoules for comparison. It is not uncommon to calculate the "precombustion energy" of a subsystem. The difference between combustion and precombustion of energy is what is included. Combustion energy is the energy contained in a unit volume, such as 175,000 BTU per gallon. If a gallon of this material was burned, it would release 175,000 BTU of energy. However, if obtaining the fuel took an additional 25,000 BTU of energy (drilling and production of the material, transportation, etc.), the total "precombustion" energy is 200,000 BTU. The inclusion of the precombustion energy is analogous to extending the boundaries of the system for energy. The inclusion or exclusion of the precombustion energy should be clearly stated. In most cases the energy used comes from commercial sources or is totally or partially generated on site. The inclusion of electrical energy from a public utility can be indicated as kilowatt hours and in dollars. The kilowatt hours can be converted to megajoules for comparison if necessary. Natural gas is usually obtained from a utility or gas supplier. The gas can be recorded as cubic feet and be converted to BTU or megajoules. Gasoline or diesel fuel for transportation is usually purchased from a retailer. Here too, the energy can be reported as gallons and converted, if necessary, to BTU or megajoules. In the case of most energy, it is considered coming from nonrenewable sources unless otherwise noted. The use of hydroelectric power would be an exception. Even in these cases, it is not uncommon for a utility to "mix" the sources of the electrical power from plants burning coal or oil with that from hydroelectric. An example of a power grid electrical source mix is

Fuel	%
Coal	5
Nuclear	20
Hydroelectric	10
Natural gas	10
Oil	4
Other[a]	<1

[a] Includes wood and waste to energy sources, geothermal, wind, but excludes cogeneration sources.

The theoretical conversion of kilowatt hours to common fuel units (joules) is 3.61 MJ/KWh. However, the user may use 11.3 MJ/KWh to reflect the actual use of fuel to deliver electricity to the user from the power grid.

Water volume requirements should be included in a life cycle inventory. How should water be included? The goal is to measure, per unit product, the amount of water that represents the water not available for beneficial use.

Water drawn from a stream, used in a process, and replaced in essentially the same quantity, location, and condition should not be counted in the analysis. This water is considered flow through. On the other hand, water taken from a groundwater source and discharged to the surface must be considered. The groundwater is not directly being replaced. Water from a utility and discharged to the sewer is considered. In the process of conducting the life cycle analysis, the analyst will consider the net amount of water consumed.

A life cycle analysis takes into consideration five types of outputs: airborne wastes, waterborne wastes, solid waste, products, and coproducts. Each of these categories of outputs is quantified during the study for each subsection and rolled up to higher levels as appropriate. In the past, some analysts have used just reportable wastes in the analysis. It is now the practice to report all waste discharges where the data can be obtained.

Air emissions are reported on a weight basis. The amounts should be the actual amounts of waste. It is permissible to report only the waste being emitted to the environment and exclude those being trapped or treated in a waste abatement system. However, the study will need to consider the treatment system as a subsystem and model it accordingly. If the waste treatment system is complex, it may be beneficial to treat it as a subsystem. Fugitive emissions and those from production or transportation are reportable. Typical atmospheric emissions include, but are not limited to

- Volatile organic compounds (VOCs)
- Sulfur oxides (SO_x)
- Nitrogen oxides (NO_x)
- Carbon monoxide (CO)
- Ammonia (NH_3)
- Lead (Pb)
- Chrome (Cr)
- Particulates

Carbon dioxide and water vapor are not usually included. If obtaining the data on these two substances is not too difficult, they should be included.

Waterborne wastes are reported in units of weight and include all substances. When possible, it should include all waterborne waste and not just those required to be reported by law. In general the broader the definition of wastes used and reported in the analysis the better the evaluation of the MANPRINT the product and process has on the environment. Any accidental discharges to the environment are reportable in the study. Some of the more commonly reported waterborne wastes and waste indicators are

- Biological oxygen demand (BOD)
- Chemical oxygen demand (COD)
- Suspended solids (SS)
- Settleable solids (SS)

- Dissolved solids (DS)
- Fats, oil, and grease (FOG)
- Phenols
- Metal ions (copper, iron, chrome, etc.)
- Anions (such as sulfides, chlorides, fluorides, etc.)
- Phosphates
- In some cases bacteria or virus
- Sludge or filtered solids

The above list is not all inclusive. Actual wastes will vary for each system depending on type of industry, process, and the range of water carrying wastes related to the product or process. For example, the waste from a food processing plant making corn chips is primarily corn meal. While not truly hazardous, much corn can be discharged. This will drastically raise the BOD, COD, and suspended solids levels. The owners of the plant might consider a treatment system enabling them to sell the waste corn meal as animal feed and reusing the water for cooling towers before discharge. The owners would now have a secondary product and get more "bang for their buck" with the additional use of the water.

Solid waste includes all solid material disposed of from all sources within the system being studied. Solid wastes are reported by weight. Depending on the comparisons, solid wastes may be converted to volume for comparisons in landfill disposal (see Figure 2-2). If volume numbers are used, weight should be reported as well.

It is sometimes desirable to segregate the wastes by type. This aids in determining which process may be capable of modification to reduce the wastes.

Solid wastes are also differentiated by production and postconsumer wastes. Postconsumer wastes are those wastes generated from product/packaging. This includes the packaging materials that are discarded by the user and the disposal of the product after its intended use.

Process wastes are those wastes generated during the manufacturing cycles of the product(s). This includes trim wastes, sludges, or any solid used to make the product that is not shipped as part of the product. All solid waste is considered, both hazardous and nonhazardous.

The depth that the analyst takes with wastes including solid depends on the effective boundary conditions set for the study. One may or may not include wastes from the refining of the fuels used at the production site(s) or for transportation, mining tailings from ore production, and slag from refining.

Products identified for the templates are defined by the system and subsystem being studied. At a top system level, the end product shipped by the company is the product. At subsystem levels, the "product(s)" are the output of that subsystem. In the case of the example at Acme Plastics & Plating, the end product is the plastic plated "widget" that is shipped. At the injection molding step, the product is the plastic molded widget. At this point, the widget

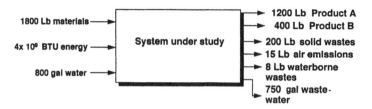

Figure 4-4. Mixed product subsystem.

is not yet complete, but it is the output of that particular process; thus, it is the product for that subsystem. Each subsystem has a product and possible coproducts that are components or subassemblies of the final product. Anything else produced at each system or subsystem level that is not disposed of as a waste and gets further processing into another product or is sold as a raw material is considered a coproduct.

If a process or subsystem has coproducts, it is the custom to allocate all inputs and outputs to each product being produced. This allows for the evaluation of resources and wastes (Figures 4-4 through 4-6). While it is customary to consider all coproducts, each system being studied needs to be handled on a case-by-case basis. Coproducts are of interest only to the point where they no longer affect the primary product being considered. Subsequent steps past the point of interest to the primary product are beyond the scope and boundary of the study and need not be included past that point. If during the study sufficient details can be found about the coproducts to facilitate the study, then they may be summed at the point of interest. This reduces the time and effort required in modeling. For chemical processing, this can become quite complex. In cases such as these, mass allocation may be necessary. Where it is not possible to allocate separate coproducts, it will be necessary to lump them together as joint wastes. An example is the electrolytic treatment of brine. This produces sodium, hydrogen, and chlorine as coproducts. In this case, one might want to consider the emissions containing chlorine alone. However, the electrolytic cell also produces sodium and hydrogen at the same time. The cell cannot produce sodium and hydrogen alone. Chlorine will be coproduced. In this case all three may be lumped as a joint waste. Any allocation of power will need to be done on a mass weight allocation basis.

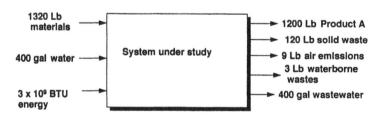

Figure 4-5. Coproduct allocation — Product A.

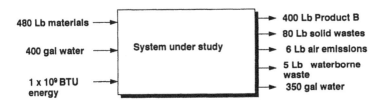

480 Lb materials

400 gal water → System under study

1 x 10⁹ BTU energy

→ 400 Lb Product B
→ 80 Lb solid wastes
→ 6 Lb air emissions
→ 5 Lb waterborne waste
→ 350 gal water

Figure 4-6. Coproduct allocation — Product B.

Data quality greatly influences the end results. In the case of life cycle analysis, this is especially true. The development of uniform criteria is critical for the selection and reporting of data types and sources. Some basic objectives for data quality should be specified by the analyst based on the purpose of the study. In life cycle analysis, data can be considered being composed of two parts:

- Process and activity measurements that are amenable to standard statistical treatments
- Sets of assumptions and rules used for combining the data sets into a system

For purposes of this text, we will consider the process and activity. When collecting the data, careful consideration should be given to the age and frequency of the measurements. This is because technology or equipment can change and drastically affect the data. The frequency of the data acquisition is important to ensure that seasonal or other variability in the system is adequately captured. In addition, traditional indices of data quality such as precision, detection limits, completeness, and accuracy should be evaluated. The most accurate and recent data are desirable in a life cycle analysis. All data received must be carefully reviewed regarding the source and content before the data are used.

Much of the data being used will be from direct facility measurements or indirect estimates from published sources. Thus, accuracy is determined by the quality of the measurement and the estimation procedures used where all the variables were not known or controlled or by the averaging process used for representative systems. The use of industry data which have been averaged may be from different plants with different processes and equipment. They may also produce several products from the same process at each plant sight. Therefore, some engineering estimation and judgment is used when preparing the data for a particular product or process. Thus, the average data present for use may not be characteristic of any existing plant.

The quality of the data may be affected by confidentiality of the data. If the data are to be given to the public, it will tend to be more aggregated and more general in nature than if the data are generated to be confidential. Care must be exercised when using public or data from "industry" sources.

Detailed sources for all the operations in a life cycle inventory are not always available. The analyst may have to resort to periodicals, public databases, and textbooks which tend to be less accurate and lack the detail of direct measurements. In general, formal data quality criteria are not included in such sources. To overcome this issue the data may be compared to data from similar processes and estimates of their validity can be drawn. Where uncertainty is not understood, the analyst must note the condition, sources, and estimate of the degree of uncertainty.

Uncertainties in data are unavoidable. All data are not created equally. Some data have a greater impact on the outcome of the life cycle inventory than others. It is also not possible to establish the significance of any individual piece of datum to the final inventory set. The true test of whether an element of datum is significant to an inventory is the sensitivity of the final result to the elements inclusion or exclusion. The typical sensitivity analysis is conducted by evaluating the range of uncertainty in the input data and recalculating the model's output to see the result. Thus, the higher the degree uncertainty in strongly related variables, the less acceptable if the objectives of the study are to be met. As a rule, if an estimate of the true variability, such as measured statistical variance, is known, it should form a basis for the high and low range uncertainty estimates. The 95% confidence bounds are generally used for this purpose. For many inputs, the variability may not be known or may reflect variations of a process over time for which the analysis is being performed. It is usual in these cases to vary the input data by a range around its expected mean value. This may be as little as 3 to 5% for some variables and as much as an order of magnitude for others.

Order of magnitude estimates are sometimes used for setting the boundaries of an inventory. Deciding how far back to go, such order of magnitude estimates may be used to decide which inputs require a higher level of accuracy. In setting the boundaries, the analyst may want to determine if a process should be included or if order of magnitude estimates are acceptable. Running calculations with and without the data or a given process, it is possible to decide whether a variable has a large or small impact on the results. The analyst must keep in mind what the end use of the life cycle analysis is and who is the end user. In some cases, highly detailed sensitivity analysis is not needed or is minimized. For example, in one case the reporting of VOC in air emissions is adequate for the intended use. VOC is a measurement of a host of volatile chemicals in an air stream. The total VOC may be adequate. In another case the constituents of the VOC measurement will be needed as will the level of contribution of each one. In the first case, the user does not mind variability in the individual components. In the second case, care must be exercised to quantify each contributing chemical's presence and contribution to the total VOC measurement.

SPECIAL CONSIDERATIONS

Certain other conditions relative to data need to be highlighted. The first is the time period used for collecting the data. The time period needs to be long enough to smooth out any deviations or variations in the normal operating of the facility. A second condition is the geographic specificity. Natural resources and environmental consequences occur at specific sites but there are broader implications. It is important to describe the scope of interest in an inventory (local, national, international). Most inventories are done domestically and relate only to the country where the plant and customers are located. However, some studies are international in nature due to the location of natural resources, multiplant locations, or international use of the product(s). If no specific geographical data exist for a particular country when conducting an inventory, it is customary to use data from the U.S., Canada, Western Europe, or Japan where more accurate data most likely exist.

Care must be exercised to consider the technologies being used. For a life cycle analysis for a specific company, this can be relatively easy. For the use of industry data, the mix of technology may be more involved. It is wisest to use as much direct data as possible; however, the use of market share data to appropriate the data may be necessary. Accidental discharges or fugitive emissions need to be addressed. Whenever possible, fugitive and routine emissions and accidental emissions should be included. If data on fugitive emissions are not available, and quantitative estimates cannot be obtained, they may be omitted as long as this condition is duly noted. For accidental discharges, more frequent low-level discharges should be included. Low-frequency, high-level discharges, such as a major oil spill, probably would not be included. Tools other than a life cycle analysis may be more appropriate. In most cases, inputs and wastes from personnel at the site are not included. This includes such things as air conditioner emissions, lunch trash, wastewater from sanitary facilities, etc. Waste disposal of plant waste must be considered. Waste disposal in the total length of the life cycle must be considered. This includes such items as process wastewater treatment or disposal, product packaging wastes, and ultimate product disposal. The actual disposal method needs to be examined. For example, a "sanitary" landfill has emissions that are, or can be, hazardous to the environment. These include

- Methane gas (usually burned on site)
- Contaminated water from seepage and decomposition
- Sulfur compounds including hydrogen sulfide gas

The emissions from a landfill and how they are treated at the site are important. However, trying to determine how much is related to the product under study may be difficult. If the breakdown products are known, or if there isn't any noticeable breakdown for years, then determining the contribution by the product is not important. However, the product will take up space and that is important, especially if the company is comparing its product with competing product.

Specific Life Cycle Stages

5   RAW MATERIALS AND ENERGY INVENTORY

The boundary conditions establish how far back in the materials chain the analysis will go. In most cases the analysis starts with the aquisistion of raw materials and ends with the first manufacturing stage that refines the raw material. There are two kinds of raw materials: primary and secondary. The primary form is raw material that has not been recycled/reused. Secondary raw materials are those that are recycled/reusable materials. Secondary materials are given serious consideration beacuse of the following:

- Reduction in use of primary raw materials
- Process involved with preparation for use
- Emissions and environmental impacts of the processes

After the materials have been refined they are inventory. However, in some life cycle inventories, the inventory is considered raw material because the boundary conditions were set accordingly.

There is also the condition where the raw material for a process is provided as a premanufactured good. For example at Acme Plastics & Plating Company, the proprietary plating solutions used are purchased from a supply house. The impact of the manufacturing of the proprietary plating solutions may or may not have a major impact on the analysis, depending on what is being considered. In either case, data for the raw materials would most likely be summarized at the raw material's input point of the appropriate subsystem. If the analyst wished to go all the way to the mining of the appropriate ores, making of the acids, and compounding the solutions, it would be possible, but time consuming and expensive. Industry data would most likely suffice. The analyst may want to stop with the proprietary chemicals as the materials input to a product study and stop there. This would most likely be the case for a site study or one that uses chemicals such as plating. The major impact Acme would have on the chemicals it buys would be to change the plating processes if possible. This could reduce Acme's MANPRINT but may or may not do anything for the supplier.

Primary raw materials can be produced by cultivation, harvesting, and replenishment such as farm products or some types of wood or can be mined such as fossil fuels, ores, water, and air. All forms of transportation associated with the materials are also considered.

The inputs for the basic raw materials used in a life cycle analysis can be categorized into three groups.

The first is energy utilization. Detailed information on the type and mix of the energy sources utilized must be included in the database for each stage. Electrical energy should be reported as kilowatt hours. Other energy sources should be reported in appropriate units of use, such as gallons or liters of fuel or cubic feet of gas (see Appendix C). Energy use is then converted to megajoules and reported as such. The type of energy should be reported as renewable or nonrenewable. A review of primary energy sources is shown in Figure 5-1.

Materials that are consumed during the maintaining of the raw material source should be included, such as pesticides, fertilizers, etc. (Figure 2-1).

Various types of infrastructures should be included, such as construction and equipment. These include roads, buildings, drilling rigs, and equipment used to explore, mine, extract, or harvest the materials.

The outputs generated during the raw materials acquisition system can be generalized into a number of categories: air emissions, waterborne emissions, solid waste, other environmental releases, habitat changes, and the raw material itself.

One of the reasons to seriously consider the raw material acquisition phase as a subsystem in the life cycle analysis is the potential environmental impacts the acquisition process has on the environment. This includes agriculture runoff, oil spills, leaching of mine tailings, etc. These types of considerations

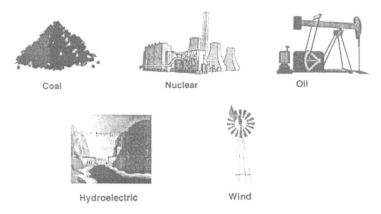

Coal   Nuclear   Oil

Hydroelectric   Wind

Figure 5-1. Primary energy sources.

can have a larger environmental impact than the sum of the rest of the product life cycle combined. Sometimes these impacts are difficult to quantify, such as aesthetic degradation and destruction of habitat. It is desirable to characterize these types of impacts in some way so they can be accounted for in the overall analysis.

Primary energy raw materials include petroleum, coal, natural gas, nuclear, wind and hydroelectric. A distinction is made between nonrenewable (coal, oil) and renewable (wind, biomass, hydroelectric) fuels. Fossil fuel raw materials inputs are reported as megajoules (MJ). This reflects their nonrenewable origin. A correction factor (precombustion energy) is applied to account for the energy required to obtain the raw material. Electrical energy is determined by stating the fuel inputs required to produce the net electrical energy consumed by the various processing stages. The distribution of electricity can be assumed to be off the national energy grid unless the analyst knows that the source is local. The consideration of the type of energy, the type of fuel used to generate it, and the amount used by the processes being studied is important. The cost of energy is of concern; however, the environmental impact of the energy source figures in to the overall MANPRINT of the processes and products being studied.

Secondary sources of energy include thermal energy derived from waste heat, combustion of biomass, combustible waste gases, combustible waste solvents and solids, and cogeneration from waste heat. The energy from these sources will be considered. To simply handle these sources, one can treat them as a process step (see Figure 3-6). Whether to call the energy from waste products a coproduct or an alternative energy source is up the analyst; however, it is important to remember to quantify it in the model.

Raw materials used in the study, excluding energy, can be in the form of solids, gases, and liquids. Water is usually categorized as an entity unto itself. While water is a renewable material, good quality water is becoming scarce. Wastewater may have to be treated before discharge, thus involving another process to be included in the model. The number of other raw materials that are extracted from the earth to produce the wide variety of products is surprisingly small. A typical list of basic raw materials would include those shown in Table 5-1. There is no simple way to characterize these materials. They are usually reported in units of weight. Gases can be in cubic feet or in weight units. The environmental sensitivity of the raw material must be identified and noted: Some materials are in short supply and are nonrenewable. The environmental impact of obtaining these resources should also be identified. Some involve processes and materials that are extremely hazardous to the environment. Since the use of renewable resources is deemed desirable, these materials should be flagged for special attention. Both renewable and nonrenewable resources must be accounted for in the inventory.

While a fundamental concept is to include all raw materials all the way to their source, it may not be practical. The importance of establishing the

Table 5-1 Typical Raw Materials List

• Barites	• Iron ore	• Water
• Bauxite	• Iron chromate	• Wood
• Biomass (cotton, wool, corn, soybeans, etc.)	• Lead	• Zinc
• Brine	• Limestone	• Gold
• Chalk	• Magnesium	• Silver
• $CaSO_4$	• Managnese	• Platinum
• Clay	• Coal	• Sand
• Copper	• Sodium nitrate	• Selenium
• Fieldspar	• Nickel oxide	• Oil
• Ferromanganese	• Uranium	• Natural gas
		• Rutile

appropriate boundaries is obvious. The extent of the boundaries and the magnitude of the study must be tailored for the individual application. The analyst must understand the intended use of the analysis and include the levels of detail required to make the report meaningful while not driving the client into bankruptcy.

DATA GATHERING

Because the data gathering is complex and critical, three basic approaches have been utilized for this stage:

- Primary data collection, where the raw materials producer directly describes how they produce their product and provides as much of the necessary data as possible.
- Secondary data, where published data such as articles, studies, and surveys are used.
- Assumptions, where the analyst makes assumptions about the parameters of the products use.

No single source is usually sufficient to conduct the life cycle inventory. In most cases, the data come from a combination of the above sources. Each source has its own limitations, advantages, and disadvantages as discussed below.

Primary Data Collection

Primary data collection can be done by statistical sampling. Here, the primary data collection is designed to capture a representative sample of data producers can provide on the parameters of their products. For example:

- Other materials used in conjunction with the product's raw materials acquisition and manufacture.
- How long the process has been in operation. Details about its operation, such as continuous service or interrupted, operating conditions.
- Method of by-product disposal or use for by-products.

Frequently, the producer cannot directly supply information on inputs and outputs. The producer may be able to supply information on how the product was obtained from which inputs and outputs can be derived. Most of this information the producer may have. Some of the information such as energy inputs and air/water/solids emissions and wastes may have to be derived by alternative means. This type of data collection takes several forms:

- Mail survey. A questionnaire is mailed to selected recipients
- Personal interviews
- Telephone survey

Each form has its advantages and disadvantages. This type of data collection can be difficult and expensive. National surveys have been conducted in a statistically valid fashion with methodologies that are well defined and codified. Most of this type of data collection is done by independent survey research companies.

Primary data collected that are statistically significant have common phases:

- Experimental design and protocols — A description of the objectives of the research, population of interest, and information to determine the sample size, the source of the list to be used for sample selection, sampling frequency, survey time frame, means of handling nonresponse, and other information.
- Survey instrument — The questionnaire used to collect the data, including instructions to the interviewer.
- Data tabulation and extrapolation — The tabulation and presentation of the survey and means to show that the sample is representative. A description of the methods used to extrapolate to the studied population.

When the source of the data is statistical sampling, even if well designed, there are issues that include the following:

- Cost
- Representativeness of the sample
- Bias in the questionnaire

- Respondent bias
- Nonrespondent bias
- Statistical interpretation

There are other sources of primary data. These include a smaller sample size and may not be representative of the total population. However, for materials that are produced by a small segment of the population, are used on a regional basis, or are geared for a certain segment of industry, the following techniques may be employed.

- Focus groups — This is a group of 8 to 15 producers that are assembled in a room to answer questions about the processes. This is usually conducted by professional marketing or survey companies. For raw materials suppliers, this isn't as difficult as one would expect.
- Suppliers of similar materials.
- Trade associations.
- Manufacturers of equipment associated with the process.

Issues associated with small groups or limited primary data collection are similar to those of the statistical sampling. The advantages include lower cost.

Secondary Data Sources

Secondary data sources are any published or unpublished data articles, reports, or studies relating to the materials that are available in published form. In many cases, good secondary data can be more comprehensible than limited primary data collection. Examples of secondary data sources include

- Trade, professional, or industry reports
- Articles in trade or professional journals
- Industry market survey and studies
- Federal government reports and statistical data documents and studies
- Reports of government rule-making hearings

The data from secondary sources may have been created for another purpose; therefore, some of the desired data may not be directly present. Some government reports may include most of the data needed for this phase of the life cycle inventory.

Issues with secondary data include

- Cost — Usually less than primary data.

- Bias — Depending on the secondary source, the data could be biased in favor of the product or manufacturer or against it. Care must be taken to ascertain any bias in the data.
- Timeliness — Secondary data are usually compiled at a time prior to the current study. It is imperative that the data be representative of current practices.

ASSUMPTIONS

Assumptions are used when primary or secondary data are not available. Assumptions can be based on data that are not specific to the process or service being analyzed. In most cases, the assumptions are used because data are not fully available.

It should be noted that the obtaining of data and the sources for all the stages of the life cycle inventory is pretty much the same. The analyst will use primary or secondary data or assumptions. The treatment of the data should be similar to what is discussed above, no matter what stage the analysis is in.

6

MANUFACTURING, FORMULATION, AND PROCESSING

The manufacturing, formulation, and processing step (hereafter known as manufacturing) in a life cycle analysis converts the raw materials into final products. This includes on-site storage and handling. The manufacturing step is considered complete when the product is transferred to distribution. All packaging required for the transfer of the product to the first distribution site is considered part of manufacturing.

Depending on the intended use of the analysis, the boundaries will include the raw materials to the processes. The end of the manufacturing step is at the distribution point. Figure 6-1 provides a conceptual view. Figure 6-2A indicates the "normal" type of multipath product flow. Figure 6-2B shows a just-in-time-type manufacturing flow. This is to indicate that both types of manufacturing systems have multistage operations and the boundaries must be made to accommodate them both. A manufacturer will be mainly concerned with the following:

- Principle raw materials
- Manufacturing of the product
- Energy
- Packaging
- Disposal/reuse/recycle
- Customer image

We will examine each of these as it relates to the design and manufacturing operations.

The boundary conditions will have defined the extent that the analysis goes back into the acquisition of raw materials. Certain materials will be of greater importance than others. These may include materials that are in short supply, environmentally sensitive, expensive, require large amounts of energy

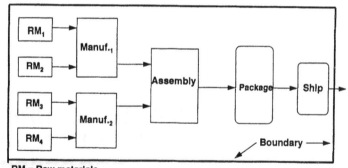

RM = Raw materials
Manuf$_x$ = manufacture of subassemblies 1 through X

Figure 6-1.   Manufacturing boundary concept.

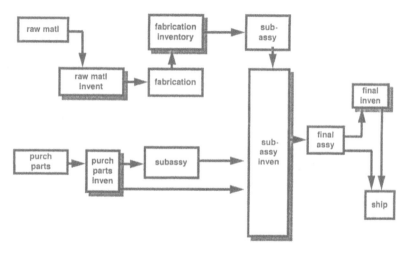

Figure 6-2A.   Normal material flow.

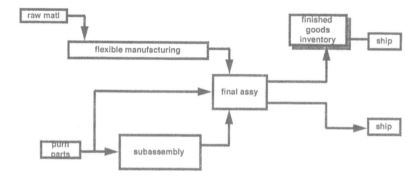

Figure 6-2B.   Just-in-time-type material flow.

to produce, and are major components of the products. Other raw materials may include recycled materials from other sources or from the company's own "take back program". Some of the recycled materials may be from an in-house waste treatment facility or a regrinding center in the case of plastics. The recycle facility must be included in the analysis. These facilities are usually considered manufacturing processes which have their products shown as material inputs to a manufacturing process. The net result is less actual raw materials used. This includes water (see Figure 3-7). In this concept diagram, the raw materials are transformed into subassemblies. These are then combined into a product. The figure also represents the packaging. This can include packing materials including foams and Styrofoam "popcorn", boxes, cartons, pallets, and shrink wrap.

As illustrated in Figures 6-1, 2-4, 3-5, and 3-6, products are usually made by a series of submanufacturing centers and assembly processes building to a final product. The overall assembly of a product consists of, as a minimum, the following:

- Raw materials for the product
- Energy
- Labor
- Materials, energy, and labor for tooling, fixtures, and assembly aids
- Manufacturing scrap and replacement materials and labor
- Rework materials
- Ancillary materials
- Packaging materials

The first three items on the above list have been discussed. It is paramount that the analyst consider the use of tooling. Tooling and fixtures used in manufacturing are of equal importance to an environmental life cycle analysis as the products. The use of exotic or environmental-sensitive materials for tooling is not uncommon. Management may not be aware of how extensive the tooling requirements are in a manufacturing environment. In a large percentage of cases, the need for special tooling can be reduced by modifications to product hardware designs.

Tooling can be made by machining metals such as alloys of steel, stainless steel, aluminum, brass, copper alloys, titanium, molybdenum, and others. Molds are made from the metals described as well as water-soluble salts, plastics, and plaster. Tools, molds, and fixtures are sometimes plated or coated to impart the desired properties to the tool. The use of chrome plate to increase wear resistance and coating with plastisol-type materials are examples. The use of the basic materials and subsequent coatings can have as great or greater impact on the environment than the actual product. Figure 3-6 illustrates the inclusion of tooling in the process flow modeling. The block in Figure 3-6 relating to tooling would be further expanded (blown up) to detail the processes involved. The modeling of the tooling process will divulge the quantities, types, and materials/coatings used and where used. This will allow for the appropriate level of analysis.

Scrap and associated replenishment materials must be considered. The level of scrap produced for a process adds not just to the environment, but to the overall cost of the final products. Facts that should be gathered about scrap include but are not limited to the following:

- Location of the generation of the scrap
- Quantity of scrap materials
- Type of scrap materials
- Disposition of the scrap (recycle in-house, third party recycle, land-fill, etc.)

Scrap is a subject of interest to most manufacturing companies. However, actual hard data quantifying scrap may be difficult to come by. There are two types of scrap. The first type is scrap from a process that involves the scrapping of a component that is a part of the product. The second type of scrap is surplus material left over from a process such as flashing from a molding process or metal turnings from a machining process.

The first type, product scrap, is the most costly. Product scrap may be handled as a contingency factor as a percentage of raw material purchased. This can mean the company overbuys raw materials and waste disposal or is constantly rushing to replace scrap materials. It also costs the company in labor. Most companies do not really know what their scrap rate is or where it is generated. The analysis of scrap will be of interest to senior management but may be difficult to develop. Scrap has a significant impact on the environment. It is a total waste, even when recycled. Someone put labor and other associated costs such as a percentage of the tooling costs into it before it was scraped. While recycling saves the material from the landfill and reduces the requirement for more raw material for the new user, the company generating the scrap has costs involved and must replace it with new material.

The second type of scrap is the process scrap. This includes materials used in the product that are scrap because of the nature of the process. Flashings and runners from molding operations and meat turning are examples. Spent solvents, rags, etc., are considered process wastes for the purposes of the analysis and not scrap. Process scrap should be noted and quantified. This can be of use to manufacturing and design engineers as well as management. While a certain level of process scrap may be mandatory by the nature of the process, efforts may be made to minimize it through design, tooling, or process changes.

When a company makes a design change for a performance requirement, it must look at the total ramifications. For example, automobile manufacturers were required to improve fuel efficiency. One aspect of the reduction was to use plastic parts, where possible, as a substitute for steel. This change helped reduce the average automobile curb weight 25%, from about 4100 to 3100 pounds. This raised the fuel efficiency from about 14 mpg in 1973 to about

28 mpg in 1995. The use of plastics and downsizing provided for the improvement in fuel usage. While the use of plastics helped reduce fuel usage, most plastic used in automobiles is not recovered. The use of plastic, therefore, increases the solid waste generated at disposal. The plastic generated at the shredder operation is called "fluff". The fluff has been increasing constantly. If the plastices cannot be recovered and recycled, in a practical manner, before or during the shredding operation, the shredding process may become uneconomical. Thus, to solve one problem, the automakers have created another one. In this example, the automakers have changed the type of scrap at their plant sites from primarily metals to a mix of metal and plastics as well as created an environmental impact at disposal.

The disposal practices for scrap should be included in the life cycle inventory. The method and quantity of scrap materials being disposed of has an affect on the MANPRINT of the processes and ultimately the associated product. If the materials are being added to a landfill, the volume as well as the costs are important. The disposal in a landfill has the greatest environmental impact of the three methods noted. If the material is considered hazardous, then additional considerations must be noted:

- The use of class I landfills
- Special transportation and packaging issues
- *Long-term liability*
- Limited on-site storage
- Special on-site storage requirements
- Additional training for employees

The long-term liability of hazardous waste disposal/treatment needs to be fully documented and evaluated in the life cycle inventory. There is not just the present impact to the environment but serious long-term considerations and potential litigation.

The on-site recycle of scrap materials will be included in the model as a process. This might be as simple as a regrinder for thermoplastics for reuse in molding. The recycled scrap material may end up in the original product, such as used ABS plastic at Acme Plastics & Plating being returned to the injection molding machine for reuse. It may be reused in a different product. A major automotive company makes closeout panels for one of their model cars from the material from minivan bumpers.

Off-site recycling can include the use of the scrap materials by another company. It will be indicated on our inventory as a scrap/waste that is used for raw material for a third party. It will have a lesser impact on the environment. Examples include an automotive firm where old tires are becoming foot pedals and old soft drink bottles are truck grills. Serious consideration should be noted in the life cycle inventory for the company's use of recycled materials as raw feed stocks. Companies that make copiers and printers usually have a "take back" program. The end user, in these cases, returns the used cartridge to the manufacturer via prepaid postage in the box the cartridge came in. The manufacturer then remanufactures a cartridge for resale by reloading and servicing the returned item. This reduces the overall impact of the company's MANPRINT by utilizing a "waste" from another company or consumer, removing it as a source of landfill material and reducing the MANPRINT of their product.

As noted above, most companies do not have a good handle on scrap. Even more surprising to the nonindustrial person is the fact that most companies do not have a handle on rework or repair either. Rework differs from repair by its definition.

- Rework returns an item that does not meet the drawing or engineering requirements to a condition that does meet the requirements.
- Repair means the item is made to comply with the drawings but does not meet the requirements. Using fill and paint as a means of repairing a dent on a car fender is an example. It looks like the original, does the job, but is not the same as the original.

Repair and rework at a manufacturing facility need to be included in the life cycle inventory. This is because the repair/rework processes require materials to be scraped and replaced and special tooling may be required as well as possible use of chemicals for cleaning, flux, solder, etc. The rework/repair cycle causes the generation of scrap, and these materials must be resupplied. There is a definite impact on the environment and associated costs involved.

Ancillary materials include cleaning agents, cutting oils, grease, rags, flux, mold release, and other similar products utilized to maintain the processes but do not become part of the product. Trace amounts below the level of concern should be noted as ancillary materials.

MANUFACTURING OUTPUTS

The various manufacturing steps ultimately result in the production of products, coproducts, and wastes. A product is a marketable commodity and the principal outcome or result of the manufacturing process. It is not uncommon for a manufacturing process to have one or more coproducts that could be used for alternative purposes. Examples include

- The making of corn chips. The principal product is corn chips; a coproduct is the waste corn meal that is sold as animal feed.
- The "boiling" of beef hides and bone for the making of gelatin. The first boil is the principal product; it is used for gel used on good-quality film. The second boiling produces the gel used on photographic paper to develop photos. The third boil is used for cooking

gelatin and food stuff. The last boil was used for glue manufacture. The resultant waste products are used as bone meal and fertilizer.

- Meat processing produces meat (beef), the principal product. It also produces beef tallow used in the production of soap, leather, and bone that is used for bone meal. The remaining materials are considered waste as they have no intrinsic value or alternative function and are disposed of in the environment.

Because of the multiple products that may be generated, it is important to clearly separate products early in the life cycle inventory so that the relative proportion of waste and energy may be properly assigned. For the corn chip producer, the energy and wastes would be apportioned over the corn chips and animal feed.

To assist in the quantification of relevant impacts of raw materials, energy, and waste emissions, it is common to assign weighted averages allocated on a weight basis. Exceptions to this should occur only when actual source data are clear enough to distinguish that an impact is caused by one product or a coproduct.

Wastes are to be considered at point of emission and after any waste treatment. That means wastes are evaluated only after processing through all in-line or on-site waste treatment and control systems to reflect direct emissions to the environment. Some wastes escape during the manufacturing cycle and never see the waste treatment abatement or control system. These are "fugitive emissions" and must be considered in the life cycle inventory. These types of emissions may be difficult to quantify. In these cases, the identification of the emission and a qualitative estimate may be required.

The manufacturing cycle can be simple or extremely complex. Each step in the manufacturing process must be scrutinized and the outputs noted. The wastes from all the subprocesses are totaled for the evaluation of the total wastes. However, it is imperative that the analyst review and report on the outputs, including wastes, at each stage of the manufacturing process. By reporting the wastes at each submanufacturing step, management can get a better look at the details of their company's MANPRINT and identify processes for further evaluation for MANPRINT reduction. Care must be taken to appoint all outputs to a proper input. The product output of a subprocess must be indicated as the input to a subsequent process. The wastes are shown as an input to a waste treatment/handling/storage or disposal process. The use of the modeling scheme depicted in Chapter 3 allows modeling down to the most appropriate level in an efficient manner.

There are practical limits to the amount of time, cost, data availability, and variations in technology throughout industry to necessitate the use of certain assumptions in the life cycle inventory. It is important to the quality of the analysis that these assumptions be made explicit. These assumptions should be understood and analyzed to ascertain the sensitivity of the assumption to the life cycle analysis.

Most people do not think about the processes involved with packaging and shipping as part of manufacturing. When the products are completed they must be prepared for transportation. The packaging of the product therefore involves three considerations as a minimum:

- Internal material handling
- Product packaging
- Storage and shipping

Internal material handling includes *special* racks, fixtures, and enclosures used during manufacturing to build and protect the hardware. It is important to note the quantity and type of packaging involved, materials used, an estimate (if not directly quantifiable) of energy consumed, and wastes generated (see process model Figure 3-6).

Product packaging must satisfy at least the following conditions:

- Product protection from handling
- Protect the product during storage
- Look pleasing for the end user
- Identify the product and manufacturer (and other legal requirements)

Product packaging may be almost any size, shape, and form, constructed out of almost any material(s). For example, the product may be held on a cardboard "platform" using a vacuum-molded clear plastic covering, shrink wrap of cardboard boxes containing the product, or be placed in a cloth-lined wooden box or anything in between. The use of foam for shock absorption or containment is especially noted for possible environmental considerations during the analysis. The important issue is to consider the packaging as a process and measure all the inputs and outputs in the same manner as other process.

Product shipping must, as a minimum, satisfy the following requirements:

- Protect the product during warehousing and internal transportation, i.e., forklifts, etc.
- Protect the product from the elements
- Protect the product during loading and shipping
- Protect the product until unpacked for sale or by the end user

The same considerations must be made for the final shipping of the product. The packaging for shipping is another manufacturing process and should be modeled as such.

Packaging is a science unto itself. The analyst must consider the processes involved in product and shipping/distribution packaging as unique processes that are an integral part of manufacturing.

SENSITIVITY

Energy variables should be noted. This includes electricity, which, if possible, should have its source noted. Other factors include whether it was from renewable or nonrenewable fuels. It will include whether the source was domestic or imported.

The variations in process waste releases and how they are accounted for is noted. If the waste is released to a treatment facility (on site or off site), it will be noted as well. The type of waste treatment facility, technology used, level of treatment, and location will be noted. The above is important as the type of technology used for a specific type of waste as well as its effectiveness and may vary within an industry. Whenever possible, the treatment plant should be modeled just like a manufacturing process. This allows all the appropriate materials, energy, and outputs to be measured or accounted for.

A number of authors in the life cycle literature refer to energy and materials balances. These are, simply put, attempts to quantify the amount of energy and materials used in a given process. The idea is basically to quantify all the inputs to a process and then quantify all the outputs for each material and amount of energy used. To a certain extent this can be done. However, with complex products and the relative size of most companies, the quantification of this is almost impossible. The most practical approach is to use the modeling system from Chapter 3 and model the manufacturing operations to the lowest level practical. Then, with the best data available, plug in the numbers for all the inputs and outputs. There will be some pieces of data that are not available or measured. The idea is to account for everything going into a process and the outputs as much as possible. If fugitive emissions are taken into account, this may be the best you can do, especially if cost is important. Parts of the product may be subcontracted, such as fabricating printed wire boards (PWBs) used in electronics. It will be necessary to model the PWB fabrication process and allocate energy and materials used for your particular PWBs. Assumptions may be necessary. Care must be used in this example because technology and equipment may vary from one supplier to another. The use of material and energy balances were commonly used in the remediation of hazardous waste sites. It became evident to more enlightened regulators and owners that materials and energy balances were the brainchild of consultants. The real value of an extensive energy and material balance is dubious at best. There are usually more assumptions than facts in them. The cost of them must be weighed against the expected result. Conducting the process modeling and plugging in the appropriate data will provide a balance, that is, in most cases, adequate to conduct a life cycle analysis and be relatively accurate. The use of the models will also highlight what data are not available and the assumptions that are made.

Care must be taken not to compare the processes of different-sized facilities. The use of different processes, technologies, and equipment will also slant comparisons. An understanding of this concept is important, especially when discussing the results with management. Another area to be sensitive about is the capacity of a plant. Executives sometimes misapply the term "capacity". They mistakenly refer to capacity as output. Capacity means the amount of output the company could get running a specified number of shifts and specified number of days with the existing equipment. Output means the output under existing condition. Utilization is the ratio of the two. For example with the present suite of equipment, Acme Plastics & Plating would have one number for a capacity at 1/8/5. This means one shift at 8 hours per shift for 5 days a week. It would be different at 2/8/5, (two shifts at 8 hours each for 5 days per week). 2/8/6 means two shifts of 8 hours each, 6 days per week. It is important, when discussing capacity, to take into consideration such things as experience, age of equipment, yields, and accident rates.

The usefulness of the analysis gains importance when the magnitude of the variables is tested for their effect on the results and the likelihood of variation is considered. The probability of change as well as the magnitude should be reflected in any sensitivity analysis performed.

The use of recycled materials must adhere to a constant convention if the material is brought into the manufacturing system, especially if different recycled materials are used at different steps. The inventory must include energies, other materials used in recycling, and waste releases connected to the recycling and distribution processes. For closed-loop recycling, the processes related to recycling must be considered as a step in manufacturing.

DATA GATHERING

Because data gathering is complex and critical, three basic approaches have been utilized for this stage:

- Primary data collection, where the manufacturer directly describes how to produce the product and provides as much of the necessary data as possible.
- Secondary data, where published data such as article, studies, and surveys are used.
- Assumptions, where the analyst makes assumptions about the parameters of the product's manufacture.

No single source is usually sufficient to conduct the life cycle inventory. In most cases, the data come from a combination of the above sources. Each source has its own limitations, advantages, and disadvantages as discussed below.

Primary Data Collection

Primary data collection can be done by statistical sampling. Here, the primary data collection is designed to capture a representative sample of data manufacturers can provide on the parameters of the products. For example,

- Other materials used in conjunction with the product's and coproduct's manufacure.
- Frequency of product repair or maintenance (warranty).
- Length of time the processes used for manufacture have been in production, details about their operating conditions, etc.
- Other coproducts produced from the same set of processes.
- Method of product disposal when the end user was through with the product.

Frequently, the manufacturer cannot directly supply information on inputs and outputs. The manufacturer may be able to supply information on how the product was produced and from which inputs and outputs. Most of the details of this information the end user may not be aware of unless the manufacturer has an outstanding accounting system. Information from the industry can sometimes be used, but with caution. Not all producers of a product use the exactly the same processes. This type of data collection takes several forms:

- Mail survey. A questionnaire is mailed to selected recipients.
- Personal interview.
- Telephone survey.

Each form has its advantages and disadvantages. This type of data collection can be difficult and expensive. National surveys have been conducted in a statistically valid fashion with methodologies that are well defined and codified. Most of this type of data collection is done by independent survey research companies.

Primary data collected that is statistically significant have common phases:

- Experimental design and protocols — A description of the objectives of the research, population of interest, and information to determine the sample size, the source of the list to be used for sample selection, sampling frequency, survey time frame, means of handling nonresponse, and other information.

- Survey instrument — The questionnaire used to collect the data, including instructions to the interviewer.
- Data tabulation and extrapolation — The tabulation and presentation of the survey and means to show that the sample is representative. A description of the methods used to extrapolate from the studied population.

When the source of the data is statistical sampling, even if well designed, there are issues that include the following:
- Cost
- Representativeness of the sample
- Bias in the questionnaire
- Respondent bias
- Nonrespondent bias
- Statistical interpretation

There are other sources of primary data. These include a smaller sample size and may not be representative of the total population. However, for products that are made by a small segment of industry and are used on a regional basis, the following techniques may be employed.

- Focus groups — This is a group of 8 to 15 manufacturers that are assembled in a room to answer questions about the product. This is usually conducted by professional marketing or survey companies.
- Suppliers of raw materials — For example, soap manufacturers for washing machines.
- Trade associations.
- Manufacturers of equipment associated with the product.

Issues associated with small groups or limited primary data collection are similar to those of the statistical sampling. The advantages include lower cost.

Secondary Data Sources

Secondary data sources are any published or unpublished data articles, reports, or studies relating to the product that are available in published form. In many cases, good secondary data can be more comprehensible than limited primary data collection. Examples of secondary data sources include

- Trade, professional, or industry reports
- Articles in trade or professional journals
- Industry market survey and studies

- Federal government reports and statistical data documents and studies
- Reports of government rule-making hearings

The data from secondary sources may have been created for another purpose; therefore, some of the desired data may not be directly present. However, it may provide valuable information on the processes used to make the product and methodologies used to estimate the current data. Some government reports may include most of the data needed for this phase of the life cycle inventory.

Issues with secondary data include

- Cost — Usually less than primary data.
- Bias — Depending on the secondary source, the data could be biased in favor of the product or manufacturer or against it. Care must be taken to ascertain any bias in the data.
- Timeliness — Secondary data are usually compiled at a time prior to the current study. It is imperative that the data be representative of current practices.

ASSUMPTIONS

Assumptions are used when primary or secondary data are not available. Assumptions can be based on data that are not specific to the product or service being analyzed. For example, data on taking photos with a particular camera could be extrapolated to a single photo, or washing a load of dishes in a dishwasher could be extrapolated to washing glasses. In most cases, the assumptions are used because data are not fully available.

7 DISTRIBUTION AND TRANSPORTATION

Virtually every product manufactured has a distribution and transportation stage in its life cycle. Any life cycle analysis that does not include this stage is deficient.

The most common attribute for distribution and transportation is that it involves a change in location or physical configuration of the product, not a transformation of the product. Boundaries are not always sharp in this area and therefore must be defined at the onset of the analysis. An example is the freezing of meat or food products during transportation. If it is already frozen at the plant, moving frozen meat or food products is just transportation under special conditions. If it is frozen during transportation then it is in this fuzzy area as to definitions. The making of concrete in the truck on the way to a job site is another example.

For the purposes herein, we have defined distribution and transportation as follows:

- Distribution is all nontransportation activities carried out to facilitate the transfer of manufactured products from their final manufacture to their ultimate end user. This includes activities in a warehouse or retail establishment. This includes warehousing, wholesaling, retailing, and support activities carried out at these locations such as repackaging.
- Transportation is the movement of energy or materials between operations at different locations. (This includes moving raw materials from their source to the production facility, moving finished goods to a warehouse, moving products from the warehouse to retailer and ultimately from the point of sale to the end user, and the movement of electricity from generator to user.) This does not include the transportation or movement of product within the production facility during manufacturing. That movement is a process in manufacturing.

Table 7-1 Common Transportation Modes

Pipeline	Electrical power lines
Airplane	Railroad
Truck	Automotive
Barge	Freighter
Tanker	Electronic

The quantification of inputs and outputs related to transportation must be clearly mapped out. When fuel for the transporting equipment is considered, the environmental impact of the production and delivery of the fuel along with the associated costs must be taken into account. The relative amount of emissions and their contribution to the MANPRINT of the product must be included.

In the analysis of both transportation and distribution, where appropriate, environmental controls such as maintaining temperature and humidity are to be included.

For each mode of transportation, measures will be described that with a given quantity of product will allow the determination of energy, materials, and waste requirements. Examples of common transportation modes are given in Table 7-1.

The purpose of a life cycle inventory is to assess all the requisite process to get a product from raw material to the intended end user and assess the environmental impact. We can consider the transportation step a "process". Like the processes used and modeled in manufacturing, a simple model can be fabricated for transportation. A top-level model is shown in Figure 7-1. The model has inputs to be determined and quantified and outputs that need to be identified and quantified. These data can then be used to ascertain the environmental impacts and what possible improvements could be made. The shipping or transportation cycle might involve multiple operations. The steps should be modeled as with production (Chapter 3). The sublevel that the model goes down to will depend on the boundary condition set and the amount of detail required. An example is shown in Figure 7-2. A similar set of models could be made for pipeline or electrical transportation systems (Figures 7-3 through 7-5). A fundamental difference in transportation systems is that the movable transportation system (trucks, boats, airplanes) moves batch lots and is thus called a batch carrier. The fixed transportation system (pipelines, electric cables, ducts, etc.) moves continuous amounts of products. Batch carriers may have integral containment (tank truck) or separable containment such as container truck or railroad box car.

The previous chapters have discussed the requirements for the early establishment of boundary conditions. The area of transportation and distribution is no different. Hereto, they must be explicitly defined. There is no "right or wrong" set of boundaries. The boundaries are determined by the intended use

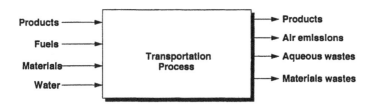

Materials = oils, lubricants, antifreeze, rags, ropes, tires, filters, belts, hoses, etc.

Figure 7-1.   Transportation model format.

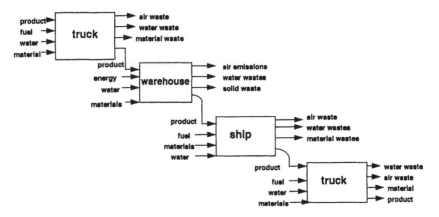

Figure 7-2.   Multilevel transportation.

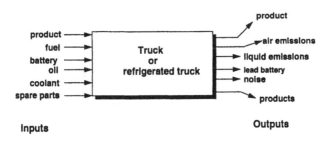

Figure 7-3.   Examples of truck transport.

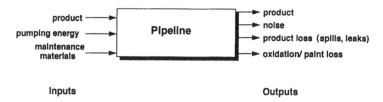

Figure 7-4. Typical pipeline transportation.

of the study and the relative costs associated with expanding boundaries. For example, the use of trucks in our model might only incorporate the operation of the truck. At a higher level, it could be expanded to include maintenance and spare parts and at a still higher level it could include the making of the truck. The usual levels include the basic to first levels only. In some cases, we need to consider the inclusion of multiple products during a life cycle analysis. Such things as home computers come as separate components (CRT, CPU, keyboard, cables and printers, modems, etc.). It takes all of the subsystems to make a computer that the user can operate. Each of these items was a product at the factory. When considering a product such as a home computer, the analysis must have all the requisite parts, and it needs to consider the trans-portation and distribution of each component in the system.

The distribution step in a life cycle inventory sometimes gets short changed. After all the effort in the manufacturing stage and transportation, distribution doesn't appear to spark the interest of analysts. The distribution stage can have multiple opportunities for environmental improvements and does have a large influence on the MANPRINT of the product.

The warehouse activity accounts for numerous areas for environmental impact. These include recycle or disposal of the packaging used for the initial shipping. The methods of storage and the use of motorized equipment need to be assessed. Repackaging for distribution to retail outlets, pallets, and water and energy requirements are necessary inputs. Outputs will include heat, noise, office, air, and waster wastes as well as the product.

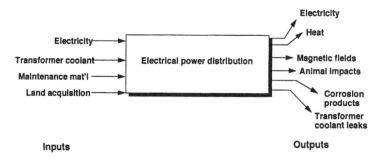

Figure 7-5. Electrical power transportation and distribution.

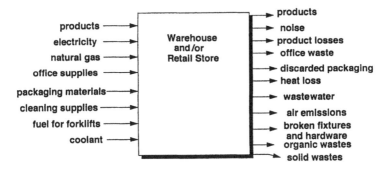

Figure 7-6. Warehouse and retail model.

The retail outlet has most of the opportunities as the warehouse plus the use of boxes, bags, and other consumer packaging for consumer transportation of the product. Figure 7-6 is a top view of the distribution model. It can be broken down to the level necessary to meet the boundary conditions of the inventory being undertaken.

The types of environmental impacts the distribution system has are drastically different from those of manufacturing. At the retail site, for example, there is the normal handling of the products by the staff as well as by customers. This will contribute to the breakage and product loss. The parking lot itself has an environmental impact that is not shown in Figure 7-6. The inclusion of the parking lot will depend on the boundary conditions and items such as who owns the parking lot, whether it is shared by multiple retailers, etc. The parking lot is considered a point source for pollution. Parking lots can contain, as a minimum, the following:

- Oil on it from leaking vehicles
- Antifreeze
- Solid waste from careless or inconsiderate customers
- Animal waste
- Grease
- Broken carts, fixtures
- Discarded automotive parts
- Dead animals
- Possible industrial emissions (directly or from precipitation from the air)

When it rains or snows, these materials can run off into creeks, streams, and rivers or slowly soak into the ground and groundwater. Because of this the U.S. EPA has regulations governing these areas. However, the analyst must consider whether to consider the parking lots in the study or omit them. If they are omitted, there should be a clear explanation as to why they were excluded and any overt observations.

The inclusion of detailed modeling of the warehouse/retail distribution should be reviewed as to the impact the company's specific product is having on the MANPRINT at this step and, conversely, how much the retail step contributes to the MANPRINT of the product. This will depend on the product and the warehouse/wholesale/retail network. It will obviously different for a refinery distributing gasoline as compared to an electronics company selling personal computers. The packaged electronic hardware will have the container or packaging materials as the largest environmental impact during distribution, whereas the refinery has the gasoline with virtually no packaging except the pipelines, tanker trucks, and underground storage tanks. Leaks at any part of the transportation and distribution phase could be catastrophic. The boundary conditions will define the extent that the distribution step is modeled. When looking at the distribution step, the inputs and outputs must be attributed for each product. This insures that each product gets its share of the inputs and outputs, such as wastes associated with that particular product. In the case of the gasoline, the inputs and outputs at the gas station are appropriated over the amount of gasoline, oil, grease, spare parts, and anything else sold. Since gasoline and oil are usually the greatest volume of materials sold, most of the inputs and outputs are attributed and distributed to them. The sale of maps, for example, is small by comparison. This can get more complicated for a personal computer sold at a Target store, for example. Target sells thousands of products; the computer is only one and is not sold in the same volume as towels, clothing, or hardware and automotive products. Trying to attribute the inputs and outputs at a Target store to the personal computer might be extremely costly and almost impossible to accomplish. To add to the problem, Target has different-size stores and sells different products in different parts of the country. There isn't much call for snow shovels in Southern California, but there is in Minnesota. In this example, it might be better to estimate the impact or consider it negligible. An example of a simple way to handle the computer sales of Brand X computers at Target would be to approximate the cost and amount of utilities, etc., for all products sold in a year. Then calculate the per cent of total volume or per cent sales dollars the Brand X computers are of the total sales or amount of merchandise sold. The analyst would then allocate the appropriate amount of utility usage to the Brand X computers. This method may not be pretty, but it saves much time and money. The amount of energy in kilowatt hours for electricity, and terms or BTU of gas, can be found in utility bills or from the local utility companies. These units can be easily transfered to megajoules.

The data requirements for the distribution and transportation stages are driven by the specific inputs and outputs associated with each transportation and distribution operation that is defined in the life cycle model. It is imperative to use the model technique. The data collected will vary depending on the product and transportation-distribution system used.

The life cycle inventory describes the total quantities of the inputs and outputs for each transportation and distribution operation. The quantities of each of the inputs and outputs are calculated from knowledge of the amount of product that is delivered to the end user. These quantities are usually reported as items per unit level of each of the transportation and distribution operations. An example includes the energy required to move a kilogram of product over 1 kilometer. In this case the analyst would convert the fuel consumption from gallons to energy. Therefore, the reported quantity would be in megajoules per kilogram-kilometer.

Some further examples would include but are not limited to

- Megajoules per kilogram-kilometer.
- Engine pollution emissions NO_x/Kg-Km (NO_x is reported in kilograms).
- Discarded and additional packaging materials (weight of materials in kilograms per kilogram of transported-distributed product).
- Product loss rate (kilograms of product loss per kilograms of product moved or distributed).
- Gallons or kilograms of water used per kilogram of product.
- Supplies required (kilograms of wood pallets per kilograms of product moved or sold).

Obtaining the data for the transportation and distribution step can be somewhat difficult. Fortunately, some of the data exist as factors and are available in the public sector. Trucking/shipping companies have some of it; regulatory agencies can provide some as well. The U.S. Departments of Transportation and Energy have data available to the public. Data relating to energy use and environmental emissions can also be obtained from regulatory agencies in most areas of the country. Some of the data are proprietary and may or may not be released to the analyst. Portions of the data will need to be developed. The models used for transportation can be somewhat generalized as the basics are the same for a wide range of products. Simple models can be constructed for the different types of transportation, see (Table 7-1). For the model of a truck moving between two locations, the model will need, as a minimum, the amount of energy used to transport the product, the amount and type of product, emissions released, noise and heat generated, and the routing schemes used. The model can be further refined as required. The extent to which this is done will depend on the boundary conditions which were established based on intended use of the study and cost considerations.

8

USE — REUSE — MAINTENANCE

How the product is used, maintained, and reused will have an important impact on the environment. Much of the impact is predetermined by the engineering design of the product. The materials of construction, product packaging, and required maintenance are predetermined by the design of the product and the design engineers. Understanding of the customer requirements and how the product will actually be used by the end user is critical for the designer. If the designer is to reduce the environmental impact of the product, he or she must understand the total life cycle of the product. This chapter deals with specific issues related to the end user stage of the product's life cycle. To accomplish this, we need to address, as a minimum, the following:

- Boundaries
- Activities in the user-reuse-maintenance (URM) stage
- Presentation of inputs and outputs
- Modeling
- Data sources
- Recommendations

The URM stage of the life cycle takes place after the distribution step and ends at the point where the end user discards the product or it enters a waste management system. This stage can be as complex as the manufacturing stage. The boundaries for this stage are illustrated in Figure 8-1. The figure shows that the URM stage begins when the end user takes possession of the finished product, including the packaging, and uses or consumes the product and ends when the used product is discarded. This definition can encompass all products from commercial products, defense weapons systems, and equipment. Everything from paper clips to aircraft carriers fits into this system.

The actual delivery of the finished product to the end user is considered part of the distribution system. This includes any means of delivery including the U.S. mail, UPS, Federal Express, private shipping service, boat, pipeline

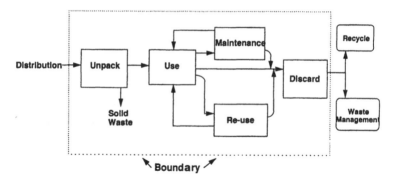

Figure 8-1.   User-reuse-maintenance stage boundaries.

or airplane (remote locations), etc. The product delivery can be from a take-out restaurant, retail outlet, mail order company, or other distribution source.

The first step in the boundary is the unpack step (Figure 8-1). During this step, the finished product is removed from its packaging and prepared for use. Wastes from this step include the packaging and shipping materials (i.e., shipping boxes) used to protect the product during transportation, storage, and distribution. The amount of discarded materials will be noted per actual unit of finished product. This is usually provided in units of weight.

The second step is the actual use of the product. In this step the product is placed in service or is consumed by the end user (Figure 8-2). This step includes all activities involved in the use or consumption of the product. Examples include the use of a refrigerator; power for a hair dryer; natural gas for heating water and the water for washing with soap, natural gas, and electricity for a furnace; water, power, and chemicals for a swimming pool; water and power/gas for the preparation of food; gasoline, water, antifreeze, grease, and oil for an automobile, etc. Each material, energy, and water input and output requirement will be quantified for inclusion in the model. Obviously, these will vary drastically by the nature of the product. The materials, energy, water, gases, or air consumed during use of the product must be identified and quantified in units that are compatible for the purposes of the study.

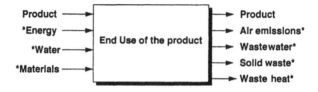

* = The extent to which these items are considered depends
on their existence based on the nature of the end product.

Figure 8-2.   Use of the finished product model.

Includes cleaning, supplies, misc. transportation effects.

Figure 8-3. On-site maintenance.

Maintenance is considered for most products. This can include grease, oil, filters, tires, paint, etc., for automobiles and trucks, polish of silverware, replacement cartridges for copy machines and printers, shingles for a house roof, cleaning units for VCRs, and parts and lubricant for industrial machines. The maintenance step may occur at the site of the end user or at an off-site location. The maintenance may be accomplished by the end user or people on the user's staff (Figure 8-3) or by a contract repair facility. Off-site maintenance (Figure 8-4), therefore, includes transportation to and from the maintenance site. All materials, gas, water, and energy must be identified and quantified for this stage of the process. If there is transportation of the product to and from an off-site maintenance facility, all transportation inputs must be included.

Reuse includes any on-site reuse and off-site reuse (Figure 8-5). On-site reuse may include intentional reuse of the product for the original purpose or incidental reuse for a different application. Examples include the use of an old coffee can to store screws, nuts, and bolts; old bottles to store old paint brushes; tires used as children's swings; and tire inner tubes used as water floats. A user may also reuse materials for an intended purpose. For example, the "reject" parts and scrap runners from Acme Plastics & Plating Company's

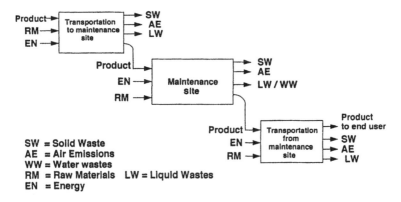

Figure 8-4. Off-site maintenance.

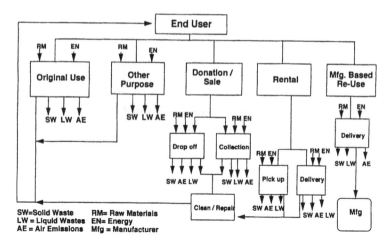

Figure 8-5.   Reuse.

injection molding process may be ground up, dried, mixed with virgin material, and reused in the injection molding process.

Reuse also includes reuse by another party for the product's intended use or return of the product to the manufacturer to be reused for its original purpose. Examples include refillable beverage bottles, computer keyboard components, and copier toner cartridges. The use by another user-party may entail the sale of the product by the original user or donation of the product. The product may be refurbished before reuse. Any energy or materials used to facilitate reuse must be included in this stage.

Discard involves the actual discarding of the product (Figure 8-6). The product will enter into either a waste management or a recycle system. At this point, the end user has taken the product out of service and will no longer use it. The waste management or recycle system will be addressed in further chapters.

The depth of the data acquired in this step is dependent on the intended use of the life cycle analysis. During the URM stage, the product may have a serious environmental impact or MANPRINT. The automobile, for example, uses nonrenewable fuel. It uses, for the most part, lubricants from nonrenewable sources. Spare parts are recycled to some extent. Most plastics currently used in automobiles are not recyclable. New paint applied to automobiles is not environmentally friendly and requires air pollution control measures that in turn use energy from nonrenewable sources. Water used for cooling contains antifreeze which requires special disposal techniques.

Gathering the data for this stage of the analysis can be very difficult. Similar users may have different environments for the product's use and have different energy sources. For example, a home computer used in one part of the country may have electrical energy supplied by hydroelectric generators; another may have nuclear, while another could easily have coal- or natural

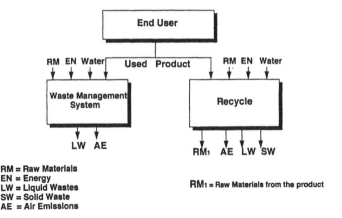

RM = Raw Materials
EN = Energy
LW = Liquid Wastes
SW = Solid Waste
AE = Air Emissions

RM₁ = Raw Materials from the product

Figure 8-6.   Discard.

gas-fired generators. Each of these sources has a different environmental impact. Breaking this down for an analysis for a computer company would be almost impossible. Making note of it would be acceptable. The analysis would therefore consider the amount of energy only and mention the potential sources. Because the data gathering is complex and critical, three basic approaches have been utilized for this stage:

- Primary data collection, where the end user directly describes the product is used and provides as much of the necessary data as possible.
- Secondary data, where published data such as article, studies, and surveys are used.
- Assumptions, where the analyst makes assumptions about the parameters of the product's use.

No single source is usually sufficient to conduct the life cycle inventory. In most cases, the data comes from a combination of the above sources. Each source has its own limitations, advantages, and disadvantages as discussed below.

PRIMARY DATA COLLECTION

Primary data collection can be done by statistical sampling. Here, the primary data collection is designed to capture a representative sample of data end users can provide on the parameters of the products use. For example,

- Other materials used in conjunction with the product's use and maintenance.
- Frequency of product repair or maintenance.

- Length of time the product remained in service. Details about its service, such as continuous or interrupted, operating conditions.
- Other uses for the product beyond its intentional use.
- How the product was disposed of when the end user was through with the product.

Frequently, the end user cannot directly supply information on inputs and outputs. The end user may be able to supply information on how the product was used from which inputs and outputs can be derived. Most of this information the end user may not be aware of unless the user is an institution or commercial user who may have some of the information such as energy inputs and air/water/solids emissions and wastes. This type of data collection takes several forms:

- Mail survey. A questionnaire is mailed to selected recipients.
- Panels of users that maintain logs or diaries of the products use.
- Personal interviews.
- Telephone survey.

Each form has its advantages and disadvantages. This type of data collection can be difficult and expensive. National surveys have been conducted in a statistically valid fashion with methodologies that are well defined and codified. Most of this type of data collection is done by independent survey research companies.

Primary data collected that is statistically significant have common phases:

- Experimental design and protocols — A description of the objectives of the research, population of interest, and information to determine the sample size, the source of the list to be used for sample selection, sampling frequency, survey time frame, means of handling nonresponse, and other information.
- Survey instrument — The questionnaire used to collect the data, including instructions to the interviewer.
- Data tabulation and extrapolation — The tabulation and presentation of the survey and means to show that the sample is representative. A description of the methods used to extrapolate from the studied population.

When the source of the data is statistical sampling, even if well designed, there are issues that include the following:

- Cost
- Representativeness of the sample

- Bias in the questionnaire
- Respondent bias
- Nonrespondent bias
- Statistical interpretation

There are other sources of primary data. These include a smaller sample size and may not be representative of the total population. However, for products that are used by a small segment of the population, are used on a regional basis, or are geared for a certain segment of industry, the following techniques may be employed.

- Focus groups — This is a group of 8 to 15 end users that are assembled in a room to answer questions about the product. This is usually conducted by professional marketing or survey companies.
- Suppliers of raw materials — For example, soap manufacturers for washing machines.
- Trade associations.
- Manufacturers of equipment associated with the product.

Issues associated with small groups or limited primary data collection are similar to those of the statistical sampling. The advantages include lower cost.

SECONDARY DATA SOURCES

Secondary data sources are any published or unpublished data articles, reports, or studies relating to the product that are available in published form. In many cases, good secondary data can be more comprehensible than limited primary data collection. Examples of secondary data sources include

- Trade, professional, or industry reports
- Articles in trade or professional journals
- Industry market survey and studies
- Federal government reports and statistical data documents and studies
- Reports of government rule-making hearings

The data from secondary sources may have been created for another purpose; therefore, some of the desired data may not be directly present. However, it may provide information on the expected or actual useful life of the product, maintenance of the product, and methodologies used to estimate the current data. Some government reports may include most of the data needed for this phase of the life cycle inventory.

Issues with secondary data include

- Cost — Usually less than primary data.
- Bias — Depending on the secondary source, the data could be biased in favor of the product or manufacturer or against it. Care must be taken to ascertain any bias in the data.
- Timeliness — Secondary data are usually compiled at a time prior to the current study. It is imperative that the data be representative of current practices.

ASSUMPTIONS

Assumptions are used when primary or secondary data are not available. Assumptions can be based on data that are not specific to the product or service being analyzed. For example, data on taking photos with a particular camera could be extrapolated to a single photo; washing a load of dishes in a dishwasher could be extrapolated to washing glasses. In most cases, the assumptions are used because data are not fully available.

When dealing with the end user, the patterns of user behavior should be included. The useful life of a product is not always included in an environmental life cycle analysis. However, to do an adequate job of assessing the MANPRINT of the product, the useful life should be included. The useful life of the product has three critical factors. The first is how the product was designed and built. This includes the materials of construction. The second is the environment and frequency that it is used and the third is how the end user perceives the product's usefulness.

The first determinate is built in by the manufacturer. If the product is used according to its intended use and maintained as specified, the product will have a life expectancy close to what the manufacturer states in the product literature. The second factor is more closely related to the user patterns. How well the end user follows directions and maintains the product can add or subtract useful life from the product. The third is basically how the user sees the product. If the product were tires on a front end drive car and the user didn't rotate the tires but otherwise kept them properly inflated, and didn't abuse them, it is not uncommon to get double the life out of the rear tires. If paper diapers are to be made to support a baby over a specific period of its life, the manufacturer would need to know how many times the "average" baby is changed per day during the time period of interest. In the case of detergents, if the manufacturer makes the detergent stronger so the user doesn't require as much to wash a load of wash, that should save the user costs. However, if the user doesn't change the way he or she thinks and acts about the product, there will be either no savings or it will actually cost the user more money to use what he or she thinks is the same product.

How the end user thinks about the product will have a major impact on its success. In some areas, the addition of certain environmental considerations can improve the product's chances in the market; an example is Body Shop's skin care products which are environmentally and animal-friendly products.

It should be noted that the obtaining of data and the sources for all the stages of the life cycle inventory is pretty much the same. The analyst will use primary or secondary data or assumptions. The treatment of the data should be similar to what is discussed above, no matter what stage the analysis is in.

9   RECYCLE — WASTE MANAGEMENT

The product has undergone most of its life cycle at this point. It has been manufactured, distributed, sold, used, and now it has reached the end of its expected life. In the past, the natural termination of the product would have been, most likely, a landfill if it were a solid object, the sewage treatment plant by way of a sewer if a liquid. The environmental movement started the country thinking about the rate the landfills were filling up and the amount of "stuff" that was being dumped in sewers. The effects of these practices were put under a magnifying glass. We did not like what we saw. For example, thousands of hair dryers are dumped into landfills every year. The main problem with most of them is that the on/off switch is broken. The whole hair dryer goes into the landfill. The landfill gets, on a daily basis, such things as paper wastes, yard wastes, glass, plastics, metals, etc. In some locations around the country, there are recycle programs for certain wastes. Typical recycle wastes are shown in Figure 9-1. The main reason any recycle program is successful is money. If it is cost effective to recycle a particular material, a higher percentage of it will be collected and recycled. The other form of financial incentive is fines for not recycling a material. Both incentive programs are based on money. If it costs more to collect and transport the materials than they are worth (i.e., it's cheaper to use virgin materials) then the materials will go into a dump.

Normally, people think of recycle and waste management as something that is done with paper, plastics, glass, and metals such as newspaper, plastic bottles, glass containers, and metals such as automobile bodies (auto recyclers). In the case of plastic bottles, the high-density polyethylene (HDPE) and polyethylene terephthalate (PET) plastics have a fairly well-established recycling infrastructure in the U.S. For the other recyclable thermoplastics, the infrastructure is somewhat weak. Up until recent times, corporations and institutions looked at recycling much the same way as the average American. Corporations and institutions "recycled" materials such as those shown in Figure 9-1. Recycling to most companies also includes the reuse of materials

87

Typical Recyclables in the Waste Stream

Office	Retail Store	Restaurant
ledger paper, white	ledger paper, white	cardboard
ledger paper, color	ledger paper, color	aluminum cans
computer paper	computer paper	ferrous metals
cardboard	cardboard	glass containers
newspaper	aluminum cans	polystyrene
mixed paper	glass containers	plastic bottles
aluminum cans	polystyrene	grease
glass containers	film plastic	newspaper
polystyrene	wood	computer paper
toner cartridges	unsold inventory	
obsolete office supplies	office supplies	

Schools	Industrial Facility	
ledger paper, white	Materials are specific to the type of industry,	
ledger paper, color	but may include:	
computer paper		
cardboard	ledger paper, white	wood
newspaper	ledger paper, color	waste oil
mixed paper	computer paper	solvents
aluminum cans	cardboard	mylars
ferrous metals	newspaper	precious metals
glass containers	mixed paper	obsolete office supplies
polystyrene	aluminum cans	recoverable inventoty
plastic bottles	ferrous and nonferrous metals	polystyrene
wood	glass containers	film plastic

Figure 9-1.   Typical recyclables in the waste stream.

in-house during the manufacturing process. The concept of taking a used product back and recycling it was a foreign concept.

The next major stage in the life cycle inventory is "discard" (Figure 9-2). At this point, the intended end user has determined that the product is no longer suited for continued use as designed. There are multiple approaches to the discarding of the product. The major methods include but are not limited to:

- Donation/sale — If the product is still usable but no longer fits the end users requirements, the product can be sold as used equipment or donated to a charity, university, school, etc. Examples include old personal computers, industrial machines, copiers, etc.
- Recycle — The product is transferred to a recycle location for dismantling and salvage of useful materials and components. Sub-assemblies and components may be returned to the original manu-facturer for cleaning/refurbishment and reuse in a new product. Examples include computers, electronic equipment, automobiles

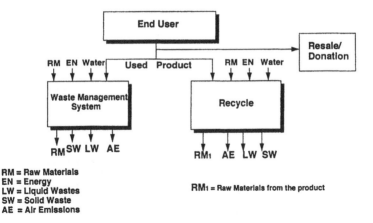

RM = Raw Materials
EN = Energy
LW = Liquid Wastes
SW = Solid Waste
AE = Air Emissions

RM₁ = Raw Materials from the product

Figure 9-2.   Recycle/waste management.

and automotive components, scrap metals, "sludge" from plating wastes that contain certain heavy metals, copier and printer cartridges, plastic bottles, and scrap thermoplastics (see Figure 9-1).

- Waste management — The product is transferred to a waste management facility. This facility may be a sanitary landfill, hazardous materials landfill, incinerator, composting system, or other termination technology. However, in the past few years, waste management has added the waste minimization banner. In this mode, efforts are made to reduce waste before it is generated, reuse materials, recycle/recover materials, and ultimately dispose of by-products and nonrecoverable-nonrecyclable materials.

DONATION/SALE AND RECYCLE

In the discard stage of the inventory, careful consideration of the boundary conditions is required. If the analyst is not careful, this phase of the study can become extremely expensive. In each of the scenarios shown above, certain sets of data will be required for the life cycle inventory. The "usual" condition involves multiples of the steps shown above. The following discussion will provide some guidance in the conditions surrounding each of the above.

The donation/sale of the product to a third party after the primary user is finished with the product is a growing factor in electronics and industrial equipment. The end user can recover some of the initial investment (which he has already written off) or gain a tax advantage. This is also a boon for the recipient. The new owner probably could not afford new equipment, and this approach provides a winning situation for both parties. The analyst must decide where to draw the boundaries. If the boundary conditions stop at the point where the new user takes possession, the inventory for this stage is complete. However, if the requester of the analysis wants the total life cycle, the inventory

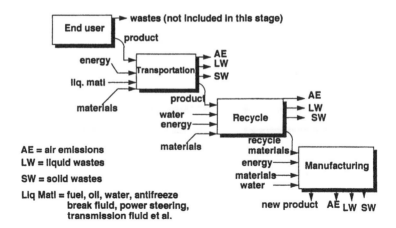

Figure 9-3.   Recycling.

will include a new end user and a secondary disposal activity downstream. In this case the techniques discussed in Chapters 8 and 9 will be repeated.

Recycled materials are those postconsumer materials and by-products that have served their intended use by a consumer (including businesses) and have been separated from solid wastes for the purpose of recycling (Figure 9-3). The two most prevalent types of recycling are the open and closed loop approaches. In the closed loop system (Figure 9-4), the product is recycled back into the same or similar products. In this scenario, the recycled materials have reduced the requirements for the production and disposal of by-products of virgin materials. This scenario does include the impacts of the recycle process (e.g., shredding, washing, melting, transportation) and any impacts incurred resulting from the use of recycled materials. The recycle process can run from the simple to very complex. An example of simple recycling is the return and reuse of glass milk bottles. A complex recycle can include the recycle of some metals, plastics, and recycle processes that are multiple steps. These processes, including all incoming attributes such as energy, materials and water, and outgoing items such a recycled materials, liquid wastes, air emissions, and solid wastes, must be accounted for.

The other scenario is open loop. In this case a product or parts of the product are recycled into alternative product or products (Figure 9-5). The overall change in the sequences of independent product A and product B is the introduction of recycled materials from product A. This has reduced or eliminated wastes from product A and reduced the requirements for virgin raw materials for product B. Figure 9-3 defines the basic data requirements for recycling, both open and closed loop types. The transfer step shown in Figure 9-3 should be handled in the same manner as the transportation steps earlier in the life cycle inventory. The basic reason for including the transportation step is to gain both a total and real picture of the MANPRINT and to assess the costs associated with this step. For example, Xerox, Canon, and others

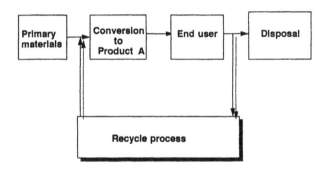

Recycle of materials/product to similar or same product

Figure 9-4A.   Closed loop recycling. Recycle of materials/product to similar or same product.

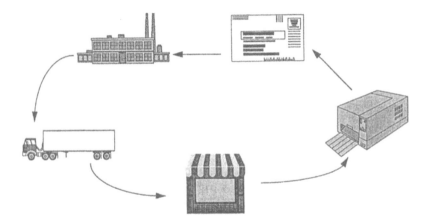

Figure 9-4B.   Recycle of toner cartridges.

supply a prepaid mailer for the return of toner cartridges from their copiers, laser printers, and facsimile machines. 3M ships its bulk videotape in plastic foam packaging, then collects the used packaging at the customer's plants and reuses it. The Big Three automakers recycle used paint for use as filler in road repair and truck underbody paint.

Some products do not undergo open or closed loop recycling exclusively. The use of recycling is dependent on costs associated with the process, transportation, and the marketability of the recycled materials. Some recycled materials go into multiple products. Plastic bottles can be recycled into insulation, other bottles, carpet or clothing fabric, park benches, and plastic pallets. Some "new" products will be manufactured with varying amounts of multiple recycled materials. In general, recycled materials are mixed with virgin materials in the product. This is especially true in the case of molded plastics. The

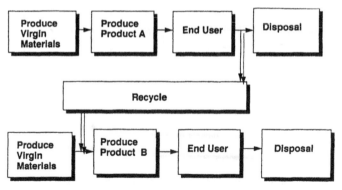

Recycled materials used in an alternative product

Figure 9-5.   Open loop recycling.

use of recycled or reused materials can degrade or change the physical properties of the product to varying degrees. Therefore, the molder will use a percentage of recycled/reused material with virgin material. By doing this, the molder reduces the demand for virgin materials while not endangering the quality of his product.

Composting is another form of recycling. It is usually considered a type of open loop recycling.

The life cycle inventory process has been divided into stages. The data inputs for the recycle and sale/donation phases should be collected as a separate stage as well. The basic input requirements are shown in the model in Figure 9-3. If the original product is donated or sold, the data on transportation, use, and ultimate disposal should be added. That the product has a "second" life is important to the analysis. The maintenance step in the second life of the product may be drastically different from that of it's "primary" life. The aging and wear of the product may require more frequent repairs. An example of this is the typical used car. The primary owner doesn't usually scrap the car when he or she is finished with it. The car is traded in on a new model and the "old" car is resold to a new owner. Data on the life cycle inventory for "second" owners may be available as averages based on the type of product involved. These figures were gathered and analyzed over long periods of time and, depending on the product, were considered fairly accurate for most life cycle inventories. This data collection is similar to the processes and models in Chapters 8 and 9. The inclusion of the data from the sold/donated stages is to be predetermined by the user of the life cycle analysis. All emissions and wastes from the transportation and recycling process are to be noted. The use and disposal of hazardous materials from a recycle process should be defined and accounted for. This can have a greater impact on the environment than if the product were simply disposed of by landfilling or incineration. All wastes from the recycling process should be noted and quantified.

As recycling technology improves in the coming years, it will complicate the models we have used. The newer technologies will allow products to be increasingly recycled in both open and closed loop fashion. This will present increased difficulty in the allocation of costs. Every effort to determine the costs split between recycled output is needed. In some cases, even though the output materials have multiple uses, they are produced by the recycler in one form, in the case of most plastics, as a powder or granular form. The next users (same or similar product or different product) obtain the material in one form. The total cost of recycling is determined, and the costs can be allocated based on sales to different customers.

For recycling, some of the same data sources used in the use/reuse and maintenance stages are applicable. Data on recycling activities may be more limited but many good primary and secondary data sources are available. The actual recycling companies themselves as well as professional organizations and the producers of the raw materials can supply a surprising amount of good-quality data. Government agencies and technical and trade journals are excellent sources. For products and materials in which recovery and recycling rates are low or recycling is relatively new, the data will be much more limited.

WASTE MANAGEMENT

This section describes the handling of wastes from the processes that have not been reused or directly recycled. It is important to note, early in the discussion, the difference between wastes and coproducts or secondary products. Coproducts and secondary products are products that are made concurrently with the principal product or they are made from the same or semiprocessed materials from the production of the principal product. The main differentiation of these coproducts or secondary products is that they have an intrinsic value or function to the company and to a customer. Wastes by definition are no longer of value and are to be disposed of. The models used for the life cycle inventory have indicated wastes after each stage and at the end for final disposal of the product. The treatment of waste management will be applicable to all the waste disposal throughout the model.

Products and coproducts must be clearly distinguished to assign the proper proportions of materials, water, wastes, and energy associated with their production. Life cycle inventories have typically used either the proportional amounts of the inputs and outputs (chemical equivalent or mass) or the relative economic value in proportioning the inputs and outputs. Most life cycle inventories use the proportional method. If an industry, particular company, or process has a high level or potential level of accidental releases, these will be added to the intentional releases.

For purposes of this text, waste management is defined as the methods used to handle, treat, and dispose of materials prior to their entering the environment. This includes waste minimization steps inside a facility, waste treatment (liquid or solids), or emission abatement systems (air) and landfills.

For purposes of the discussion, there are basically two types of waste: hazardous and nonhazardous. Hazardous waste examples include acids, strong bases, corrosives, and flammable and toxic materials including metals in solution, cyanides, radioactive wastes, incinerator wastes, mine tailings, biohazardous wastes, etc. Nonhazardous waste examples include most household wastes, paper, most solid metals, yard wastes, treated municipal wastewater treatment sludge, construction and demolition wastes, etc.

The environmental community has established and codified most states and in the U.S. Environmental Protection Agency (U.S. EPA) a hierarchy of preferences of waste management techniques. The hierarchy includes six preferences in descending order:

- Waste minimization/waste reduction
- Reuse
- Recycle/material recovery
- Composting
- Treatment (physical, thermal, chemical, or biological)
- Disposal (landfill, ocean dumping, groundwater or deep well)

Waste minimization and reuse are at the top of the list because of their importance to pollution prevention, resource conservation, and economic efficiency. Waste minimization reduces wastes by not creating them in the first place. Recycle-reuse minimizes the requirements for virgin raw materials. At this time, in the U.S., this occurs less frequently than waste minimization. The primary reasons for this are

- Management and technical people understand design and manufacturing better than recycle-reuse. Reducing the need for a material or reducing a material waste is "part of their job."
- There are intermediate steps such as collection, hauling, washing, grinding, sterilization, refining, etc., involved.
- Efficiency of recycle-reuse varies with the product, materials involved, distance to recycle-reuse locations from source, and the market for the materials.

Waste minimization and recycle-reuse reduce the environmental loading of a product but are, or can, be difficult to baseline. Recycle-reuse is easier to quantify because it could be measured. As for waste minimization, a baseline of where the company is at in a given point in time must be used. Reduced environmental loading at future dates can be measured relative to the established baseline.

The remaining waste management alternatives involve collection, processing, and ultimate disposal by or at a waste management facility. The inclusion of the waste management phase of a products life cycle is very important.

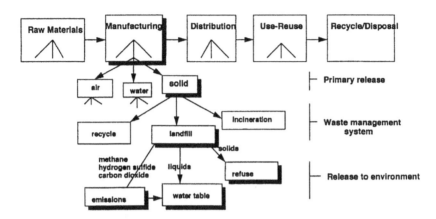

Figure 9-6.   Waste management/disposal. Generic pathways to the environment.

This is the phase where the waste or spent product now reenters the environment. Up to this point, the product has caused certain wastes/emissions to enter the environment from its manufacture, transport, use, and maintenance. The product has now become obsolete, and the portions, if any, that can be recycled have been extracted. The whole or parts of the product remaining will now need to be disposed of. This is the final contribution to its MAN-PRINT on the environment. Figure 9-6 shows the generic relationship of waste management/disposal to not just the final stage but all the previous stages as well. The establishment of boundary conditions is important in this stage as well. The boundary of waste management system starts where the waste is generated. While there are, or may be, multiple waste management systems that can be employed, the analysis will only take into consideration whenever possible the actual waste management system used. For certain classes of products, this is straightforward. In other cases, the specific or multiple geographic location of the product's use will need to be factored in. For example, if the only viable disposal method for a product is a landfill, the analyst will focus on the contribution the product makes to the landfill and any "discharges" it may contribute to while in the landfill (methane, etc., from decomposition). In Figure 2-2 the volumes of 1000 plastic and paper bags from a grocery store were compared. The height of 1000 plastic bags stacked together was 4 inches. The same number of paper sacks was 46 inches. Obviously the paper has a larger volumetric impact. Neither one decomposes well in a sanitary landfill, so the volume is important. On the other hand, some locations may facilitate an incineration process as well. Materials have varying amounts of latent heat or energy stored in them. A comparison of internal energies for different products is shown in the Appendix. In this case, the product's emissions from both waste management processes will need to be considered. The technologies for waste management vary widely on a geographical basis.

There are multiple methods used for performing the life cycle inventory on disposal methods. The method selected should be the one most cost effective for the type of inventory being developed. The most common method used is based on weight or volume of materials. The outputs are then normalized to the inputs based on a weight-to-weight or volume-to-volume basis. It is almost impossible to do a complete materials balance, especially if a biological or some chemical process is involved. This is due to contributions not included in the incoming materials input data (examples include hydrogen, oxygen, enzymes, etc.).

Waste management includes the treatment, if any, and disposal of wastes from the life cycle inventory as noted in Figure 9-6. Three categories of wastes to be addressed are solid, liquid, and air emissions. All the treatment schemes that are used today to treat waste emissions are designed to transform the waste materials from their existing form to another form that is less toxic or has less impact on the environment and health of organisms around it. The real effectiveness of these treatments can be debated. It should be noted that one type of treatment for each generic type of waste will not work. For example, treating some industrial wastes, containing heavy metals such as copper, as domestic sewage will not only not work, it will prevent the sewage treatment facility from adequately treating the domestic sewage. Table 9-1 provides a general listing of types of waste management technologies. Most municipalities require industrial discharges that include materials that are hazardous to the sewage treatment plant to be pretreated to prevent upset of the sewage treatment facility. Some municipal treatment works also require industrial pretreatment for waste streams that will input a high organic load on the plant, thus requiring extra treatment capabilities. This is usually noted as BOD or COD levels (see Figure 9-7). Domestic sewage treatment technology has not changed much in the past 80 years. However, good secondary or

Table 9-1 Waste Management Technologies

Solid wastes	Liquid wastes	Air emissions
Landfilling (nonhazardous wastes)	Sewage treatment	Incineration/combustion
Landfilling (hazardous wastes)	Industrial treatments	Activated carbon
Incineration	Incineration	Condensation
Composting	Underground injection	Dust collectors
Landspreading	Lagooning	Scrubbers
Vitrification	Filtration	Filters
Fixation/cementation	Solidification	
Autoclaving/microwaving		
Recycling		
Illegal dumping		

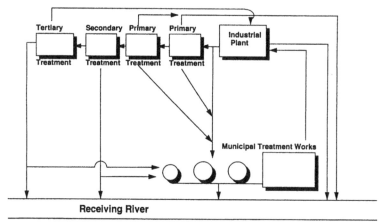

Multiple possible flows of Industrial Waste Treatment Systems

Figure 9-7.   Industrial/municipal treatment.

tertiary treatment of sewage does produce wastewater that can be disinfected and, in reasonable amounts at a time, be safely discharged to waterways. Industrial waste treatment has changed slightly in the past 50 years. Note again that different types of industrial waste require different treatment methods. There might also be more than one method for treating a particular industrial waste. The analyst must determine the method(s) used for the particular wastes for the product being investigated.

LIQUID WASTES

Liquid wastes in question need to be segregated by type and treatment methods required. The treatment method used will determine the required inputs and outputs. Most on-site treatments systems can be easily modeled with associated materials and costs from company records. For example, an on-site treatment system for plating wastes will have multiple waste streams for inputs with limited outputs (water, solid sludge; air emissions are included but may be extremely small). The inputs will vary, but will all be coming from the metal finishing operations at the plant. For example, chromate wastes and cyanide wastes will be from different plating lines. The analyst needs to determine what plating processes and rinses the product went through to allocate the contribution to the operation of the waste treatment plant. Off-site treatment is a different issue. In this case, wastes from the transportation method should be considered, unless it is insignificant compared to the actual treatment process. Off-site treatment processes need to be modeled to properly assign values to the input and output streams for the wastes from the specific product being studied (see Figure 9-8). The generic model block takes into

Notes: 1 Sludge may have commercial value
       2 Air emissions may be in the form of mists
       3 Solid material inputs may be thickeners, precipitation facilitators etc.

Figure 9-8.   Liquid waste model.

consideration all the treatment systems used for water/liquid wastes. This includes but is not limited to the following examples:

- Reverse osmosis
- Precipitation/clarification
- Lagooning
- Filtration
- Underground injection
- Incineration
- Biotreatment
- Oxidation
- Land farming

The treatment of liquid wastes involves mainly in-solution treatments. However, the analyst should understand that treatment systems vary. Therefore, he or she should be familiar with the specific treatment system being employed. This will aid in determining the pathways for emissions from the treatment system to the environment. For example, a waste treatment facility might use aeration as a means of improving biological oxidation of the waste stream. The aeration process can and usually does release small amounts of the waste liquid into the air (environment) as well as some dissolved gases, volatile organic compounds (VOCs), aerosols, water vapor, and heat. The reader may, at one time or another, have had the misfortune of being downwind from a sewage treatment plant and been quickly able to determine his or her error in location. There are also the intended treated liquid effluents and usually solids in the form of sludge. Sometimes the liquid or solids from a treatment have commercial value. Sludges from a treatment system handling metal finishing wastes may have a high enough concentration of certain metals to qualify as an ore and be sold to refiners as raw material. In other cases the solids will find their way to a landfill.

Depending on the type of landfill, the analyst can usually count on the fact that the landfill leaks. Water-based seepage is trapped and treated on site in some landfills. Others seep into the ground or to nearby streams, lakes, or groundwater. Quantifying this seepage, if not captured and treated on site, will be difficult. The analyst should note that the condition exists or could exist. If there are data from public records at local agencies to help quantify it, the data should be gathered. The American Water Works Association, Water Pollution Control Federation, and other environmental organizations have valuable information on sources of wastewater. There are magazines and organizations that specialize in landfills as well. The data from these sources are reliable and as accurate as can be expected for generic settings. Local chapters of environmental organizations and Air Quality Management Districts may have quantifiable data on a specific local landfill. Local, regional wastewater control agencies, the U.S. EPA or the U.S. Army Corps of Engineers may have data on discharges to natural watersheds such a streams, rivers, lakes, and ocean outfalls. There are stringent requirements and permits needed for discharges to storm drains, wetlands, and waterways. These can be researched at the local offices of the local, state, and federal agencies. The requirements for determining the specifics for the "normal" inputs and outputs are obvious. The analyst should investigate leaks, spills, or overflows as well. These are potential pathways to the environment.

SOLID WASTE

The disposal of solid wastes is what people usually think of as garbage. This text uses solid disposal where most refer to land disposal. This is because land disposal is not the only method of treating solids that is available today. The disposal of solids includes

- Landfills
- Incineration
- Vitrification
- Alternative treatments (microwaving, etc.)
- Recycling
- Landfarming
- Composting
- Fixation/cementation

Landfills are the most common waste management practice. The other methods listed have niche applications. For example, composting is used primarily for natural organic wastes such as gardening and organic garbage. Incineration is used for liquid and solid materials that usually have some caloric value. Each has a set of inputs and outputs that will need to be noted and quantified most accurately as possible (see Figure 9-9). The emissions

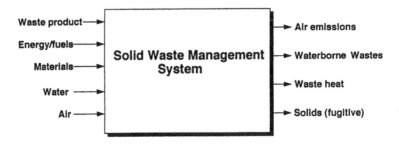

Figure 9-9.   Solid waste model.

from an industrial incinerator are readily known by the operators of the equipment. This is because of the requirements of their permits. Typical emissions from incinerators are indicated in Figure 9-10A and B. Determining the allocation to a specific product, unless it is a captive system or the product constitutes a major part of its feedstock, will be difficult. The use of percentages will usually suffice. The other methods of waste management will offer varying degrees of challenges. For landfills, the following are considered the major outputs or pathways to the environment:

- Airborne emissions — Methane, VOCs, volatile liquid wastes, waste handling equipment emissions, landfill gas combustion products.
- Water emissions — Groundwater releases, leachate production and treatment processes, soil erosion, surface runoff.
- Solid particulate — Soil erosion, dust, sludge particles, chemicals applied to soils, compost, litter.
- Energy releases — Waste heat, landfill gas combustion.
- Fugitive emissions — Spills/accidental releases, containment system failures, waste handling equipment releases.

A similar set of pathways should be developed for the type(s) of waste management systems used for the disposal of the product or products being studied in the life cycle inventory.

AIRBORNE WASTE

Air emissions result from nearly every stage of the life cycle inventory. The emissions may or may not pass through some sort of waste treatment/control technology before reaching the environment. The concern of air emissions is the wider-spread impact air emissions can have on the environment. Solid-based wastes tend to stay in a relatively small area after discharge to the environment. Liquid wastes are capable of movement and can contaminate a wider area including groundwater. This movement can be fast (minutes) or extremely slow (years). Air pollution on the other hand cannot just spread over

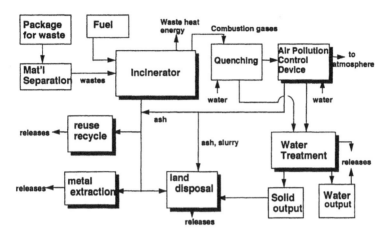

Figure 9-10A. Pathways for emissions from incinerators.

· **Emissions from incinerators include:**

    – carbon dioxide   - water vapor

    – water   - heavy metals

    – dioxins and furans   - waste heat

    – ash   - particulate organic chemicals

    – products of incomplete combustion

    – product specific pollutants

Figure 9-10B. Pathways for emissions from incinerators.

a vast area in a short period of time, it can contaminate soil and water, including both surface and groundwater, in a very short duration of time (see Figure 9-11). The boundaries used for airborne wastes and by-products need to be flexible. The extent of the inventory and associated costs need to be considered. To gain the most from an environmental life cycle inventory at a reasonable cost, the inventory should draw boundaries that include the major considerations and note the lesser ones. Air emission studies from waste management systems have been and continue to be studied. The U.S. EPA, air quality management districts, technical associations, and universities are good sources for quantitative information. The actual waste management organization may also be willing to provide information. Care must be taken with any data provided by a waste management facility. It is always a good practice to consider any such data as privileged and treat it as such. As with water and

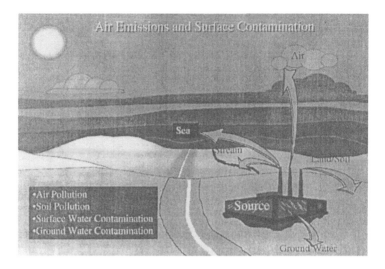

Figure 9-11.   Air emissions and surface contamination.

solid wastes, the units used to measure the inputs and outputs must be consistent. The units are usually in volume/volume or weight/weight relationships. It is confusing to mix volume and weight measurements. Therefore, it is necessary that the analyst

- Compiles a comprehensive list of emissions and pollutants from local, state, and federal laws, permits, and reporting requirements.
- Develops a standard measurement and reporting method.
- Develop consistent standards to fill in the gaps.

When the analyst is developing the data from air pollution control devices that involve a chemical transformation, care must be taken in rationalizing the data. For example, oxidation processes may *not* convert all or most of the product being treated to carbon dioxide. There are conditions that may exist that convert initial breakdown products into other compounds. These compounds may not be detected because no one is looking for them.

The collection and reporting of the data used for characterization of the waste generation and treatment will be a set of building blocks. Air, water, and solid wastes will be analyzed independently, recognizing that many processes will involve all three types of waste. It will also recognize that waste management processes may reduce wastes in one category only to raise wastes in another category. For example, look at a manufacturer, who, while trying to reduce airborne emissions of VOCs, changed from a solvent cleaning operation to aqueous cleaning. He reduced his airborne emissions but increased the amount of water he was using and increased the waterborne wastes emissions and increased his surcharges for BOD and COD.

Release	Amount	Comments
	Solid Wastes	
Hazardous		
Nonhazardous		
Municipal Waste	X kg	other units or
Municipal sludge		releases as neceaasry may be added
Compost		
	Airborne Wastes	
Regulated		
Particulate		
Toxic		other units or
Carcinogenic		releases as neceaasry
Nitrogen oxides	Y Kg	may be added
Sulfur oxides		
Carbon Dioxide		
VOCs		
Benzene		
other		
	Waterborne Wastes	
COD		
BOD		
TOC		other units or
Suspended Solids	Z Kg	releases as neceaasry
Settleable Solids	or applicable units	may be added
Carcinogens		
Heavy Metals		
Toxic Materials		
Benzene		
Sewage		

Figure 9-12.   Total releases for the life cycle inventory component.

As shown in the fundamental modeling in Chapter 3, each phase of the product's life can be broken down into smaller steps until a fundamental understanding and model can be made. At this level the collection and quantifying of data including waste management can be handled easily. Once the data for each small step are generated (Figure 9-12), they can be aggregated up to the next level and so forth to finally produce the desired information at the required levels of the model.

The disposal model is the most complicated due to fact that wastes are generated all through the life cycle inventory model. The disposal section is treated like all the previous model steps with the addition of the wastes from all the prior steps. It is not uncommon to consider the wastes generated at each step as part of that step and use the models for the disposal step for the actions that take place at the end of the life cycle inventory. This approach simplifies the model and *makes the actual impact at each stage stand out*. The author recommends treating wastes generated at each stage at the particular stage where they are generated. Only the waste emissions generated at the disposal stage should be included at this stage level. Others may disagree. When it comes to methods to perform a life cycle analysis, there are no specifications regarding what must be included where in the study. If it is easier and more meaningful to include the wastes at each stage, then do it. If it is a minor consideration, due to the nature of the study, then place all the disposal/wastes in the disposal section. It is up to the analyst and the requirements and intended use of the life cycle analysis.

10   SUMMARY

The purpose of the life cycle inventory is to develop a life cycle assessment of a product. This assessment is chartered by the company management to aid in part of the product's design. The company may be interested in the impact it is having directly or indirectly through its products for any number of reasons. Most of the time it is due to some regulatory concern or to improve the company's image and customer market share. The life cycle analysis will provide an estimate of the impact the company is having on the environment or its MANPRINT. It will point out areas where the impact is the greatest and allow the user to compare his or her design or product to another competing design or product. It will not, however, directly determine what to do about any impacts. Waste minimization is another step. However, the life cycle analysis will provide guidance regarding where to put the emphasis on waste minimization and possible product/design improvements. It will also provide information to the design community to consider improvements during the design stage. That the designers cause most of the pollution from the product is not often clear to a design engineer. The use of the information from a life cycle analysis will help the designer better understand his or her role in a nonthreatening manner.

Knowing the various impacts the product has at each stage of its life will aid the company and its manufacturing management and the designers in determining what changes can be made and at which stage in the product's life cycle to reduce the product's MANPRINT. As mentioned in an earlier chapter, some copier and printer manufacturers have a no-cost return policy for their toner cartridges. This reduces the amount of refuse in landfills as well as the requirements for raw materials. The U.S. Army, during the early stages of a tactical missile program, instructed the missile contractors to do a MAN-PRINT study. They found that changing some materials and design callouts reduced the MANPRINT during manufacturing. They also studied what happens when they go into the field on training exercises. By making changes to fuel delivery systems, modifications missile support/launch vehicles, and troop operations, the Army could drastically reduce its MANPRINT on the environment (not counting the explosions when the missiles hit a target).

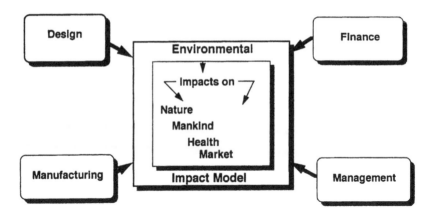

Figure 10-1.   Impact assessment.

Sometimes it is satisfactory to provide the producer of the product(s) with information on the effects of its product on energy, raw materials utilized, disposal impacts such as volume in landfills, etc. Newer assessments have been taking a longer look at the assessment, more as a risk assessment.

At this point the life cycle inventory has become the life cycle analysis or environmental impact assessment. This is especially important to the management community. The impact analysis evaluates the environmental impacts caused by the product and its use/disposal. On the most basic level, resources are depleted and residuals are generated for each product and subproduct system. Resource depletion and wastes or residuals from the product and product manufacturing, distribution, use/maintenance, recycle/reuse, and disposal processes all contribute to the degradation of the ecosystem. Because of this, organizations such as design, manufacturing, finance, management, and marketing will be impacted by the results of the life cycle assessment. Figure 10-1 provides a simple diagram of this.

Environmental impacts can be organized into the following categories:

- Degradation of ecological systems
- Resource depletion
- Human welfare effects
- Human health effects

The type of models used to translate the life cycle inventory data to useful information will vary. The nature of the potential impact and the scope of the analysis will determine how much detail is required. For example, the release of chlorofluorocarbons (CFCs) into the atmosphere is reported to cause a degradation of the ozone in the upper atmosphere. This phenomena results in increased levels of ultraviolet light reaching the Earth's surface. This in turn is said to cause an increase in skin cancer. The models to show this are quite complex and the ability to ascertain the exact contribution of a company's CFCs contributed to the "problem" is almost impossible. In this case it would be sufficient to just state that the release of CFCs is contributing to the degradation of the ecosystem and possibly contributing to human health effects. It may be enough to simply estimate the impact on the company to eliminate CFCs. For a designer (product design or process design), the impact of the design on the environmental life cycle is one of the most challenging he or she will undertake. The following describes several aspects of environmental impact assessments on ecosystems.

DEGRADATION OF ECOLOGICAL SYSTEMS

Environmental life cycle assessments have largely focused on human health issues and to some extent on resource depletion. Up until recently, the degradation of the ecological systems has been largely ignored. This position is changing. This is because science has demonstrated a strong link to the health and welfare of humans to the health and welfare of the oceans, wetlands, forests, and other natural ecosystems. Mankind cannot as yet fully understand and recreate his ecosystem. This was demonstrated in the biosphere experiment. In this experiment, the oxygen levels in the biosphere went down to a level requiring outside ventilation. Some plants died. The reason was the cement used in the walls interfered with the carbon cycle, removing carbon dioxide that the plants needed to produce oxygen for the air and carbon for their cells. Bacteria created the carbon dioxide but the concrete absorbed enough to upset the cycle. It has been shown that if the oceans die, so does man. Therefore, governments and scientists are now starting to understand the fragile relationship man has with his ecosystem.

Ecological risk or impact assessment is modeled after human health risk assessments but is more complex. Each ecosystem the product will come in contact with will be evaluated based on the impact the product has on that system. Ecosystems need to be bounded as well. The whole world is an ecosystem; however, this approach may be too vast in most applications. In the case of CFCs, mentioned earlier, the atmosphere around the world was considered an ecosystem and the impact of CFCs on it was studied. Subecosystems, mainly human interaction, was added as part of the risk assessment.

Ecosystems are never static. They are living systems and as such tend to respond to stimuli or stress. Stress in the ecosystem world can be chemical (toxic waste dumping, pesticides, etc.), physical, (habitat destruction due to construction, logging, farming, etc.), or biological (introduction of a foreign or exotic species) in nature. These stimuli or stresses cause the ecosystem to respond in some manner. The risk involved to the ecosystem will elicit a distinct response. The response may range from a mild adjustment to a destruction of the existing ecosystem and the evolution of a new one. The risks to an ecosystem are classified as follows:

- Type of ecological response based on indicator's response
- Intensity of the potential effect
- Time scale for recovery after stimuli removal
- Spatial scale (local, regional, global)
- Transport media

The rate of recovery of an ecosystem from a stress is important. In some cases the effect is permanent changes in the biocommunity and species extinction. Stresses tend to be cumulative, finally resulting in large-scale changes and problems. Habitat destruction and atmospheric changes are widespread examples. Care must be exercised in this area. The use of renewable resources may be misleading, e.g., the use of wood to make paper and other wood products. The first thought and the advertisements from the lumber industry indicate that the "forests" are replaceable. The wood that the lumber mills want is, to some extent, replaceable. It can be grown on tree farms. These tree farms are *not* the same ecosystems that were placed here by nature. They do not harbor the same plants and animals that the original forest, that was cut down, did. Is this the same thing as the original? No. Is the wood replaceable? Yes. Is there an impact to the environment, Yes. Should this be taken into consideration during an environmental impact analysis? Yes!

Determining the potential risks and likely effects is the first step in the ecological assessment. The data have been provided by the life cycle assessment. Now the user must evaluate the data to determine the possible effects the product's design and life cycle will have on the environment and what, if any, changes can be made to reduce, mitigate, or eliminate the potential environmental impact.

RESOURCE DEPLETION

The extraction and consumption of natural resources is divided into two categories. The first one is renewable resources such as hydroelectric and wind-generated power and certain biomasses such as corn and other crops. The second category is nonrenewable resources. There are finite amounts of minerals in the earth. Oil, coal, iron, copper, chrome, and in some areas water, etc., are not being "remade" at any noticeable rate. Certain minerals are obtained only in specific locations in the world. Because of this, wars have and will be fought. Up until recently, most people considered minerals to be almost inexhaustible. People have had the "frontier" mentality of "rip it up, use it, and throw it away — we can get more" philosophy. The problem is we do not have infinite amounts of resources. Fresh water is becoming scarce because of overuse, leaching of minerals and pesticides, and the disposal of sewage and industrial wastes. The producer of products needs to understand what the demands on the environment and natural resources are and how to prolong their life. The life cycle analysis will provide the understanding that, with the present design of the product, the company will require "X" thousands of pounds of thermoplastic, "Y" thousands of pounds of steel screws, nuts, bolts, washers, "Z" gallons of water, etc. Now, armed with those data, the design and manufacturing engineers can work on how to reduce the requirements. This may involve the reuse of waste plastic, recycle of solvents, redesigns to reduce components parts, and more efficient or reduced use of water, thus reducing the number and types of fasteners such as nuts, bolts, washers, resources, etc. This can have major cost reduction implications. Examples include

Company	Operating change	Benefit
3M	Developed an adhesive for sealing of boxes that didn't require solvent	Eliminated the need for $2 million in pollution prevention equipment
Reynolds Metals	Replaced solvent-based ink with water based in packaging plants	Cut emissions by 65% and saved $30 million in pollution control equipment
Hughes Aircraft	Cut off unnecessary air sparging to a plating line	Reduced chemical costs, improved quality of the plating, and saved over $50,000 in pollution abatement equipment
	Recycle of materials and materials reduction including just-in-time chemical acquisition and use	Over $ 1.5 million saved Floor space saved >17,000 tons of materials recycled

The engineers can design the product for ease of consumer recycling of critical and expendable components such as toner cartridges. The designers can think of recycling and reuse as "mining" the old product for materials to reuse in the same design product or another product. *Mining the scrap* can be as profitable as mining for the natural resource. The designers may require some initial training in design for assembly (DFA)/design for disassembly (DFD-A) and design for the environment (DFE). They are all very closely related. DFE includes DFD-A. If the recycler or customer can't *easily* get to the components that are to be recycled/reused, it isn't cost effective and, if it isn't easy, the recycler/customer won't do it.

As noted above, the depletion of natural forests and the substitution of man-made ones is a resource destruction. Students at California State Polytechnic University at Pomona noticed this during their study of the comparison of plastic grocery bags to paper ones. After their study, plastic won out based on multiple environmental impact analyses.

HUMAN HEALTH AND WELFARE ISSUES

The one thing most manufacturers do not want is to have their product cause human health problems. Most do not want their products to harm animals either. Having a product unintentionally cause sickness, injury, or death to man or animal can have devastating effects on the company. Beyond the "normal" precautions taken during the design phase of the life cycle, the assessment can determine any long-term effects the product may cause. The cause may be indirect. The design may cause the manufacturing organization to use solvents, solutions, or materials that are hazardous to humans. The effects on humans is dose related but the requirements for the materials is caused by the designers. The effects of the product on humans and the local ecosystems is determined by the life cycle analysis. This will include not just direct effects but indirect.

Another aspect of human health and welfare is the loss of the natural environment, e.g., loss of forests, wilderness areas, wildlife, streams, etc. Most people don't understand nature — some appreciate it more than others — but the natural environment is not man-made greenbelts. When our products and activities cause the destruction and loss of natural environments, we all lose.

The use of a life cycle analysis to ascertain the impact a product or company has on the environment is a noble undertaking. The company using the tool may find out facts that it does not want to hear. Using the data to improve the environmental impact will benefit not just the company but the world outside as well. Companies that have taken the reduction of wastes and MANPRINT seriously have had some or all of the following benefits:

- Improved market share
- Reduced costs
- Additional advertising material

The use of the data must begin at the top of the organization. Management must be committed to reducing their company's impact on the environment. The design organization must understand management's commitment and use the life cycle analysis as a guide for reducing environmental impact through the design of the product. In most cases, training can be beneficial.

The training should be from companies that understand not just environmental issues (environmental rules, waste minimization, assessments, and life cycle analysis), but materials and processes (M&P), design (including DFA/DFE/DFD-A), and manufacturing. Most environmental consultants do not understand product design or manufacturing. Consulting or training firms that have the capabilities listed above to conduct this type of training are not easy to find (Figure 10-2). They must have people that have experience in all three areas. The following companies have the background to perform the necessary training and consulting required:

Company			
Name of consulting company:			
Address:			
Telephone/Fax. number:			
Contact name:			

Skill Summary			
Skill matrix:	Yes	No	Comments
Industrial design experience			
Direct manufacturing experience			
Environmental areas of experience			
Waste minimization			
Lifecycle analysis			
Remediation			
Site assessments			
Envir. management assessments			
Teaching/ training experience			
Waste treatment system design			
Publication/patents in fields			
Estimated costs			

Figure 10-2.   **Consultant-training checklist.**

Orion Management Company
Principal offices at
24000 Alicia Parkway # 17
Box 211
Mission Viejo, CA 92691

Edward C. Lai & Associates
Principal offices at
2424 229th Street
Torrance, CA 90501

Coopers & Lybrand
Offices throughout the U.S.

Arthur D. Little
Offices throughout the U.S.

The use of the life cycle analysis can range from a directed product/process or potential impact area to a full life cycle analysis starting from a figment of the designer's imagination through ultimate disposal. The type of analysis chosen will depend on the intended use of the study and the amount of time and money the company wants to spend in it. There is no one-and-only way to conduct a life cycle audit. Using the models shown earlier as templates, the analysis can be varied to accommodate the needs of the company.

The data from the models must be modified into a format or sets of formats that turn the data into information usable by the company. The use of charts and graphs will aid in the understanding of the technical data. The user wants information that can be readily used without laborious calculations and manipulations to translate into something usable in the designs. Figures 10-3 through 10-6 illustrate the use of graphic formats as part of the final report.

Each life cycle inventory has its own set of limitations. These limitations must be contained in the report and study notes. It must contain statements on components of the study that were not quantified or omitted and for what reasons, the base year of the study, special conventions used, data ranges, efficiencies, whether the study was peer reviewed, if reviewer comments were included, and any other limitations. Below are some examples of possible limitations that would be documented as such:

- How deep and broad was the study? How were the boundaries drawn?
- Are there any significant limitations that affect the data?
- Do facilities and processes meet minimum regulatory requirements?
- Sources of generated information. Type of data being used (primary, secondary, assumptions, tertiary). Statements as to reliability of the data.
- How did the analysis address any missing data?
- How does, or did, changing technology affect the study?
- How can the data best be delivered to intended users?
- How much proprietary information was used and how much can be made available to the intended users of the report? Was proprietary

PROCESS	ENERGY	ENVIRONMENTAL IMPACT	MANUFACTUREABILITY	RECYCLABILITY
Paper	• 1,340,000 megajoules per bag required • Numerous equipment transfers to complete a finished product • Paper uses approximatley 2 times the energy than it takes to produce plastic used for grocery sacks	• Odor producing process • Produces air and water pollutants • Inorganic fillers such as adhesives and inks, produce large quantities of wastes • Deforestation and loss of ecosystems • Carcinogenic products produced • Limited biodegradability • Large amounts of solid wastes	• Messy manufacturing operations • Numerous operations to finished product • Government regulations have caused a large increase in capital improvements to control pollutants • Increased off shore production where environmental laws are less stringent or can be overlooked	• Low profit margin in recycling paper bags • Limited degree of reprocessing • Secondary fibers are of a lower quality • Increased solid wastes • Very high capital investment

Figure 10-3. Data summary sheet.

Process	Energy	Environmental Impact	Manufactureability	Recyclability
Plastic	• 580,000 megajoules per bag required • Can be incinerated has latent heat content • Uses approximately 1/2 the energy required than it takes to produce paper sacks • Takes less energy to recycle	• Thermal decomposition produces aldehydes • Water pollutants; waster wastes through production and polymerization • Toxic additives used in processing facilities • Littering of post consumer plastic; trash in streets, oceans and wilderness areas • Take much less volume in a landfill than paper sacks	• Inert final product • Low energy consumption • Gas blown • Polyethylene pellets used • Water based ink • Uses additives such as oxidizing agents/ colorants	• Loses desired properties • Contamination losses • Chemical additives • Additional additives required for biogradability or photodegradability • Easier to recycle than paper sacks • Less pollutants recycling plastic bags than paper

Figure 10-3. *Continued.*

Wt	Attribute	Plastic	Paper
5	*Environmental Impact*	*8*	*6*
4	*Recyclability*	*7*	*5*
3	*Generated Waste Mtrl*	*8*	*5*
2	*Energy*	*9*	*5*
1	*Manufacturability*	*7*	*6*
	TOTAL (ATT X SCORE)	*117*	*81*

Figure 10-4.   Table comparing key attributes for plastic and paper.

information manipulated to avoid the exact proprietary nature thus allowing general use of the data?

- What trade-offs were made in selecting the boundaries for the study?

The final report should include, but is not limited to, the following elements:

1.0 Executive summary
    1.1 An opening paragraph describing the nature of the study
    1.2 A brief summary of the results
2.0 Introduction
    2.1 A description of the purpose of the study
    2.2 A description of the products the study included
    2.3 The dates over which the study was undertaken
    2.4 The names of companies, institutions, government agencies, and individuals who were contacted during the study
    2.5 Limitations of the study

The Environmental burden per 1 million paper bags

Subject	Polyethylene bags	Paper bags
Energy required	580,000 megajoules	1,340,000 megajoules
Air pollution produced (kilograms)		
Sulfur dioxide	198	388
Nitrogen oxides	136	204
Hydrocarbons	76	24
Carbon monoxide	20	60
Dust	10	64
Waste water (kilograms)	10	512

Figure 10-5. The energy dilemma. The environmental burden per 1 million bags.

2.6 Boundaries and assumptions used during the study
2.7 A summary of the environmental impact analysis
3.0 Stages of the inventory
    3.1 A description of each stage and sublevels in each stage
    3.2 Boundary conditions imposed and qualifications
    3.3 A description and *quantification* of inputs and outputs for each stage at the top level for each stage; describe anything

	Kraft		
Item	Unbleached	Bleached	Groundwood
Virgin material (dry)	1.0 ton	1.1 ton	1.1
Waste water Volume	24 x 10^3 gal	47x 10^3 gal	10x 10^3 gal
Energy	16 x 10^6 BTU	22 x 10^6 BTU	18x 10^6 BTU
Solid wastes	135 lbs	225lbs	164 lbs
Air emissions	50 lbs	64 lbs	65 lbs
Waterborne wastes *	46 lbs	90 lbs	25 lbs

* includes BOD

Figure 10-6. Environmental impacts of manufacture on one dry ton of wood pulp.

outstanding at each stage (outstanding = any obvious issue or opportunity)

    3.4 Procedural activities, limitations, assumptions

    3.5 Summary of sources for each stage

4.0 Top level or product level summary or product/design comparisons

    4.1 Discuss rollup of the environmental impact and comparisons to other similar designs/products if any exist

    4.2 Discuss limitations and assumptions

    4.3. Highlights of where the heaviest environmental impacts are located, causes (if known)

    4.4 Comparisons to other products or processes that are pertinent

    4.5 Conclusions

    4.6 Recommendations

Appendix

Holds major tables, drawings, references, and support information

The final report is provided during the exit briefing to management and others that have interest in the analysis. The exit briefing provides for the presentation of the pertinent information and delivery of the final report. The exit briefing is an excellent time for management to reestablish the importance of the report and define near and long-term activities. Management support for future activities must be made clear if the life cycle analysis findings are to be utilized.

For results from the life cycle analysis to have a long-term impact, employees and management may have to change the way they think and act. This will not happen by itself. To facilitate changes throughout the organization, the individuals will need to understand what is going to be required and why. By addressing the unasked question "What's in this for me?", the company will not get the total expected results. To accomplish this, training will be necessary (Figure 10-7). Most of the training, for the organization, will be common. However, each department will have unique training that is required for their specific function. For example, accounting may be figuring out how to easily account for environmental costs above what is presently reported. This will allow management to easily review the TOTAL environmental costs. The collection of scrap and rework costs may be part of their training. The design engineers will get different training such as how to set up and use a "green design system," materials training, how design impacts the environment, and a crash course in manufacturing technology. Manufacturing will be concentrating on pollution prevention, tooling/packaging, etc.

The life cycle analysis and report is not the end of the process. If the study and report are to be of value, the report and subsequent findings must be used to reduce the environmental impact of the product or processes that were studied. Two areas that will have major impacts will be the design engineering organization and manufacturing.

Figure 10-7. Training for life cycle analysis.

The design engineering function determines not just what the product looks like and how it works but what the materials of construction are and to a large extent what manufacturing processes are used. The design engineering function therefore determines the environmental destiny of the product. Aspects of the design determine how it is packaged for shipment and the amount of energy and materials required for use, maintenance, and repair. The final destiny of the product upon disposal is also preordained by the design engineers. The design community must consider the following for each product:

- Cost of the product
- Legal aspects of the design and product use
- Cultural aspects (the product's name, color, shape, etc.)
- Performance of the product
- Materials and processes for production
- Environmental destiny

Obviously, all the items listed above are interrelated. The life cycle analysis study, however, allows the designer to see where in its life cycle the product has the greatest impacts. This can provide the designer with some ideas as to what aspects of the design could possibly be changed to reduce the impact. Because the designer knows, by means of the study, how the product impacts

		Raw Materials	Mfg/Processes	Distribution	Use/Reuse	Recycle	Disposal
Product	inputs						
	outputs						
Processes/ Mfg.	inputs						
	outputs						
Distribution	inputs						
	outputs						
Waste Management	inputs						
	outputs						
Use/Reuse	inputs						
	outputs						

Figure 10-8. Conceptual matrix.

the environment at each stage, he or she can more easily estimate the impact the proposed change will have on the environment and the product. A conceptual requirement matrix is shown in Figure 10-8. Using the knowledge of impacts the designer can focus his or her energy at reducing the environmental effects. The designer must, however, consider the functionality and cost of the product. If making the requisite changes drastically increases the cost, what will the impact be to the end user? Will the user go someplace else for a similar product? Sometimes the company can actually charge more for an environmentally sound product or gain increased market share. The marketing department needs to understand the changes to better sell the product. The changes to reduce environmental impact may start in the factory. The materials of construction, coatings, and cleaners required are predetermined by the designers. The company may want to institute a program of design reviews with manufacturing people or have designers spend time in manufacturing actually seeing, firsthand, how the product is actually built and what their callouts on drawings actually do to production. In most cases, the design engineers do *not* actually know the details of how the product is manufactured. What they think and what really happens are usually quite different.

Manufacturing engineers and management must also review the life cycle analysis. Manufacturing creates many materials that cause an environmental impact for the plant site. The impacts come from

- Solid waste such as paper, wood, plastics, metals, etc.
- Sludge from water treatment facilities for such operations as painting and plating lines. These can have high concentrations of heavy metals or paint sludge.

- Liquid wastes such as solvents, hot water, cooling water, process water, cooling agents, wash water, etc.
- Air emissions such as solvents from coating operations, vapor degreasers, lamination processes, welding/brazing processes, and microelectronics fabrication procedures.

Manufacturing operations in a company usually handle most of the chemicals used. Therefore, they create the largest amount of hazardous waste as well as nonhazardous wastes. Manufacturing can and should undertake a waste minimization program that includes

- Reducing the amount of chemicals used
- Changing to more environmentally friendly chemicals or processes whenever possible
- Reducing solid wastes
- Recycling/reusing as much material as possible
- Working with design engineering to reduce the requirements for environmentally unfriendly materials and processes

There are books on the market detailing waste minimization techniques:

- *Hazardous Waste Minimization Handbook* by T. E. Higgins (Lewis Publishers, 1989).
- *Waste Minimization as a Strategic Weapon* by D. F. Ciambrone (CRC/Lewis Publishers, 1995).

The largest single factor in the successful use of a waste minimization program as well as the life cycle analysis is *management.* Management must be the driving force behind the use of the life cycle analysis. Management will drive engineering and manufacturing to do their respective jobs. However, management must include marketing and finance as well. The evaluation of the position of a product with respect to its future and the amount of time and money that will be spent improving its environmental impact are management, finance, and marketing decisions. Figure 10-9 illustrates a matrix method of determining what to do with a product. It takes into consideration real and perceived environmental impacts. The real impacts can be determined from the life cycle analysis. The perceived impacts are determined by marketing listening to the consumer. Each product will position itself somewhere in the matrix. From its respective position, management must decide what strategy and leadership is required. A perceived impact is just as real to the user as an actual impact.

If the position of the product is in the high-perceived but low-actual impact area, management will be looking at marketing and communication strategies.

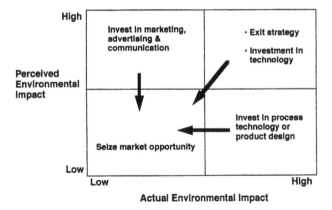

Figure 10-9.   Actual vs. perceived environmental impact.

If the product is in the high-actual impact but low-perceived impact area, the management will be considering process or product improvements. This will be an investment in engineering or manufacturing.

The high-perceived and actual-impact area may mean that management will have to invest in processes or product changes as well as new marketing approaches. The other alternative is to exit the product market. There might be cases where the product is in this block area and the market is still strong. Management may consider possible changes to the next-generation product and leave the present one alone.

For the product that falls into the low-perceived and low-actual impact area, the strategy should be to seize the advantage and try to improve market share by advertising the product's environmentally friendly nature, especially if the competing products by other companies are not as environmentally friendly as yours.

More companies are increasingly recognizing that, to achieve an environmentally competitive advantage, communication is necessary. Employees are possibly the single most important group to communicate to. Employees, if communicated to, will

- Strive to improve a successful situation. If you are doing well in reducing environmental impacts and tell employees how their efforts are helping insure the company's and their future, they will strive to make more improvements. Everyone wants to be part of a winning situation.
- Tell others about their company's product's low environmental impact. This is more believable to outsiders than an advertisement from marketing.

The company needs to tell customers, distributors, local community leaders, shareholders, and the general public. There will be opportunities during the product's life for this kind of communication.

Environmental issues will continue to be important to corporation's strategies and opportunities. Management has to direct the company through a myriad of issues on a daily basis. The use of the life cycle analysis can help management position its products for the future.

REFERENCES

1. World Wildlife Fund and The Conservation Foundation, *Product Life Assessments: Policy Issues and Implications, Summary of a Forum*, Washington, D.C., August 1990.
2. U.S. Environmental Protection Agency, *Information Resources Directory — Fall 1989*, Springfield, VA, U.S. Dept. of Commerce, National Technical Information Service, October 1989.
3. Hunt, R. G., Sellers, J. D., and Franklin, W. E., *Resources and Environmental Profile Analysis: A Life Cycle Environmental Assessment for Products and Procedures*, Environmental Impact Assessment Review, Elsevier Science, New York, Spring 1992.
4. Battelle and Franklin Associates, *Life Cycle Assessment; Inventory Guidelines and Principles*, U.S. EPA Risk Reduction Engineering Laboratory, Office of Research & Development, Cincinnati, OH, EPA/600/R 92-086.
5. Stoop, J., Scenarios in the design process, *Appl. Ergon.*, 21(4), 304, 1990.
6. Nemerow, N. L. and Dasgupta, A. D., *Industrial and Hazardous Waste Treatment*, Van Nostrand Reinhold, New York, 1991.
7. Ciambrone, D. F., *Waste Minimization as a Strategic Weapon*, CRC Press, Boca Raton, FL, 1995.
8. Boothroyd, G. and Dewhurst, P., *Product Design for Assembly*, Boothroyd and Dewhurst, Inc., Wakefield, RI, 1989.
9. Sellers, V. R. and Sellers, J. D., *Comprehensive Energy and Environmental Impacts for Soft Drink Delivery Systems*, Franklin Associates, Prairie Village, KS.
10. Little, A. D., *Disposable versus Reuseable Diapers: Health, Environmental and Economic Comparisons*, Arthur D. Little, Inc., Cambridge, MA, 1990.
11. Fabrycky, W. J., Designing for the life cycle, *Mech. Eng.*, 109(1), 72, 1987.
12. Saaty, T. L., *The Analytical Hierachy Process*, McGraw-Hill, New York, 1980.
13. SETAC, *A Technical Framework for Life Cycle Assessment*, The Society for Environmental Toxicology and Chemistry, Washington, D.C., 1991.
14. Little, A. D., Identifying Strategic Environmental Opportunities: A Life Cycle Approach, *Prism*, Arthur D. Little, Cambridge, MA, 1991.
15. Meadows et al., *The Limits to Growth*, Universe Books, New York, 1972.
16. *A Blueprint for Survival*, Club of Rome, Universe Books, New York, 1972.
17. Higgins, T. E., *Hazardous Waste Minimization Handbook*, Lewis Publishers, Boca Raton, FL, 1989.

GLOSSARY

Biodegradable   Capable of being broken down by natural, biological processes

Compatible Material   When combined compatible materials do not cause unacceptable impacts

Composting   An aerobic biological process employed to breakdown natural organic materials and organic garbage into compost for use in agriculture

Cross Disciplinary Team   A team consisting of representation from all affected operations

Concurrent Design   A design approach that causes the concerns and ideas from production and engineering to be considered at the same time during the design phase of a program

Downcycle   The recycling of a material or product for a less-demanding use

Embodied Energy   Energy contained in a material that can be recovered for use through combustion or other means

Life Cycle Analysis   Draw on the information from the life cycle inventory and identify issues that are pertinent to the particular process or products under consideration

Life Cycle Inventory   The portion of the life cycle study process that gathers the specific data on each of the product's stages and quantifies them

Impact Analysis   Assesses the environmental impact and risks associated with various products or activities; an impact analysis interprets the data from an impact inventory

Improvement Analysis   The strategic evaluation of the options for reducing environmental impact of the product and the initiation of actions

Inventory Analysis   Identifies and quantifies all inputs and outputs associated with a product and processes including materials, energy, and residuals

MANPRINT   The impact on the environment caused by humans and their equipment/products and processes

Physical Life Cycle   The series of physical activities that form the framework for materials and energy flows in a product life cycle

Pollution   The unwanted by-product or residual produced by human activity

Pollution Prevention   The reduction of anything that produces an impact on the environment or health risks that is released into the environment

Postconsumer Materials   Any material that has served its intended purpose and has been discarded before any recovery activities

Recycling   The reprocessing, reforming, or in-process reuse of waste materials; this includes collection, separation, and processing

Renewable   Capable of being replaced with a like entity quick enough to meet present, near-term, and future demands

Residual   The remainder; what is left over after a process or use of a product; the wastes remaining after all usable material has been used or recovered

Reuse   The additional use of a component, product, or material after it has been removed from a clearly defined product or process stage even if some cleaning or processing is required

Sustainable   Able to be maintained through time

System Boundaries   Define the extent of system or activities; boundaries define the limits of activities

Usable Life   Measurement of how long a system, process, or product will operate safely in its intended manner

APPENDIX A

**Example
Process Flow Diagram**

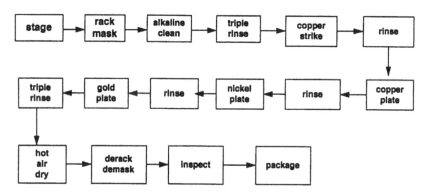

Example of process flow diagram. (From *Waste Minimization as a Strategic Weapon,* **Ciambrone, D. F., Ed., CRC/Lewis Publishers, Boca Raton, FL, 1995.)**

APPENDIX B

Issues to Consider for Assessing Environmental Impacts

Materials

Amount	Character	Impacts
Type	Virgin	Health and safety
Direct	Recovered (recycled)	Ecological
Product related	Reusable	Residuals
Process related	Resource-based factors	Energy
Indirect	Location	
Fixed capital	Scarcity	
Source	Quality	
Renewable	Regulations	
Lumber	Transportation	
Fishery	Restoration	
Agriculture/	Sustainability	
biomaterials		
Nonrenewable		
Metals		
Nonmetals		
Petrochemicals		

Energy

Amount	Source	Impact/character
Quantity purchased	Renewable	Resource-based factors
Embodied in materials	Wind	Location
Quantity used	Solar	Scarcity
	Hydroelectric	Quality
	Geothermal	Restoration
	Biomass	Impacts
	Nonrenewable	Materials
	Fossil fuel	Residuals
	Nuclear	Ecological
		Health and safety
		Net energy

Residuals		
Type	**Character**	**Environmental fate**
Waterborne	Nonhazardous	Containment
Suspended	Types	Degradability
Biological	Quantities	Bioaccumulation
Emulsified	Hazardous	Mobility
Chemical	Types	Atmospheric
Dissolved	Toxicity	Surface water
Airborne	Concentrations	Biological
Aerosol	Radioactive	Groundwater
Particulate	Type	Treatment impacts
Gas	Amount	Health and safety
Solid	Concentration	effects
Semisolid	Half-life	Materials
Liquid	Potency	Energy
Solid	Medical	Residuals
	Type	Contamination
	Quantity	
	Toxicity	
	Pathogen form	

Ecological factors		
Type	**Stress factors**	**Scale**
Chemical	Sensitive species	Local
Biological	Interrelationships	Regional
Physical	Sustainability	Continental
	Diversity	Global
	Rarity	

Health and safety issues		
Risk to	**Toxicology characteristics**	**Accidents**
Workers	Mortality	Types
Users	Morbidity	Frequency
Community	Exposure routes	Nuisances
	Inhalation	Noise
	Skin contact	Odors
	Ingestion	Sight
	Dose rate	Congestion
	Duration	
	Frequency	
	Concentration	

APPENDIX C

Examples of Energy Storage

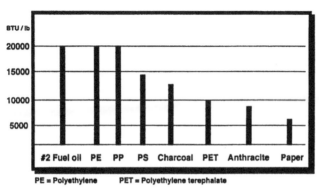

PE = Polyethylene	PET = Polyethylene terephalate
PP = Polypropylene	Anthracite = Hard coal
PS = Polystyrene	

APPENDIX D
MAJOR FEDERAL LAWS

CLEAN AIR ACT

Provisions include

Section 3 — National ambient air quality standards
Section 4 — State implementation plan
Section 5 — New source performance standard
Section 6 — Prevention of significant deterioration program
Section 7 — Nonattainment areas
Section 8 — National emissions standards for hazardous air pollutants
Section 9 — Acid rain provisions
Section 10 — New permitting requirements
Section 11 — Mobile source and fuel requirements
Section 12 — Ozone protection

CLEAN WATER ACT

- Grants for construction of treatment works
- National pollution discharge elimination system (NPDES)
- Water quality standards
- New source performance standards
- Toxic and pretreatment effluent standards

COMPREHENSIVE EMERGENCY RESPONSE, COMPENSATION AND LIABILITY ACT (CERCLA) AND SUPERFUND AMENDMENTS AND REAUTHORIZATION ACT (SARA)

- Definitions of hazardous wastes

- National contingency plans
- Liability of responsible parties and financing options for remedial actions

SARA TITLE III

Subtitle A — Emergency response and notification for extremely hazardous substances
Subtitle B — Reporting and notification requirements for toxic and hazardous substances

POLLUTION PREVENTION ACT

- Expand EPA's role in encouraging pollution prevention
- Creates an office in EPA to coordinate all agency pollution prevention activities
- Establishes grant program for training
- Requires the establishment of a clearinghouse to compile and disseminate information on source reduction and to serve as a technology transfer resource
- Mandates that EPA collect data on source reductions, recycling, and treatment of chemicals listed on the TRI reporting forms

RESOURCE CONSERVATION AND RECOVERY ACT (RCRA)

- Responsible to protect human health and the environment, reduce waste and conserve energy and natural resources, and eliminate the generation of hazardous wastes
- Provides for the identification and listing of particularly hazardous wastes for regulation and standards for generators, transporters, and owners/operators of hazardous waste treatment, storage, and disposal facilities (TSDs)
- Establishes recordkeeping, labeling, and manifest systems and proper handling methods
- Requires permits to be granted for treating, storage, or disposal of listed substances; imposes standards applying to financial aspects, groundwater monitoring, minimum technology usage, and closure procedures
- Provides for site inspection and enforcement
- Imposes a requirement on states to compile an inventory describing the hazardous waste storage and disposal sites with each state; encourages each state to take over responsibility for program implementation and enforcement from the federal government

- Establishes guidelines for minimum requirements for solid waste disposal
- Regulates underground storage tanks

TOXIC SUBSTANCE CONTROL ACT (TSCA)

- Provides for the testing of certain substances to determine if they present an unreasonable risk to health or the environment
- Provides for the notification of the EPA before producing a new chemical substance and submits any required test data
- Regulation of substances that present jan unreasonable risk to health and the environment
- Provides for the seizure of substances that are an imminent hazard through civil actions
- Provides for required recordkeeping by manufacturers

FEDERAL INSECTICIDE, FUNGICIDE AND RODENTICIDE ACT (FIFRA)

- Regulates all pesticides, fungicides, and rodenticides and requires that they be registered with the EPA; labeling regulations are included

NATIONAL FOREST MANAGEMENT ACT

- Establishes procedures for sale of forest timber
- Mandates Department of Agriculture to maintain a renewable resource program

OCCUPATIONAL HEALTH AND SAFETY ACT (OSHA)

- Provides for worker health and safety
- Sets standards
- Defines employer duties
- Defines inspection and enforcement
- Hazard communication standard — worker right-to-know laws

SURFACE MINING CONTROL AND RECLAMATION ACT

- Abondoned mine provisions
- Regulates surface coal mining's environmental impact

APPENDIX E
BASIC RECYCLE CODES
FOR PLASTICS

For consumers, the plastics industry indentifies resins by seven basic codes:

 PET (polyethylene teraphthalate) — 1- and 2-liter soda bottles, some foods, sauces, and sundries packaging

 HDPE (high density polyethylene) — gallon milk and juice containers, some food packaging

 PVC (polyvinyl chloride) — food and mineral water bottles

 LDPE (low-density polyethylene) — food product containers and lids, plastic grocery and shopping bags

 PP (polypropylene) — cereal box liners and medical cases

 PS (polystyrene) — deli, cookie and muffin trays, fast food cutlery

 OTHER multiple plastic resins from which layered products such as deli trays and potato and corn chip bags are made

(From *Waste Minimization as a Strategic Weapon,* Ciambrone, D. F., CRC/Lewis Publishers, Boca Raton, FL, 1995.)

INDEX